Figurative Language Comprehension
Social and Cultural Influences

Social and Cultural Influences

Figurative Language Comprehension
Social and Cultural Influences

Edited by

Herbert L. Colston
University of Wisconsin–Parkside

Albert N. Katz
University of Western Ontario

LAWRENCE ERLBAUM ASSOCIATES, PUBLISHERS
2005   Mahwah, New Jersey   London

Lawrence Erlbaum Associates, Inc., Publishers
10 Industrial Avenue
Mahwah, New Jersey 07430

Cover design by Katherine Houghtaling Lacey

Cover artwork by Linda K. Williamson .
Table Figures, 1994; charcoal on paper, 20 × 25 cm;
Private collection.

Library of Congress Cataloging-in-Publication Data

Figurative language comprehension : social and cultural influences /
edited by Herbert L. Colston, Albert N. Katz.
     p. cm.
    Includes bibliographical references and index.
ISBN 0-8058-4506-2 (cloth : alk. paper)
1. Sociolinguistics. 2. Figures of speech—Social aspects. 3. Psycholinguistics. I. Colston, Herbert L. II. Katz, Albert N.
P40.5.F54F54 2003
306.44—dc22   2003049526
                                         CIP

Books published by Lawrence Erlbaum Associates are printed on acid-
free paper, and their bindings are chosen for strength and durability.

Printed in the United States of America
10 9 8 7 6 5 4 3 2 1

To Brigitte, for her love, patience, support,
and willingness to entertain reading aloud,
and to Raymond W. Gibbs, Jr.,
whose mentoring and friendship
enabled my work

—Herbert L. Colston

To Al Paivio, who, by demonstration,
showed me what it was to be a scholar
and to Bill and Mollie Katz who, by demonstration,
tried to show me how to be a mensch

—Albert N. Katz

Contents

Preface

How is it that when I open my mouth and I say something such as, *"well, you all know that I am the Barry Bonds of my department's hockey team"* that I expect I will be understood? And why is it that I am not surprised that my comment may be understood differently by people who do not know me (and take my comment as a self-serving metaphoric bragging) from those who know me well (who will, alas, understand the comment as self-deprecating irony). And why is that when we utter a comment that we sometimes do so with two audiences in mind—one in the "know" and one "in the dark"—so that two different messages are being sent intentionally (see, e.g., Katz & Lee, 1993)? And why is it that when we read or listen to the satire of Lenny Bruce we recognize the "truth" in his comment that the wisest of philosophers talking in a deep Southern accent will be ignored, whereas a fool talking in a cultured new England accent will be honored; this is a "truth" based on how our prejudices about people, social class, and culture influence our reactions to what is being said. These examples, and many others, all point to the centrality of social and cultural factors in the production and comprehension of language.

Despite their seeming centrality, the history of linguistics and psycholinguistics has evolved to marginalize, and even ignore, social and cultural factors. For instance, in about the mid-19th century August Schleicher (see the nice review by Yngve, 1996) conceptualized language "as an object of nature" (p. 26) and, thus, as an entity to be studied on it's own, independent of human interaction. Later theorists took a similar line of argument. Ferdinand de Saussure (1959), for instance, made his well-known distinction between *langue* (language) and *parole* (speech) and asserted that understanding the *langue* is the true role of the linguist. Speech and the human element were relegated to a secondary role, best studied by other disciplines,

ix

a point also made by Leonard Bloomfield (1926/1957) who explicitly expelled phenomena related to people from the study of linguistics.

It was, of course, with Noam Chomsky (1957) that the modern era in linguistics began. But like the linguistics just cited, Chomsky was interested in language as an abstract entity, autonomous from secondary human-related performance factors. According to this view, language should be considered an autonomous function, separate from other cognitive functions. And these other cognitive functions would and should include the belief structures that govern what we hold about people, social class, and culture. Thus, what I have called central to our understanding of the production and comprehension of language is, in the Chomskian perspective, secondary and not a part of mainline language at all! In fact, the Chomskian perspective dismissed much more than sociocultural factors and relegated any expression that did not meet certain criteria for grammaticality as worthy of mainline study. Thus, expressions such as, "Been there, done that" or "You're no Jack Kennedy," are considered by those in this tradition to be nongrammatical despite the fact that they are often used and easily understood. (see Turner, 1998, for examples of how cognitive linguists treat these expressions as indeed grammatical).

The distinction between natural and nonnormal language has gone beyond the study of what is and is not grammatical to what is basic and derived in other language-related domains, especially to forms of language considered literal from that considered nonliteral. The nonliteral language here includes metaphor, irony, indirect requests, proverbs, and all forms of language in which what is being expressed differs from what the speaker intends to convey. In many ways linguists, psycholinguists, and various specialists in experimental psychology have made a concerted effort over the past 10 to 15 years to break the false dichotomies just described that have treated language as an entity separate from human beliefs and knowledge systems and have separated so-called literal from nonliteral forms of language.

An examination of the work of the past 10 to 15 years has shown that, for instance, one cannot examine an autonomous syntactic structure (the backbone of the Chomskian revolution) without examining the immediate effects of pragmatics and semantic knowledge (see review by Katz, 1998). One cannot relegate nonliteral language to a secondary and derived form of communication (see Gibbs, 1994; Gluckberg, 2001). One cannot examine language as a cognitive object of nature independent of the social interactions of people in communication (Clark, 1996). In these ways the understanding of language that is emerging is of a complex interactive system that, even at the earliest moments of production and comprehension, simultaneously evaluates and integrates knowledge of linguistic structure—that is, how language is used and the sociocultural factors of relevance.

Despite the work of the past 10 to 15 years, there is still a lack of systematic examination of social and cultural factors in language processing, especially with so-called nonliteral language. In fact, one can argue that nonliteral language, because it is so contextual and reflects speaker's intention above and beyond what is being expressed, is an ideal crucible for examining the effects of social and cultural knowledge. This book is intended as a conduit, bringing together many of the strings that are promoting and supporting the importance of the human agent in our understanding of language processing. In this volume you will find the most recent research by a range of scholars from linguistics, psycholinguists, and experimental psychology, who, in their own ways, attempt to reintroduce the human element into language production, comprehension, and use.

—*Albert N. Katz*

REFERENCES

Bloomfield, L. (1957). A set of postulates for the study of language. In M. Joos (Ed.), *Readings in linguistics* (pp. 26–31). Washington, DC: American Council of Learned Societies. (Original work published 1926)

Chomsky, N. (1957). *Syntactic structures.* The Hague, The Netherlands: Mouton.

Clark, H. (1996). *Using language.* Cambridge, England: Cambridge University Press.

Gibbs, R. W., Jr. (1994). *The poetics of mind.* New York: Cambridge University Press.

Glucksberg, S. (2001). *Understanding figurative language.* New York: Oxford University Press.

Katz, A. (1998). Figurative language and figurative thought: A review. In A. Katz, C. Cacciari, R. W. Gibbs, Jr., & M. Turner (Eds.), *Figurative language and thought* (pp. 3–43). New York: Oxford University Press.

Katz, A., & Lee, C. (1993). The role of authorial intent in determining verbal irony and metaphor. *Metaphor and Symbolic Activity, 8,* 257–279.

Saussure, F., de. (1959). Course in general linguistics. Translated by W. Baskin. New York: The Philosophical Library (reprinted, New York: McGraw-Hill, 1966).

Turner, M. (1998). Figure. In A. Katz, C. Cacciari, R. W. Gibbs, Jr., & M. Turner (Eds.), *Figurative language and thought* (pp. 44–87). New York: Oxford University Press.

Yngve, V. (1996). *From grammar to science: New foundations for general linguistics.* Amsterdam: Benjamins.

1

On Sociocultural and Nonliteral: A Synopsis and a Prophesy

Herbert L. Colston
University of Wisconsin–Parkside

The past several decades of psychological and linguistic empirical research and theorizing on nonliteral language has branched into a few key directions. Much of this work has focused and continues to focus on the comprehension of forms of figurative, indirect, and other kinds of nonliteral language. Some of this work concerns specific, step-by-step, online processing; other work is directed at the products of the comprehension and interpretation processes. A related line of work has attended to the sorts of pragmatic accomplishments that these kinds of language perform for interlocutors. This work seeks explanations of what is done by forms of nonliteral language and how these achievements are brought about. A growing interest in the production of nonliteral language is also emerging, as is a concern for authenticity. And the theoretical efforts to account for the accumulating empirical findings continue in light of these developments as well as related phenomena like situational irony.

One implicit idea emerging in much of this work is that of a growing appreciation of the importance of social and cultural influences to the comprehension, processing, use, pragmatic accomplishments, and so on of nonliteral language forms. Scholars have increasingly focused on variables such as gender, status, cultural background, age, and others in their observations, experiments, examples, and so on used to gain an understanding of nonliteral language cognition.

    This book is offered as a first attempt to summarize and synthesize this appreciation of sociocultural influences. The chapters were prepared by a wide variety of talented scholars of nonliteral language, with a diversity of backgrounds in cognitive psychology, psycholinguistics, linguistics, social psychology, and other areas. Thus, there is no universal theoretical or methodological underpinning or agenda to this work. Rather, the chapters reflect the diversity of approaches and mechanisms in the study of nonliteral language. But the fact that these different perspectives have all unearthed the need to pay much greater attention to social and cultural influences underscores the importance of these influences.

    A number of themes can be distilled from the chapters presented here. These range from (a) the kinds of mechanisms discussed for nonliteral language comprehension to (b) the variety of types of nonliteral language treated, (c) the twin ideas of what is a social and what is a cultural variable, and (d) what the actual influences in interlocutors might be. A number of theoretical backgrounds are also used in the chapters. These emerging themes and theories served to help organize the structure of the book. In this chapter I discuss each briefly and follow with a short discussion of the likely direction research on nonliteral language cognition should take given this heightened awareness of sociocultural influences. First, however, a very brief comment on the organization of the book is in order.

    Categorizing the chapters into coherent, separable sections according to their content proved to be a very difficult task. Organization schemes based on the kind of theoretical approach, type of nonliteral language, particular form of sociocultural influence, and so on were not viable because many of the chapters discuss multiple approaches, several nonliteral forms, various influences, and so forth. Instead, divisions based on the primary topic or strength of the chapters were created. The resulting four parts are Sociocultural Knowledge Influences, Sociocultural Phenomenological Influences, Sociocultural Processing Influences, and New Sociocultural Influences. Please note, however, that the content of a given chapter may supercede the section in which it was placed.

MECHANISMS IN NONLITERAL LANGUAGE COMPREHENSION: COMMON GROUND, SUPPRESSION, NEGATION, SOCIAL PSYCHOLOGICAL PRINCIPLES, CONTRAST, SCHEMAS, AND PRIMING

The role of common ground in the processing and comprehension of the meaning of instances of nonliteral language was taken up in two of the chapters—those by Gerrig and Horton and by Barr and Keysar. In particular, Gerrig and Horton argue that people necessarily interpret contextual expressions against both communal and personal sources of common ground.

An alternative view that egocentrism is more prevalent in everyday language than mutual knowledge would allow is offered by Barr and Keysar. This chapter makes a case that, contrary to the traditional view in pragmatics, conventions in language use can emerge without appeal to mutual knowledge between interlocutors. Rather, conventions can emerge, "as by-products of dyadic-level mechanisms of coordination" (Barr & Keysar, chap. 2, this book).

This is a fascinating development in that such contrary claims with evidence can be provided. My suspicion is that both claims are in a sense true, in that common ground is used, on occasion necessarily so, for important aspects of comprehension of many language forms. But there may also exist parallel lower level interaction mechanisms, as described by Barr and Keysar, as well as some others (e.g., mimicry, response in kind, script adherence, priming, chaining, attitude display, acting, and mere continuance) that are also influential. Future work might attempt to substantiate the separation of these mechanisms and address related questions such as how the mechanisms work individually and interactively, their possible interdependence, when are each used, and so on.

Another emerging mechanism involved in nonliteral language comprehension is that of negation. Giora, Balaban, Fein, and Alkabets' chapter bolsters an ongoing attack on the notion that negation markers (e.g., *not*) suppress their target concepts. Although applicable much more broadly to other language forms, this attack on suppression, or more specifically on obligatory suppression, plays a key role in some forms of indirect language (e.g., litotes). This chapter presents experimental evidence that meanings suppressed via negation markers are retained and influence later processing.

Gibbs and Izett's chapter highlights a variety of cognitive and, in particular, social psychological mechanisms of persuasion, including contrast, reciprocity, cognitive dissonance, analogical reasoning, and others, in its review of the persuasive ability of verbal irony. This chapter poignantly demonstrates the great need for more cross talk between social psychologists who study the mechanisms for how people influence one another, through language and other means, and psycholinguists and linguists who study the pragmatic accomplishments of forms of language.

Last, Blumentritt and Heredia's chapter discusses the mechanisms of schema processing in the form of stereotypes, as well as priming, and how they can influence the comprehension of forms of metonymy and metaphor. This chapter is of particular value in its coupling of standard mechanisms of cognitive functioning–language processing with a timely, important, and heretofore generally ignored sociocultural variable—stereotypes.

A few other mechanisms are also discussed, including conversational implicature and constraint satisfaction, but these are treated in the following sections, along with the theoretical approaches.

TYPES OF NONLITERAL LANGUAGE

The second theme of this book is that it brings together work that addresses the commonly studied forms of nonliteral language with work on relatively understudied nonliteral forms. The chapters report studies on metaphor and verbal irony, as well as on metonymy, proverbs, asyndeton, contextual expressions, idioms, scalar statements, "What is X doing Y" constructions (WXDYs), conventional indirect requests, analogies, litotes, and metaphorical signs.

One goal of the book was to assess whether any points of discussion might emerge in the treatments of these diverse nonliteral forms, in terms of the theoretical approach, mechanistic requirements, and so on. At least three of these points are considered.

The first is the degree to which language forms depend on contexts of different sorts to enable appropriate comprehension. The chapters by Curcó, Gerrig and Horton, Holtgraves, and Barr and Keysar deal with this issue explicitly, and indeed all of the chapters deal with it implicitly in their recognition of the importance of the social and cultural influences, which are certainly part of the contextual component of comprehension.

What might be emergent from these discussions, however, is the varying degree of dependence on different kinds of contexts in the comprehension of the different types of nonliteral language, particularly those having to do with these sociocultural variables. Beyond the related issues of idiomaticity, conventionalization, fixed expressions, and the like, which have received extended treatment in many other venues, the extent of nonliteral forms treated here and their relative dependence on social and cultural variables for comprehension might shed new light on the role of context. Consider that, clearly, all forms of language—nonliteral and others—require some degree of context for appropriate comprehension. But there is an arguably greater role played by context in many instances of nonliteral language comprehension, because of the less direct correspondence between the utterance meaning and the intended meaning. Comprehension thus must rely on something else.

So, comprehension of nonliteral forms relies more on context. But, and this point is less often made, such comprehension also relies more on sociocultural pragmatic reasoning. Moreover, this shift toward contextual and sociocultural sources of information may vary depending on the kind of nonliteral form being comprehended. Arguably, verbal irony, metaphors, and metonymies based on stereotypes, and possibly other forms, might rely more on sociocultural information than other aspects of context. Asyndeton, contextual expressions, idioms, analogies, litotes, and scalar statements, conversely, might rely more on other aspects of context than on sociocultural information. Granted, this observation is speculative at this point, but it certainly behooves us to look more at different sources of context, including sociocultural information, and how different nonliteral forms would rely on these sources to varying degrees, and then perhaps attempt to determine why this is the case. This observation has been made by other scholars concerning the relative dependence of verbal irony versus metaphor (Colston & Gibbs, 2002), but it might ought be expanded to include the entire continuum of nonliteral forms.

The second emergent point in consideration of the many nonliteral forms treated here concerns an argument I made elsewhere about whether nonliteral language comprehension should be approached with an inclusive or a piecemeal theoretical goal (Colston, 2002). The former approach is demonstrated powerfully in Holtgraves' chapter, wherein a classification of a number of nonliteral language forms according to different kinds of implicatures is presented. Several of the other chapters might be seen as espousing the more fragmented approach, whereby the mechanisms they cover might apply only to one nonliteral form or family (e.g., Gibbs and Izett's contrast and verbal irony, Giora's suppression and litotes, and Blumentritt and Heredia's schema activation and metonymy). Whether Holtgraves' approach can account for all kinds of nonliteral language and whether it can provide a detailed enough explanation to account for all the rich pragmatic accomplishments of the different forms (whether it should be required to explain the latter, however, is an open question) remains to be seen. Nevertheless, this classification is just the sort of work that is needed to evaluate whether we can build an explanation of language comprehension in general, based on such mechanistic or theoretical tenets, or whether different families of nonliteral (and literal) forms will each require their own set of explanations.

The last point of discussion to emerge in the chapters' treatments of many nonliteral forms is that of possible mixtures of mechanisms and processes, some of them contradictory and others complementary or parallel (see Gibbs & Colston, 2002, for a discussion of these possible mixtures for ironic communication), that might underlie nonliteral language use and comprehension. One example is the reliance on common ground versus more dyadic-level mechanisms of coordination already discussed for the comprehension of contextual expressions and referential precedents in the chapters by Gerrig and Horton and by Barr and Keysar, respectively. A second example might be the varying degree to which suppression of meaning occurs in nonliteral language comprehension. Giora notes that suppression, although not obligatory, does nevertheless occasionally occur. There may thus be different mechanisms at play, one in which suppression occurs and one in which it does to a lesser degree. A third example might be the conflict between contrast effect mechanisms and tinge mechanisms in verbal irony comprehension (see Colston, 1997, for a review of this debate). The former is discussed in Gibbs and Izett's chapter, the latter is treated in Giora's chapter (although not for verbal irony). Another example might be the mix of processes that underlie the intergroup conflict phenomenon discussed in Colston's chapter. Here, a combination of language comprehension processes, social tension and cognitive load, and social psychological principles were shown to combine to produce and maintain communication difficulties between different sociocultural groups.

The bottom line here is that nonliteral language use and comprehension is a very complicated matter. The rich nuance of clever meaning exchange and pragmatic accomplishment achieved by nonliteral language motivates its existence, but it is also made possible only by the interplay and, on occasion, conflict between an array of complex cognitive, linguistic, social, developmental, and other processes. It may not, therefore, be the case that a particular processing mechanism (e.g., activation of a conceptual metaphorical mapping, creation of a blended space, contrast between context and utterance meaning, inflated perception of an expectation–reality discrepancy, and a host of others) plays a role in each and every usage and comprehension of a particular nonliteral form. Granted, there may be general tendencies, but the true complexity of nonliteral forms and, in particular, the often found clever blends of nonliteral forms (e.g., an echoic, ironic, hyperbolic metaphor delivered laterally) might make straightforward deterministic explanations of nonliteral language incapable of accounting for the entire phenomenon.

WHAT IS "SOCIAL" AND "CULTURAL"?

The third theme that arose from the chapters concerns different ideas about what it means for something to be a social or a cultural influence or variable. Perhaps this discussion is best begun with a listing and description of the variety of sociocultural variables that the chapters cover. Gender is the most prevalent sociocultural variable discussed in the chapters. Colston, Katz, Link and Kreuz, and Pexman all offer extensive treatments of the role that gender plays in nonliteral language use, comprehension, and processing in terms of the gender of both speakers and listeners. The social relationship between interlocutors (e.g., close friends vs. strangers) is taken up in the chapters by Gerrig and Horton, Gibbs and Izett, Katz, and Pexman. Social role (e.g., high vs. low status or power) is treated in the chapters by Katz and Holtsgraves. Occupation (e.g., high irony [comedian] vs. low irony [nun]) is discussed by Katz, Pexman, and Holtgraves. Geographic origin is included in the discussion of proverb comprehension by Curcó, as was religious background—a very clever insight and possibly a sociocultural variable that has not been considered previously in discussions of nonliteral language use and comprehension. Political background is treated by both Giora et al. and

Blumentrit and Heredia. These same chapters also discuss speakers' and listeners' ethnicity. Ethnicity and other kinds of cultural background—including the idea that the mere degree of cooperativeness in communication or degree of indirectness prevalence may be a cultural difference—are reviewed by Holtgraves. Personality traits are discussed in Pexman's chapter, and the medium of language (e.g., spoken vs. signed)—also a very important sociocultural variable that has received relatively little past attention—is discussed extensively by Marschark.

As already alluded, these variables have also been treated in a variety of ways. Occasionally, a sociocultural variable is treated as a predictor of the likelihood of using a particular kind of nonliteral language (e.g., men use sarcasm more than women). Other times it is considered a predictor of how a nonliteral utterance will be comprehended (e.g., a person from outside a given culture will be less likely to interpret correctly the nonliteral meaning of a proverb). Still other times they are treated as more global predictors of use or comprehension extent, quality, and so on (e.g., cultures with more indirectness will use and comprehend nonliteral language more often than cultures with less indirectness). In some cases a sociocultural variable is also considered along with another expressive phenomenon (e.g., men use more nonliteral language for negative vs. positive emotional expressions).

Other chapters discuss the role that sociocultural variables play at different levels of nonliteral language cognition. Katz's chapter in particular provides a detailed discussion of both on- and offline effects of sociocultural variables. Gibbs and Izett's chapter talks about the variety of ways that social influence principles are at play in the use or comprehension of verbal irony, both in terms of online language processing and in broad effects of irony as an influencer (e.g., as an effective tool in advertising campaigns). Curcó's chapter discusses the influence of degree of experience with a given language as well as degree of acculturation in comprehension of native language proverbs—and concomitant with this, the variety of levels at which proverbs can be interpreted (e.g., as a nonliteral language form as well as a form of extollation). Finally, Marschark's chapter's treatment of metaphorical sign language can easily be seen as an example of nonliteral language being processed at a variety of different levels (visual processing, linguistic processing, interpretation, etc.).

Still other chapters treat the sociocultural variables as important components of the contextual backdrop in which nonliteral forms are always interpreted. These discussions focus less on sociocultural variables' influence per se, but rather they use sociocultural variables as examples of how important consideration of all aspects of context are when considering language, particularly nonliteral language, comprehension.

Despite how sociocultural variables were treated, the extent and variety of these variables attest to their prevalence and demonstrate their rising importance in scholars' thinking and research about nonliteral language cognition.

WHAT ARE SOCIOCULTURAL INFLUENCES?

What does it mean for a variable to have an influence on nonliteral language cognition? This question constitutes the final theme derived from the chapters in this book. In general, we can divide this theme into two issues—the direction of an influence and the type of influence—and discuss several versions of each. The direction aspect is considered first.

If we consider an individual person as the object of analysis, then influence can flow in a variety of directions. A person can hold a number of roles in a language exchange, and sociocultural influences can impact on or emanate from that person in several ways. If a person is the addressee, for instance, then sociocultural variables in the speakers can affect the addressee (e.g., comprehension is different if the speaker is wealthy vs. poor). Such variables can also exist in overhearers and affect the addressee (e.g., comprehension is different if the conversation is being overheard by a man vs. woman). Sociocultural variables also exist in audiences, coaddressees, strangers, cospeakers, and a variety of other roles, and many of these could have an influence on the addressee's comprehension (and this is all just to consider comprehension, other influences are taken up later). Indeed, even to the extent that sociocultural variables can vary within the same person (e.g., I am an authority figure to my students in the lab but a regular guy to them if we go out to lunch), such variation might affect one's own comprehension of the same utterance from the same speaker when heard in these different roles.

If instead the person in question is the speaker, then sociocultural variables in other people (e.g., addressees, coaddressees, audiences, overhearers, and cospeakers) can affect production. It can also affect the monitoring of comprehension, which in turn can affect subsequent production, subsequent monitoring, and other aspects of the negotiation of meaning exchange.

If the person is in one of the other roles just discussed, then sociocultural variables in the speaker, the addressee, or in other people holding other roles can affect the cognition of the person. Moreover, these mixtures of sociocultural variables might interact in very complex ways. For example, if I am obviously overhearing a conversation in which the addressee is known to be a religious person, I might comprehend a given utterance differently than if the addressee were known to not be religious. But this switch in my comprehension might only hold if the speaker were, for instance, of high social status. If the speaker were of low social status, then my comprehension might be more stable across the sociocultural variable in the addressee. Of course this particular example may not necessarily be true, but interactions such as this might hold.

Next, the types of influence on a person encountering nonliteral language as an addressee, overhearer, audience, and so on are considered. Individuals or groups of people who encounter nonliteral language can be influenced by sociocultural variables both in terms of processing or comprehension and in broader pragmatic effects. For instance, a person hearing a nonliteral utterance might process it faster or more slowly; comprehend it more or less extensively; resolve ambiguity to a lesser or greater extent; compute additional, fewer, or different types of meanings (literal or nonliteral); make different inferences; or do a variety of other kinds of processing differently as a result of a sociocultural variable in some role in the interaction. People who encounter a nonliteral utterance may also be broadly affected in terms of their emotional response; their attitude toward the speaker, other person, or some issue; the degree to which they are persuaded or insulted; their level of surprise; their subsequent thinking; their subsequent behavior; and so on all as a result of such sociocultural variables in the speaker(s) or other people.

Sociocultural variables in other people can also have an effect on individuals' or groups' production of nonliteral language. Speakers might use more or less, or perhaps different kinds of, nonliteral language depending on sociocultural variables in the addressees, overhearers, audiences, witnesses, and so on. Speakers might also blend literal, nonliteral, and types of nonliteral language in different ways according to such variables. Indeed, an often discussed phenomenon of nonliteral language is that it affords incredible flexibility in communication. An adroit user of nonliteral language can simultaneously communicate several distinctly different messages individually to several different addressees with the same nonliteral (or even literal) utterance.

So, in summary, influence can flow in a number of different directions, and it is comprised of changes to processing, comprehension, production, use, emotional response, and broader pragmatic functioning. This level of complexity once again attests to how important it is that future work on nonliteral language continues to explore social and cultural aspects to this domain of human cognition.

THEORETICAL APPROACHES

In addition to the aforementioned themes that emerged, a number of theoretical approaches were also used in various chapters. These bear brief discussion as they link with the point discussed earlier concerning whether nonliteral language cognition is best attempted by a unified theory or a family of explanations. A few of these approaches might be candidates for the former approach, whereas mechanisms discussed in other chapters illustrate the latter strategy.

Holtgraves' chapter uses Gricean and neo-Gricean distinctions of conversational implicatures to attempt to build a classification scheme of a variety of kinds of nonliteral language and their comprehension. Katz's chapter introduces the possibility of using constraint satisfaction as a global theoretical mechanism for explaining nonliteral use and comprehension, an approach that holds much promise. Giora et al. discusses suppression and salient meaning, which have been put forth previously as components of an account for nonliteral language cognition. Lastly, the role of common ground in comprehension is discussed, albeit with differing conclusions, in the chapters by Gerrig and Horton and by Barr and Keysar. Each of these approaches could be an underpinning for a global account of nonliteral language processing, comprehension, and possibly use, although they would clearly need much work to enable explanation of all the nuance to these aspects of nonliteral language cognition.

Colston's chapter illustrates a number of potential cognitive and social psychological theoretical phenomenon that could underlie gender differences in nonliteral language use, Gibbs and Izett's chapter also outlines a number of important social psychological theoretical principles that could underlie nonliteral language comprehension, pragmatic effects, and use. Link and Kreuz's chapter offers a variety of potential theoretical sources for gender differences in nonliteral language use. Pexman's chapter discusses some theoretical components of individual differences. Blumentritt and Heredia's chapter discusses some psycholinguistic and cognitive theoretical underpinnings, and both of these chapters apply these components to account for sociocultural differences in nonliteral language cognition. Lastly, the chapters by Curcó and Marschark provide some key potential theoretical underpinnings to explain nonliteral language cognition in two novel ways—the kind of nonliteral language used (proverbs and metaphorical signs) and the sociocultural variable(s) that might be of interest (religious background, among others, and language media). These chapters all offer components that might be incorporated into a global theoretical attempt at explaining nonliteral language cognition, or, and perhaps more likely, they might supply components for more disparate explanations.

Given the incompleteness of both the potential global and disparate theoretical strategies, it is premature to argue which approach will likely win out. Nevertheless, if forced to make a prediction at this point, I would have to opt for the latter strategy. Given the wide variety of basic cognitive, linguistic, social, and even perceptual processes that have been shown to play a role in the processing, comprehension, and use of different nonliteral forms (e.g., contrast effects, assimilation effects, conceptual metaphor, distinctiveness, memory processes, analogical processes, relevance, foot-in-the-door, social alignment, and many others), and particularly, the lack of universality of many of these processes across forms of nonliteral language, then a global account appears untenable. One exception to this speculation, however, might be a global approach that is flexible with respect to what kinds of mechanisms might be at play in a given form of nonliteral language processing, comprehension, or use. Katz suggested a constraint satisfaction approach that allows the particular constraints to vary according to nonliteral language type and contextual situation but maintains some fixed theoretical construct for what pragmatic constraint satisfaction would be might make for a successful compromise.

FUTURE DIRECTIONS FOR NONLITERAL LANGUAGE RESEARCH

The topics, empirical findings, explanations, and the emergent themes and theoretical approaches from the chapters in this book help outline some key issues that nonliteral language research is facing. I briefly discuss some of these and offer some suggestions for the future of this field. This is not a conclusive list, and items are not offered in any particular order of importance.

Authenticity

A number of the chapters alluded to a growing concern with authenticity in the study of nonliteral language. Indeed, the recognized importance of sociocultural variables that motivated this book supports this concern. Most of the methodologies discussed in the chapters as well as those used in empirical research on nonliteral language involve experimentation. For purposes of control and manipulation, well known to most psychologists and many linguists as a means of identifying cause–effect chains, studies typically involve the presentation of carefully designed, experimenter-crafted situations and utterances to participants who are ideally representative of populations of interest. The sets of situation–utterance items are manipulated somehow to introduce variables that are potential causal agents. Participants are then asked to perform some language-related task(s) involving the items, and a wide variety of measurements are taken to tap into potential effect agents. Although the specific details of the application of this methodology to psycholinguistic studies may not be widely known to all scholars of nonliteral language, the general technique is pervasive in psychological research and is very familiar to a psychological and possibly linguistic audience.

Not widely known among psychologists or even among all psycholinguists, however, is a potentially damning problem with this methodology discussed among a number of fields also interested in nonliteral cognition. The essential criticism is that the rich, sociocognitive nuance of actual nonliteral talk concerning an infinity of contexts and topics, among varieties of kinds of interlocutors, with their rich subjective experiences and mutual knowledge of these, is severely compromised with the introduction of strict laboratory methodologies, items, tasks, and measures. Although there may be some very low-level auditory, phonological, morphological, or perhaps higher phenomena that can be studied with laboratory techniques, so the criticism goes, many phenomena at those levels, and any phenomenon perhaps involving syntax or semantics but certainly concerning pragmatics, are made insurmountably artificial if not studied in situ. Proponents of this criticism, therefore, use observational methodologies designed to capture, as best as possible, actual language used in a variety of real-world settings and then study recordings and rich transcripts of that language to determine its nature and to draw inferences about speaker–listener cognitive processes, intentions, language functioning, and so on.

Countercriticisms offered against this conversational or discourse analysis methodology are typical of arguments against observational methods: Although they might allow cursory descriptive accounts of language phenomena, they afford no means of reliable generalizeability across participant or language type populations, the precise identity of causal agents is indeterminate, the cognitive state of the interlocutors is relatively inaccessible, and so on.

Whatever position one takes in this debate, there is nonetheless something to be said for the importance of authenticity in studying nonliteral language cognition. Although it may be true that the use of strict control, which actually may not necessitate the use of inauthentic items, impacts, for example, the processing or comprehension of nonliteral language so minimally that its disadvantages may be overlooked, the delicacy and complexity of nonliteral language cognition lean heavily against this view. Indeed, the recognition by the scholars in this book, as well as others of the importance of attending to sociocultural variables and their impact on nonliteral language cognition demonstrates the appreciation of the richness of nonliteral language. My view is that attempts should be made to find compromise methodologies that make use of recorded authentic language and then adopt more controlled mechanisms to enable causal determinations.

For example, I (Colston, 2004) recently used a methodology wherein people were placed in contrived, controlled social situations that varied some key factor (e.g., how much the participant respected his or her addressee) and required the participant speakers to produce a particular form of language in that situation—specifically, gratitude acknowledgments (e.g., "no problem" and "anytime"). These verbatim utterances were then given in written form to a separate group of participants who rated the degree of nonliteralness of the utterances.

The evaluation of the pragmatic functions accomplished by gratitude acknowledgments was made in this study with a methodology that thus provides an appealing compromise between purely experimental and purely field- or corpus-based studies. By collecting real utterances offered by normal, every-day speakers, instead of using experimenter-crafted comments, a much-needed improvement in ecological validity is gained. Indeed, the authentic gratitude acknowledgments collected in this study were much richer than what would likely have been created by an experimenter. They are often grammatically questionable (e.g., "I'm sure good" and "I'm real sorry your bike got stole"). They do not always use complete sentences (e.g., "Refresh on old stuff" and "You could have"). They refer to subtle details of the contexts (e.g., "The jacket looks good on you" and "How was the party"). They make use of colloquialisms (e.g., "No sweat" and "it's all good"), and so on.

Conversely, by manipulating people into producing these utterances in reasonably controlled situations rather than simply capturing usages in fully natural settings, some of the looseness in fieldwork in terms of causal agents or links, generalizeability, replicability, and so on, is reduced. Future work might continue to make use of such compromise methodologies as an alter-native to more extreme procedures.

Nonliteral Blends

Both the concern for authenticity and the work that is needed on prevalences of kinds of nonliteral language (discussed next) call for more at-tention to be placed on blends of nonliteral forms of language, not just on blends of metaphorical language (see Lee & Barnden, 2001) but on blends of different kinds of nonliteral language (Colston, 1998). Although some of this work has begun to appear in the recent literature (e.g., Colston & Gibbs, 2002), my strong suspicion is that corpus and fieldwork will highlight the prevalence of this kind of talk. Moreover, as already discussed, given the po-tential offsetting nature of some mechanisms of nonliteral language cogni-tion (suppression vs. no suppression, tinge vs. contrast effects, etc.), investigation of such blended forms will become very important. Production of such blends is also an important understudied area. This issue is taken up in the Production section.

Prevalence of Nonliteral Language

Although there have been a number on studies of the prevalence of forms of nonliteral language amid certain targeted populations (e.g., Gibbs, 2000), as well as some very recent corpus work just emerging on this issue for figura-tive language (Lee, 2003; also see an upcoming special issue of *Metaphor and Symbol* devoted to corpus work on metaphor), there has yet to be any large-scale measurements of actual talk in a wide array of settings and cultures for a large number of forms and mixtures of nonliteral language.

Such work is crucial to help evaluate our emerging and refining explana-tions. For instance, if 70% of hyperbolic utterances are of a certain type (e.g., specific quantified magnitude overstatements) and a smaller percentage are of another type (e.g., extreme case formulations) and different comprehension or use explanations are supported by these different types, then the prevalence data can help weigh the comprehension explanations accordingly.

Benchmarked longitudinal studies of prevalences of nonliteral language would also allow a better evaluation of mechanisms like grammaticalization, and concomitantly the different comprehension accounts that rely on or dismiss such processes, and the impact that sociocultural variables play in these and similar processes.

Continued Empirical and Theoretical Work

The diversity of theoretical approaches and mechanisms and the relatively underexplored nature of many kinds of nonliteral language also speak to the huge need for continued work that addresses new nonliteral forms and new nonliteral processing, comprehension, or use mechanisms—similar to what has already been conducted. I do not believe that certain summary or evaluation attempts such as this book should cease, but there is much more territory to be explored before the process of map making will become entirely fruitful.

Production

Until very recently, there has also been a dearth of work on the production of forms of nonliteral language (see Barr, in preparation; Gibbs, 2000; Horton & Keysar, 1996; and Link & Kreuz, this book). One standard reason for processing and comprehension work outpacing that of production lies with the greater difficulty in conducting work on production. Electronic communication technologies that enable relatively easy recording of nonliteral productions are changing this situation, but these suffer from the constraints inherent in the medium (Hancock & Dunham, 2001a, 2001b). Although such computer mediated work is useful and should continue, parallel work that investigates spoken nonliteral language is also crucial and should receive more attention.

More work on production of nonliteral language will help evaluate some of the theoretical perspectives emerging in the literature. Katz's constraint satisfaction approach in particular might benefit by more production research; one could test whether speakers are attempting to satisfy a host of complex cognitive, linguistic, and social goals and constraints in how they talk nonliterally.

More production work could also help delineate sources for differences in the quality of nonliteral language use, factors that lead to development of such use, limits on such skills, and so on. In particular, production work could help evaluate how people use clever blends of nonliteral language forms to accomplish complex mixtures of often conflicting social and communicative goals (e.g., to defend one's position from attack but to also maintain appropriate politeness).

Last, production work could also help address the empirical issues discussed thus far concerning the impact of sociocultural variables. Recall that, for instance, some findings have shown more production of particular kinds of nonliteral language across some sociocultural variables (e.g., men use sarcasm more often than women). Production work could help continue the exploration of these differences and their sources.

APPLICATIONS OF FINDINGS

Aside from the important directions for the basic research on processing, comprehension, and use of nonliteral language, a number of important applications of nonliteral language might warrant further investigation.

As discussed in Colston's chapter, nonliteral language comprehension and its breakdown might underlie some aspects of group conflict. Future work to refine this potential mechanism and, ideally, to circumvent it (e.g., does knowledge of the mechanism on the part of interlocutors act to derail or slow the communication breakdown?) could be important to alleviate this source of social problems.

Indeed, the field of conflict resolution could potentially be benefited by increased work on the role that nonliteral (and literal) language processing, comprehension, and use play in misunderstandings, misinterpretations, and other communication difficulties. Although there is already an enormous cottage industry surrounding this kind of endeavor, it is unclear to what extent the practitioners make use of the most recent findings from research on nonliteral language.

Given the work discussed in some chapters about the pragmatic effects of various forms of nonliteral language (e.g., persuasion in Gibbs and Izett's chapter and extollation in Curcó's chapter), some applied work might also address how nonliteral language is useful for educational purposes (see Barnard & Colston, 2000, for one example).

There may also be room for improvement to legal systems that in many ways are built on the tenet that language is literal and people state what they mean. Courtroom procedures, interrogation policies, beliefs surrounding testimony, and a host of other aspects of how many legal systems operate are based on some archaic notions about language and its use. Research on nonliteral language comprehension applied to these issues might also help to improve such systems.

Last, and related to the aforementioned argument, there are enormous benefits to be gained simply by educating populations much more broadly on what language, nonliteral and literal, is and how its comprehension and use work. I very recently read an article from a local newspaper (Barton, 2002) that illustrates this point poignantly:

> Joke empties plane: Man ticketed and sent home as passengers scurry to resume travels.
>
> As he boarded a commuter plane at the Dane County Regional Airport Tuesday morning, 33-year-old Steven M. Wiese of Cottage Grove peeked around the cockpit door and made a joke: "I hope you haven't been drinking."
>
> The pilot didn't think it was funny. Neither did the other passengers.
>
> "(The pilot) could see the other passengers' heads popping up like gophers coming out of their holes," said Lt. Michael Krembs of the Dane County Sheriff's Department. "The whole plane could hear. He said it really loud."
>
> In an instant, Wiese's holiday travel plans were ruined. The flight was delayed. The other passengers had to re-book on other flights on Christmas Eve. And the pilots were checked to make sure they indeed had not been drinking.
>
> Wiese and his wife have not flown since their honeymoon nine years ago. He had planned a trip to New York as a surprise Christmas gift for her.
>
> "I shouldn't have said it. I regret saying it," Wiese said Tuesday afternoon. "I meant it as a joke. I had a smile on my face. But they took it the wrong way." Atlantic Coast Airlines flight 6302, with 26 passengers aboard, was delayed. The crew reported to a medical facility to be tested for alcohol and drugs, in compliance with Federal Aviation Administration guidelines.
>
> "Since 9–11, you can't joke about anything in an airport," Krembs said.
>
> Wiese apologized to his fellow travelers as they got off the plane at the Madison airport and lined up at the ticket counter, hoping to be re-booked. Then he and his wife got in line, too.
>
> "The deputies pulled them out of line and said, 'Oh, no. You're not going anywhere today,'" Krembs said.
>
> The deputies then ticketed Wiese for disorderly conduct. He must pay a $225 fine.
>
> That's not all.
>
> The FBI and the U.S. attorney's office will discuss the incident after the holidays and decide whether the man should face the more serious charge of interfering with a flight crew, a federal felony that carries a

maximum 20-year prison term, said Monica Shipley, FBI spokeswoman.

All of the other passengers were re-booked to their final destinations, said Rick Delisi, spokesman for Atlantic Coast Airlines. The members of the flight crew all tested negative for alcohol and other controlled substances. Their plane departed more than four hours late, at 2:05 p.m.

Delisi said the pilot followed the proper procedures. "The crew is never meant to ask whether (people are) joking or what their motivations are," he said. "… People just don't realize the seriousness of what they're saying."

For Wiese, that realization came at a high price—and not just the cost of the nonrefundable plane tickets. Instead of taking the trip, he and his wife now plan a quiet holiday at home trying to recover from the ordeal.

Wiese has weighed in his mind exactly what he should have done differently.

"I should have said, 'Merry Christmas.' "

If such well-intended endeavors as ensuring the safety of air travel were not victim to these sorts of ill-placed policies stemming from a widespread simplistic notion of language and its use, perhaps these and other important efforts could be channeled in more effective directions.

REFERENCES

Barnard, K., & Colston, H. L. (2000, November). *How to teach people about the web: Image-schematic metaphor and the construction of the information highway.* Paper presented at the meeting of the Society for Computers in Psychology, New Orleans, LA.

Barr, D. J. (in preparation). Paralinguistic correlates of discourse structure.

Barton, G. (2002, December 24). Joke empties plane: Man ticketed and sent home as passengers scurry to resume travels. *Milwaukee Journal Sentinel.*

Colston, H. L. (1997). Salting a wound or sugaring a pill: The pragmatic functions of ironic criticism. *Discourse Processes, 23,* 25–45.

Colston, H. L. (1998, July). *On the viability of a multi-trope account of figurative language processing.* Poster session presented at the meeting of the International Pragmatics Association, Reims, France.

Colston, H. L. (2002). Pragmatic justifications for nonliteral gratitude acknowledgments: "Oh sure, anytime." *Metaphor and Symbol, 17,* 205–226.

Colston, H. L. (2004). *On why people don't say what they mean: An analysis of authentic formulaic language.* Manuscript submitted for publication.

Colston, H. L., & Gibbs, R. W., Jr. (2002). Are irony and metaphor understood differently? *Metaphor and Symbol, 17,* 57–80.

Gibbs, R. W., Jr. (2000). Irony in talk among friends. *Metaphor and Symbol, 15,* 5–27.

Gibbs, R. W., Jr., & Colston, H. L. (2002). The risks and rewards of ironic communication. In L. Anolli, R. Ciceri, & G. Riva (Eds.), *Say not to say: New perspectives on miscommunication* (pp. 181–194). Amsterdam: IOS.

Hancock, J. T., & Dunham, P. J. (2001a). Impression formation in computer-mediated communication revisited: An analysis of the breadth and intensity of impressions. *Communication Research, 28*(3), 325–347.

Hancock, J. T., & Dunham, P. J. (2001b). Language use in computer-mediated communication: The role of coordination devices. *Discourse Processes, 31,* 91–110.

Horton, W. S., & Keysar, B. (1996). When do speakers take into account common ground? *Cognition, 59*(1), 91–117.

Lee, M. G. (2003, January 10). Corpus-Based Approaches to Figurative Language Workshop. Message posted to the Cognitive Linguistics electronic mailing list.

Lee, M. G., & Barnden, J. A. (2001). Reasoning about mixed metaphors within an implemented artificial intelligence system. *Metaphor and Symbol, 16,* 29–42.

PART I

Sociocultural Knowledge Influences

2

Making Sense of How We Make Sense: The Paradox of Egocentrism in Language Use

Dale J. Barr
University of California, Riverside

Boaz Keysar
University of Chicago

Language users routinely face the problem of making sense out of language: Speakers must design utterances that listeners can understand, and listeners must interpret utterances the way they were intended. Because ambiguity is pervasive in language use, pragmatic theories assume that speakers and listeners should strive to speak and understand against the background of a mutual perspective. However, our findings indicate that speakers and listeners are egocentric to a surprising degree. With respect to many current frameworks in psycholinguistics, these findings are anomalous: They suggest that language users are not properly designed for the task of making sense. Our goal in this chapter is to review these findings and to try to sketch out a new framework against which such egocentric behavior makes more (theoretical) sense. We propose that language users can rely on simpler mechanisms than current theories require because the work they are assumed to do to achieve a mutual perspective is actually distributed among processes in the language use environment.

The research presented in this book exemplifies how the meanings of figurative and other so-called "indirect" language can vary with social and cultural context. In this regard, it echoes a refrain that one encounters time and again in the literature on language use—that meaning is underdetermined in the sense that the same string of words can convey anything from a benign comment to vicious sarcasm. One of the reasons why people continue to marvel at this idea is that we are still lacking a clear picture of how, in the face of vast ambiguity, people are able to make sense with and out of language. What we require is a better understanding of the mechanisms that underlie how people coordinate with each other.

One point on which all can agree is that speakers and listeners will only properly understand one another if they process utterances against a similar background set of assumptions and beliefs. In an influential study, Clark and Marshall (1981) characterized this background as *mutual knowledge*, the set of knowledge that is mutually held between interlocutors. Mutual knowledge is different from knowledge that is merely shared, because it is not only shared but is known to be shared. According to Clark and Marshall, mutual knowledge is essential because it is the only true guarantee of successful communication. They demonstrated this by showing that there are circumstances under which utterances that are based on information that two individuals have in common—but do not know they share—will fail. Because Clark and Marshall developed the theory extensively for the case of definite reference, it makes very clear predictions about how people should behave when producing and understanding referential expressions.

In definite reference, a speaker uses language to establish some object as the intersubjective focus of attention. Based on the cooperative principle, when speakers describe referents to listeners they should strive to be optimally informative (Grice, 1975). This means that they should provide no more and no less information than is necessary for the purpose of securing the listener's attention. Yet, what counts as "optimally informative" is defined by their mutual knowledge (Clark & Marshall, 1981). Imagine that Henry and Mabel are sitting at a table and there is a candle and a box placed between them. Henry wishes to get Mabel to put the candle in the box. What should he say? Clearly, he can simply tell her to "put the candle in the box." He should not say "the small candle" even if he is thinking of other larger candles that were on the shelf where he purchased the candle—these other candles are not part of their mutual knowledge. Similarly, Mabel will know that Henry is talking about the candle on the table and not the one that Ted bought for her yesterday, of which the small candle reminds her, because she knows that Henry does not know about Ted's candle. She will not ask "Which candle?" because she will know, by virtue of their mutual knowledge, that Henry is referring to the candle on the table.

As cognitive psychologists, we became interested in the mutual knowledge theory because of its strong implications for language processing. Even though much of the literature on mutual knowledge shuns explicit discussion of psychological mechanism, the theory's proponents have on various occasions made clear assumptions that mutual knowledge should serve as a guiding principle in the access of information during language processing (Clark & Carlson, 1981; Gerrig, 1986) as well as in the organization of memory (Clark & Marshall, 1981) and the lexicon (Clark, 1998). Thus, speakers should design utterances with their specific addressee in mind (Clark & Murphy, 1982), and comprehenders should restrict the information they consider to mutual knowledge (Clark & Carlson, 1981). These proposals assume that language users can directly compute mutual knowledge on the fly and, therefore, call for the existence of powerful and efficient cognitive mechanisms that can guide the formulator and parser in their processing decisions. Building mutual knowledge directly into the language processing system seems advantageous not only because it would guarantee successful communication, but it would also reduce uncertainty and thus the complexity of the problem that language users face (Clark & Carlson, 1981).

From this vantage point, we were surprised to find from our own experiments on language use that speakers and listeners commonly violate their mutual knowledge when they produce and understand language. Thus, Henry will often refer to the candle as "the small candle" (Barr, 1999; Horton & Keysar, 1996), and Mabel will often consider the candle that Ted bought her as the referent or ask "Which candle?" even though there is only one candle that is uniquely defined by their mutual knowledge (Keysar, Barr, Balin, & Brauner, 2000; Keysar, Barr, Balin, & Paek, 1998). This behavior is egocentric because it is rooted in the speakers' or listeners' own knowledge instead of in mutual knowledge.

We have also observed effects in other domains that confirmed the generality of this egocentrism. Overhearers violate mutual knowledge in assessing whether an addressee will perceive an utterance as sarcastic (Keysar, 1994). Addressees interpret referential expressions according to naming precedents established by a previous speaker even though the current speaker was absent when the precedents were established (Barr, 1999; Barr & Keysar, 2002). Moreover, people turn out to be quite poor estimators of what others know. Speakers systematically underestimate the ambiguity and overestimate the effectiveness of their utterances (Keysar & Henly, 2002). When taught the meaning of an opaque idiom such as *the goose hangs high*, people overestimate the likelihood that others who are unfamiliar with the idiom will perceive its meaning (Keysar & Bly, 1995).

These findings might appear to conflict with other studies that purport to show effects of mutual knowledge on comprehension (e.g., Clark, Schreuder, & Buttrick, 1983; Greene, Gerrig, McKoon, & Ratcliff, 1994). However, Keysar (1997) noted that these studies suffer from a design flaw which confounds information that is mutual (i.e., known to be shared) with information that is simply known to the self (see also Lea, Mason, Albrecht,

Birch, & Myers, 1998). Once this flaw has been corrected, these methodologies yield the same systematic egocentrism as the studies just reviewed.

The evidence that language users are more egocentric than the mutual knowledge theory predicts is too abundant and too robust to be ignored. Yet, in light of the assumption that mutual knowledge is the only true guarantee of successful communication, it raises something of a paradox. How can language users be egocentric and still communicate effectively? In other words, how can people get away with being so alarmingly unsophisticated in dealing with the sophisticated problem of making sense?

We suggest that the only way to really make sense of this seemingly erratic behavior is to take a closer look at the circumstances under which it was designed to operate: the language use environment. Although certain aspects of the language use environment have been closely studied by researchers in disparate fields, there has been little effort to fit these pieces back together so that they can yield their full impact on theories of language use. In what follows, we examine the structure of the language use environment with the hope of showing how, counterintuitively, an egocentric way of speaking and understanding can make sense. Language users' egocentric behavior does not necessarily reflect a badly designed processing system; instead, we argue that it reflects the operation of simple heuristics that are adaptive given the normal circumstances of spoken language use. The burden of computing mutual knowledge is not one that individual language users carry alone; rather, it is one that they share by distributing it over processes in the environment. The richness of the environment enables language users to compensate for their limitations. In other words, language users have a bag of simple tricks that makes them look more sophisticated than they actually are. These tricks work because they are specifically designed to exploit the structure of the environment.

DOMAINS OF THE LANGUAGE USE ENVIRONMENT

What do we mean by the language use environment? We propose a typology that divides the environment into three subdomains: cognitive, interactional, and cultural (see Table 2.1). These domains are defined by the social and language units that constitute the primary units of analysis. By analogy, the set of domains can be construed as a set of lenses of varying power of magnification through which the theorist observes language use. Looking through the strongest lens, we can observe language use at its finest level of resolution, the cognitive domain. In this domain the basic social unit is the individual language user and the basic language unit, the single clause or utterance. This domain corresponds to the traditional level of inquiry in psycholinguistics, whose task is to understand the moment-by-moment processes underlying the production and comprehension of single utterances.

TABLE 2.1
Basic Domains of the Language Use Environment

Domain	Social Unit	Language Unit	Characteristic Processes	Theoretical Import
Cognitive	Individual	Clauses or utterances	Judgment and decision making Attention Memory Categorization	Places constraints on computation
Interactional	Dyad or group	Conversational turns	Epistemic exchanges Grounding (Clark & Brennan, 1991) Multimodal communication	Promotes shared understanding among the dyad or group
Cultural	Community	Languages	Establishment or diffusion of conventions	Promotes commonality of semantic representation among community members

The majority of our own research has primarily focused on understanding processes within this domain. What this research has shown is the existence of certain limitations on computation that prevent speakers and listeners from effectively deploying mutual knowledge when they process language. Any theory of how people establish shared understanding needs to take these limitations into account.

The broader domain in which the individual language user is embedded is the interactional domain, wherein the basic social unit of analysis is the dyad or larger group of conversational interactants and the basic language unit is the conversational turn. The focus at this level is on the interactive processes by which individuals manage the interaction (Sacks, Schelgloff, & Jefferson, 1974) and establish shared understanding (Clark & Brennan, 1991; Garrod & Anderson, 1987). Research on the interactional environment provides two extremely important insights. First, in conversation a shared perspective can be negotiated through an interactive process between interlocutors (Clark & Brennan, 1991; Clark & Wilkes-Gibbs, 1986). Second, it shows that language as traditionally construed is really part of a multichannel system of communication (Clark, 1996) that includes paralinguistic information conveyed through the spoken channel

(Barr, 2003; Clark & Fox Tree, 2002) as well as body movements such as gestures that are conveyed visually (McNeill, 1992).

Much of what we currently know about the interactional domain is due to research by Clark and by other proponents of the mutual knowledge theory. In their view, interaction works at a metarepresentational level; that is, it is used as a vehicle for building models about what others know. Instead, we suggest that interaction works not indirectly at the metarepresentational but directly at the representational level in that it serves to coordinate individuals' conceptions of the discourse. This hypothesis is supported by some of our findings which indicate that people egocentrically apply what they have learned with one interlocutor when talking to the next one despite the fact that this violates mutual knowledge (Barr, 1999; Barr & Keysar, 2002). What is important about interactional processes, we argue, is that they greatly reduce the amount of work that must be done by processes in the cognitive domain.

Last, it is useful to remind oneself that communication is only made possible by the existence of shared semantic representations in the language community. The degree to which individual perspectives diverge or converge depends on the degree of overlap in how people in the community represent linguistic and world knowledge. With little overlap in semantic representations, communication will seem difficult. With large amounts of overlap, communication will seem effortless. To understand what is necessary for successful communication, it is important to evaluate the degree of overlap on which language users can typically rely. This requires an understanding the mechanisms that generate similarities or differences in semantic representation among the members of a language community.

Having completed this overview of the domains of the language use environment, we now put on our first set of lenses and take a closer look.

The Cognitive Domain

The reader might question our classification of the mind of the individual language user as a domain within the larger *environment* because this term has traditionally been used to refer to the set of information that is outside the mind of the individual. However, following Herbert Simon (1996) we view the structure of the human mind as a kind of an environment for thought. We propose that the cognitive domain is relevant to pragmatic inquiry because it imposes limits on the kinds of computations that language users can make during real-time conversation. Furthermore, the so-called "external" environment is itself made possible through the existence of cognitive structures that encode, store, and retrieve information. Therefore, accessing information while planning and interpreting utterances will partake of such basic cognitive processes as judgment, categorization, attention, and memory, and it will thus reflect inherent features of how they operate.

Mechanisms of Decision Making in Language Use. Because utterances are inherently ambiguous, speakers and listeners face a high degree of uncertainty when they attempt to convey their own or decode another's intention on the basis of linguistic evidence. They may have insufficient information about what their interlocutor knows, or they may lack good evidence on which to base their assumptions. Our research shows that language use is no different from other domains in which people must make judgments under conditions of uncertainty. Specifically, we find that speakers and listeners employ the same anchoring and adjustment heuristic in understanding language as they do in other forms of problem solving.

When people make judgments to solve a problem, they tend to anchor their judgments in available information regardless of whether this information is actually useful for solving the problem. They then adjust away from this initial anchor, although the adjustment is typically insufficient; their ultimate response is skewed toward the initial anchor. For example, Tversky and Kahneman (1974) found that a group of high school students who were asked to estimate the multiplicative product of a sequence of numbers listed in descending order came up with higher estimates than a group who was asked to estimate the product of the same sequence with the numbers listed in ascending order. The explanation for this difference was that the students anchored their responses in the initial numbers of the sequence. Similarly, Epley and Gilovich (2001) showed that people often anchor on related, self-generated anchors and then make adjustments. When asked when Washington became president, they anchored on 1776, the lowest possible value, and then adjusted upward.

Likewise, research by Keysar and colleagues suggests that the same anchoring and adjustment principles apply to language processing, including how people perceive the meanings of figurative language (for a more extensive review of the anchoring and adjustment approach to language processing, see Keysar & Barr, 2002). Keysar (1994) showed that people's assessments of how others will perceive sarcasm are anchored in their own knowledge. In his study, participants read a passage involving two protagonists. For example, in one passage June recommends a certain restaurant to Mark. Mark goes there for dinner and has either a positive experience (i.e., enjoys the restaurant) or a negative experience (i.e., hates the restaurant). The next day he leaves a note for June that says, "The restaurant was marvelous, just marvelous." Participants were asked whether June would construe Mark's statement as sarcastic or sincere. Keysar found that respondents tended to think that June would perceive Mark's attitude even though she was missing the crucial information about the valence of his attitude. The interpretation of this finding is that respondents anchored their estimate in their own understanding, and they failed to sufficiently adjust to the perspective of the uninformed addressee.

In addition, Keysar and Bly (1995) reported evidence that people anchor their assessments of how others will perceive the meanings of idioms in their own knowledge. In their study, they selected archaic English idioms such as *the goose hangs high* whose meanings were unfamiliar to modern day college students. The idioms were presented in the context of one of two passages by which the reader could infer either the original meaning or its opposite. For instance, in one passage, *the goose hangs high* was used to express optimism in the future. In a second passage, the same idiom was used to express foreboding about the future. Then, each participant read a passage in which a person used the idiom in conversation with a stranger but in a context that did not reveal its meaning. They were asked what they thought the stranger would take the idiom to mean. Sixty-two percent of respondents tended to think that the stranger would take the meaning to be the same thing they learned in the first place, whereas only 32% believed the stranger would understand the opposite meaning. In short, the respondents' anchoring of their judgments in their own knowledge of the meanings of the idioms led them to believe that the idioms were more transparent than they actually were.

In sum, these findings underscore the relevance of processes of cognition for theories of language use. Language users egocentrically anchor their judgments in available information and fail to fully adjust to the perspectives of others, just as they do in standard decision-making tasks. This suggests that the mechanism by which people assess shared perspective in speaking and understanding and the one they use in nonlinguistic problem solving are one and the same and, therefore, will be subject to the same sort of limitations.

The Control of Attention and Capacity Limitations.   Attentional processes determine what information becomes accessible to cognitive systems in the normal course of their operation. We propose that to operate at a speed that is fast enough to cope with conversation, language processing systems are designed to operate on information that is made available by attention regardless of whether this information is part of mutual knowledge.

Many problems of pragmatics, such as formulating and disambiguating referential expressions, are problems that concern the control of attention. Speakers produce referential expressions to guide listeners' attention to referents. The expression that a speaker chooses in referring to some object— from an elaborate, full noun phrase to a simple pronoun—will depend on the degree to which the referent is in the focus of attention in the discourse (Ariel, 1998; Chafe, 1976; Gundel, Hedberg, & Zacharski, 1993). Likewise, listeners use the speaker's level of specificity as a cue to guide them in their search for referents. For example, when listeners hear pronouns, they will assume that the referent is the current focus of attention.

However, under certain circumstances, a speaker's and a listener's focus of attention may not coincide. Suppose that your sister is telling you about her husband's trip to China, which her husband already told you about when you saw him yesterday. Feeling somewhat bored, your attention strays off, and you remember that you have not caught up with your friend Ben since he returned from Mexico. Just as you are thinking about Ben, your sister asks, "Have you talked to him yet?" The question is, will you consider Ben as the referent of the pronoun *him*, albeit temporarily, even though your brother-in-law has been established as the topic of discourse?

Because the attentional foci of speakers and listeners may not coincide, to avoid miscommunication it would seem optimal for comprehension systems to restrict the search for referents to mutually known information (Clark & Carlson, 1981). We put this restricted search hypothesis to the test by creating such a situation in our laboratory (Keysar et al., 1998). In this experiment, listeners wore a set of headphones while they helped a confederate director fill in missing details on a target picture (e.g., a picture of an airplane). At a critical moment, the listener's attention was distracted by a voice in the headphones that instructed him or her to look at a competitor picture. Just at the moment that the listener's eyes were focused on the competitor, the confederate asked a question about the target picture; for instance, "What color are its wings?" When the competitor picture that was at the focus of the listener's attention was a picture of a woman, listeners were faster to move their eyes back to the target picture than when it was a picture of a bird. This delay indicates that listeners mistook their own private thoughts as the referents of speakers' utterances. This is strong evidence against the restricted search hypothesis, and it supports our contention that language processing systems are designed to rapidly exploit the information made available by attentional processes regardless of its mutuality.

The finding that language processing systems do not initially restrict themselves to mutual knowledge suggests that misunderstanding will be systematic and pervasive. Yet, we know that people can compute the shared perspective when asked. Perhaps the reason why they fail to do this during routine language processing is because of capacity limitations; that is, the system must operate at such a time scale that it cannot accommodate inferences about mutual knowledge.

Horton and Keysar's (1996) study provides evidence in support of this view. In this study, participants described a target shape to a listener. The target shape was paired with a context shape that the speaker could see, but the listener could not. For instance, a target circle appeared next to a larger context circle that only the speaker could see. The question was whether the speaker would describe the target circle as "the small circle" or just "the circle," with the former case representing a failure to consider the listener's lack of knowledge of the context circle. Horton and Keysar found that speakers were more likely to produce such egocentric utterances under the pressure of a response deadline than they were when they were allowed to respond at leisure.

We believe that this series of findings strongly implicates that language processing systems are designed to quickly settle matters of referential ambiguity by making rapid use of available information, regardless of its mutuality. Speakers and listeners routinely ignore even the most blatant cues to a referent's mutuality, such as whether it is occluded from the other's view, when they process utterances. In other words, language processing is anchored in the assumption that what is salient or accessible to oneself will also be accessible to one's interlocutor. Against the theoretical background in which mutual knowledge is taken as the only true guarantee of successful communication, the idea that the design of the language processor would embody such an assumption in its design is perplexing. Yet, we contend that although there are no guarantees of mutual understanding, there are powerful mechanisms in the interactional and cultural environments that promote shared perspectives among interlocutors, which can compensate for these limitations.

The Interactional Domain

One response that we sometimes encounter when we discuss our findings is that perhaps in real interaction, as opposed to in the psychological laboratory, people will be less egocentric. The assumption seems to be that to make interaction work, people will have to be more careful about adhering to mutual knowledge. Yet, we suggest that the opposite of this assumption may hold true: People are much more busy during real conversation than they are in the slow-moving and informationally rarified environment of the psychological laboratory; therefore, they will have fewer resources with which to constantly monitor what others know. However, because conversation is interactive and multimodal, it affords speakers and listeners copious feedback on their performance which affords them the opportunity to be more egocentric.

Even though conversational interaction is the fundamental setting of language use, the study of interaction has had little influence on the study of the psychology of language use. In many ways studies of conversational interaction developed in parallel with the laying of the foundations of sentence-level pragmatics in the Gricean and speech act traditions. The field of psycholinguistics, with its focus on single utterances and the isolated speaker, listener, or reader, has as its primary object the cognitive domain, and it has yet to gain the full impact of insights from studies of interaction.

One reason why research on interaction should cause people to rethink pragmatic theories is that it shows that pragmatic expectations are surprisingly flexible, such that speakers and listeners adapt them to suit their conversational experience. Consider the generalized pragmatic expectation that speakers should be optimally informative in designing referring expressions: They should provide their listeners with no more and no less information than is necessary (Grice, 1975). When choosing the word by which to refer to some object, speakers typically have a wide variety of choices available, each of which reflects different ways of categorizing the object (Brown, 1958). For instance, a shoe can be referred to as *the thing, the shoe,* or *the loafer.* Cruse (1977) suggested that speakers must determine the proper level of lexical specificity or their utterances can generate unintended conversational effects. For the purpose of definite reference, he argued that speakers should choose a specific term only when it is required, or they should default to a conventionally neutral level. For instance, if there are two shoes of different styles, the speaker might call the intended shoe *the loafer.* However, if there is only one shoe, the specific term *loafer* will sound especially "marked" and the speaker should default to the conventionally neutral, basic-level term *shoe.*

Brennan and Clark (1996) reported an experiment that challenges the generality of this pragmatic expectation. In their experiment, speakers played a game with listeners that required them to make reference to the same pictures over and over in contexts requiring different levels of lexical specificity. For instance, they referred to a shoe as *the loafer* multiple times because it appeared in the constraining context of another shoe. But when they were later presented with a test trial in which this same shoe appeared without the constraining context of the other shoe, they continued to use the specific term *loafer* even though it was now overly specific. Brennan and Clark took this as evidence that the dyad had established a mutually accepted "conceptual pact" to refer to this particular shoe as *the loafer.* Moreover, they found that speakers attempted to continue to use the overly specific term even when the test trial took place with a new listener who was absent when the pact was established.

We conducted an experiment that was similar to Brennan and Clark's (Barr & Keysar, 2002, Experiment 3) except that we examined listeners' expectations about the informativeness of speakers. Our experiment had a similar design, in which listeners learned to expect that a speaker would refer to a particular car as *the sports car* because it appeared recurringly within the constraining context of a station wagon. Likewise, the speaker established the precedent of referring to a particular flower as the *carnation* because it appeared in the context of a daisy. In a later posttest they saw a picture containing only the car and the flower and listened to a speaker refer to one of the objects. The question was, would listeners expect the terms *sports car* and *carnation* which were overinformative in this context, or would they expect *car* and *flower* which were sufficient? What they actually heard was the word *car*. Note that if they expected to hear the overly specific terms, they would tend to mistake the word *car* as the initial phonemic segment of the word *carnation*. By tracking listeners' eye movements, we found that listeners expected the overly specific precedents, as revealed by more fixations to the carnation than in a baseline condition. More important, we found this expectation of the precedent to be equally strong among listeners who performed the posttest with a new speaker, one who could not have known of the precedent's existence.

The research on referring precedents is striking because it shows that interlocutors consider their conversational experience more important than prevailing norms of informativeness. Through interaction, speakers and listeners are able to adapt their language use to suit their own purposes. By relying on precedents, interactants reduce the complexity of the problem they face. Speakers will face fewer options during lexical selection; hence, listeners will benefit from less uncertainty in lexical identification. One reason why speakers might use naming precedents and listeners might expect speakers to use them is because they are part of their mutual knowledge. Another reason is because over the course of the interaction repeated use has simply made the lexical item strongly available and the underlying conceptualization strongly entrenched. These explanations differ in that the former assumes that interaction creates changes at the metarepresentational level, in terms of what is mutually accepted and mutually known, whereas the latter assumes that the changes are occurring directly at the representational level. The fact that speakers and listeners both use precedents in ways that violate mutual knowledge offer support for the latter interpretation. Furthermore, this interpretation is consistent with other research that shows how conversational interaction leads to conceptual convergence in how people represent the content of the discourse (Garrod & Anderson, 1987; Markman & Makin, 1998). To be clear, we do not dispute the idea that interacting speakers and listeners can and do keep track of what others know. But because interaction naturally causes speakers and listeners to similarly represent discourse information, we suggest that they need not always consult this metaknowledge to successfully communicate.

A second way in which interaction makes coordinating understanding easier is that it enables people to engage in what we call the *epistemic exchange*, an interactive exchange that serves as a proxy for the direct computation of mutual knowledge. We propose that certain interactive episodes in conversation represent instances of what Kirsh and Maglio (1994) termed *epistemic action*—cases in which people gain information about the world through direct action instead of through computing that information. In an epistemic exchange, speakers or listeners proceed on the basis of an egocentric assumption and gather information about what their interlocutors know through feedback, even though they could have directly computed the partner's perspective. In the case of conversation, interaction provides interlocutors with ample opportunities to learn about what other people know or do not know without having to expend effort computing it themselves.

For example, imagine you are sitting across the table from Henry, and between you there are two candles that you both can see. In addition, there is a smaller candle that is obscured from Henry's view and is even smaller than the two mutually visible candles. When Henry tells you to "pick up the small candle," you could potentially compute the intended referent as the smaller of the two visible candles, because you know that he does not know about the even smaller hidden one. In Clark and Marshall's (1981) terms, only the visible candles are physically co-present and part of your mutual knowledge. However, you might simply pick up the smaller one without really thinking or feel confused and ask, "Which candle?" It might be easier (and more accurate) to get information about Henry's perspective from Henry himself, even though you could derive the identity of the referent on the basis of your mutual knowledge.

We revisited a set of data reported in Keysar et al. (2000) and looked for evidence that addressees engage in such epistemic exchanges. We found that under circumstances such as the one in this example, 27% of the time listeners performed the following actions: (a) asking for clarification (10%), (b) moving the small candle and then being corrected by the speaker (14%), or (c) both (3%). In contrast, in our control condition wherein the object corresponding to the hidden small candle was replaced with a nonreferent (i.e., a glass), in the vast majority of cases addressees were able to go right for the intended referent and required an interactive exchange only 6% of the time. In summary, even when addressees are presented with clear cues to what is mutually known, they often opt to resolve ambiguity by engaging in an epistemic exchange rather than computing the referent themselves. Especially given our finding that people are poor estimators of what others know, it makes a lot of sense for addressees to exploit the dynamics of interaction to distribute the burden of reference resolution rather than try to compute it themselves.

Another dimension of conversation that gives interaction its dynamism is multimodal communication. Despite the conventional terminology, a speaker does more than just speak and a listener does more than just listen. Speakers look and gesture as they speak. Listeners watch, nod, and make facial expressions as they listen. This background of multimodal activity provides interactants with a channel by which they can continually monitor their level of mutual understanding, and one that is backgrounded so as not to obtrude upon the official business of the conversation (Clark, 1996; Clark & Brennan, 1991). When speakers witness an uncomprehending look from a listener midsentence, they can choose to elaborate on or repair their utterances. Listeners can nod and provide other back-channel information to show their continuing attention and that they are following the thread of the discourse. In other words, speakers and listeners not only communicate in the traditional sense but use the backgrounded multimodal channel to give constant evidence of their level of understanding. As with the interactive dimension of conversation, the multimodal character of conversation makes things much easier on language users.

Kelly, Barr, Church, and Lynch (1999) showed that listeners can read a speaker's pragmatic intention from their gestural behavior. In their study, viewers were presented with a video clip in which two actors acted out an everyday scenario that ended with a pragmatically ambiguous target utterance such as *it's hot in here*. The target utterance could potentially be construed as either a literal statement or an indirect request (i.e., to open the window). In one condition, speakers pointed to an object while delivering the target utterance, such as a closed window, that pertained to the intended meaning of the indirect request. In another condition, speakers kept their arms at their sides as they delivered it and maintained eye contact with the addressee. In the former condition, listeners were far more likely to interpret the utterance as an indirect request, showing that gesture can indexically ground the meaning of utterances. Yet, not only did the gesture disambiguate the speech, but the speech served to disambiguate the gesture—people were better at identifying what the speaker was pointing to when they heard the accompanying speech (which did not mention the object) than when they simply saw the pointing gesture. These findings suggest that speech and gesture work together to convey pragmatic meanings.

Another set of studies by Barr emphasizes how even a single vocal channel of communication can carry multiple dimensions of signals that enhance conceptual and linguistic coordination. In one study, listeners learned a set of novel color categories from a pretrained expert by viewing instances of each category and hearing prerecorded labels from the speaker (Barr, 2003). Listeners were able to detect the speaker's level of certainty in the classification from paralinguistic cues such as filled pauses (e.g., *um* and *uh*), hesitations, and rising or falling intonation. Given that people are more certain about the classification of typical than atypical instances, the speaker's paralinguistically conveyed certainty enabled listeners to differentiate good from bad examples and thereby facilitated learning of the categories.

Finally, these same kinds of paralinguistic cues can guide listeners in the identification of referents. Barr (2001) found that speakers produce different "hesitation signatures" when they formulate descriptions of new referents as compared to when they retrieve established precedents to refer to old referents. New referent signatures contained longer hesitations and were more likely to contain a filled pause. A follow-up comprehension experiment found listeners to be sensitive to these signatures. When listeners heard a description of a new referent that was preceded by a hesitation signature containing a filled pause, they were over 300-ms faster at comprehending the description than when the filled pause was replaced by incidental noise. It is surprising that something as humble as an *um* can yield such a large advantage to comprehension, and such a finding suggests that listeners determine the identity of referents not only by what speakers say but by the apparent effort that they put into saying it.

In this discussion of the interactional domain of language use, we attempted to show how the interactive and multimodal processes of conversation simplify the coordination of mutual understanding by reducing the corresponding burden of processes in the cognitive domain. Although many of the same practitioners of the mutual knowledge theory have been the prime champions of research on interaction and multimodal communication, what differs is our interpretation of the implications of this domain for cognitive processing. Because these approaches have tended to eschew explicit discussion of mechanisms, they fail to fully appreciate the degree to which interaction serves as a proxy for the explicit computation of a shared perspective. Interaction serves as a vehicle not only for coordinating the metarepresentations of language users but for the representations themselves. It affords speakers and listeners the opportunity to engage in epistemic exchanges that help them learn about others' perspectives with a minimum of effort. Finally, the multimodal nature of conversation provides language users with immediate feedback and extra channels for communication. In short, the interactional domain enables language users to be more egocentric because it distributes the work that must be done to achieve mutual understanding over other processes in the environment.

The Cultural Domain

Whereas the interactional domain focuses on patterns of language use within a dyad or group of interactants, the cultural domain looks at language use through a wide-angle lens that encompasses the broader language community. We construe the culture as the repository of conventional practices that the members of a community have in common. The cultural domain is relevant to theories of pragmatics because it informs us about how much language users can take for granted when they interact with other members of their communities.

When interactants establish temporary patterns of language use to communicate effectively, they build on preestablished cultural patterns of language use—specifically, linguistic conventions—that the broader language community has shaped over time. The amount of work that language users will need to do to understand one another, whether through direct computation of mutual knowledge or through interactive exchanges, will depend on the degree to which they proceed from the same starting assumptions about the meanings of conventions. If everyone had exactly the same knowledge and experience, there would be little need for mutual knowledge because people could count on others knowing what they know. Conversely, if everyone had wildly different representations, communication would be extremely difficult. The need for communities to develop common representations among members presents a massive problem of social coordination. How do communities solve this problem? On what level of commonality of representation can two average members count? And how do these commonalities come about?

Traditionally, the field of pragmatics has sought to explain the establishment and use of linguistic conventions as a product of the accumulation of mutual knowledge among the members of a language community (Lewis, 1969). According to this view, individuals adhere to community-wide conventions because they have a preference to conform to the practices of other members of their community. Over the course of their experience, they build up a representation of how the modal member of their community will behave. Lewis stated, "If one has often encountered cases in which coordination was achieved in a certain problem by conforming to a certain regularity, and rarely or never encountered cases in which it was not, he is entitled to expect his neighbors to have had much the same experience" (p. 40). Mutual knowledge gives individuals a justification for conforming to the conventions in that it gives them reason to expect others to do the same. In essence, what this view assumes is that there can be no conventions without mutual knowledge.

Barr (in press) reported a series of multiagent computer simulations that shows that mutual knowledge is not necessary for the establishment and maintenance of semantic conventions in language communities. He argued that such representations of communal knowledge are unnecessary because conventions emerge as by-products of dyadic-level mechanisms of coordination. In the simulations, individual agents played a simple signaling game with other agents in the community. Each agent had a lexicon that mapped four symbolic forms onto four meanings. Initially, the form-to-meaning mappings were randomized for each agent. During each round of the simulation, each agent played the signaling game with a randomly selected partner from the community. The agent would attempt to communicate a random sequence of four meanings to its partner, and the partner would attempt to match the speaker's meanings. Agents received feedback as to whether they were correct or incorrect, but they did not receive any information about the other agent's mapping. Agents updated their mappings and then went on to play the next round with new partners.

Although these agents had no representation of what was going on in the community, but just adjusted their lexicons based on their experiences during a sequence of isolated interactions, the communities converged quite robustly to a single set of conventions. Even when they did not establish a single system, they typically converged on several spatially organized signaling systems or dialects, which are hallmarks of human language.

These simulations suggest that coordination can be achieved in language communities as a by-product of the work that language users do in the dyad rather than as the result of high-level calculations about what others know. In addition, it demonstrates that the work that individual language users do to coordinate with their language partners ultimately subserves the purpose of making their representations ever more similar to other members of their community. The fact that they can count on other members of their community having similar experiences with language greatly reduces the work they must do when they speak to others who are like themselves.

CONCLUSION

We began this chapter with a discussion of the paradox of egocentrism in language use. Although the underlying assumption of cooperation requires language users to speak and understand against the background of their mutual knowledge, language users appear to routinely disregard this knowledge. They expect an addressee to perceive sarcasm even when the addressee lacks crucial evidence about the speaker's attitude. They routinely consider hidden objects and private thoughts as the intended referents of speaker's expressions. They expect speakers to follow linguistic precedents that were established by another speaker. All of these findings show that language users are not designed to the exacting standards of pragmatic theories. According to these theories, language users' egocentric behavior does not make sense.

We argued that to make it make sense, we need to look not at the nature of the problem that language users must solve but at the structure of the environment in which language use is embedded. The environment can be divided into three subdomains, which is like looking at a single picture through lenses of different powers of magnification. Our research has focused on the cognitive domain, and it has uncovered limitations on language users' ability to effectively deploy mutual knowledge when processing single utterances. If we are to take these limitations seriously, then we must look elsewhere to find mechanisms that can compensate for these limitations.

The finding of egocentrism in language use need not imply that language users are somehow not adequately designed for the purpose of coordinating understanding. In fact, the processing system's rapid use of available information is exquisitely tuned to provide maximally efficient processing given the interactional and cultural domains in which it operates. In essence, what we are claiming is that language users can get away with a large degree of egocentrism because the work of achieving shared understanding is distributed over interactive, multimodal, and cultural processes in the environment. Interactive processes such as the epistemic exchange allow language users to discover what other people know through negotiation without having to compute it themselves. Multimodal channels of communication enable language users to simultaneously convey and perceive multiple dimensions of meaning, including online feedback about their level of understanding. Cultural processes serve to indirectly coordinate the representations of the individuals in a community, greatly reducing the work they must do in the dyad. In essence, language users can be simpler than pragmatic theories require because part of the burden of coordination is distributed over the domains of dyadic and communal interaction.

To be clear, we do not intend to cast doubt on the possibility of mutual knowledge either as a theoretical construct or as a factor that is operative in conversation. Yet, we wish to emphasize that whether or not a speaker or listener uses mutual knowledge on a particular occasion is an empirical question. The coincidence of perspectives is not a fortuitous event but rather a direct consequence of the operation of background processes in the language use environment. Thus, the mere observation that a speaker produces an utterance that is in alignment with mutual knowledge does not warrant the inference that she or he directly computed that knowledge as mutual at any time. The speaker may have or may have simply used information that was simultaneously available and salient to him or her and the interlocutor.

Moreover, our purpose is not to question people's ability to compute metarepresentations about what others know. Yet, our results imply that the cognitive system is designed to operate efficiently on representations, not metarepresentations. However, this does not preclude the use of such higher order representations to monitor and correct problems that arise during conversation. Thus, speakers' and listeners' ability to compute mutual knowledge might be operative primarily when communication fails. According to our findings, it appears that mutual knowledge is most likely to be implemented as a mechanism for detecting and correcting errors instead of an intrinsic, routine process of the language processor.

Faced with the findings reviewed so far, we think it is important to rethink exactly what it means to be cooperative, a concept that is at the heart of most theories of language use. For one, the supposition that speakers strive to be maximally informative in lexical selection does not seem to fit what they actually do. Perhaps a better description of what they do is simply rely on their past and current discourse experience and select the term that is most strongly available to them. As the simulations by Barr (in press) show, one's own conversational experience can often be a reliable guide to what is

conventional in the community. That said, there are probably social politeness norms that will cause speakers to be more careful about their lexical selection (e.g., whether to refer to a woman as *my mother, mom*, or *Mrs. Smith*).
Just when and how speakers will heed social circumstances during lexical selection are questions that warrant further investigation.

The presence of epistemic exchanges, hitherto unnoted in the literature,
also calls for us to rethink the notion of cooperation. If speakers and listeners
really had as strong expectations of cooperation as the theory says they
should, then they would routinely be confronted with behavior that seemed
uncooperative. Perhaps language users tolerate some slack over the short
run because it is the most effective way to share the burden of coordinating
understanding over the long run. Perhaps it is not through the individual
sentence by which language users demonstrate they are cooperative, but
rather it is how they behave over the course of the conversation.

In closing, the inherent ambiguity of language creates a complex problem
for language users and seems to call for correspondingly complex mechanisms that enable language users to successfully communicate in the face of
such vast uncertainty. Our message is that this complexity should not be
sought within the head of the individual language user but rather in the cognitive, interactional, and cultural domains that comprise the environment
of language use. Language users can be simpler than theories require because the environment is more complex than these theories envision. It is
only by considering the behavior of language users against this background
that we can truly make sense of how we make sense.

REFERENCES

Ariel, M. (1988). Referring and accessibility. *Journal of Linguistics, 24*, 65–87.

Barr, D. J. (1999). *A theory of dynamic coordination for conversational interaction.* Unpublished doctoral dissertation.

Barr, D. J. (2001). *Paralinguistic correlates of discourse structure.* Paper presented at the
43rd annual meeting of the Psychonomic Society, Orlando, FL.

Barr, D. J. (in press). The emergence of conventions in language communities. In J.
C. Trueswell & M. K. Tanenhaus (Eds.), *Approaches to studying world-situated language use: Bridging the language-as-product and language-as-action traditions.* Cambridge, MA: MIT Press.

Barr, D. J. (2003). Paralinguistic correlates of conceptual structure. *Psychonomic Bulletin & Review, 10*, 462–467.

Barr, D. J., & Keysar, B. (2002). Anchoring comprehension in linguistic precedents.
Journal of Memory and Language, 46, 391–418.

Brennan, S. E., & Clark, H. H. (1996). Conceptual pacts and lexical choice in conversation. *Journal of Experimental Psychology: Learning, Memory, and Cognition,
22*, 1482–1493.

Brown, R. (1958). How shall a thing be called? *Psychological Review, 65*, 14–21.

Chafe, W. L. (1976). Givenness, contrastiveness, definiteness, subjects, topics, and point of view. In C. N. Li (Ed.), *Subject and topic* (pp. 26–55). New York: Academic Press.

Clark, H. H. (1996). *Using language.* Cambridge, England: Cambridge University Press.

Clark, H. H. (1998). Communal lexicons. In K. Malmkjær & J. Williams (Eds.), *Context in language learning and language understanding* (pp. 63–87). Cambridge, England: Cambridge University Press.

Clark, H. H., & Brennan, S. E. (1991). Grounding in communication. In L. B. Resnick, J. M. Levine, & S. D. Teasley (Eds.), *Perspectives on socially shared cognition* (pp. 127–49). Washington, DC: American Psychological Association.

Clark, H. H., & Carlson, T. B. (1981). Context for comprehension. In J. Long & A. Baddeley (Eds.), *Attention and performance IX* (pp. 313–330). Hillsdale, NJ: Lawrence Erlbaum Associates.

Clark, H. H., & Fox Tree, J. E. (2002). Using *uh* and *um* in spontaneous speaking. *Cognition, 84,* 73–111.

Clark, H. H., & Marshall, C. R. (1981). Definite reference and mutual knowledge. In A. K. Joshe, B. L. Webber, & I. A. Sag (Eds.), *Elements of discourse understanding* (pp. 10–63). Cambridge, England: Cambridge University Press.

Clark, H. H., & Murphy, G. L. (1982). Audience design in meaning and reference. In J. F. Le Ny & W. Kintsch (Eds.), *Language and comprehension* (pp. 287–299). Amsterdam: North-Holland.

Clark, H. H., Schreuder, R., & Buttrick, S. (1983). Common ground and the understanding of demonstrative reference. *Journal of Verbal Learning and Verbal Behavior, 22,* 245–258.

Clark, H. H., & Wilkes-Gibbs, D. (1986). Referring as a collaborative process. *Cognition, 22,* 1–39.

Cruse, D. A. (1977). The pragmatics of lexical specificity. *Journal of Linguistics, 13,* 153–164.

Epley, N., & Gilovich, T. (2001). Putting adjustment back in the anchoring and adjustment heuristic: Divergent processing of self-generated and experimenter-provided anchors. *Psychological Science, 12,* 391–396.

Garrod, S., & Anderson, A. (1987). Saying what you mean in dialogue: A study in conceptual and semantic co-ordination. *Cognition, 27,* 181–218.

Gerrig, R. J. (1986). Process models and pragmatics. In N. E. Sharkey (Ed.), *Advances in cognitive science* (Vol. 1, pp. 23–42). New York: Wiley.

Greene, S. B., Gerrig, R. J., McKoon, G., & Ratcliff, R. (1994). Unheralded pronouns and management by common ground. *Journal of Memory and Language, 33,* 511–526.

Grice, H. P. (1975). Logic and conversation. In P. Cole & J. Morgan (Eds.), *Syntax and semantics: Vol. 3. Speech acts* (pp. 41–58). New York: Academic Press.

Gundel, J. K., Hedberg, N., & Zacharski, R. (1993). Cognitive status and the form of referring expressions in discourse. *Language, 69,* 274–307.

Horton, W. S., & Keysar, B. (1996). When do speakers take into account common ground? *Cognition, 59(1),* 91–117.

Kelly, S. D., Barr, D. J., Church, R. B., & Lynch, K. (1999). Offering a hand to pragmatic understanding: The role of speech and gesture in comprehension and memory. *Journal of Memory and Language, 40(4),* 577–592.

Keysar, B. (1994). The illusory transparency of intention: Linguistic perspective taking in text. *Cognitive Psychology, 26*(2), 165–208.

Keysar, B. (1997). Unconfounding common ground. *Discourse Processes, 24,* 253–270.

Keysar, B., & Barr, D. J. (2002). Self-anchoring in conversation: Why language users don't do what they "should." In T. Gilovich, D. W. Griffin, & D. Kahneman (Eds.), *Heuristics and biases: The psychology of intuitive judgment* (pp. 150–166) Cambridge, England: Cambridge University Press.

Keysar, B., Barr, D. J., Balin, J. A., & Brauner, J. S. (2000). Taking perspective in conversation: The role of mutual knowledge in comprehension. *Psychological Science, 11,* 32–38.

Keysar, B., Barr, D. J., Balin, J. A., & Paek, T. S. (1998). Definite reference and mutual knowledge: Process models of common ground in comprehension. *Journal of Memory and Language, 39,* 1–20.

Keysar, B., & Bly, B. (1995). Intuitions of the transparency of idioms: Can one keep a secret by spilling the beans? *Journal of Memory and Language, 34,* 89–109.

Keysar, B., & Henly, A. S. (2002). Speakers' overestimation of their effectiveness. *Psychological Science, 13,* 207–212.

Kirsh, D., & Maglio, P. (1994). On distinguishing epistemic from pragmatic action. *Cognitive Science, 18,* 513–549.

Lea, R. B., Mason, R. A., Albrecht, J. E., Birch, S. L., & Myers, J. L. (1998). Who knows what about whom: What role does common ground play in accessing distant information? *Journal of Memory and Language, 39,* 70–84.

Lewis, D. (1969). *Convention: A philosophical study.* Cambridge, MA: Harvard University Press.

Markman, A. B., & Makin, V. S. (1998). Referential communication and category acquisition. *Journal of Experimental Psychology: General, 127,* 331–354.

McNeill, D. (1992). *Hand and mind: What gestures reveal about thought.* Chicago: University of Chicago Press.

Sacks, H., Schelgloff, E. A., & Jefferson, G. (1974). A simplest systematics for the organization of turn-taking for conversation. *Language, 50,* 696–735.

Simon, H. A. (1996). *The sciences of the artificial* (3rd ed.). Cambridge, MA: MIT Press.

Tversky, A., & Kahneman, D. (1974). Judgment under uncertainty: Heuristics and biases. *Science, 185,* 1124–1131.

3

Contextual Expressions and Common Ground

Richard J. Gerrig
William S. Horton
State University of New York at Stony Brook

In his autobiographical account of his rise to the top of corporate America, Jack Welch revealed that one of his favorite expressions during business discussions was, "Don't Walter Cronkite me!" (Welch, 2001, p. 43). Fortunately, Welch immediately provided an interpretation of his somewhat idiosyncratic meaning: "That [the utterance] was understood by everyone to mean: 'You report the bad news, but you don't tell me how you're going to fix it.' " It was not, presumably, Walter Cronkite's responsibility as a newscaster to do more than report the news. Thus, the special meaning Welch wished his underlings to take from the verb phrase "to Walter Cronkite" needed to have been acquired through interactions with Welch himself.

In this chapter, we discuss *contextual expressions*—the class of linguistic phenomena to which "to Walter Cronkite" belongs. We begin by delimiting this class of expressions and describing how, as in the case of "to Walter Cronkite," speakers produce them against the background of appropriate assessments of the common ground shared with their addressees. We then discuss the ways in which addressees understand these types of expressions. We structure this latter discussion around the questions that have dominated research on other types of pragmatic phenomena. The conclusion we draw is that addressees are well-prepared to understand the types of contextual expressions that arise frequently in social interactions.

COMMON GROUND AND THE PRODUCTION
OF CONTEXTUAL EXPRESSIONS

The verb phrase "to Walter Cronkite" fails to appear in a standard dictionary. Rather than being a conventional part of the language, the phrase takes on meaning by virtue of the discourse context in which it appears. This is the hallmark of contextual expressions: "Their senses depend entirely on the time, place, and circumstances in which they are uttered" (H. H. Clark, 1983, p. 300). As such, each contextual expression has an infinite number of potential meanings. Jack Welch's use of "to Walter Cronkite" provides a good example of this infinite flexibility. Most *eponymous verb phrases*, the category of language to which "to Walter Cronkite" belongs, are based on salient acts of the eponym (H. H. Clark & Gerrig, 1983; Rapp & Gerrig, 1999). This is true of Welch's use of "to Walter Cronkite" (i.e., Cronkite did deliver the news), but his meaning transcends that starting point. We see immediately how speakers, by using proper contexts to focus attention, can weave infinite variations on the salient acts associated with a famous individual. For "to Walter Cronkite," we also might think of "to show great empathy in the face of a national calamity" or "to host the Kennedy Centers Honors."

Eponymous verb phrases are one of a wide variety of contextual expressions (H. H. Clark, 1983). Because we provide tokens throughout the chapter, we only give a small number of examples here. We wish to give a brief sense of the range of these expressions, from those that blend in to those that call attention to themselves:

- Recently—thinking a *mountain vacation* would cheer me—I sublet my apartment to a handsome but somber newlywed couple, who turned out to be every bit as responsible as I'd hoped (noun–noun combination, italics added, Jen, 1999, p. 40).
- In between those times, Pino's was home to a few regular drunks, and the kitchen was taken over by cockroaches as big as barn cats. I ate at Pino's in spite of the *roach rumor* because Anthony Pino made the best pizza in Trenton (noun–noun combination, italics added, Evanovich, 1999, p. 45).
- 'I'm going door-to-door with Fred's photo,' I told her [Lula]. 'Want to help?'

  'Sure, you just give me one of those posters, and I'll *door-to-door* the hell out of you' (denominal verb, italics added, Evanivich, 1999, p. 132).
- All he knew was that, assuming, to begin with, that she was willing, he couldn't sleep with a woman like Cindy and then leave her flat. She could *you folk* him, he could never *us folk* her (denominal verb, Jen, 1999, p. 32).

Each of these examples provides circumstances in which a contextual expression fills a gap in the mental lexicon. For that reason, we also use the term *lexical innovation* to describe many tokens of contextual expressions.

We left one of these examples mysterious on purpose: What precisely do the verb phrases "to you folk" and "to us folk" mean? It is likely to be the case that a reader could get a general sense of what these expressions mean, but a more precise understanding requires an accumulation of experiences over the course of a short story. In the story, an Asian-American businessman, Art, has accidentally reserved a room at a welfare hotel. An African-American woman, Cindy, who lives in the hotel comforts him after he has been knocked unconscious (Jen, 1999, p. 30):

'Sure musta been a shock,' she said, 'End up in a place like this ....'

'What about you? It's no place for you, either, you and your kids.'

'Maybe so,' she said. 'But that's how the Almighty planned it, right? You folk rise up while we set and watch.' She said this with so little rancor, with something so like intimacy, that it almost seemed an invitation of sorts.

Somewhat later, Art reflects on Cindy's utterance (p. 31):

You folk. What folk did Cindy mean?

This reflection eventuates in Art's (mental) assertion, "She could *you folk* him, he could never *us folk* her."

This example illustrates the way in which contextual expressions rely on the *common ground* shared between the speaker and addressee. That is, the meanings of such expressions can only be determined when addressees take into account the appropriate knowledge mutually known to both interlocutors. In this literary example, the reader is not exactly an addressee, but the author still wrote with an expectation that the expressions have shared experiences as their foundation (Gerrig, 1993). More generally, common ground is established between individuals either as the result of common membership in particular sociocultural groups or on the basis of joint personal experiences. H. H. Clark (1996) described this distinction as one between *communal* common ground and *personal* common ground; both types of common ground are important for understanding particular contextual expressions.

Communal Common Ground and Contextual Expressions

Communal common ground, which we also call *community membership*, is the shared body of knowledge possessed by individuals who belong to particular cultural communities. These communities can be reasonably well-defined, such as "members of the psychology department" and "Canadians," or they may exist on a more ad-hoc basis, such as "people who were standing on a subway platform while a performer sang 'The Way You Look Tonight.' " H. H. Clark (1996) listed a number of types of communities based on everything from nationality to occupation to political stance to hobbies. Every individual is simultaneously a member of multiple social and cultural groups, and as a result, every individual shares partially overlapping sets of common ground with every other individual who belongs to the same groups.

Community membership is important for providing the background for many types of language use. Within particular communities, for example, it is often assumed that all of the members of that group will have knowledge of a certain vocabulary or jargon (e.g., psychology jargon such as *dependent variable* or *ANOVA*). In these cases, the specialized vocabulary in use within a community has a set of meanings and functions like any other set of lexical items. Contextual expressions, by contrast, put the knowledge mutually known to community members to use in innovative, unconventional ways.

The example with which we began, "to Walter Cronkite," provides an excellent example of a contextual expression that relies on community membership. Understanding of this phrase requires, to start, membership in the community of individuals who remember that Cronkite was a news anchor. Speakers should only use this phrase when they have good reasons to believe a priori that their addresses are members of that community. Consider another eponymous phrase uttered by a character on the situation comedy "Undeclared": "You better shut up man, or I'm gonna Van Damme your head off." Although this statement can be generally understood as a threat, its particular meaning will be clear only to individuals belonging to the community who are aware that Jean-Claude Van Damme is the star of several violent martial-arts movies. The sitcom's writers presumably believed that the members of their target audience were overwhelmingly members of the appropriate community.

In fact, because contextual expressions have shifting senses, the meanings of particular eponymous verb phrases may differ from community to community and may change within a community over time. For example, there was probably a moment in time when "to do an O.J." meant to dash athletically through an airport. As of 1995, however, "to do an O.J." took on divergent new meanings (cited in Rapp & Gerrig, 1999, p. 613):

- *From an essay by Martin Amis:* A coinage has forged itself within the media community of the West Coast: "O.J.," as a *verb*. Thus, "to O.J." Or, passively (and much, much more commonly), "to be O.J.-ed" or "to get O.J.-ed." "O.J.-ing," generally, has nothing to do with sports or movies, or sexual jealousy. It has to do with media reschedulings caused by extra coverage of the O.J. Simpson trial.

"People are always getting O.J.-ed off of things," explains Kathi Goldmark, my media escort in San Francisco.

"So for example you'd say … ?"

" 'Norman Mailer was going to do national TV, but he got O.J.-ed off of it.' "

"I glance at my schedule and say, "Look! I'm meant to do a radio interview at eleven-thirty. Live. But it says here they'll tape it if I get O.J.-ed."

• *From a letter in response to the original essay:* Martin Amis … notes that in Los Angeles "O.J." has become a verb …. In New Jersey, this verb has a different meaning. Recently, I was standing in line at a local deli behind a customer who asked the counterman to "O.J." his sandwich. Without a word of inquiry, the employee lifted his knife and cut the sandwich in half.

We suspect that, given the divergence of opinion with respect to O.J. Simpson's guilt, the phrase "to do an O.J." was used quite variously. Such is, of course, the nature of contextual expressions.

Eponymous phrases are a class of contextual expression that clearly require consideration of information held in common between speakers and addressees. Moreover, understanding such phrases engages a hierarchy of beliefs on the part of addressees about the ways in which speakers have assessed background information (H. H. Clark & Gerrig, 1983). Each of these beliefs makes reference to information that is in communal common ground. First, there is the identity of the eponym. If an addressee has no idea who Jean-Claude Van Damme is, then the expression "van Damme your head off" will not have its full intended effect. Next, particular acts of the eponym must be in common ground, and there must be one or more acts that are relevant to the situation. Jean-Claude Van Damme has a number of acts that are potentially associated with him and known to his fans, including "bad acting" and "showing his bare chest a lot," but presumably only something like "bloodying opponents through kickboxing" is relevant in a threatening context. Finally, the speaker must assume that the addressee will be able to identify the relevant act upon hearing the eponymous verb phrase. Thus, when speakers produce a phrase such as "Van Damme your head off" they are signaling their own belief that they have made an appropriate judgment about the community knowledge—with an appropriate level of detail—that they and their addressees have in common.

In this section, we focused on phrases involving eponyms because they appear to be circumstances in which contextual expressions engage community membership. Note, in addition, that speakers also make assessments of community membership as a part of the process through which words or phrases that began as contextual expressions become conventionalized (E.

V. Clark & H. H. Clark, 1979; Gerrig & Gibbs, 1988). For example, within his community Jack Welch's utterance "Don't Walter Cronkite me!" presumably had a meaning that had achieved the status of a conventional idiom. In general, speakers must be aware that expressions that function as conventional in some communities may still be contextual in others. Consider this example (Michaels, 2001, p. 111):

> [Norbert] is always broke, but he doesn't think about getting a job. He schemes day and night. And he dollars me. You know the expression? 'Nachman, lend me a dollar.' He never pays me back.

By uttering "You know the expression?" this speaker evokes a community for which "to dollar" can be conventionally understood to mean "ask for a dollar" but suggests that his addressee may not be part of it. Thus, speakers must make judgments of community membership to determine whether they must continue to provide context for what began as contextual expressions.

Personal Common Ground and Contextual Expressions

Personal common ground is the set of information shared between two (or more) individuals arising from their joint perceptual or physical experiences, like conversations (H. H. Clark, 1996). In the parlance of H. H. Clark and Marshall (1981), personal common ground is based on physical or linguistic copresence, and it is built up over the course of interactions between individuals. Suppose an introductory psychology lecture is interrupted by a loud bang outside the classroom. When the professor utters, "What was that?" he is making the assumption that, by virtue of physical copresence, the reference of "that" will be clear. Suppose the same professor has caught two students cheating on an extra-credit assignment. When the professor informs his colleague, "It's happened again," he is making the assumption, by virtue of linguistic copresence, that his addressee will recall their conversation about the ubiquity of cheaters. Both types of personal common ground provide ample opportunities for speakers to produce contextual expressions.

With respect to physical copresence, contextual expressions often serve the function of identifying some object or activity in the environment. For example, Downing (1977) provided an anecdote about a friend who was "instructed to sit in the *apple-juice seat*" (p. 818). The intended meaning of the phrase—"the seat in front of which a glass of apple juice had been placed"—was clear by virtue of physical copresence. Downing observed that the constraints on these types of deictic noun–noun combinations "appear to be less severe than those which govern compounds suitable as long-range category labels, usable and interpretable from situation to situation" (p. 819). That is, when speakers create novel noun–noun combinations of this sort, they need only call attention to salient physical features of the immediate context of use. Still, it is possible to find contextual expressions based on physical copresence that function more conceptually. Consider these examples from an Olympic gymnastics sportscast:

- He cowboyed it.
- He has to cowboy it a little bit.

In the original contexts, the meaning of the two uses of "to cowboy" were made clear by virtue of physical copresence: In each case, the gymnast had bowed his legs a bit to facilitate rotation.

Speakers also routinely avail themselves of linguistic copresence to produce contextual expressions that name both ephemeral and more permanent concepts. Consider this line from a short story: "And there she is, the condiment gal" (Labute, 2001, p. 121). The author presumably expected readers to be able to understand "condiment gal" because of the story's opening episode: "Now there's a nice lay, he thinks to himself, as he politely sidesteps and lets her out of line so she can carry her food over to the condiment island" (p. 120). "Condiment gal" succeeds as a referring phrase because of linguistic copresence, but it does not name any intrinsic property of the *gal*.

Other contextual expressions appear to function via linguistic copresence to create a new conceptual structure. This was true of examples we cited earlier (e.g., *roach rumor* and "you folk"). Consider an additional example (Evanovich, 1997, pp. 6–7).

'Well, of course you can do it,' I said. 'It's just that this situation is sort of … delicate.' …

'Hell,' she said, stuffing herself into her jacket. 'I can delicate your ass off.'

In this case "to delicate" seems to be a good candidate for a deadjectival verb that could potentially endure over time as a standard of behavior that the speaker was or was not able to meet.

Conversation and the Emergence of Contextual Expressions

Although we largely cited literary examples, conversational tokens of contextual expressions assume the same functions. In the most interesting cases, they emerge in conversations to serve as labels for concepts that are not otherwise lexicalized. So, for example, as a young girl watched someone remove a bicycle helmet before entering a grocery store, she volunteered,

"It's okay to wear it. It's a store helmet." In this construction *store helmet* projects a conceptualization of the world in which helmets can be discriminated as to their store worthiness.

Because these contextual expressions name unlexicalized concepts, they often represent a speaker's attempt to negotiate a perspective with an addressee. In some of our experimental work, we observed how contextual expressions unfold in time, as speakers and addressees collaborate jointly to develop expressions that aptly encode joint perspectives. Our corpus of conversational data comes from a referential communication task in which participants playing the roles of directors and matchers refer repeatedly to a set of picture cards as part of a card-matching task (Gerrig & Horton, 2001). In the opening round we often see overt negotiation with respect to particular cards—here, a fish:

Director (D): A multicolored fish.

Matcher (M): Does it have like red lines?

D: Blue, red- it looks like a flag or whatever.

The second round still involves collaboration:

D: The multicolored fish.

M: Like the flag?

D: The flag yeah.

In subsequent rounds, the expression settles in and becomes truncated. The third time the director describes this fish the utterance is "The multicolored American flag fish." The final time, the phrase became "The American flag one." Other directors and matchers negotiated other expressions for the same fish, such as "the rainbow fish." We see in these examples the process by which speakers propose contextual expressions to label novel concepts and addressees participate in accepting or modifying those proposals. In that way, contextual expressions emerge from linguistic copresence with the potential of functioning beyond their original contexts.

We now completed a brief survey of the origins and functions of contextual expressions. In each case, we showed that contextual expressions are deeply social in their origins. Speakers produce contextual expressions against the background of appropriate common ground. That is not to say that speakers are always correct in their judgments. Because assessments of common ground rely on speakers' and addressees' memory processes, the quality of those assessments will depend on the quality of those memory processes (Gerrig & Horton, 2001). We could, for example, gloss our earlier example "And he dollars me. You know the expression?" as an instance in which the speaker decided, through monitoring of his language production, that "dollars me" might not be sufficiently comprehensible without some help. Still, the query "You know the expression?" reasserts the social function of language. We now turn our attention from the social circumstances in which speakers produce contextual expressions to the mental processes that allow addressees to understand them.

PROCESSES OF UNDERSTANDING CONTEXTUAL EXPRESSIONS

The hallmark of pragmatic phenomena is that speakers' meanings depart from the meanings of the words they utter. Consider this exchange (Dennis, 1958, pp. 13–14):

> "Chilly out, dear," I said, kissing her. "Anything in the mail? I mean like especially terrible Christmas cards."

> Pegeen knew perfectly well what I meant and went on to say so. "I know perfectly well what you mean. You mean is there some word from our child or from that madwoman who carried him off. And the answer is No. Just as it's been every day for the last four months. No! No! No!"

In this excerpt, common ground provides the link between what the narrator says and what his wife, Pegeen, correctly understands him to mean. Research on pragmatics has largely been directed toward uncovering the processes and representations that allow addressees to understand what particular speakers mean on particular occasions. With respect to our analysis of the production of contextual expressions, we also pose the questions of process and representation: With what time course are addressees able to use common ground to narrow down contextual expressions' meaning from infinite possibilities to (in most cases) a single possibility? And to what extent do representations of out-of-context meanings affect this time course?

How Powerfully Does Common Ground Constrain Meaning?

As we just noted, an important topic of research on pragmatic phenomena has been the relationship between speakers' words (i.e., literal meanings) and the meanings those words accrue when addressees bring common ground to bear (i.e., speakers' meanings). Consider an indirect request, such as "Could you please pass the salt?" Under appropriate circumstances, an addressee might respond "Sure" and then pass the salt. Such a response suggests that the addressee is aware both of the literal, direct force of the utterance (i.e., a question of ability) and the indirect force (i.e., a request for action; H. H. Clark, 1979). However, what is the relationship between these two types of meaning? We consider, in turn, two aspects of this question that have been addressed by researchers on pragmatics. (Because it is not entirely clear how the concept of literal meaning applies to words, for contextual expressions we speak of out-of-context meanings rather than literal meanings.)

Do Out-of-Context Meanings Have Temporal Primacy?   Because most theories of comprehension have been theories of literal meaning, they have most often made an implicit or explicit assumption that addressees recover literal meaning as a necessary step along the way to recovering speaker's meaning. On these accounts, if one examines the time course of comprehension, the literal meaning also comes first. What has come to be called the *standard pragmatic model* suggests just such temporal primacy (Grice, 1975; Searle, 1979). According to this model, when a speaker performs an indirect request (or uses irony, metaphor, and so on), the addressee must construct the literal meaning and determine whether it is the entirety of the speaker's intended meaning before doing anything else. As such, addressees should take less time to understand utterances conveying just literal meanings.

The temporal predictions of the standard pragmatic model have been tested and disconfirmed with great regularity (for a review, see Gibbs, 1994). For example, Gibbs (1979) contrasted reading times for utterances used either as literal or indirect requests. Gibbs recorded readers' times to read the target sentences ("Must you open the window?") and to verify a paraphrase of the intended literal or indirect meaning. The sum of these times was reliably shorter for the indirect requests than for the literal requests—a clear contradiction of the prediction that literal meanings have temporal primacy. These types of experiments have allowed researchers to rule out the standard pragmatic model as a general account of language processing. The results suggest that addressees are swiftly able to put common ground—in this case, story context—to use to arrive at appropriate understandings of speakers' utterances.

Contextual expressions provide an opportunity to assess the time course with which addressees engage common ground at the level of the lexicon. Consider this sentence: "She had never done so much wadding as she did now, packing up to move from the fun house" (Jen, 1999, p. 193). The phrase "fun house" has a conventional meaning as an attraction at an amusement park. However, in this particular discourse setting "fun house" referred to a nonamusement park house and "fun" was intended ironically (Jen, 1999, p. 182):

It was at least with a feeling of mutuality that they started to call the house *the fun house* ....

—'It mocks us,' Sven said, 'with its air of being at our service, when if fact we live in service to it.'

"Fun house" provides an example of a *preempting innovation*—contextual expressions that are identical to conventional expressions (Gerrig, 1989). Such preempting innovations are relatively common particularly because most instances of metonymy qualify. For example, in its original conversational contest the utterance "Let me give you your orange juice" was used to mean "Let me give you a coupon for free orange juice."

How do addressees understand preempting innovations? There are at least two possibilities. The first possibility—the *error recovery model*—gives temporal primacy to the conventional meaning. In parallel to the standard pragmatic model, the error recovery model suggests that addressees first process the conventional meaning fully. Thus, the model would anticipate that readers would access the lexicalized meaning of "fun house" and try to create a representation of the utterance in which the conventional meaning could function appropriately. Only when the conventional meaning proved to be in error would the reader engage other processes to recover. An alternative possibility—the *concurrent processing model*—suggests that processes of developing conventional and innovative meanings function in parallel.

To contrast these models, Gerrig (1989) wrote a series of stories that were based on pairs of noun–noun combinations such as "door man" and "cave man." For each pair, one story ended with an utterance in which the noun–noun combination was used in its conventional sense:

> A movie company is making a new multimillion dollar film. This afternoon they are supposed to film a strange dream sequence. At the beginning, a Neanderthal man is seen standing by a cave. Suddenly he becomes the man guarding the door of a posh hotel. The director realized that no one had been hired to play this part. He said, "We really ought to get the door man."
>
> (or:) He said, "We really ought to get the cave man."

A second story created innovative meanings for each combination:

> The Fine Arts Department was hiring a new faculty member. The department needed people in two areas. They no longer had faculty who taught about caves or doors. Unfortunately they could afford only one new professor. Professor Rogers had an opinion about the best choice. He said, "We really ought to get the door man."
>
> (or:) He said, "We really ought to get the cave man."

For the conventional uses, it should be the case that the one or the other of the two noun–noun combinations will be easier to understand (because, e.g., one of the two combinations has a higher frequency of use). As such, the error recovery model makes two predictions. First, innovative uses of the combinations should inevitably take longer to understand than do conventional uses (because error recovery presumably takes time). Second, the time to understand a preempting meaning for a relatively slow conventional use should also be relatively slow. Suppose, for example, readers take longer to understand the utterance using the conventional sense of *door man* than the parallel utterance using *cave man*. Assume that, all other things being equal, processes beyond conventional meaning (e.g., error detection) add a standard increment to comprehension time. In that case, readers should also take longer to understand *door man* in its innovative use. Thus, the ordering of reading time (e.g., for the uses of *door man* and *cave man*) should remain stable across the conventional and innovative contexts. By comparison, the concurrent processing model predicts no particular relationship between the conventional and innovative uses of the combinations.

Participants in the experiment read 20 stories each of which included a compound noun with a conventional or innovative meaning (i.e., participants read only one of the four versions for each pair) as well as 20 filler stories. The reading times for the sentences with the noun–noun combinations contradicted the predictions of the error recovery model. Gerrig (1989) sorted the pairs of combinations to gather together those that were relatively fast (mean reading time = 2.10 s) and relatively slow (mean = 2.53 s) for conventional uses within each pair. The error recovery model suggests that the same difference should be observed for innovative uses. In fact, the pattern was reversed. Innovative uses based on "fast" conventional uses took more time to read (mean = 2.97 s) than innovative uses based on "slow" conventional uses (mean = 2.51 s). These means suggest, in addition, that the innovative uses of the noun-noun combinations did not inevitably take longer to understand than the conventional uses. Although overall the reading times were longer for the innovative uses, those times for the "slow" member of each pair converged (i.e., the mean reading times were 2.53 and 2.51 s). These data are consistent with the concurrent processing model's suggestion that the processes that give rise to lexical and innovative meanings operate in parallel. In addition, the reversal in the pattern of "slow" and "fast" hints that the processes may be competing for the same resources. That is, when the conventional meaning is accessed quickly (i.e., the "fast" cases) it was relatively difficult for readers to create the innovative meaning.

The rejection of the error recovery model strongly echoes the rejection of the standard pragmatic model. These experiments extend the important conclusion that common ground has a powerful effect—early and often. For these stories, linguistic copresence, as encoded in the accumulating context, enables readers to overwrite ready-made meanings. These results foreshadow the suggestion we make somewhat later that the processes that allow addressees to understand contextual expressions have wider application than just for those expressions. Any word or phrase could be a preempting innovation. As such, the processes that allow them to be understood must be in perpetual readiness to generate appropriate readings.

Do Out-of-Context Meanings Have Conceptual Primacy? Recall circumstances in which the addressee of the utterance "Could you please pass the salt?" replies "Sure" and then passes the salt. In this case, it seems that the addressee has recovered both the literal and indirect meanings. However, is it necessarily the case that addressees inevitably recover literal meanings—that is, even if literal meanings do not always come first, do they always come? Researchers have considered this question in various ways (for a review, see Gibbs, 1994). Consider an experiment in which participants were asked to read stories that provided contexts that generated either literal or indirect meaning for the same sentence (Gibbs, 1983). Gibbs demonstrated that literal meanings were not particularly accessible in indirect contexts. This result suggests that readers did not inevitably construct literal meanings for these utterances. Rather, addressees used common ground to short circuit or eliminate construction of literal meanings.

For many types of contextual expressions, it would be quite hard to define an out-of-context meaning. It is not clear, for example, how addressees might represent the phrases "to delicate" or "to Van Damme" without immediately assessing them with respect to common ground. Still, one type of contextual expression has generated a good deal of research as an out-of-context phenomenon. Specifically, researchers have used noun–noun combinations as a way to study *conceptual combination*—the processes through which the independent meanings of different concepts (e.g., *roach* and *rumor*) interact to yield innovative combinations (e.g., *roach rumor*; e.g., Coolen, Van Jaarsveld, & Schreuder, 1991, 1993; Gagné & Shoben, 1997; Murphy, 1990; Wisniewski, 1996; Wisniewski & Love, 1998; Wisniewski & Middleton, 2002). With few exceptions, researchers have studied conceptual combination by presenting experimental participants with noun–noun combinations with no supporting context. Researchers then build theories about processes of conceptual combination based on the comparative difficulty of interpreting phrases in isolation.

The difficulty with this approach is that the results for out-of-context interpretation (and the corresponding theories) may prove to be of little or no value with respect to a theory of how addressees understand noun–noun combinations (and carry out conceptual combination) in discourse contexts that are defined by richer common ground. Not surprisingly, researchers who routinely engage participants in out-of-context interpretation have defended this practice. For example, Wisniewski (1996, pp. 450–451) argued, "It makes sense to first identify how the meanings of the constituents (i.e., prior knowledge) affect interpretation. Then the role of discourse setting may be more meaningfully understood in light of these prior knowledge effects." This argument is strikingly similar to the claims some theorists have made for the conceptual primacy of literal meaning. However, as we observed, research results suggest that literal meanings are not inevitably present in understanding. To assess the validity of the output of the conceptual combination enterprise, it is important to determine the extent to which these results generalize to contextual expressions.

The evidence on the temporal primacy of out-of-context meanings is relevant to this issue. If it does not inevitably take longer to understand a literal use of, for example, *cave man* then we have reason to wonder whether out-of-context meanings always contribute to understanding in discourse contexts. In fact, Gerrig's (1989) experiments provided suggestive evidence that the recovery of the two types of meaning interfere with each other. This hint of interference provides the basis for a broader test of the relationship between out-of-context and discourse contexts interpretation of noun–noun combination.

In particular, Gerrig and Bortfeld (1999) contrasted two views of this relationship. In one view, the two types of meaning recovery are *interdependent*. This view, represented by Wisniewski's (1996) quotation, suggests that readers represent out-of-context meanings as a first step toward understanding the expressions in context. In this view, trouble should arise when there is a discrepancy between the two interpretations. Suppose, for example, that in the absence of discourse context most people believe *doll smile* means "the smile on a doll's face," but in a particular story context it is given the meaning "the smile a child gets when she is given a doll as a present." The interdependence view suggests that the readers should find it relatively difficult to understand *doll smile* in the story use—relatively difficult, that is, with respect to a comparable expression (e.g., *baseball smile*) that has no immediately available out-of-context meaning. A contrasting view—the *independence* view—suggests that the two types of meaning recovery do not necessarily depend on one another. As such, the independence view does not predict interference when noun–noun combinations that have strong out-of-context meanings are placed in discourse contexts.

To begin their contrast of the interdependence and independence views, Gerrig and Bortfeld (1999) identified pairs of noun–noun combinations that differed reliably in the accessibility of meanings out of discourse contexts. They used three different methods to construct these pairs. In an initial experiment, participants saw one member from each of 30 pairs of noun–noun combinations (e.g., *doll smile* vs. *baseball smile, family lunch* vs. *tax lunch,* and *zebra horse* vs. *ostrich horse*). Their task was to read each noun phrase and rate how difficult it was to come up with a meaning on a scale ranging from 1 (*very easy*) to 7 (*very hard*). The data generally confirmed the experimenters' intuitions with respect to the probable accessibility of meanings: The 1mean difficulty rating for those noun–noun combinations they anticipated would have relatively more accessible meanings was 2.62; for those noun–noun combinations they anticipated would be relatively less accessible the mean rating was 3.58. The 20 pairs that yielded the largest differences were passed along to later experiments (with mean ratings of 2.24 vs. 3.70).

The next pair of studies measured the accessibility of meanings in speeded tasks. The two accounts of processing—the interdependence and independence views—make different predictions about the time course with which contextual expressions will be processed. The two speeded tasks provided evidence that the participants' intuitions about meaning accessibility out of context also had an impact on processing time. In the first study, Gerrig and Bortfeld (1999) asked participants to push a response key to indicate when they had thought of a meaning for each noun–noun combination. Participants responded considerably more quickly for the (rated) highly accessible tokens from each pair (mean response time = 5.61 s) versus the less accessible tokens (mean = 8.54 s). In the second study, Gerrig and Bortfeld used a task more closely patterned on previous processing time analyses of noun–noun combinations: They asked participants to indicate as quickly as possible whether they found a phrase meaningful (Murphy, 1990). Once again, participants made responses more swiftly for highly accessible tokens (mean = 1.92 s) than for less accessible tokens (mean = 2.44 s). This response time pattern was further corroborated by the rates at which participants judged the phrases to be meaningful. Participants responded "yes" for 81.2% of the highly accessible tokens versus only 43.4% of the less accessible tokens.

This series of results provide an appropriate context for the contrast between the interdependence and independence views. The two populations of noun–noun combinations are reliably different out of discourse context. As such, the interdependence view anticipates a greater degree of interference when the relatively more accessible noun–noun combinations are placed in discourse contexts that endow them with innovative meanings. Consider the pair *family lunch* versus *tax lunch.* Out of discourse context, *family lunch* has a meaning that is considerably more accessible. However, an appropriate context creates meanings for both *family lunch* and *tax lunch* that are conceptually quite similar:

Each day Maggie ate lunch with her friends. They all sat together and talked about concerns in their lives. Generally, they agreed on the topic ahead of time. One day, they discussed how to avoid paying extra income tax. Another day, they discussed how to deal with family problems. Maggie found the family lunch to be very helpful.

(or:) Maggie found the tax lunch to be very helpful.

The interdependence view predicts that readers should experience interference when they experience *family lunch* in this context that is at odds with their out of context expectations. To provide a final index of the relative accessibility of the meanings of the noun–noun combinations without particular contextual support, Gerrig and Bortfeld (1999) also used stories that provided neutral contexts:

Each day Maggie ate lunch with her friends. They all sat together and talked about concerns in their lives. Generally, they agreed on the topic ahead of time. Sometimes Maggie wasn't always sure the conversations were worthwhile. She thought back over the topics they'd covered over the last few days. Maggie found the family lunch to be very helpful.

(or:) Maggie found the tax lunch to be very helpful.

Given the sparse contextual support, readers should find it easier to eke some sort of meaning out of those combinations that have an out-of-context advantage.

In fact, participants' reading times for the final sentences in the neutral contexts did replicate the pattern of accessibility from the out-of-context studies: Participants read the sentences with the noun–noun combinations that had been otherwise highly accessible in reliably less time than they read the sentences with the other members of the pairs (3.74 s vs. 4.34 s). However, contrary to the interdependence view, there were no hints of interference when the combinations appeared in the innovative contexts. The (nonreliable) trend was for readers still to take less time to understand the highly accessible combinations (3.61 s vs. 3.71 s).

This pattern of reading times is consistent with the independence view—that meaning recovery in and out of discourse contexts are independent of one another. However, the reading times alone cannot confirm that participants understood the noun–noun combinations in the way that was intended. The rejection of the interdependence view relies on the assumption that, in innovative contexts, readers represented, for example, *family lunch* and *tax lunch* with equal specificity. To address this concern, Gerrig and Bortfeld (1999) conducted a final experiment that added paraphrase judgments to the ends of each of the innovative versions of the stories. (Because it was not entirely clear what paraphrases to give for the noun–noun combinations in the neutral contexts, the experiment omitted those stories.)

In this final study, the reading times for the highly accessible tokens were reliably faster than those for the less accessible tokens (2.80 s vs. 3.04 s). This result is not consistent with a view that predicts interference. However, the result also raises the disturbing possibility that participants may not have arrived at the appropriate innovative meanings for the noun–noun combinations: Readers might have been indicating that they had understood the highly accessible combinations particularly quickly because they were defaulting to the out-of-context meanings. Fortunately, the paraphrase judgments allow this possibility to be dismissed. Readers agreed with the correct paraphrases in roughly the same amount of time for highly accessible (mean = 3.88) and less accessible combinations (mean = 4.05). They also made roughly the same number of errors (7.5% vs. 11.0%).

These converging measures lead to the strong conclusion that the relatively high accessibility of out-of-context meanings for noun–noun combinations did not lead to interference when these combinations were endowed with innovative meanings. Thus, the results support the contention that meaning recovery in and out of discourse contexts is relatively independent. As such, Gerrig and Bortfeld's (1999) research questions the overall value of research that focuses on out-of-context meanings. The norm, presumably, is for people to encounter noun–noun combinations (as well as other types of contextual expressions) in rich contexts. It is curious, in that light, that most research on so-called conceptual combination has used paradigms in which participants interpret expressions with no contextual support. Of course, Gerrig and Bortfeld only used one type of noun–noun combination with some unknown range of accessibility. The possibility remains that there would be some subset of noun–noun combinations for which the out-of-context meaning would be so highly accessible that interference would arise. As we discussed earlier, readers experienced interference for some preempting innovations (e.g., *door man* vs. *cave man*). However, the burden clearly lies with researchers who use out-of-context tasks to demonstrate that their results have relevance to any type of ordinary language understanding.

In this section we showed that out-of-context meanings for contextual expressions have neither temporal nor conceptual primacy. Rather, addressees appear able to use common ground to arrive at speakers' intended meanings without considering how words or phrases might have been used, had they been used out of discourse context. This is an important conclusion because it brings common ground's penetration into the process of comprehension down to the level of the word and the phrase. We turn now from the relative primacy of meanings in and out of context to the processes that yield those meanings.

Does Common Ground Constrain Meaning Via Special Processes?

In the previous section, we reviewed evidence that contextual expressions share properties with other pragmatic phenomena with respect to the divergence between what a speaker said and what the speaker meant. We concluded that out-of-context meanings do not have temporal or conceptual primacy with respect to those meanings recovered in discourse contexts. Still, that leaves open the question of whether the actual processes that bring about the two types of meaning recovery are identical (Gibbs & Gerrig, 1989). It could be the case that two different streams of mental processes yield their own types of meaning (i.e., out of context vs. common ground sensitive) with the same temporal endpoint. However, researchers on pragmatic phenomena have argued in various ways that the processes are, in fact, identical. Keysar (1989), for example, examined the functional equivalence of the processes that recover literal and metaphorical readings of the same utterances. Consider the utterance, "Bob Jones is a magician." Keysar demonstrated that readers' comprehension was affected by the extent to which Bob Jones was consistently a magician, both literally (i.e., he sawed women in half) and metaphorically (i.e., he was good with money). Keysar suggested that consistency mattered because the same processes yielded both literal and metaphorical readings. Results of this type support the contention that pragmatic phenomena do not require special mental processes. Rather, the same processes give rise to a variety of representations (Gibbs & Gerrig, 1989).

By contrast, contextual expressions appear to demand special processes. Consider a sentence without any (apparent) contextual expressions: The cat is on the mat. Accounts of language processing universally include as a critical step *sense selection*: For each word (e.g., *cat* and *mat*) addressees select a contextually appropriate reading from the mental lexicon. This process is most complicated when words are ambiguous, in which case addressees must combine sources of information to select the appropriate sense. As we note somewhat later, the details of this selection process have been the topic of prolonged psycholinguistic debate. Still, it is clear that sense selection will not work for contextual expressions: They are infinitely ambiguous, and (for the vast majority of cases) none of those infinite number of meanings are listed in the mental lexicon. For these reasons, H. H. Clark and Gerrig (1983) proposed that the understanding of contextual expressions requires addressees to engage in processes of *sense creation*. These processes of sense creation use common ground to constrain speakers' meanings for *roach rumor* and its peers.

Support for sense creation as a process apart from sense selection comes from research with older adults. Zelinski and Hyde (1996) examined the hypothesis that older adults come to have a semantic processing deficit that prompts them to form general rather than specific interpretations. This deficit has implications for the understanding of contextual expressions because contextual expressions require addressees to recover specific interpretations of expressions that are, on the surface, quite general. In their experiments, Zelinski and Hyde asked younger adults (mean age = 22) and older adults (mean age = 68) to interpret eponymous verb phrases such as "do an Elvis Edmunds" in story contexts. In the stories, various activities were attributed to the characters (e.g., Elvis Edmunds). In some stories, the sentence using the eponymous verb phrase included restricting information (e.g., "Later your friend says that he has thought about doing an Elvis Edmunds to the apples he bought."); in other stories, the use of the phrase did not include such information (e.g., "Later your friend says that he has thought about doing an Elvis Edmunds."). The question is whether readers would be able to use the added information about doing an Elvis Edmunds "to the apples" to constrain their understanding of the novel eponymous phrase. The younger adults were more likely to use the cue to restrict their interpretation than were the older adults. These data suggest that the processes that give rise to appropriate interpretations of contextual expressions can be selectively impaired as a cognitive concomitant of aging.

We just briefly made the case that addressees require special processes to recover the meanings of contextual expressions. The error here, however, would be to conclude that because special processes are needed for contextual expressions, addressees only engage those processes when they encounter contextual expressions (H. H. Clark, 1983; Gerrig, 1986). That is, the processes that addressees use to understand contextual expressions only seem special because psycholinguistic research has been so narrowly focused on sense selection. We argue instead that the processes of sense creation—the processes through which addressees use common ground to fix the precise meanings of words—function quite broadly in ordinary comprehension. In this light, sense creation looks special only because people have studied it almost exclusively with respect to contextual expressions. We now discuss three types of evidence that the processes of sense creation function quite ubiquitously.

Construal and Negotiation.   One of the central assumptions of theories of sense selection is that meanings reside ready-made in a mental lexicon. Thus, addressees need only access those ready-made meanings for *cat* and *mat*, combine them in the way indicated by English syntax, and the interpretation of "The cat is on the mat" becomes clear. However, most words have the potential to take on different shades of meaning, depending on the context. Consider these uses of *tomato* (Johnson-Laird, 1975):

- She sat on a tomato.
- She likes tomato.
- Her face was like a tomato.

Suppose the same information for *tomato* is accessed via sense selection in each of these contexts. If that is the case, the addressees are clearly not done: They need to show the same ability to adjust the representations to context that is required for contextual expressions. Most research on meaning has focused on how addressees settle on one or another reading of an ambiguous word (e.g., *bank* or *scale*). We suggest, by contrast, that processes of sense creation function within discourse contexts to narrow down the variability within senses.

To make this observation more concrete, we return to the notion that speakers and addressees often negotiate to establish a perspective on objects and activities in the environment. Recall our referential communication experiment that gave rise to contextual expression *American flag fish*. We suggested that the directors offered perspectives that were adjusted through interaction with the addressees. Now consider the phrases *green fish* and *orange fin*. There is nothing about these expressions that seems, on the surface, contextual. Still, they emerged through a process that was much the same as *American flag fish*. In the first round of our task, one director performed this utterance:

"Number twelve is like a dark green fish, it's got like an orangy fin."

In this utterance, the director hedges the description in two ways. She says that the fish is "like a dark green" and that the fin is "orangy." In both cases, the director signals to the matcher that she is taking a perspective that is open to adjustment. The matcher replies, "Dark green fish, orangy fish, got it." In the next round, the hedges have fallen away:

"Number fourteen is the green fish with the orange fin."

Thus, although *green fish* and *orange fin* do not look like contextual expressions, they are. It is quite likely that other addressees, who were not participants in the negotiations, would find it relatively more difficult to identify the appropriate picture (among the other pictures of fish). We base this suggestion on research by Schober and H. H. Clark (1989), who demonstrated that experimental participants who listened to full conversations in a referential communication task—but did not themselves participate in negotiations—were at a comprehension disadvantage with respect to direct participants. In general, we see a commonality in the construal of *tomato*, *green*, and *orange*. In each case, we can evoke the processes of sense creation to explain how addressees recover the correct specific meaning.

Memory Processes and Meaning.   We noted earlier that, within the study of sense selection, the topic of ambiguity resolution has been one of nearly constant controversy. Consider the word *bank*, which has at least two meanings as "a financial institution" and "the side of a river." Debate has centered on the question of under what discourse circumstances are one or both of these meanings accessible. As research methods have evolved, each of several models has held sway for months or sometimes years (for a review, see Simpson, 1994). In some periods, psycholinguists have believed that addressees automatically access all meanings equally at all times, or that all meanings are accessed but some more so than others. In other periods, psycholinguists have believed that only contextually appropriate meanings are accessed. Because contextual expressions have infinite possible meanings, they provide an opportunity for researchers to test the generality of their conclusions about ambiguity resolution. Specifically, researchers can use contextual expressions to determine whether conclusions narrowly drawn about sense selection are really true of more general cognitive processes.

For example, the two meanings of *bank* are unequal (Onifer & Swinney, 1981): "A financial institution" is the more frequent dominant meaning; "the side of a ride" is the less frequent subordinate meaning. Research on ambiguity resolution has often suggested that dominant meanings are privileged with respect to subordinate meanings. For example, Tabossi and Zardon (1993) wrote sentences that created biases toward the dominant and subordinate readings of ambiguous words. Using a cross-modal lexical decision task, they demonstrated that dominant meanings were primed irrespective of context, but subordinate meanings were primed only when the context was specifically biased toward those readings. Experiments of this sort presuppose that the privilege of dominance reflects the representation of ready-made meanings in the mental lexicon.

By contrast, Rapp and Gerrig (1999) sought to demonstrate that the privilege of dominance extends to uses of eponymous verb phrases. In the initial phase of their research, they normed eponymous verb phrases to construct a set with well-defined dominant and subordinate meanings. Rapp and Gerrig asked participants in the norming study to provide interpretations of phrases such as "do a Neil Armstrong" and "do an Albert Einstein." The instructions were patterned after production tasks for ordinary lexical ambiguities: "Your task is to write down the three most likely meanings of each verb phrase. Pretend that you have just heard the phrase during a conversation. What would be some meanings that seem most natural to you?" After transcribing participants' responses, Rapp and Gerrig created categories that drew together responses similar in meaning (e.g., they considered "to set foot on the moon," "jump up and down on the moon," and "be the first to walk on some planet" all variations on the same interpretation of "do a Neil Armstrong"). From an initial pool of 45 eponymous verb phrases, Rapp and Gerrig found 28 phrases for which the average rate at which the dominant meaning was produced was roughly 42% higher than the rate at which the subordinate meaning was produced (72.4% vs. 29.8% respectively). This difference between production frequencies is comparable to that used in experiments using ordinary ambiguities (e.g., Onifer & Swinney, 1981). Note that although the subordinate meanings were given less often, they were not particularly obscure (e.g., for "*do an Albert Einstein*," the dominant meaning was "accomplished a scientific milestone" and the subordinate meaning was "have unkempt hair").

The norming study provided the set of eponymous verb phrases Rapp and Gerrig (1999) needed to test the relative accessibility of dominant and subordinate meanings. For the next phase of their research, they wrote stories that supported one of these two meanings. Consider this story that engaged the dominant meaning of "*do a John Travolta:*"

> Rick and his sister had found some old 70s records in the attic. They put one on the player and laughed while they listened. Then Rick began to move in time to the music. He announced, "Watch me do a John Travolta."

An alternative story engaged the subordinate meaning:

> Rick was once the most valuable player on his soccer team. A drug habit had affected his skills, and he was removed from the team. Now he was in rehab, hoping to kick his habit and return to the sport. He announced, "Watch me do a John Travolta."

The purpose of the experiment was to test the hypothesis that readers would consider the dominant meaning of the eponymous verb phrase even in the subordinate contexts. To assess this prediction, Rapp and Gerrig (1999) asked participants to accept or reject paraphrases of the sentences including the following eponymous verb phrases:

> Rick is going to try to disco dance [dominant paraphrase], and

> Rick is going to try to make a comeback [subordinate paraphrase].

For each of 20 eponymous verb phrases, participants read a story that supported one of the two senses and ended with one of the two paraphrases. Participants took nearly the same amount of time to agree with both of the appropriate paraphrases—dominant paraphrases to dominant senses (mean = 3.10 s) and subordinate paraphrases to subordinate senses (mean = 2.97 s). As expected, however, response times for the inappropriate paraphrases were reliably longer for the dominant paraphrases in subordinate contexts (mean = 3.03 s) than subordinate paraphrases in dominant contexts (mean = 2.66 s).

These data support the contention that dominant senses are relatively available even when the context does not support their relevance. As such, they suggest that claims for the privilege of dominant meanings for ordinary ambiguities should not unreflectively be attributed to properties of lexical memory. Rather, common ground appears to play a broader role in shaping experiences of ambiguity. The extension of dominance effects to at least one type of contextual expression weakens faith in one assumption for sense selection—the existence of ready-made meanings in the mental lexicon.

Contextual Expressions and Parsing. We have been focusing on the implications of contextual expressions with respect to theories of lexical access and meaning. However, contextual expressions also have implications for other aspects of language processing. In particular, H. H. Clark (1983) argued that contextual expressions pose enormous problems to standard accounts of parsing. Consider his famous example from one of Erma Bombeck's columns (H. H. Clark, 1983, p. 298):

We thought we were onto a steam iron yesterday, but we were too late. Steam irons never have nay trouble finding roommates. She could pick her own pad and not even have to share a bathroom. Stereos are a dime a dozen. Everyone's got their own systems. We've just had a streak of bad luck. First, our Mr. Coffee flunked out of school and went back home. When we replaced her, our electric typewriter got married and split, and we got stuck with a girl who said she was getting a leather coat, but she just said that to get the room.

Once readers get the hang of this paragraph—that *steam iron* and so on are the possessions of once and prospective roommates—there does not seem to be anything particularly challenging about the recovery of grammatical structure. Still, Clark suggested that standard accounts of parsing will lead to a pair of errors: *nonparsing* and *misparsing*. Non-parsing occurs when the parser would be stumped by a construction. For example, because "married" requires human participants, "our electric typewriter got married" would cause most parsers to fail. Misparsing occurs when the parser yields an incorrect representation. For example, "stereos are a dime a dozen" yields the interpretation "phonographs are very common." This is not what Bombeck intended.

To accommodate these parsing problems, Clark (1983) suggested that a shift in emphasis was necessary from standard parsers to what he called *intentional parsers*. He suggested that parsing should be "viewed not simply as dividing a sentence into its parts—the traditional view—but as identifying the goals and subgoals the speaker had in uttering each part of the sentence" (p. 324). In Clark's view, the goals and subgoals refer to the speaker's intentions. The recovery of those intentions require the parser to use information about common ground (p. 325):

With contextual expressions, reference to speaker's and addressee's common ground is mandatory. When Bombeck wrote *Our electric typewriter got married*, she intended us readers to make use of the fact that she had just written about roommates and their possessions. She intended us to use this common ground in conjunction with the fact that she was uttering the phrase *our electric typewriter* and was predicating of its referent, that it got married. She intended us to use both sources of information in inferring her hierarchy of goals.

Despite Clark's strong arguments, theorists of parsing have not moved in the direction of intentional parsers and, for that matter, have not provided alternative accounts of how utterances including contextual expressions might be parsed.

The omission of contextual expressions from theories of parsing has at least two consequences. First, as Clark (1983) argued, if parsing theories cannot accommodate contextual expressions, they will be incomplete or incorrect. Second, as in other instances, contextual expressions provide an interesting control for the generality of conclusions with respect to certain aspects of parsing. For example, research attention in parsing has often focused on the extent to which different verbs have associated with them *parsing preferences*. Consider a series of studies by Shapiro, Nagel, and Levine (1993) that explored (among other things) the consequences of verbs' preferences for taking or not taking a direct object. In a norming study, participants were asked to indicate which of two sentence forms they preferred for common verbs such as *taught*:

The aging pianist taught his solo with great dignity.

The aging pianist taught with his entire family.

This norming study allowed Shapiro et al. to construct minimal pairs with opposite preferences. In these sentences, *read* has a transitive preference and *sang* has an intransitive preference:

1. The baby-sitter read the # story to the sick child.
2. The baby-sitter read to # the sick child.
3. The baby-sitter sang the # story to the sick child.
4. The baby-sitter sang to # the sick child.

If verbs' preferences play a role in parsing, readers should find it easier to recover the structures for Sentences 1 and 4 (which respect the verbs' preferences) than Sentences 2 and 3. To test this prediction, Shapiro et al. asked participants, while listening to the sentences, to perform a lexical decision task (to unrelated words) at the positions marked by the #. The premise was that performance on a secondary task would be slowed when parsing processes were constructing nonpreferred representations. The data bore out this prediction: Participants took reliably more time to make lexical decision judgments when the sentence provided a nonpreferred complement (mean = 0.80 s) than what it provided a preferred complement (mean = 0.77 s).

In the types of experiments exemplified by Shapiro et al.'s (1993) research, the strong assumption is made that the parsing preferences are stored along with each verb's "entry" in the mental lexicon. Although this may be the case, we have data that suggest that readers also have rather strong preferences with respect to the complements that should occur with innovative denominal verbs. In a pilot experiment, 40 participants provided the same type of norming information Shapiro et al. had gathered. Specifically, they were asked to choose which of two sentences sounded better to them:

1. The young mother potato-chipped the casserole to make it extra crispy.
2. The young mother potato-chipped while she watched a game show.
3. The yuppie BMW'ed his girlfriend to her dance class.
4. The yuppie BMW'ed to the grocery store to buy some caviar.

In the norming data, participants showed a strong preference for "to potato-chip" to serve as a transitive verb (Sentence 1) and for "to BMW" to serve as an intransitive verb (Sentence 4). Because these verbs do not appear in the mental lexicon, these data present the immediate problem of explaining how the preferences arise. Suppose, furthermore, that response time studies produced costs and benefits for mismatches and matches similar to those Shapiro et al. disclosed. With lexical innovations, it would be impossible to attribute such results to information precompiled in the mental lexicon. Of course, parallel results (should the speculation be correct) would not necessitate identical mental processes. Still, these pilot data illustrate another way in which contextual expressions provide an important control for claims about the structure and content of the mental lexicon. Ultimately, experiments with contextual expressions could provide strong evidence for H. H. Clark's (1983) notion of intentional parsers, with common ground at their core.

CONCLUSIONS

We conclude this chapter with a final example of a contextual expression. Consider this brief literary excerpt (Costello, 2002, p. 213):

Gretchen said, 'What is this, Vi, a college road trip? Thirteen your butt to Portsmouth and stay there, got it?'

In this excerpt, the ordinary number "thirteen" is being used as a verb. In this chapter, we suggested that contextual expressions arise through speakers' (and, in this case, authors') assessments of common ground. We suggested that speakers produce contextual expressions—some for the nonce, some to endure—with appropriate sensitivity to communal and personal co-presence. In fact, the meaning of *thirteen* is established much earlier in the novel, in a memorable fashion (Costello, 2002, p. 81):

> Gretchen said, *Felker, that's a negative. Thirteen your ass right back here.* 'Thirteen' was borrowed cop code. It meant do it now.

In this original instance, the reader learns that Gretchen (who works for the Secret Service) has borrowed the verb use of *thirteen* from ordinary police. The unmarked return to *thirteen* late in the novel suggests that the author believed he had successfully extended the verb to a new community—readers of his book.

In the second part of the chapter, we examined the processes that make it possible for contextual expressions like the latter use of *thirteen* to succeed. We saw that processes of sense creation are highly integrated into the ordinary time course of language understanding. That is why, for example, readers are not baffled when *thirteen*—which, for most readers will previously only named the quantity between 12 and 14—can become a verb with minimal (or zero) disruption. In that light, our major conclusion is that the processes of sense creation function quite broadly, allowing addressees to recover the specific meanings that speakers intend.

ACKNOWLEDGMENTS

Material for this chapter was based on work supported by the National Science Foundation under Grants No. IRI9980013 and No. ITR0082602. Correspondence concerning this chapter should be sent to Richard J. Gerrig, Department of Psychology, State University of New York at Stony Brook, Stony Brook, NY 11794–2500. E-mail: rgerrig@notes.cc.sunysb.edu

REFERENCES

Clark, E. V., & Clark, H. H. (1979). When nouns surface as verbs. *Language, 55*, 767–811.

Clark, H. H. (1979). Responding to indirect speech acts. *Cognitive Psychology, 11*, 430–477.

Clark, H. H. (1983). Making sense of nonce sense. In G. B. Flores d'Arcais & R. Jarvella (Eds.), *The process of understanding language* (pp. 297–331). New York: Wiley.

Clark, H. H. (1996). *Using language.* Cambridge, England: Cambridge University Press.

Clark, H. H., & Gerrig, R. J. (1983). Understanding old words with new meanings. *Journal of Verbal Learning and Verbal Behavior, 22,* 591–608.

Clark, H. H., & Marshall, C. R. (1981). Definite reference and mutual knowledge. In A. K. Joshi, I. Sag, & B. Webber (Eds.), *Elements of discourse understanding* (pp. 10–63). Cambridge: Cambridge University Press.

Coolen, R., Van Jaarsveld, H. J., & Schreuder, R. (1991). The interpretation of isolated novel nominal compounds. *Memory & Cognition, 19,* 341–352.

Coolen, R., Van Jaarsveld, H. J., & Schreuder, R. (1993). Processing novel compounds: Evidence for interactive meaning activation of ambiguous nouns. *Memory & Cognition, 21,* 235–246.

Costello, M. (2002). *Big if.* New York: Norton.

Dennis, P. (1958). *Around the world with Auntie Mame.* New York: Harcourt Brace.

Downing, P. A. (1977). On the creation and use of English compound nouns. *Language, 53,* 810–842.

Evanovich, J. (1997). *Three to get deadly.* New York: St. Martin's Paperbacks.

Evanovich, J. (1999). *High five.* New York: St. Martin's Press.

Gagné, C. L., & Shoben, E. J. (1997). Influence of thematic relations on the comprehension of modifier–noun combinations. *Journal of Experimental Psychology: Learning, Memory, and Cognition, 23,* 71–87.

Gerrig, R. J. (1986). Process and products of lexical access. *Language and Cognitive Processes, 1,* 187–195.

Gerrig, R. J. (1989). The time course of sense creation. *Memory & Cognition, 17,* 194–207.

Gerrig, R. J. (1993). *Experiencing narrative worlds.* New Haven, CT: Yale University Press.

Gerrig, R. J., & Bortfeld, H. (1999). Sense creation in and out of discourse contexts. *Journal of Memory and Language, 41,* 457–468.

Gerrig, R. J., & Gibbs, R. W., Jr. (1988). Beyond the lexicon: Creativity in language production. *Metaphor and Symbolic Activity, 3,* 1–19.

Gerrig, R. J., & Horton, W. S. (2001, November). *Judgments about common ground in language production.* Paper presented at the meeting of the Psychonomic Society, Orlando, FL.

Gibbs, R. W., Jr. (1979). Contextual effect in understanding indirect requests. *Discourse Processes, 2,* 1–10.

Gibbs, R. W., Jr. (1983). Do people always process the literal meanings of indirect requests? *Journal of Experimental Psychology: Learning, Memory, and Cognition, 9,* 524–533.

Gibbs, R. W., Jr. (1994). *The poetics of mind.* Cambridge, England: Cambridge University Press.

Gibbs, R. W., Jr., & Gerrig, R. J. (1989). How context makes metaphor comprehension seem "special." *Metaphor and Symbolic Activity, 4,* 145–158.

Grice, H. P. (1975). Logic and conversation. In P. Cole & J. Morgan (Eds.), *Syntax and semantics: Vol. 3. Speech acts* (pp. 41–58). New York: Academic Press.

Jen, G. (1999). *Who's Irish?* New York: Knopf.

Johnson-Laird, P. N. (1975). Meaning and the mental lexicon. In A. Kennedy & A. Wilkes (Eds.), *Studies in long term memory* (pp. 123–142). London: Wiley.

Keysar, B. (1989). On the functional equivalence of literal and metaphorical interpretations in discourse. *Journal of Memory and Language, 28,* 375–385.

Labute, N. (2001, May 28). Layover. *New Yorker, 77,* 120–121.

Michaels, L. (2001, November 12). Nachman from Los Angeles. *New Yorker, 77,* 110–121.

Murphy, G. L. (1990). Noun phrase interpretation and conceptual combination. *Journal of Memory and Language, 29,* 259–288.

Onifer, W., & Swinney, D. (1981). Accessing lexical ambiguities during sentence comprehension: Effects of frequency of meaning and contextual bias. *Memory & Cognition, 9,* 225–236.

Rapp, D. N., & Gerrig, R. J. (1999). Eponymous verb phrases and ambiguity resolution. *Memory & Cognition, 27,* 612–618.

Schober, M. F., & Clark, H. H. (1989). Understanding by addressees and overhearers. *Cognitive Psychology, 21,* 211–232.

Searle, J. (1979). Metaphor. In A. Ortony (Ed.), *Metaphor and thought* (pp. 92–123). Cambridge, England: Cambridge University Press.

Shapiro, L. P., Nagel, H. N., & Levine, B. A. (1993). Preferences for a verb's complements and their use in sentence processing. *Journal of Memory and Language, 32,* 96–114.

Simpson, G. B. (1994). Context and the processing of ambiguous words. In M. A. Gernsbacher (Ed.), *Handbook of psycholinguistics* (pp. 359–374). San Diego: Academic Press.

Tabossi, P., & Zardon, F. (1993). Processing ambiguous words in context. *Journal of Memory and Language, 32,* 359–372.

Welch, J. (2001). *Jack: Straight from the gut.* New York: Warner Business Books.

Wisniewski, E. J. (1996). Construal and similarity in conceptual combination. *Journal of Memory and Language, 35,* 434–453.

Wisniewski, E. J., & Love, B. C. (1998). Relations versus properties in conceptual combination. *Journal of Memory and Language, 38,* 177–202.

Wisniewski, E. J., & Middleton, E. L. (2002). Of bucket bowls and coffee cup bowls: Spatial alignment in conceptual combination. *Journal of Memory and Language, 46,* 1–23.

Zelinski, E. M., & Hyde, J. C. (1996). Old words, new meanings: Aging and sense creation. *Journal of Memory and Language, 25,* 689–707.

PART II

Sociocultural Phenomenological Influences

4

Context
and the Comprehension
of Nonliteral Meanings

Thomas Holtgraves
Ball State University

Conversations abound with nonliteral meanings; sarcasm, irony, meta-phors, hyperbole, indirect requests, hints, backhanded compliments, and so on all occur with great frequency (Gibbs, 1994; Holtgraves, 2001a). Nonliteral language, however, is not a monolithic phenomenon. Instead, there are a multitude of ways in which nonliteral meanings can be conveyed and comprehended, and one of the most important ways in which these meanings differ is in terms of their sensitivity to the context. Context always matters, of course, but sometimes it matters more than others. In this chapter I focus on the dimension of contextual sensitivity and argue that many types of nonliteral meaning—especially figurative expressions—are rela-tively immune to the context; their recognized meanings transcend their oc-casions of use. In contrast, other types of nonliteral meaning—especially violations of the relation maxim—are completely context dependent. These differences in contextual sensitivity have a corresponding effect on how these different forms are comprehended; contextual variables that ef-fect the comprehension of the latter will not have a corresponding impact on the comprehension of the former.

In this chapter I begin with a brief review of what has become known as the standard pragmatic model for comprehending nonliteral meanings, Grice's (1975) theory of conversational implicature, and research designed to test various aspects of this model. This model has not held up well, partly because most research has focused on nonliteral meanings that are contextually independent. Next, I review Grice's distinction between generalized (contextually independent) and particularized (context dependent) implicatures and attempt to classify various types of nonliteral meanings with this scheme. Then, I describe my research on the comprehension and interpretation of utterances yielding particularized implicatures, as well as the role of context (face management concerns, status, and perspective) in these processes. Finally, I discuss cultural differences in the interpretation of nonliteral meanings.

THE GRICEAN MODEL

Grice's (1975) theory of conversational implicature is the starting point for most attempts to explain the comprehension of indirect meanings; in the psycholinguistic literature this has become known as the standard model (e.g., Gibbs, 1994; Glucksberg, 1991). Grice argued that interlocutors abide by what he termed the *cooperative principle* (CP), a principle stating that one should: "Make your conversational contribution such as is required, at the stage at which it occurs, by the accepted purpose or direction of the talk exchange in which you are engaged" (p. 45). This general requirement is further specified in terms of the following four conversational maxims:

1. *Quantity*—Make your contribution as informative as required (i.e., do not be either overinformative or underinformative).
2. *Quality*—Try to make your contribution true, one for which you have evidence.
3. *Manner*—Be clear. That is, avoid ambiguity, obscurity, and so on.
4. *Relation*—Make your contribution relevant for the exchange.

It is usually the case that people will mutually assume adherence to the CP and corresponding maxims, and this assumption serves as a frame for the interpretation of a speaker's utterances. In other words, speakers' utterances will be interpreted as if they were clear, relevant, truthful, and informative. For example, saying "Can you pass the salt?" at the dinner table is a violation of the relation maxim (i.e., in this context, inquiring into another's ability to pass the salt would not be a relevant contribution). But because the hearer assumes the speaker is being relevant, she or he will search for an ulterior meaning and interpret the utterance (i.e., generate a conversational implicature) in such a way so as to maintain adherence to the conversational maxims.

The "Pass the salt" example is an instance of an implicature that arises to preserve adherence to a specific conversational maxim. In addition, speakers will sometimes intentionally flout or violate a maxim, in which case it is simply not possible for the hearer to assume the speaker is adhering to the maxims. For example, abrupt topic changes ("I really think the Cubs will win the pennant") in response to personal questions ("How did you do on that history exam?") function as relevance violations and convey much more than their strictly literal meaning (possible gloss: I didn't do well on the exam). In this case, it is obvious the speaker is not complying with the relation maxim. Still, the hearer will usually assume overall cooperativeness on the part of the speaker and generate a conversational implicature that makes sense of the violation.

PROCESSING NONLITERAL MEANINGS

Is the Gricean model an accurate description of how people interpret instances of nonliteral meaning? Research on politeness (Clark & Schunk, 1980; Holtgraves, 1997a; Holtgraves & Yang, 1990, 1992) and responses to polite requests (Clark, 1979) provide some indirect support for this model, primarily for the claim that both the literal and nonliteral meanings of indirect requests are activated. For example, Clark (1979) demonstrated that when people respond to indirect requests for information (e.g., "Can you tell me what time you close?"), they frequently address both the literal meaning (i.e., do you have the ability to tell me when you close) and the indirect meaning (i.e., tell me what time you close) of the request (e.g., "Sure, 8:00 p.m.").

Moreover, research on politeness also suggests that people recognize the literal meaning of many indirect utterances. This is because the politeness of an utterance is based on the remark's literal rather than indirect meaning. For example, "Could you shut the door?" is more polite than "I want you to shut the door," even though both are indirect requests to shut the door. There is fairly extensive research demonstrating that the perceived politeness of requests is influenced by variations in literal wording (Clark & Schunk, 1980; Holtgraves & Yang, 1990, 1992). There must be some awareness of the literal meaning if politeness judgments vary in this way. Along similar lines there is some evidence that people encode the specific wording of an utterance when that wording varies in politeness (Holtgraves, 1997a). In these studies, people spontaneously remembered the politeness wording of utterances at better-than-chance levels. And even when they did not remember the exact wording, they did seem to retain some gist of the politeness of the utterance. For example, if people had heard "I'd like you to read the list," they were more likely to recall an equally polite form (e.g., "Could you read the list?") rather than an impolite form (e.g., "Read the list"). These results also suggest some activation of literal meaning.

The fact that people are attentive to variations in politeness suggests that there must be some awareness of both the literal and the nonliteral (or conveyed) meaning of utterances. The problem with politeness research, of course, is that it is not direct evidence; there is no evidence regarding the actual cognitive operations involved in the comprehension of requests. For example, it is possible that the politeness of a request is recognized simultaneously with (rather than prior to) the recognition of the conveyed (indirect) meaning. Furthermore, it is conceivable that some wordings have conventionalized politeness values that determine perceived politeness without any activation of the literal meaning of the remark. For example, "Can you X?" might be conventionally more polite than "I want you to X." It is possible that this difference in wording could affect perceived politeness without any activation of the literal meaning of the utterance.

More direct tests of this model have been provided by psycholinguists who have examined in detail the processing of figures of speech. In general, this research has not supported Grice's (1975) model. For example, consider the claim that a nonliteral meaning is the result of an inference process. An inference process is time consuming; thus people should take longer to comprehend figures of speech than their direct equivalents. However, numerous studies have demonstrated that an inference process is not required for these forms. People simply do not take more time to understand the meaning of figurative expressions (e.g., "He spilled the beans") than they do equivalent literal expressions (Gibbs, 1980; Ortony, Schallert, Reynolds, & Antos, 1978).

Moreover, in the standard pragmatic view, activation of the literal meaning of a remark is obligatory and must occur prior to the (optional) recognition of the nonliteral (figurative) meaning. But research indicates that for many figures of speech, the literal and figurative meanings are assessed simultaneously; in some cases, they are assessed in a reversed order.

For example, several studies have demonstrated that the nonliteral meaning of a figure of speech is activated even when the literal meaning is acceptable in context (Gildea & Glucksberg, 1983; Glucksberg, Gildea, & Bookin, 1982; Keysar, 1989), and sometimes people recognize the literal meaning only after first considering and then rejecting the nonliteral meaning, which is the reverse of the predicted ordering (Keysar, 1994).

Finally, most interpretations of Grice's (1975) model claim that once a literal meaning has been rejected, it will no longer play a role in determining the meaning of an utterance. But this too appears not to be the case. Rather, the literal meaning of the words in a metaphor can continue to influence the manner in which the metaphor is interpreted (Cacciari & Glucksberg, 1994; Titone & Connine, 1994).

GENERALIZED VERSUS PARTICULARIZED IMPLICATURES

For the most part, psycholinguistic research on nonliteral meaning has focused on a narrow range of utterance types, primarily figures of speech (which are highly idiomatic) and conventional indirect requests (which are also highly idiomatic). But clearly there are many different ways to convey indirect meanings, with corresponding differences in how those meanings are processed. Of particular importance for processing models is Grice's (1975) distinction between generalized and particularized implicatures. The basic difference between the two is that generalized implicatures are context independent; they have preferred interpretations that occur without reference to the context. Particularized implicatures, however, are context dependent; their recognition requires a consideration of the utterance in terms of a context, most notably the prior discourse context. Much of the figurative language examined in prior psycholinguistic research appears to produce generalized implicatures. For example, most metaphors and idioms seem to be interpretable independent of any discourse context. Regardless of the context, people will usually interpret "He spilled the beans" as meaning "He revealed a secret." Support for this comes from the fact that the nonliteral meaning of many metaphors is not optional; even when the context supports a literal reading, the nonliteral meaning is still activated (Gildea & Glucksberg, 1983; Glucksberg et al.,1982; Keysar, 1989). (But see Levinson, 2000, for an alternative view.)

It is not only metaphors and idioms that produce generalized implicatures. In fact, there is a very large class of utterance forms that possess preferred interpretations regardless of the context in which they are used. Scalar implicatures (e.g., some and few) are common and generally result in what Levinson (2000) referred to as *Q-implicatures*. For example, "Some of the students attended class" implies that not all of the students attended class. Note that this is an implicature because the sentence would be true even if all of the students attended class. Other examples of generalized implicatures include sentences such as "Mark has three children" and "Harry tried to play the stock market." The former yields the inference that Mark has no more than three children (even though the sentence would be true if Mark did have more than three children), and the latter yields the inference that Harry failed at playing the stock marker (again, even though the sentence would be true had he been successful). Empirical evidence regarding the specific manner in which these forms are comprehended is lacking, although it is clear that contextual features will play little role in their comprehension.

One particularly interesting utterance type that yields a generalized conversational implicature is referred to as a "what is X doing Y" (WXDY) construction (Kay & Fillmore, 1999). Examples include "What you doing in my chair?," "What is this coffee doing on the carpet?," and so on. These constructions typically are interpreted as indicating a state of affairs that is incongruent with what is normally expected in these situations (that you should not be in my chair, that coffee should not be on the carpet, etc.). Although empirical research on the processing of these forms is lacking, intuitively it seems that these are the default interpretations for these forms, and there is little processing cost associated with their use (i.e., a Gricean inference process is not required).

Even illocutionary force—the speech act (e.g., promise, request, apologize, and warn) performed with an utterance—can be considered a generalized implicature. Note that with the exception of performative utterances (e.g., I order you to shut the door), the illocutionary act is usually implicit and not literally present in the utterance that performs the act (e.g., "I'll definitely do it tomorrow" does not contain the speech act verb *promise*). Yet, people do appear to routinely and automatically recognize this level of meaning during comprehension. For example, we have found evidence for the online activation of illocutionary force (Holtgraves & Ashley, 2001) using both a recognition probe reaction time procedure (Experiments 1 and 2) and a lexical decision task (Experiments 3 and 4). Specifically, when participants read utterances that performed a specific speech act (e.g., warn and remind), their responses to probes representing the performed speech act were slowed in Experiments 1 and 2 and facilitated in Experiments 3 and 4. Although illocutionary force appears to be activated during comprehension, the process by which it is activated has not been investigated.

Finally, conventional indirect requests have received a fair amount of empirical attention, and these too appear to be generalized implicatures. Conventional indirect requests (e.g., Could you shut the door?) usually contain the imperative form of the request (shut the door), allow for the insertion of *please* (Could you please shut the door), and are related to the felicity conditions underlying the performance of the request (e.g., hearer's ability). Research has demonstrated that conventional indirect requests are processed directly and quickly and without an inference process (Gibbs, 1983) and that their recognition is not affected by contextual variables such as the status of the speaker (Holtgraves, 1994).

Overall, then, generalized implicatures represent instances when speaker meaning—what a speaker intends to accomplish with an utterance—is recognized in a relatively direct fashion, without need of a Gricean inference process. Now it is obvious that some type of inferential processing is required to recognize a generalized implicature. But the process outlined by Grice (1975)—recognize and then reject a literal meaning—does not appear to be involved. And, of course, contextual independence is far from absolute. It is relatively easy to envision contexts in which a generally accepted generalized implicature is not appropriate. For example, the literal meaning of "He spilled the beans" might be taken seriously (and exclusively) in the context of one's youngest son spilling a pot of beans. Generalized implicatures may be default implicatures, but they (at least some of them) can be overridden by a context that strongly biases how the utterance is to be interpreted. However, this will probably involve a time-consuming, effortful process.

PARTICULARIZED IMPLICATURES, RELEVANCE VIOLATIONS, AND FACE MANAGEMENT

In contrast to generalized implicatures, particularized implicatures are heavily dependent on the context and, in fact cannot be interpreted apart from a context. A prototypical particularized implicature would be a violation of the relation maxim (be relevant). Consider the following example (from Holtgraves, 1998b, p. 1): Bob and Al are students in the same history class and Bob has just given a presentation in this class. The following exchange then takes place:

Bob: What did you think of my presentation?

Al: It's hard to give a good presentation.

How is Al's reply to be interpreted? Obviously he is asserting the belief that the act of giving a class presentation is difficult. But most people would probably conclude that he really means something more; the most likely interpretation would be that he did not like the presentation. Unlike a generalized implicature this interpretation is not conventionally associated with this utterance. It is only in the context of the preceding question that this interpretation can be derived (and hence, it represents a particularized rather than generalized implicature).

Our research on relevance violations has focused on several issues. One major question has concerned the specific interpretation that recipients of a relevance violation will tend to generate. This is not trivial; in theory there are an infinite number of implicatures a recipient might produce. Grice (1975) was not particularly clear in this regard. He argued that the implicature would be one that makes the utterance a cooperative response, one that would fit in the conversation. This makes perfect sense, but in many instances there are numerous possible interpretations that would fit in the conversation; the theory narrows down these possibilities somewhat but does not specify exactly how an utterance will be interpreted. And, of course, it is impossible to specify precisely, in advance, how an utterance will be interpreted. Still, it seems likely that additional interpretive constraints could be developed. Research has focused on how face management (Goffman, 1967) may play a role in the interpretation of relevance violations.

I assume that the recipient of a relevance violation will construct an inference that represents an attempt to explain why the violation occurred. This assumption is consistent with attribution research demonstrating that people attempt to explain why unexpected or unscripted actions occurred (e.g., Hastie, 1984). It is also consistent with text processing research (e.g., Singer, Halldorson, Lear, & Andrusiak, 1992) demonstrating that readers generate causal inferences as a means of achieving coherence in their representation of a text (a property of text that is similar to the conversational requirement of relevance) and with Graesser, Singer, and Trabasso's (1994) model of text comprehension that is based on a search after meaning (i.e., readers' representations are influenced by their attempts to understand why something is mentioned in the text).

Although there are no doubt many reasons why people might violate the relation maxim and speak indirectly (e.g., see Roberts & Kreuz, 1994), a fundamental motivation for indirectness is face management. According to P. Brown and Levinson (1987), indirectness is an important mechanism for conveying politeness, and all politeness is motivated by concerns for managing face. The essence of politeness is the performance of a face-threatening act in a manner that simultaneously attends to the face needs of the interactants. For example, people frequently perform requests indirectly (e.g., Could you open the door?) rather than directly (e.g., Open the door); in this way they attend to the face of the recipient by symbolically lessening the implied imposition of the act. Research has documented that indirectness (as a form of politeness) is motivated by face management concerns (R. Brown & Gilman, 1989; Clark & Schunk, 1980; Holtgraves, 2001b; Holtgraves & Yang, 1990, 1992). Note that this relationship has been found for replies to personal information questions; people will be indirect and violate the relation maxim as a means of managing face (Bavelas, Black, Chovil, & Mullet, 1990), and replies that do this are perceived as more polite (Holtgraves, 1986).

Almost all research on face management has focused on how speakers' produce polite remarks; there has been virtually no research on how face management might impact the manner in which a recipient interprets a speaker's remark. But there is a straightforward extension here. Because face management is a major reason for violating Gricean conversational maxims, it is reasonable to assume that when faced with such a violation hearers will consider the possibility that the speaker is trying to engage in face management. This recognition then can serve as the basis for generating an interpretation of what the speaker actually means with an utterance. This reasoning seems very likely to occur for replies to personal questions. So, when Al replies "It's hard to give a good presentation," in response to Bob's request for feedback, Bob is likely to infer that Al is engaging in face management. Now, because it is a negative opinion about Bob's presentation that would be face threatening in this situation, the most likely inference is that Al does not have a positive opinion of the presentation. If the information was positive, there would usually be no need to violate the relation maxim; a positive opinion would not be face threatening. The claim, then, is that in these situations relevance violations will be interpreted as conveying nonliteral meanings; because it is negative information that would be most face threatening in these situations, the most likely interpretation is that the speaker is conveying negative information. Note that not all relevance violations will be interpreted as conveying negative information. Rather, the claim is that they will be interpreted as conveying negative information if it is negative information that is face threatening.

I found support for this reasoning in several experiments (Holtgraves, 1998b). In these experiments participants read brief descriptions of situations, each followed by a question–reply exchange (similar to the example provided earlier). Two types of situations were created, an opinion situation in which the requested information pertained to the person asking the question (e.g., "What did you think of my presentation?") and a self-disclosure situation in which the requested information pertained to the recipient of the question (e.g., "How did you do on the chemistry test?").[1] The reply always violated the relation maxim either by completely changing the topic or by providing an excuse for why the requested information might be negative. The information requested by the questions was described in the scenario as being either positive, negative, or no information was given. Sample scenarios are presented in Table 4.1.

In the first experiment participants were asked to interpret each reply and indicate their degree of confidence in their interpretation. Their interpretations were coded in terms of whether they were literal or indirect and, if the latter, whether the interpretation was positive, negative, or neutral. Obviously, participants should interpret the replies as conveying negative information when they are told that the requested information is negative (the negative information condition in Table 4.1). When no information is provided (the no information condition in Table 4.1), however, participants could infer a number of different things (e.g., that the information is negative, that it is positive, that the speaker is not really giving an opinion at all). But if participants attempt to uncover a reason for the relevance violation, if a major reason for violating the relation maxim is to manage face, and if (as in the present situations) it is negative information that is face threatening, then participants should be most likely to infer that the information is negative. That is exactly what happened. Participants were far more likely to interpret the replies as conveying negative information rather than positive or neutral information. And, more important, they were just as likely to interpret the replies as conveying negative information when no information was provided (62.2%) as when they were told explicitly that the requested information was negative (66.4%).

---

[1]In general, I found no meaningful differences between these two types of situations. Accordingly, in this chapter differences between opinions and disclosures are not discussed.

TABLE 4.1
Sample Experimental Materials

Opinion

Nick and Paul are taking the same history class. Students in this class have to give a 20-min presentation to the class on some topic.

No information: Nick gave his presentation and then decided to ask Paul what he thought of it.

Negative information: Nick gave his presentation, and it was truly terrible. He decides to ask Paul what he thought of it.

Positive information: Nick gave his presentation, and it was excellent. He decides to ask Paul what he thought of it.

Nick: What did you think of my presentation?

Paul: It's hard to give a good presentation. (excuse)

Paul: I hope I win the lottery tonight. (topic change)

Indirect interpretation target: I didn't like your presentation.[a, b]

Neutral target: I gave her roses for Valentine's Day.[b]

Self-Disclosure

Jim is in seventh grade. Report cards were due today, and Jim's mother is curious about how well he did.

No information: Jim just got home from school, and his mother met him at the door.

Negative information: Jim is having a bad semester and flunking several classes. Jim just got home from school, and his mother met him at the door.

Positive information: Jim is having a great semester and getting As in all but one class. Jim just got home from school, and his mother met him at the door.

Mom: How were your grades this semester?

Jim: I don't think the teacher grades fairly. (excuse)

Jim: It snowed very hard last night. (topic change)

Indirect interpretation target: My grades are not very good.[a, b]

Neutral target: His wallet was stolen.[b]

---

[a]Experiment 2, Holtgraves, (1998b).
[b]Experiments 1 through 3, Holtgraves, (1999).

A second experiment tested this logic further. The same materials were presented to participants on a computer screen, and the time taken for them to comprehend the replies was recorded. After reading the replies, participants also indicated whether an indirect interpretation was a reasonable interpretation of the preceding reply (see Table 4.1). When the vignette makes clear that the requested information is positive (the positive information condition), then the comprehension of relevance violations should become quite difficult and time consuming because there is no apparent reason for the violation. In contrast, in the no information and negative information conditions, the hearer can reasonably assume the existence of face management as a reason for the violation. Consistent with this logic, participants took far longer to comprehend replies in the positive information condition (2766 ms) than in the no information (2281 ms) and negative information (2263 ms) conditions. Note that the difference between the latter two conditions was not significant. Judgment speeds for the interpretations paralleled these results. Participants were far slower at judging the indirect interpretation in the positive information condition (2791 ms) than in the negative (2147 ms) and no information (2090 ms) conditions.

These results provide support for the idea that the specific interpretation given to a relevance violation is guided by beliefs about the reason for the violation. Again, I do not claim that relevance violations will always be interpreted as conveying negative information; I do claim that if face management is recognized as a motivation for the violation, then the utterance will tend to be interpreted as conveying face-threatening information. Occasionally, it might be positive information that is face threatening. For example, imagine a conversation between two siblings, Mark and John, in which Mark always outperforms John in school, much to John's chagrin. Mark is aware of John's feelings and generally tries to manage John's face. Now, when John asks Mark how he did on his chemistry test, and Mark fails to answer directly (e.g., "Let's go get a pizza"), John will probably interpret the reply as conveying positive information (i.e., he did well on his exam) rather than negative information. In this context it is positive information that may be face threatening, and so the reply will tend to be interpreted as conveying positive information.

Do people automatically generate indirect interpretations of relevance violations when they comprehend the utterance, or are these interpretations constructed in a post hoc manner when people are asked to interpret them? In the two experiments just described, participants were explicitly asked to interpret the replies (Experiment 1) or to judge the adequacy of interpretations of the replies (Experiment 2). It is possible, then, that our results reflect a post hoc judgment process rather than online comprehension. I conducted additional experiments to examine this issue (Experiments 1 through 3, Holtgraves, 1999).

In these experiments, participants were presented materials similar to those used in earlier research (Holtgraves, 1998b). Participants first read a (no information) scenario, question, and reply on a computer screen, and then they performed a sentence verification task. For this task a string of words appeared on the screen and participants were asked to indicate, as quickly as possible, whether or not the word string formed a sentence. Sometimes the target string was an indirect interpretation of the reply;

other times it was a neutral string that was not related to the reply (see Table 4.1). A pretest was conducted to select indirect and neutral strings that were equal in comprehension difficulty. If there is any activation of the indirect meaning when a reply is comprehended, then sentence verification judgments for the indirect interpretation targets should be faster than for the control sentence (a priming effect). This is exactly what happened. Participants were significantly faster at verifying sentences that were indirect interpretations of the reply than verifying matched control sentences. This effect occurred for excuses (Experiment 1) and topic changes (Experiment 2). Note that it did not occur when the scenarios were altered so that the reply did not violate the relation maxim. Finally, this priming effect is not the result of the indirect targets being more related to the preceding scenario than to the control targets. This possibility was eliminated in a third experiment in which participants read only the scenario and question (and not the reply). Under these conditions the priming effect did not occur, suggesting that it is the comprehension of the reply in the context of the preceding question that activates an indirect reading; facilitation of the indirect target is not a result of the indirect targets being more related to the context than the neutral targets. Take together, these results demonstrate that the indirect meaning of a relevance violation is activated when an utterance is comprehended; it is not simply the result of a postcomprehension judgment process.

Finally, I also examined whether recognition of the conveyed meaning of these replies involves a Gricean inference process (Experiments 4 through 6, Holtgraves, 1999). In two of these experiments, participants read versions of the question–reply materials described earlier. After indicating comprehension of the reply they performed a timed, sentence verification task. On critical trials the target string of words was either a literal interpretation of the reply (rather than an indirect interpretation as in the experiments already described) or a neutral sentence matched with the literal interpretation in terms of comprehension difficulty. For most of the reply types, participants were significantly faster at verifying the literal interpretations than matched controls. (One particular reply type did not demonstrate this pattern.) Unlike comprehension of metaphors and other generalized implicatures, these results are consistent with the standard pragmatic view that the literal meaning of an indirect utterance will be activated during the comprehension process. In another experiment I timed how long it took participants to read the reply as a function of whether the preceding context activated or did not activate an indirect (face-threatening) reading of the reply. Participants took significantly longer to read the replies when the indirect meaning was activated than when it was not. This too demonstrates that these types of particularized implicatures require a Gricean inference process for comprehension.

Preference Organization and Comprehending Particularized Implicatures

My research (Holtgraves, 1998b; 1999) on reply interpretation demonstrates that relevance violations are particularized implicatures and that a nonliteral meaning can only be derived in the context of the preceding question. Because the generated implicature is the product of a reasoning process, recipients should be sensitive to any features of the context that are informative as to the speaker's likely intended meaning. Thus, if face management is recognized as the motive behind a relevance violation, then any contextual information suggesting that face management processes are operative in this context should facilitate recognition of an indirect (face-threatening) meaning. I investigated this issue by examining the impact of dispreferred markers on the comprehension of indirect replies.

A question–reply sequence is an adjacency pair (Schegloff & Sacks, 1973), and as such a reply (the second pair part) is expected given the occurrence of the question (the first pair part). As with all adjacency pairs, however, there is a range of possible second pair parts that could occur, and these alternatives are not equal; some are preferred, and others are dispreferred. Dispreferred turns are turns that are marked (in the linguistic sense) in some way; preferred turns are unmarked. A common means of marking dispreferred turns is with a delay, a delay that will often include prefaces such as "well," "yes, but" (with disagreements), and apologies and/or accounts (with request refusals). In contrast, preferred turns are quick, simple, and direct. By definition, then, dispreferred turns are communicative; they signal that the current turn is not preferred. As such, dispreferred markers should help recipients comprehend replies with potential indirect meanings, particularly replies that convey face-threatening information.

My research has focused on *well* as a marker of dispreferred turns (Holtgraves, 2000). In general, the occurrence of *well* at the beginning of an utterance can be interpreted as indicating that the speaker is engaging in face management (Jucker, 1993). To refuse a request, decline an offer, and so on are threatening to the other person's face, and the dispreferred marker *well* helps soften this threat (Holtgraves, 1992). Moreover, as discourse analysts have argued, discourse markers such as *well* should signal to the recipient that the remark underway is indirect and needs to be interpreted within a context that is not immediately apparent (Jucker, 1993; Lakoff, 1973). Because of this, the occurrence of the dispreferred marker *well* in a reply should facilitate recognition of a face-threatening interpretation of that reply.

To examine this issue I modified the materials used in my earlier studies of indirect replies (Holtgraves, 1998b; 1999). The major change was to manipulate whether the indirect reply contained a *well* marker. One half of the time it did (e.g., Well, I think it's hard to give a good presentation), and one half of the time it did not (e.g., I think it's hard to give a good presentation). In Experiment 1, participants read the scenario, question, and reply on a computer screen, and then judged the adequacy of a potential interpretation of the reply. For the critical trials the interpretation was always a face-threatening paraphrase of the reply (e.g., I didn't like your presentation). As expected, face-threatening interpretations of the replies were more quickly verified when the reply contained a *well* preface (1534 ms) than when it did not (1632 ms).

It is possible that the facilitation observed in Experiment 1 occurred because participants were explicitly asked to judge the meaning of the reply. Would this facilitation occur automatically? A second experiment was conducted, using a more online measure, to examine this issue. Participants in this experiment viewed the same materials as before; one half of the time the reply contained a *well* preface, and one half of the time it did not. However, rather than providing a judgment regarding the meaning of the reply, participants performed a timed sentence verification task after reading the reply. On the critical trials, the to-be-judged target string was either a face-threatening interpretation of the reply (the paraphrases used in the first experiment) or an unrelated sentence. As in my previous research (Holtgraves, 1999), there was a substantial priming effect; verification speeds were much faster for the indirect (face-threatening) targets (1425 ms) than for the matched neutral targets (1690 ms). More important, however, this priming effect was significantly greater when the reply contained the *well* marker (a 322 ms difference) than when it did not contain the marker (a 206-ms difference). These results suggest that the impact of a *well* marker on comprehension is fairly immediate; its' presence facilitates the comprehension of indirect meanings when the reply is comprehended.

It seems likely that other markers of dispreferred turns will play a role in comprehension similar to that played by a *well* preface. And there is some preliminary evidence that they do. In an earlier study (Experiment 3, Holtgraves, 1998a) participants listened to (rather than read) question–reply exchanges. In some conditions the reply was briefly delayed (2 s). Brief delays are a common means of marking a turn as dispreferred, and in these conditions participants were faster at comprehending the reply, relative to replies that were not preceded by a brief delay. A delay, similar to a *well* marker, serves to mark the turn as dispreferred and, hence, facilitate recognition of a likely indirect reading. Taken together, these studies demonstrate clearly the role played by paralinguistic and noncontent features of talk in the comprehension of speaker meaning. This is an important avenue for future investigation as relatively little research has examined the role played by nonverbal and paralinguistic behaviors in the generation of conversational implicatures.

Perspective and Particularized Implicatures

One particularly important feature of the context is the perspective of the interlocutors. Perspective taking, of course, is crucial for language use (e.g., R. Brown, 1965; Clark, 1985; Krauss & Fussell, 1991; Mead, 1934; Rommetviet, 1974), especially for the recognition of indirect expressions. To successfully use an indirect expression requires the speaker to have some sense of how the recipient will interpret the utterance, and it requires the hearer to take the speaker's perspective in producing this particular utterance. Note, in this regard, how Grice's (1975) theory of conversational implicature requires perspective taking. Consider, for example, the quantity maxim, or stipulation that one's conversational contribution should be as informative as required. Obviously, adherence to this principle requires an assessment of what one's interlocutor knows; one cannot be appropriately informative without an assessment of the recipient's knowledge. And people are sensitive to this; the explanations they give others vary as a function of what they believe their audience knows (Slugoski, Lalljee, Lamb, & Ginsburg, 1993).

Perspective taking, however, is not perfect. For example, research suggests that interactants often exhibit an egocentric bias, producing and interpreting (at least initially) utterances from their unique perspective, without taking into account the perspective of their interlocutors (Horton & Keysar, 1996; Keysar, 1998; Keysar, Barr, Balin, & Paek, 1998; Keysar & Bly, 1995). That is, a people's conversational goals or agendas may blind them to the possibility that their interlocutors have different goals or agendas (Russell & Schober, 1999). Hence, speakers may assume they mean one thing without considering that the hearer might interpret it differently, and hearers may assume the speaker means one thing without considering that the speaker may have meant something else. So, even though theories of communication suggest that perspective taking underlies successful communication, it is possible that hearers and speakers will systematically diverge in their interpretations.

This raises the issue of whether the comprehension of indirect meaning might vary as a function of perspective. In my earlier studies (Holtgraves, 1998b, 1999, 2000) participants were asked to read and interpret replies from the perspective of the recipient of the reply, and there was a strong tendency for them to interpret relevance violations as conveying face-threatening information (i.e., a negative opinion or disclosure). This makes sense from the recipient's perspective. This person has asked for the opinion, and failing to obtain a direct and relevant reply should assume that the requested information is negative. If the information was positive, the speaker would have said so. However, these participants may have been engaged in means–end reasoning (Levinson, 2000). That is, they interpreted a relevance violation (the means) as reflecting face concerns (the end); hence, they interpreted the replies as indirectly conveying negative (i.e., face-threatening) information. Logically, of course, this is fallacious (affirming the consequent in deductive logic). That is, the means (a relevance violation) may occur for reasons other than face management. Consider a relevance violation in response to a request for an opinion. Perhaps the speaker's opinion was not well-formed or was ambiguous, or perhaps it did not even exist or was one that the speaker would prefer not to convey. All of these possibilities could be handled with a relevance violation, an utterance that functions to avoid providing a specific opinion rather than conveying a negative one. As a result, a speaker's intention in producing a relevance violation could sometimes be at odds with the recipient's interpretation of the same utterance.

To test this possibility I asked participants to interpret replies from either the perspective of the recipient of the reply or the perspective of the speaker, the person who produces the reply (Holtgraves, 2003). The materials for these experiments were adapted from those used in my earlier work on the role of face management in reply comprehension (Holtgraves, 1998b; 1999). If meaning simply resides in an utterance, then speakers and hearers should agree quite readily in what is being communicated. My results suggest otherwise. In three experiments, participants were far more likely to interpret relevance violations as conveying a negative opinion or disclosure when they assumed the perspective of the hearer than when they assumed the perspective of the speaker. This effect occurred for both excuses and topic changes, as well as for requests for opinions and requests for disclosures. Also, it made no difference whether participants were informed that the requested information was negative. In addition, it made no difference that participants alternated assuming the perspective of the speaker and hearer, a design that should have sensitized them to the possibility that they were interpreting the replies one way when they took the speaker's view and another way when they took the hearer's perspective. Despite these various features of the design, in the end replies were more likely to be interpreted as conveying negative information when participants took the hearer's perspective than when they took the speaker's perspective.

This research, then, suggests that there may be a systematic, interpretive bias built into the hearer and speaker roles. The tendency for hearers to interpret relevance violations as conveying negative information is consistent with my earlier research (Holtgraves, 1998b, 1999, 2000). Because indirect replies are frequently used as a means of managing face, and because interactants are generally aware that this is the case, recipients should interpret a relevance violation as conveying face-threatening information (a negative opinion or disclosure). But indirect utterances are inherently ambiguous and open to multiple interpretations. The means–ends reasoning used by a recipient to recover a face-threatening interpretation can yield errors. From the speaker's perspective, a relevance violation may be a means of signaling an unwillingness to provide the requested information. Hence, speakers may not believe that they are communicating negative information, but instead believe they are communicating an unwillingness to convey an opinion or disclosure.

Speaker Status and Nonliteral Meaning

Various speaker variables—such as his or her occupation (Katz & Pexman, 1997)—provide contextual cues regarding how a speaker's utterance is to be interpreted. One very important variable in this regard is the speaker's relative status (or power). Previous research has focused on language production and demonstrated that the greater the status of the recipient, the greater the likelihood that the speaker will use polite (or indirect) request forms (P. Brown & Levinson, 1987; Holtgraves, 2001b; Holtgraves & Yang, 1990, 1992). Because of its role in language production, it seems likely that speaker status will play an important role in comprehension. My research suggests that it does. For example, in my research on the processing of conventional and nonconventional indirect requests (Holtgraves, 1994), the status of the speaker moderated the effects of request conventionality. For conventional indirect requests (e.g., Can you shut the door?), the status of the speaker did not affect comprehension; these forms were recognized quickly and directly, without any type of inference process (they appear to be generalized implicatures). In contrast, the comprehension of nonconventional forms was affected by the status of the speaker. Participants were faster at comprehending these forms when the speaker was higher rather than equal in status to his or her conversation partner. In addition, priming experiments demonstrated that both the literal and the indirect meanings were activated for these forms when the speaker was equal status; this did not occur when the speaker was high status. These results thus demonstrate that a Gricean inference process appears to be required for the comprehension of nonconventional forms performed by an equal-status speaker, a process that appears not to be necessary when the speaker is high status.

Similar to face management, speaker status is a feature of the social context that impacts both utterance production and utterance comprehension. But exactly how does status play a role in the comprehension of requests? There are at least two possibilities. The first possibility is that knowledge that a speaker is high status may circumvent the need for an inference process; a directive interpretation may be activated prior to any activation of the literal meaning of the utterance. Thus, when a speaker is high status, a recipient may be inclined to interpret the speaker's utterances a priori as directives (cf. Ervin-Tripp, Strage, Lampert, & Bell, 1987). The finding that an inference process is not required for nonconventional indirect requests when the speaker is high status supports this possibility (Holtgraves, 1994). Additional empirical support for this idea is provided by a priming study I conducted demonstrating that directive readings can be activated based solely on the status of the speaker (Experiment 4, Holtgraves, 1994). Participants in this study first read descriptions of situations in which speaker status was varied, and then they made sentence verification judgments of targets that either were or were not possible directives in each situation. The requests themselves were not presented. When the speaker was high status, sentence verification times were significantly faster for directives than for related control targets (i.e., a priming effect), and this effect did not occur when the speaker was equal status. In short, speaker status alone (without the utterance) was sufficient for priming a directive interpretation.

A second possibility is that knowledge that a speaker is high status can facilitate an inference process if one is required. Rejection of the literal meaning of an utterance depends in part on the possibility that there are alternative interpretations of the utterance (e.g., Sperber & Wilson, 1986). People who are high status have the right to issue directives; hence, there exist possible directive interpretations of their utterances. The existence of these interpretations, then, increases the likelihood that the literal meaning will be rejected. Moreover, given that the literal meaning is rejected, knowledge that the speaker is high status can increase the likelihood that a directive interpretation will be adopted.

Regardless of how speaker status impacts the comprehension of speaker meaning, other research suggests that speaker status can influence long-term memory for a speaker's remarks. In several experiments we had participants read or listen to dialogues in which we manipulated the ostensible status of one of the speakers (Holtgraves, Srull, & Socall, 1989). In these experiments there was a tendency for the utterances of high-status speakers to be recalled as being more assertive (i.e., direct) than identical remarks uttered by an equal-status speaker. These results are consistent with our research demonstrating the impact of speaker status on comprehension (high speaker status prompts a directive reading, a reading that is then retained in long-term memory). However, I conducted additional studies demonstrating that, at times, if the wording of an utterance is at odds with normative expectations, these wordings will tend to be remembered well. In one experiment (Experiment 3, Holtgraves, 1997a) I gave participants a surprise memory test for the experimenter's instructions. The ostensible status of the experimenter was manipulated (high-status professor vs. equal-status undergraduate research assistant) as was the politeness (or directness) of his utterances. On subsequent memory tests, participants were more likely to remember the polite remarks of the high-status speaker and the impolite remarks of the equal-status speaker. In this situation, it is utterances violating normative expectancies that receive additional processing and, hence, that are remembered relatively well.

CULTURAL DIFFERENCES IN COMPREHENDING NONLITERAL MEANINGS

Nonliteral meanings, by definition, are ambiguous. Hence, there is the possibility that people will differ in their interpretation of utterances with potential indirect meanings, as my research on speaker–hearer differences suggest (Holtgraves, 2003). And there may be systematic cultural differences in this regard. In this case the cultural background of the interlocutors will play an important role in the comprehension of nonliteral meanings. This issue is related to the criticism of Grice's (1975) model as not being cross-culturally valid. For example, in a well-known article Keenan (1976) argued that people in Malagasy routinely withhold information from one another (information is a culturally prized commodity), an action that is in clear violation of the quantity maxim. Because of this, violations of the quantity maxim in Malagasy do not usually result in conversational implicatures (as presumably would be the case in most other cultures). There is a more general criticism here. It has been suggested that Grice's view, with its emphasis on individual autonomy, has relevance only in Western cultures (Fitch & Sanders, 1994). For example, Rosaldo (1982), in her analysis of Llongot speech acts, argued that directives in that culture are not particularly face threatening, referencing as they do group membership and responsibility rather than individual wants and desires. Hence, directives in that culture will usually not be performed indirectly.

It is clearly possible that the maxims people follow in communicating cooperatively may vary over cultures, perhaps reflecting differences in what is regarded as rational interaction. Note, however, that even if there are cultural differences in this regard, these differences will not alter the basic Gricean insight that if a person believes a maxim has been violated, then some interpretive work will be undertaken. In addition, Grice's (1975) fundamental point that conversational maxims (whatever they may look like) serve as a basis for rational interaction and, hence, as a framework for interpretation will not be altered.

Still, it is clearly important to determine the specific content of conversation maxims and how they might vary over cultures. This issue has been explored in various ways. One research line has been to examine overall cultural differences in the tendency to interpret utterances indirectly. This research has been guided by the cultural dimensions of individualism and collectivism (Triandis, 1995). In general, collectivism entails a relatively greater concern for the needs, feelings, and wants of one's in-groups; it represents a relatively greater concern for the face of in-group members

(Ting-Toomey, 1988). Because one of the major means for attending to face is indirectness (P. Brown & Levinson, 1987), it seems reasonable that indirectness will be more common in collectivist cultures than individualistic cultures. I examined cultural variability in indirectness using the Conversational Indirectness Scale (CIS; Holtgraves, 1997b). The CIS is a 19-item, self-report measure assessing both an interpretation dimension (the extent to which a person looks for indirect meanings in the remarks of others) and a production dimension (the extent to which a person phrases his or her remarks indirectly). My initial research demonstrated that this a reliable and valid measure of these two dimensions. For example, people scoring high on the interpretation dimension are more likely to recognize indirect meanings and to be significantly faster at doing so than people scoring low on this dimension (Experiment 6, Holtgraves, 1997b). Note that the latter difference occurred only for relatively unconventional forms (i.e., particularized implicatures), forms for which an inference process is most likely required.

To examine cultural variability I (Holtgraves, 1997b) translated the CIS into Korean and administered it to a sample of students at Korean universities. Factor analyses of the scores from this sample were highly similar to the factor analytic results based on a sample of American students. Accordingly, I compared the two samples in terms of their scores on the CIS. Overall, Korean students scored significantly higher on both the interpretation dimension (53.26 vs. 43.62) and production dimension (42.37 vs. 33.61). These results provide some support for the notion that people in collectivist cultures tend to produce and look for indirect meanings to a greater extent than people in individualistic cultures. Recently, Hara and Kim (2001) demonstrated that these broad cultural differences may be partly explained in terms of differing self-construals. Specifically, they found that individuals with interdependent self-construals were more likely to speak and interpret indirectly than were people with independent self-construals. Of course, not all collectivist and individualistic cultures are alike (e.g., Kashima et al., 1995). And cultural differences in indirectness reflect only average differences. People in all cultures will vary the politeness (and thus the indirectness) of their remarks as a function of the context. And, in fact, it appears that people in collectivist cultures are more sensitive and responsive to the context than are people in individualistic cultures (Gudykunst, Yoon, & Nishida, 1987; Holtgraves & Yang, 1992; Triandis, Bontempo, Villareal, Asai, & Lucca, 1988).

Another way in which cultural variability has been explored is in terms of cultural differences regarding which specific maxims are likely to result in conversational implicatures (Holtgraves & Drozd, 1998). Participants in this study were students at Ball State University who were from either an individualistic culture (the United States) or collectivist cultures (East and Southeast Asia). We created scenarios and corresponding dialogs with one utterance designed to convey an indirect meaning. Across these scenarios we systematically manipulated which specific maxim was violated. For violations of the relevance maxim we also included different utterance types (request refusals, opinions, and self-disclosures). Participants read a scenario and the target utterance and then chose which of three possible interpretations (one literal interpretation and two indirect interpretations) best captured the speaker's meaning in this situation. There was a reliable Culture × Maxim Type interaction. For all but one utterance type, American participants were less likely to interpret utterances indirectly than the East and Southeast Asians, a finding that is consistent with research demonstrating that collectivists tend to be more indirect than individualists. However, this pattern was reversed for violations of the quality maxim: East and Southeast Asians were less likely to interpret the utterances indirectly than were the American participants. Although these findings are preliminary, they do suggest that it is too simplistic to view collectivists as more indirect than individualists. Instead, there may be cultural variability in interpretation as a function of how the indirect meaning is conveyed (and, no doubt, as a function of many other differences as well). This is clearly an important avenue for future research.

CONCLUSION

Nonliteral meanings can be conveyed in a variety of ways, with corresponding differences in how those meanings are processed. One major distinction useful for classifying nonliteral meanings involves the extent to which recognition of their intended meaning is dependent on the immediate context. Some nonliteral meanings—generalized implicatures in Grice's (1975) terms—tend to be recognized regardless of the context in which they are used. In other words, they are highly conventionalized and the default, nonliteral, meaning is recognized in a relatively direct fashion, without need of a relatively time-consuming inference process. The empirical evidence is really quite clear in this regard. Most figurative expressions are recognized quickly and without any activation of their literal meanings. Comprehension of conventional indirect requests is also relatively quick and not influenced by features of the context such as speaker status. Although not examined empirically, it seems likely that Q-implicatures and WXDY constructions will also be recognized quickly and directly. But how exactly are these nonliteral meanings recognized? Although we know a Gricean inference process (recognize and then reject the literal meaning) is not involved, we do not know what processes are involved in their recognition. For example, which features of the utterance or the context activate the nonliteral meaning? Is the entire meaning activated at once, or does recognition occur in stages?

Although generalized implicatures have default meanings that are activated regardless of the context, it is possible that it is the literal meaning that is intended by the speaker and that will be recognized by the recipient. Thus, "He spilled the beans" might be intended literally and taken as such when reporting on the recent activities of one's preschooler. But in this case the intended meaning will be the result of an inference process of some sort as the recipient recognizes and then rejects the default nonliteral meaning. In short, even though generalized implicatures have preferred meanings that are independent of the context, those preferred meanings can be overridden by the context. And when this happens, it appears to be the result of a Gricean process in reverse—first recognize and then reject the nonliteral meaning—with the literal meaning chosen because of its fit with the conversation and the context.

In contrast to generalized implicatures, the interpretation of particularized implicatures is completely dependent on the context; the nonliteral meaning is not attached a priori to the utterance that carries it. As a result, particularized implicatures (at least those that have been investigated) require a time-consuming inference process for their recognition. And because it is a reasoning process that is required, various aspects of the context—status, face management, and so on—will play a critical role in the process of interpretation.

Particularized implicatures have not received as much empirical attention as generalized implicatures. As a result, not very much is known regarding how they operate. For example, what mechanisms, other than relevance violations, can yield particularized implicatures? And what features of the context will play a role in its comprehension? And to what extent are there cultural differences in the interpretation of particularized implicatures? Pursuing these and other questions will increase our understanding of the comprehension of nonliteral meaning.

ACKNOWLEDGMENTS

Much of the research described in this chapter was supported by grants from the National Science Foundation (SBR–9601311 and 0131877), National Institute of Mental Health (MH45747), and Ball State University Office of Research and Sponsored Programs

REFERENCES

Bavelas, J. B., Black, A., Chovil, N., & Mullet, J. (1990). *Equivocal communication*. Newbury Park, CA: Sage.
Brown, P., & Levinson, S. (1987). *Politeness: Some universals in language usage*. Cambridge, England: Cambridge University Press.

Brown, R. (1965). *Social psychology*. New York: The Free Press.

Brown, R., & Gilman, A. (1989). Politeness theory and Shakespeare's four major tragedies. *Language in Society, 18,* 159–212.

Cacciari, C., & Glucksberg, S. (1994). Understanding figurative language. In M. A. Gernsbacher (Ed.), *Handbook of psycholinguistic research* (pp. 447–478). San Diego: Academic Press.

Clark, H. H. (1979). Responding to indirect speech acts. *Cognitive Psychology, 11,* 430–477.

Clark, H. H. (1985). Language use and language users. In G. Lindzey & E. Aronson (Eds.), *The handbook of social psychology* (3rd ed., Vol. 2, pp. 179–232). Reading, MA: Addison-Wesley

Clark, H. H., & Schunk, D. (1980). Polite responses to polite requests. *Cognition, 8,* 111–143.

Ervin-Tripp, S., Strage, M., Lampert, M., & Bell, N. (1987). Understanding requests. *Linguistics, 25,* 107–143.

Fitch, K. L., & Sanders, R. E. (1994). Culture, communication, and preferences for directness in expression of directives. *Communication Theory, 4,* 219–245.

Gibbs, R. W., Jr. (1980). Spilling the beans on understanding and memory for idioms. *Memory & Cognition, 8,* 449–456.

Gibbs, R. W., Jr. (1983). Do people always process the literal meaning of indirect requests? *Journal of Experimental Psychology: Learning, Memory, and Cognition, 9,* 524–533.

Gibbs, R. W., Jr. (1994). Figurative thought and figurative language. In M. A. Gernsbacher (Ed.), *Handbook of psycholinguistic research* (pp. 411–446). San Diego: Academic Press.

Gildea, P., & Glucksberg, S. (1983). On understanding metaphor: The role of context. *Journal of Verbal Learning and Verbal Behavior, 22,* 577–590.

Glucksberg, S. (1991). Beyond literal meanings: The psychology of allusion. *Psychological Science, 2,* 146–152.

Glucksberg, S., Gildea, P., & Bookin, H. (1982). On understanding nonliteral speech: Can people ignore metaphors? *Journal of Verbal Learning and Verbal Behavior, 21,* 85–98.

Goffman, E. (1967). *Interaction ritual: Essays on face to face behavior.* Garden City, NY: Anchor.

Graesser, A. C., Singer, M., & Trabasso, T. (1994). Constructing inferences during narrative text comprehension. *Psychological Review, 101,* 371–395.

Grice, H. P. (1975). Logic and conversation. In P. Cole & J. Morgan (Eds.), *Syntax and semantics: Vol. 3. Speech acts* (pp. 41–58). New York: Academic Press.

Gudykunst, W., Yoon, Y. C., & Nishida, T. (1987). The influence of individualism–collectivism on perceptions of communication in in-group and out-group relations. *Communication Monographs, 54,* 295–306.

Hara, K., & Kim, M. S. (2001, May). *The effect of self-construals on conversational indirectness.* Paper presented at International Communication Association Convention, Washington, DC.

Hastie, R. (1984). Causes and consequences of causal attributions. *Journal of Personality and Social Psychology, 46,* 44–56.

Holtgraves, T. M. (1986). Language structure in social interaction: Perceptions of direct and indirect speech act and interactants who use them. *Journal of Personality and Social Psychology, 51*, 305–314.

Holtgraves, T. M. (1992). The linguistic realization of face management: Implications for language production and comprehension, person perception, and cross-cultural communication. *Social Psychology Quarterly, 55*, 141–159.

Holtgraves, T. M. (1994). Communication in context: Effects of speaker status on the comprehension of indirect requests. *Journal of Experimental Psychology: Learning, Memory, and Cognition, 20*, 1205–1218.

Holtgraves, T. M. (1997a). Politeness and memory for the wording of remarks. *Memory & Cognition, 25*, 106–116.

Holtgraves, T. M. (1997b). Styles of language use: Individual and cultural variability in conversational indirectness. *Journal of Personality and Social Psychology, 73*, 624–637.

Holtgraves, T. M. (1998a, July). *Interpreting indirect replies*. Paper presented at International Communication Association Convention, Jerusalem, Israel.

Holtgraves T. M. (1998b). Interpreting indirect replies. *Cognitive Psychology, 37*, 1–27.

Holtgraves, T. M. (1999). Comprehending indirect replies: When and how are their conveyed meanings activated. *Journal of Memory and Language, 41*, 519–540.

Holtgraves, T. M. (2000). Preference organization and reply comprehension. *Discourse Processes, 30*, 87–106.

Holtgraves, T. M. (2001a). *Language as social action: Social psychology and language use*. Mahwah, NJ: Lawrence Erlbaum Associates.

Holtgraves, T. M. (2001b). Politeness. In W. P. Robinson & H. Giles (Eds.), *The new handbook of language and social psychology* (pp. 341–355). Chichester, England: Wiley.

Holtgraves, T. M. (2003). *Conversational perspective taking: Diverging assumptions of speakers and hearers*.

Holtgraves, T. M., & Ashley, A. (2001). Comprehending illocutionary force. *Memory & Cognition, 29*, 83–90.

Holtgraves, T. M., & Drozd, B. (1998, May). *Cross-cultural differences in conversational interpretation*. Paper presented at the annual meeting of the Midwestern Psychological Association, Chicago, IL.

Holtgraves, T. M., Srull, T. K., & Socall, D. (1989). Conversation memory: Effects of speaker status on memory for the assertiveness of conversation remarks. *Journal of Personality and Social Psychology, 56*, 149–160.

Holtgraves, T. M., & Yang, J. N. (1990). Politeness as an universal: Cross-cultural perceptions of request strategies and inferences based on their use. *Journal of Personality and Social Psychology, 59*, 719–729.

Holtgraves, T. M., & Yang, J. N. (1992). The interpersonal underpinnings of request strategies: General principles and differences due to culture and gender. *Journal of Personality and Social Psychology, 62*, 246–256.

Horton, W. S., & Keysar, B. (1996). When do speakers take into account common ground? *Cognition, 59*, 91–117.

Jucker, A. H. (1993). The discourse marker *well*: A relevance-theoretical account. *Journal of Pragmatics, 19*, 435–452.

Kashima, Y., Yamaguchi, S., Kim, U., Choi, S., Gelfand, M. J., & Yuki, M. (1995). Culture, gender, and the self: A perspective from individualism–collectivism research. *Journal of Personality and Social Psychology, 69*, 925–937.

Katz, A., & Pexman, P. (1997). Interpreting figurative statements: Speaker occupation can change metaphor to irony. *Metaphor and Symbol, 12*, 19–41.

Kay, P., & Fillmore, C. J. (1999). Grammatical constructions and linguistic generalizations: The what's X doing Y? construction. *Language, 75*, 1–33.

Keenan, E. O. (1976). The universality of conversational implicature. *Language in Society, 5*, 67–80.

Keysar, B. (1989). On the functional equivalence of literal and metaphorical interpretation in discourse. *Journal of Memory and Language, 28*, 375–385.

Keysar, B. (1994). Discourse context effects: Metaphorical and literal interpretations. *Discourse Processes, 18*, 247–269.

Keysar, B. (1998). Language users as problem solvers: Just what ambiguity problem do they solve? In S. Fussell & R. Kreuz (Eds.), *Social and cognitive approaches to interpersonal communication* (pp. 175–200). Mahwah, NJ: Lawrence Erlbaum Associates.

Keysar, B., Barr, D. J., Balin, J. A., & Paek, T. (1998). Definite reference and mutual knowledge: A processing model of common ground in comprehension. *Journal of Memory and Language, 39*, 1–20.

Keysar, B., & Bly, B. (1995). Intuitions of the transparency of idioms: Can one keep a secret by spilling the beans? *Journal of Memory and Language, 34*, 89–109.

Krauss, R. M., & Fussell, S. R. (1991). Perspective taking in communication: Representations of others' knowledge in reference. *Social Cognition, 9*, 2–24.

Lakoff, R. (1973). Questionable answers and answerable questions. In B. B. Kachru (Ed.), *Issues in linguistics: Papers in honor of Henry and Renee Kahane* (pp. 453–467). Chicago: University of Illinois Press.

Levinson, S. C. (2000). *Presumptive meanings.* Cambridge, MA: MIT Press.

Mead, G. H. (1934). *Mind, self, and society.* Chicago: University of Chicago Press.

Ortony, A., Schallert, D., Reynolds, R., & Antos, S. (1978). Interpreting metaphors and idioms: Some effects of context on comprehension. *Journal of Verbal Learning and Verbal Behavior, 16*, 465–477.

Roberts, R. M., & Kreuz, R. J. (1994). Why do people use figurative language? *Psychological Science, 5*, 159–163.

Rommetviet, R. (1974). *On message structure: A framework for the study of language and communication.* New York: Wiley.

Rosaldo, M. Z. (1982). The things we do with words: Llongot speech acts and speech act theory in philosophy. *Language in Society, 11*, 203–237.

Russell, A. W., & Schober, M. F. (1999). How beliefs about a partner's goals affect referring in goal-discrepant conversations. *Discourse Processes, 27*, 1–33.

Schegloff, E., & Sacks, H. (1973). Opening up closings. *Semiotica, 8*, 289–327.

Singer, M., Halldorson, M., Lear, J. C., & Andrusiak, P. (1992). Validation of causal bridging inferences in discourse understanding. *Journal of Memory and Language, 31*, 507–524.

Slugoski, B., Lalljee, M., Lamb, R., & Ginsburg, G. P. (1993). Attributions in conversational context: Effects of mutual knowledge on explanation giving. *European Journal of Social Psychology, 23*, 219–238.

Sperber, D., & Wilson, D. (1986). *Relevance*. Cambridge, MA: Harvard University Press.

Ting-Toomey, S. (1988). Intercultural conflict styles. In Y. Y. Kim & W. B. Gudykunst (Eds.), *Theories in intercultural communication* (pp. 213–238). Beverly Hills, CA: Sage.

Titone, D. A., & Connine, C. M. (1994). Comprehension of idiomatic expressions: Effects of familiarity and literality. *Journal of Experimental Psychology: Learning, Memory and Cognition, 20,* 1126–1138.

Triandis, H. (1995). *Individualism and collectivism*. Boulder, CO: Westview.

Triandis, H., Bontempo, R., Villareal, M., Asai, M., & Lucca, N. (1988). Individualism and collectivism: Cross-cultural perspectives on self-ingroup relationships. *Journal of Personality and Social Psychology, 54,* 323–333.

5

Social and Cultural Influences on Figurative and Indirect Language

Herbert L. Colston
University of Wisconsin–Parkside

Accounts of language comprehension have long recognized that language is inherently underdetermined—the meaning of a statement or other instance of spoken or written language is necessarily less than or potentially different from the reasonably predictable intended comprehended meaning of a use of that language by a speaker or a writer, for a hearer(s) or a reader(s), in a context. Processes such as referential assignment, ambiguity resolution, inference generation, and others nearly always take place in language comprehension and result in intended comprehended meanings that go far beyond language meanings. Indeed, even relatively straightforward, veridical language (e.g., the oft used, "The cat is on the mat") is at best a skeleton of the meaning comprehended from that language by a hearer or reader in a real-world context.

Often considered, and in my view erroneously so, a separate and, indeed, by some scholars special category of language are those forms where underdeterminedness is just the beginning to how the language meaning and its intended comprehended meaning are separated. This category of language is comprised of indirect forms, figurative language, idiomatic, proverbial, colloquial, and so on—expressions wherein the decontextualized meaning of the language is more than just an underdetermined scaffold of the intended comprehended meaning. The mismatch between what is said and what is meant is instead (or additionally) one of seeming opposition (verbal irony), seemingly disparate topicality (metaphor), seemingly unequivalent magnitude (hyperbole), seeming unrelatedness (idioms, proverbs, colloqui-alisms, etc.), seeming laterality (emintended directives), and so on. Com-prehension of these forms is thus an arguably more complicated matter of gleaning the intended comprehended meaning from an underdetermined and nonveridical language meaning.

Generally speaking, the former veridical language category wherein underdeterminedness is the only form of separation between language meaning and comprehended meaning has been referred to as *literal language*, and the latter category where underdeterminedness is coupled with other forms of meaning separation has been called *nonliteral language*.

Whether one considers literal and nonliteral types of language to be sepa-rate categories or, as would be my preference, areas of language that, al-though potentially overlapping, typically have the tendency to be toward different ends of a continuum of language that varies from relatively little complexity, density, or richness to relatively more, one must still acknowl-edge that all language comprehension necessarily involves computation of the speaker's intended meaning. Note that this requires consideration of something other than the language meaning itself—something rather ephemeral that has typically been given the umbrella term of *context*.

Traditional comprehension explanations have handled this role of con-text typically by splitting comprehension into separate processes, one that composes a semantic meaning of what is said from lexical and syntactic, as well as semantic, information in the spoken or written language and a sec-ondary one that then uses context to assign reference, solve ambiguities, and compute inferences. Last comes a final process, whose extent is op-tional, of deriving pragmatic ramifications of the use of that spoken or writ-ten language in that context (for the given interlocutors, their social relationship, etc.) to arrive at the speakers particular full intended meaning.

Recent revisions to this general separation strategy have begun to recog-nize the interdependency or even the indistinguishability of these purport-edly separate comprehension parts, and some have even done away with some of the lexical-semantic initial processes altogether. Such accounts put much more emphasis on top-down, context-, and expectancy-driven pro-cesses in language comprehension.

A review of the history and current status of language comprehension accounts is beyond the intent and scope of this chapter. Suffice it for now to say that a movement toward incorporating contextual contributions to language comprehension both overall and as a component of lower and lower level bottom-up processing has taken place, and most accounts now grapple with the fact that an intended comprehended meaning is built from both linguistic input and context in a very complex self-dependent relationship.

However, this heightened appreciation of contextual information in language comprehension has been limited. Perhaps unfortunately, consideration of context has all too often omitted social and cultural variables of the interlocutors and instead focused on information in the present physical environment or in the memories of the parties involved. Perhaps this is due to the relatively heightened status given to the referential assignment over interlocutor pragmatic ramification stages in traditional language processing accounts. Nonetheless, until very recently, social and cultural variables have not played much of a role in explanations of literal or even nonliteral language comprehension—particularly in processing.

In this chapter I first argue for the necessity of inclusion of social/cultural variables in consideration of all forms of language processing, comprehension, and use, particularly so for nonliteral forms. Then, I briefly review some past and current research that concurs with this argument. Next, I demonstrate the necessity of attending to the social/cultural components of context by delineating how an understanding of the use of two forms of nonliteral language requires this attention. Finally, I attempt to drive home the general argument with a brief discussion of a very recent study of mine that has begun to delineate a powerful overall mechanism that strongly argues for the crucial importance of social and cultural variables in nonliteral language comprehension.

ARGUMENTS FOR CONSIDERATION OF SOCIAL/CULTURAL INFLUENCES IN NONLITERAL LANGUAGE COMPREHENSION

The relative omission to date of social and cultural influences on language comprehension in our developing accounts is unfortunate. Two compelling lines of reasoning strongly indicate that leaving social and cultural influences out of our explanations of all forms of language comprehension is limiting our understanding of this important area of human cognition. The first of these is a logical argument; the second is an argument by analogy. These arguments are then followed by a discussion concerning the relative dependence of literal and nonliteral language on social/cultural variables.

Argument 1: Contextual Structure Versus Contextual Content

To justify that heretofore acknowledged contextual influences on language comprehension—such as situation models built up from preceding text or talk or situational schematic information—are worthy of consideration, whereas other contextual influences—such as social or cultural variables of the interlocutors—are not, these sources must be shown to be fundamentally separate or different. There is very little support for such a split. Although it is possible to have different kinds of contextual support for the interpretation of some target utterance, and these different kinds of support will undoubtedly alter how that utterance is comprehended, I argue that these differences are primarily structural rather than content based; therefore, social and cultural variables should be considered to be as important as situational ones.

Consider first a concrete example of literal language usage. A variety of comprehension accounts would now acknowledge that the intended comprehended meaning of *fish*, in (1):

(1) He likes fish.

would be very different when comprehended in context (2) versus (3):

(2) Your young daughter belongs to a soccer league that is expanding. The league is planning on forming a new team, and several players have been asked to help think of names for the team. Your daughter is one of the players. She is at a loss for ideas, though, and asks for your help. You don't have a ready suggestion either, so you ask her what name her coach might like. Your daughter says,

      "He likes fish."

(3) Your widowed mother has remained single for some time now, but has finally decided to start dating. She recently introduced you to a new guy she's been seeing who you thought would be great for her. You invite them for dinner, and want him to have a good time, but you don't know what to serve. You ask your mother for a suggestion and she says,

      "He likes fish."

The intended comprehended meaning of *fish* in (2) would likely involve instances of fish such as shark, barracuda, or killer whale, whereas in (3) it would instead involve instances such as salmon, cod, or whitefish. And, important technical differences in these processing accounts aside, most accounts would also generally agree that this different intended comprehended meaning of *fish* arises very early in processing and is influenced by the preceding semantic information in the context passages.

How do these different contexts produce different intended comprehended meanings of the same word? Again, skirting technical difference in the accounts, in general they agree that the first passage builds up a semantic representation of a category of something like "names for sports teams," whereas the second passage builds up a semantic representation for the category of "foods for a dinner entrée." Thus, before encountering the word *fish*, a very different situation model is in place in the working memory of the reader or listener. These different situational models then constrain which senses of fish are activated, to use the processing jargon, when the word is read or heard, and thus a different intended comprehended meaning is derived but with a relatively equivalent time course in the different contexts.

However, such different *processing environments*, to use a broader term than situation models, are not purely dependent on a long series of sentences as in the just-noted scenarios. They can also be invoked by a variety of other sources, including social or cultural variables that can be changed with the replacement of a very few, or indeed just one, word(s). Consider the comprehension of (4) in the contexts (5) versus (6):

(4)   "Try the French place up the street, they serve an exquisite duck."

(5)   You arrive in a new city you've never visited before, and are hoping to get a good recommendation for a restaurant from a local citizen. You are walking to your hotel and you meet a small group of people waiting for a bus on the street. You strike up a conversation with a few of them and say you are new in town and ask if someone could recommend a good restaurant for dinner. A wealthy looking business man in the group says,

    "Try the French place up the street, they serve an exquisite duck."

(6)   You arrive in a new city you've never visited before, and are hoping to get a good recommendation for a restaurant from a local citizen. You are walking to your hotel and you meet a small group of people waiting for a bus on the street. You strike up a conversation with a few of them and say you are new in town and ask if someone could recommend a good restaurant for dinner. A poor looking homeless man in the group says,

    "Try the French place up the street, they serve an exquisite duck."

The different scenarios conjured up by contexts (5) and (6) would very likely alter the comprehension of (4). At the very least, even if the recommendation were taken seriously in both instances, the comprehension in (6) would likely involve a degree of curiosity, skepticism, or hint of unusualness greater than that in (5).

Note that, the source for the different interpretations in (5) and (6) is fundamentally the same as the source for different interpretations of (2) and (3)—the processing environment difference in which the target statement is comprehended. For the latter scenarios, the different processing environments are invoked by altering a very few words in a passage that change the kind of person making the statement. For the former scenarios, the processing environments are altered by broader situation model descriptions that are spelled out over several lines, which changes one's thinking regarding the kind of fish.

One could make an argument that the more concentrated method of invoking processing environment differences in the latter scenarios is a stronger manipulation than the more diluted method in the former ones. The more concentrated presentation in (5) and (6) allows for greater juxtaposition of the processing environment with the target remark. This stronger juxtaposition can enable greater contrast that can, in turn, greatly alter the comprehension of the target utterance (Colston, 2002a). Alternatively, one could also make a counterargument that the slow buildup allowed by the former scenarios can create more interpretive momentum and thus send the different interpretations of the target utterance off in broadly disparate directions.

Essentially, both of these arguments have validity. Different means of presenting distinct processing environments can afford different ways in which interpretations of a target utterance can divulge. But, aside from the means by which these processing environments are established, there is no logical reason to suppose that the processing environment differences in the latter scenarios are somehow more or less effective than those in the former. The point still holds that the social/cultural differences in the former scenario versus the situational differences in the latter scenarios are really just a matter of technique—they are not something based upon content.

Indeed, one could easily reverse the pairings of the concentrated or diluted mechanism just discussed and the kind of processing environment scenarios (e.g., social/cultural vs. situational) and alter interpretation differences accordingly. All one would need to do is invoke a social/cultural processing environment difference with several lines worth of description and invoke a situational processing environment difference with alternation of just one word; the structural processing environment mechanisms would still have their effects, but these effects would be independent of the content.

So, in essence, processing environments can differ; if arranged appropriately, these differences can make social/cultural processing environments less effective than situational ones. But if this is the case, the processing environment differences are only structural-, not content-based. One could equally arrange the processing environments such that social/cultural environments are more effective than situational ones.

Thus, it appears that the social/cultural versus situational difference in contextual information bears no impact on processing or comprehension—only structural factors seem important. But there may be reason to suppose that the difference does matter when one is interpreting nonliteral language, or at least some forms of nonliteral language (Colston & Gibbs, 2002; Winner & Gardner, 1993). For these forms (e.g., verbal irony), social/cultural variables may in fact carry more influence than situational ones. To demonstrate, recall that nonliteral language presents a relatively greater separation between language meaning and intended comprehended meaning. Thus, comprehension of nonliteral language may be more dependent on deriving speakers' intention compared to literal language. According to Colston and Gibbs (2002, p. 59), "irony says something about the speaker (i.e., his or her attitudes or opinions about the topic).... Interpreting irony requires that listeners draw particular inferences about the speaker's state of mind. More specifically, understanding irony demands that listeners draw a second-order inference about the speaker's beliefs and intentions." Knowing some key information about the speaker may then be particularly useful for comprehension of some forms of nonliteral language, and thus providing or removing this information (e.g., manipulating a social/cultural variable) would strongly influence processing or comprehension. Indeed, this claim has empirical support; Pexman and Olineck (2002) found that speaker occupation strongly influenced comprehension of verbal irony and most notably so when other contextual clues were absent (see also Katz & Pexman, 1997).

Argument 2: Analogous Omissions of Social/Cultural Influences—Conservation and Word Learning

Another way to approach this issue of whether to consider social/cultural variables as important components of context is to look at analogous domains of research that have moved from little or no consideration of social or cultural influences on some level of processing to a more contemporary understanding of how these influences matter. Such a view correctly points out how the omission of social and cultural influences in some ways is accidental and understandable, given the focus of the then-current theoretical approaches or methodologies, but at the same time is crucially inhibitive of our attempts to understand these domains of cognition.

A number of domains of developmental psychological research, for instance, were founded on principles that originally failed to consider important sociopragmatic influences. Each of these domains has since seen an important shift in that social/cultural influences are now at least entertained by many scholars as being crucial components of human cognition in those domains. Consider the domains of conservation and word learning.

Conservation used to be considered by many scholars to be a milestone exclusively of conceptual development that was essentially immune to social influences. Children in a Piagetian preoperational stage of development, for instance, were considered unable to comprehend that the magnitude of substances (e.g., a fixed amount of a liquid) was constant across various external changes to those substances (e.g., when being poured from one container to another of a different shape). Only when children reached a particular age and level of conceptual sophistication (in Piagetian terms, the concrete operational stage) did they achieve the ability to conserve. Moreover, this ability was seen as being independent of any social influences on children both in terms of the actual conservation ability as well as how such abilities were measured.

This view has experienced a significant change. Although still considered a general conceptual milestone much like I described, conservation is now also considered to be at least partially determined by sociopragmatic influences. This is best observed in how the means by which conservation was measured have come under scrutiny. Children in a classical conservation task would typically be shown a colored liquid in a transparent container of a certain size and shape (e.g., a tall and narrow cylinder). The children would also be asked if they can see how much of the liquid there is in the container by an experimenter. Children would typically respond affirmatively. Next, the experimenter would pour the liquid into a differently shaped container (e.g., a short and wide cylinder), in direct view of the child, being careful not to spill any liquid or to leave any liquid in the original container. Then, the child would be asked if he or she can see how much liquid there is in the new container and whether the amount is the same or different from what it had been in the original container. The general pattern of results was that preconserving children would say there was less liquid in the second container but conserving children would say the amount had remained constant. The typical reasoning given by the preconserving child was that the liquid did not come up as high in the container and, therefore, had to be of a lesser amount.

Consideration of the pragmatic principles involved in measuring a child this way, however, has lead to a change in our understanding of what the child who failed to conserve was thinking. In particular, one must appreciate the influence of authority, questioning, and pragmatic rules for speaking to fully understand the child's behavior. In essence, a child may have had some semblance of conservation present in their ability, but he or she still failed to conserve in a conservation task because of these additional influences. When the adult finished pouring the liquid, for instance, the child may have held an implicit understanding that the amount had remained constant. But when the adult asked the question about the amounts, the child began to question his or her current beliefs. The child may have wondered why the adult would ask him or her about something so seemingly obvious or implicit and then conclude, following a given-new assumption and the general social knowledge that adults are more knowledgeable than children, that the adult knew something about the liquid that the child did not know. Only then would the child invoke the height of the liquid as a clue and report that the amount was less.

Thus, the child was using social/cultural information about the interactant—*adults often know more about things than do children*, along with complex pragmatic rules for interaction—(*given or new contracts, relevance, etc.*) to help him or her complete what appeared to be just a relatively straightforward problem-solving task involving physical properties of the world.

Next consider an example from a linguistic developmental task—word learning. Although still a debated issue, the role of social/cultural and pragmatic principles and information in vocabulary acquisition has also recently received much greater appreciation than was the case in earlier approaches. Initial attempts to explain a variety of problems associated with word learning produced a host of constraints or assumptions that were presumed to be necessary for a child's word learning to take place as it does. For instance, consider the problem of reference. How does a child know to what a new word refers? Many things can have more than one name. For instance, a neighbor's household pet could be a *dog, doggie, pet, beagle, Musket, canine, brat, pain, joy, boy*, and so on. Apply this duplicity to all the things around a child that can be named or referred to, and the child is faced with an enormous mapping problem. Ways around this problem include simplifying the mapping so that a child learns just one word at a time for a given thing or having the child assume that each and every object has just a single name. This assumption has been proposed as being necessary for children to overcome this problem of reference and has been referred to as the *mutual exclusivity assumption*.

To test the validity of the assumption, a variety of tasks can be employed. A standard version involves a word that has never been encountered previously by a child (*flombat*) being used by a caregiver to refer to an object that is also novel to the child (a stapler). Then, the child is shown this object along with a second novel one (a flashlight), and is asked to pick out which object is the *spondut*; another word that the child has never heard before. Typically, the child will pick the second novel object instead of the original one. This selection appears to demonstrate that the child is assuming that the novel name must apply to the unnamed object because the other object already bears a name.

Consider another problem with reference. How does a child know to what a word refers when it is being applied to a single object? How would a child know, for instance, to what a newly encountered word (*finpot*) is referring when used in the context of a novel object (a rocking horse)? *Finpot* could logically apply to a number of things including the springs that support the horse, the head of the horse, the color of the paint, the material used to construct the horse, the handles on either side of the head, or the rocking motion of the horse. But children typically take the word to refer to the entirety of the object. A *whole object assumption* was invoked to explain the child's focus in such situations. Proposing that the child holds such an assumption, either innately or emergently as a necessary temporary corral to channel initial word learning, also enables this problem of reference to whole objects to be explained.

Testing for the whole object assumption is similar to that for the mutual exclusivity assumption. A child is first shown a novel object (a rocking horse). Then a reference is made that assigns the novel name ("this is a *finpot*") by an experimenter. Next, a child is shown a variety of objects, including component parts of the target object in isolation (the springs, the head, etc.), as well as the whole object. The child is then asked to pick out which object is the *finpot*. Typically, the child will pick the whole object instead of one of its component parts. This selection appears to demonstrate that the child is assuming that the name must apply to the entire object.

However, as was the case with conservation, such an approach to explaining word learning fails to appreciate the contribution of social/cultural variable and pragmatic influences. Here also one must appreciate the influence of authority, questioning, and pragmatic rules for speaking to fully understand children's behavior. In the tasks that tested the mutual exclusivity assumption, for instance, the child may not have necessarily just assumed that the new word, *spondut* must refer to the novel object (the flashlight). Instead, because the question is being posed by a knowledgeable, cooperative, adult interlocutor who had just negotiated the label for the other object (*flombat* for a stapler), it would be very unlikely and a violation of pragmatic rules governing common ground for the adult to now refer to that just-named object with another name.

For the whole object assumption, a similar argument can be made. A child in this task may not have necessarily just assumed that the label *finpot* refers to the entire object. But when given the choice between a variety of things that could be called by that name, the child again relies on the social knowledge about their interlocutor—a knowledgeable, cooperative, adult —as well as pragmatic rules governing relevance and common ground, to choose the most likely object that the adult would have meant—the one that most closely resembled the object that had been recently negotiated as being a *finpot* (Bloom, 2000; Tomasello & Akhtar, 1995).

These examples demonstrate that some important domains of human cognition have been incompletely understood due to failure to consider social/cultural influences on the cognitive activity in question. My contention is that this same form of omission has been occurring in our understanding of nonliteral language comprehension.

Next, I demonstrate how such an omission has lead to a limitation in our understanding of the use of some common forms of nonliteral and indirect language. First, though, I briefly discuss how this omission has also inhibited our understanding of the processing and comprehension of nonliteral language.

SOCIAL AND CULTURAL INFLUENCES ON NONLITERAL LANGUAGE PROCESSING AND COMPREHENSION

It is a generally accepted point that, with adequate contextual support, the processing of nonliteral language can occur as rapidly as the processing of comparable literal language. The body of work that has supported this finding has thus demonstrated that contextual information in the processing of nonliteral language is playing its role at some point during the processing of utterances. The question for present purposes is whether social/cultural variables in this contextual information also have an influence early in processing.

Before addressing this question, a brief discussion of some ways in which at least one kind of nonliteral language differs from comparable literal language is in order. Verbal irony can differ from literal language in such a way that the influence of social and cultural variables on early processing of verbal irony would almost have to be a necessity.

Consider first that the processing duration of verbal irony has revealed conflicting findings. Some studies have shown that verbal irony processing takes longer than processing of the same language used literally (Dews & Winner, 1999; Giora 1995, 1997; Giora, Fein, & Schwartz, 1998; Schwoebel, Dews, Winner, & Srinivas, 2000). Other studies have shown no difference in the time course of verbal irony and literal language processing (Gibbs, 1986; Gibbs, O'Brien, & Doolittle, 1995). To evaluate whether there might be some inherent differences in verbal irony versus literal language that could explain this discrepancy in processing duration, I conducted an evaluation of the impact of referential distance and inference complexity on the processing duration of verbal irony and comparable literal language (Colston, 2004b). The results revealed, not surprisingly, that increasing the referential distance and inferential complexity of utterances slowed processing time. This delay in processing was also shown to be equivalent for literal and ironic utterances. The key point of the study, however, was an additional demonstration that verbal irony, by its mere nature, often requires more complex inferences and more distal references relative to comparable literal language. Thus, some of the variability in processing duration of verbal irony compared to literal language is due to these additional processing factors:

> Ironic utterances often require complex inferences or distal referents … that are not required for the same utterances to be interpreted literally. The *mere nature* of ironic utterances often introduces a require-

ment of complex inferences or distal referents for successful comprehension, while other aspects of the ironic utterances remain generally equivalent to when the utterances are used in literal contexts. Complex inferences and distal referents might then account for a great deal of the occasional lag found in verbal irony processing rather than the serial argument that ironic utterances must first be interpreted literally. (Colston, 2004b)

Note that the oft found greater referential distances and inferential complexities for verbal irony makes this form particularly susceptible to social and cultural influences. To give a concrete example, the Colston (2004-b) study demonstrated that the frequently observed echoic reminder mechanism in verbal irony requires a more distal referent than a comparable instance of literal language. A given ironic utterance that uses echoic reminder is referring to an established social norm that has been violated in a particular situation but that may not have been completely salient in that situation (e.g., a speaker says, "You're so generous" to a friend who committed a disservice to the speaker). Such a reference requires processing effort on the part of the comprehender to establish the referent social norm. Clearly, social and cultural variables would have a great deal of influence here. A speaker who has a particular social or cultural characteristic that would enable references to relatively distal or nonsalient social norms to occur more readily might be comprehended more quickly than a speaker who does not have such a characteristic. For example, a speaker who is stereotypically known for pointing to social norms that have been violated (e.g., a newspaper editorialist), who makes such a reference in an ironic comment (e.g., "people are so generous"), might be processed more readily than a speaker stereotypically known for not referencing such discrepancies (e.g., a nun).

Indeed, such a prediction has been validated. Katz and Pexman (1997) demonstrated that the occupation of a speaker had a strong effect on how nonliteral utterances were comprehended. Metaphorical utterances that could be interpreted ironically or nonironically (e.g., "children are precious gems") were more likely to be interpreted ironically when the speaker was a person who was stereotypically apt to use irony, as indicated by norming data (e.g., comedians, police officers, and factory workers), than a person stereotypically less apt to use irony (e.g., clergymen, doctors, and teachers).

We thus know that social/cultural variables do have an influence on comprehension. The question now is if they influence early processing. A number of other recent studies have provided an answer to this question. Pexman, Ferretti, and Katz (2000) tested the processing duration of ironic and metaphorical statements made by either stereotypically high-irony users or high-metaphor users based on the users' occupation. The results very clearly demonstrated that the occupation had a significant effect on processing and that this effect was showing itself very early in the processing stream of the utterances (see Katz, chap. 8, this book, and Pexman, chap. 9, this book, for a synopsis of this study).

Pexman and Olineck (2002) further showed that the particular qualities of high-irony occupations—being humorous, critical, insincere, and having low social status—were what enabled those occupations to cue ironic intent. This finding fits nicely with the previous discussion that ironic language would almost necessitate an early influence of social/cultural variables. The social characteristics established by Pexman and Olineck mesh well with the process of pointing out social norms that have been violated. Being critical and humorous are particularly consistent with scrutiny of violated expectations. Having low social status makes one likely to have frequently experienced violated social norms. The insincerity factor also reflects the mechanism of using verbal irony—a statement of expectations in the midst of a violation of those expectations.

Katz, Piasecka, and Toplak (2001) also found very early processing effects of speaker gender on the processing of sarcastic utterances. Most notably, they found that gender effects emerged during the act of reading the key target sarcastic utterances, with reading times for male speakers being less than female speakers. This slowdown in the processing of sarcastic utterances by female speakers was most pronounced when the listener was also a woman.

Thus, there is some very clear evidence emerging recently in the literature that social and cultural variables, gender and occupation among them, have an influence on nonliteral language processing and comprehension. Now I discuss how these variables might have an impact on the use of nonliteral language.

SOCIAL AND CULTURAL INFLUENCES ON NONLITERAL LANGUAGE USE

A variety of studies have been conducted on social and cultural variables and their impact on the use of several indirect or figurative forms. Among the kinds of variables that have been investigated are the degree of familiarity between interlocutors (Colston, 1999a; Jorgensen, 1996; Kreuz, 1996), the amount of shared knowledge of interlocutors (Katz & Lee, 1993; Kreuz, Kassler, Coppenrath, & McLain, 1999; Kreuz & Link, 2002), the social status of interlocutors (Holtgraves, 1997a, 1997b; Kemper & Thissen, 1981; Okamoto, 2002), gender (Gibbs, 2000; Holtgraves, 1991, 1992; Katz et al., 2001), and occupation (Holtgraves, 1997a, 1997b; Katz & Pexman, 1997; Pexman et al., 2000; Pexman & Olineck, 2002). The kinds of indirect or figurative language investigated have included verbal irony, metaphor, negated sentence structure, indirect requests, and proverbs—among others.

Most of these studies have either directly or as a means of addressing some other issue surreptitiously manipulated one of these variables across speakers of the indirect or figurative remarks or across the relationship between the interlocutors. Comprehension or pragmatic effects are then measured, and any differences across the variables are noted. For instance, in the Colston (1999a) study participants read short vignettes that described two interlocutors conversing over some topic. One of the interlocutors then described some aspect of the topic with either a direct (e.g., "It was stale" or "It was fresh") or negated (e.g., "It wasn't fresh" or "It wasn't stale") comment. For some of the comparisons the interlocutors' relationship was described as being one of high common ground (e.g., they were close friends) or low common ground (e.g., they were strangers). Participants then rated the intended meanings of the speakers making the remarks (e.g., for this example, how fresh or stale the speaker is saying the bread was). For this particular study, no difference was obtained for the common ground variable. But most of the findings of this literature have shown differences across the manipulated social/cultural variables.

One shortcoming of much of this work, however, is that it does not always afford a means by which to evaluate why the particular social or cultural differences are found. Although the mere establishment of such differences is very important and, as just indicated, frequently social/cultural variables are not the primary topic of the study; thus, their causal delineation is not the highest priority, but nevertheless their presence now begs for an explanation.

The following two studies were conducted with this goal in mind—to begin an investigation of why some particular social/cultural differences are found in nonliteral language use. The studies selected gender as the social variable because gender has emerged as a fairly robust predictor of some effects in nonliteral language use. Gender differences in verbal irony and asyndeton were investigated.

GENDER DIFFERENCES IN VERBAL IRONY

The studies conducted by myself and Sabrina Lee (Colston & Lee, 2000, 2004) sought to evaluate whether and why gender differences would be found in peoples' use of verbal irony. Prior to this study, a number of areas of research had established, although not without controversy, some gender differences in language use, including differences in males' and females' verbal skills and communicative styles. Other lines of research had also begun to show that a wide variety of pragmatic functions are accomplished by different forms of indirect or figurative language. This latter research area had also begun to delineate which forms of indirect or figurative language were most adept at particular pragmatic functions and why. Thus, a straightforward extension and combination of these lines of research could seek to establish whether gender differences would be obtained in speakers' use of indirect or figurative language. Thus, we chose to investigate gender differences in verbal irony because that form had been the most widely studied to date for its pragmatic functions.

After a series of unsuccessful pilot studies that directly asked participants to rate how sarcastic male and female speakers were, when depicted making sarcastic or literal comments in short written scenarios with stereotypical male and female names, a study that indirectly probed this phenomenon did demonstrate a gender difference. Participants read a series of short scenarios depicting themselves and other characters in various generally negative situations (e.g., a person was not accepted into graduate school). No cues were given to assign gender to the characters (e.g., abstract symbols were used instead of character names, and the scenarios were designed to be gender neutral). One of the characters would then make a comment that was either literal or sarcastic, as if spoken to the participant in the experiment, at the end of the scenario, for instance: "This is just terrible" or "This is just terrific." was said after the scenario:

You and your cousin *

were on your way to another friend's house.

That friend owes * two hundred dollars.

You ring the doorbell and after two tries,

no one comes to the door.

* turns to you and says,

Participants read the scenarios and the characters' comments and rated whether speakers using the comments were *most likely male* or *most likely female* on a 7-point rating scales. The results of both male and female participants showed that verbal irony was considered more male-like than literal remarks. Four subsequent experiments then evaluated two possible causes of this gender difference—discourse goal match and risk attraction.

The discourse goal match explanation stemmed from the dual possibilities that verbal irony accomplishes a variety of pragmatic functions that are different from those of other figurative and literal forms and that men might have a different set of discourse goals on average than women. Therefore, men might be more apt to use verbal irony because their discourse goals match verbal irony's pragmatic accomplishments better than do women's discourse goals.

The risk attraction explanation arose from previous research that has documented that men are generally more risky than women in a variety of domains. Men engage in more risky behavior, take more health risks, and prefer more injury-risking sports and activities than do women. In addition, men find less risky behaviors less interesting than women (Byrnes, Miller, & Schafer, 1999; Carlson & Cooper, 1974; Howland, Hingson, Mangione, & Bell, 1996; Wiederman, 1997). Our conjecture was that verbal irony, being an indirect or figurative form of language, might pose a greater risk of misinterpretation and thus appeal more to male speakers than female speakers in part because of this risk.

Experiments 2 and 3 (Colston & Lee, 2000, 2004) tested the possibility that the particular pragmatic functions accomplished by verbal irony fit better with males' than females' typical discourse goals. To make this evaluation, we first needed to determine what pragmatic functions would be performed by verbal irony. Verbal irony had previously been shown to enable speakers to perform a variety of pragmatic functions, including to be humorous, express surprise, express mastery over some topic or issue, diminish criticism, enhance criticism, point out a deviance from expectations, show negative emotion, and others. These pragmatic functions were tested in studies that sought to determine purely what people thought verbal irony would do for speakers (Roberts & Kreuz, 1994), as well as in studies that sought to determine how and to what extent different kinds of verbal irony would perform the functions they do (Colston, 1997a, 1997b, 1999a, 1999b, 2000a, 2000b, 2002a; Colston & Gibbs, 1998; Colston & Keller, 1998; Colston & O'Brien, 2000a, 2000b; Dews, Kaplan, & Winner, 1995; Dews & Winner, 1995, 1999; Gibbs, 1986, 1987, 2000; Kreuz, 2000; Kreuz, Long & Church, 1991; Schwoebel et al., 2000; Toplack & Katz, 2000; Whaley & Holloway, 1996).

For our purposes, we selected pragmatic functions from two general sources. One source came from Roberts and Kreuz's study (1994) that tested the extent to which a large number (approx. 20) of pragmatic functions would be performed by verbal irony, among many other nonliteral forms. We chose five of the functions they measured to provide us with a range that varied from functions that were reported as not being performed at all by verbal irony (to deemphasize—none of their participants said that verbal irony did this), to functions that verbal irony was almost universally reported as accomplishing (to show negative emotion—94% of their participants said that verbal irony did this). Other functions we selected from this study were to be humorous (65%), to clarify (35%), and to manage the discourse (18%). Our second set of functions were derived from other studies that investigated the pragmatic functions of verbal irony including some of my previous work that showed that verbal irony is used to enhance negativity; (Colston, 1997b), from work by Lee and Katz (1998) that pinpointed the important role of a victim in the use of verbal irony, from a claim by Whaley and Holloway (1996) that was empirically validated by Colston (1999b), that irony can serve to socially attack people, and from the general theoretical characteristic that verbal irony is indirect. From these studies we derived the following additional pragmatic functions: to be rude, to insult, and to imply.

We then took the scenarios from Experiment 1 and presented them to a new set of participants along with rating scales for all of these functions. Participants in this experiment (Experiment 2) were asked to rate how much the remarks in the scenarios would accomplish each of the functions. The results revealed that verbal irony is thought to express negative emotion, to be humorous, to be rude, to de-emphasize, and to insult to a greater extent than literal commentary, by both male and female participants.

In Experiment 3, participants were given the same situations as were presented in Experiment 2 with slight wording alterations to place the participants in the role of the speakers of the comments, but no comments were presented. Participants were instead asked to rate the likelihood that they would wish to accomplish each of the pragmatic functions we had selected in each of the particular scenarios that was presented. The results revealed that three of the five functions accomplished by verbal irony were more sought by female participants than by male participants (to be rude, to de-emphasize, and to insult). The other two functions were equally sought by male and female participants. Thus, there is little evidence to support the idea that men use verbal irony more often than women because the pragmatic functions of verbal irony particularly suit men's discourse goals.

Experiments 4 and 5 evaluated the possibility that the heightened risk of misunderstanding presented by verbal irony relative to literal language would appeal to men. Experiment 4 presented a new set of participants with the scenarios from Experiment 1; this time the wording was altered so that the participants were not one of the characters in the scenarios, and they were asked to rate the degree of risk of misinterpretation of the comments. The results revealed that both men and women report that verbal irony poses more of a risk for misinterpretation than do literal remarks. Thus, we know that verbal irony use does involve some level of risk for a speaker that is noticeable to people.

Results of Experiment 5 indicated a preference for use of verbal irony by male participants, as the risk attraction account would predict. Here, participants were given the scenarios from Experiment 3 (the ones with the participants as the speakers), along with the comments, and the participants were asked to imagine themselves to actually be present in these situations and to then rate the likelihood that they would actually use the remark that was presented.

Taken together, these findings demonstrate that verbal irony is considered a more male-like than female-like form of communication not because the particular pragmatic functions it accomplishes fit better with males' than females' discourse goals. The results instead support the explanation that the risk of misinterpretation inherent in verbal irony appeals to males' greater degree of riskiness.

Note that the explanations we explored in this study were certainly not exhaustive. For reasons of brevity we were unable to test several other viable explanations. Among these are the emotional expressiveness of verbal irony, gender differences in attribution, aggressiveness gender differences, and mastery demonstration.

The emotional expressiveness explanation stems from work that has shown a difference in the kinds of emotions that are expressed by verbal irony versus other kinds of remarks, including literal commentary. In addition to the negative emotion expression by verbal irony demonstrated by Roberts and Kreuz (1994) and Colston and Lee (2000, 2004), Leggitt and Gibbs (2000) found that verbal irony enables expression of emotions that differ from those expressed by literal remarks. Other studies have shown that verbal irony expresses more surprise than literal comments (Colston & Keller, 1998). These findings, coupled with the varying cultural norms that influence which emotions men and women are allowed to express, suggest that men may be more likely to use verbal irony because it enables expression of the emotions that they are apt to seek to express in conversations.

The gender differences in the attribution explanation comes from work in social psychology that has shown reliable differences in how men and women attribute blame for contribution to failure. In general, when having participated in some collective task that has resulted in a failure, men are more apt to attribute blame for that failure to situational causes (e.g., there was not enough time provided, the task asked too much, and the tools or material were of poor quality). Women, however, are more likely to make personal attributions for the failure (e.g., I do not have the skill and I am not fast enough). This pattern of attribution—coupled with the notion that nonliteral language arguably presents a greater likelihood of miscomprehension, which may be considered a form of failure—might make women slightly less likely to use verbal irony. The idea is that, because women, all else being equal, are more likely to blame themselves for a conversational exchange that was misunderstood (whereas men are more apt to blame the situation or their addressee) they tend to avoid ways of speaking that present higher risks of miscomprehension and, hence, be slightly less likely to use verbal irony.

Still another explanation might come from differences in aggressiveness between men and women. Verbal irony may be considered a more aggressive form of talking than literal commentary, given work that has shown verbal irony to be more critical, condemning, and so on, than literally negative remarks (Colston, 1997b). Given other work that has shown a degree of greater aggressive in certain measures of men over women, verbal irony might be more apt to be used by men for this reason. However, note that not all studies have shown that verbal irony is more negative than literal commentary, and not all forms of aggressiveness show a gender difference.

One other possible explanation involves how nonliteral language, including verbal irony, enables a speaker to demonstrate mastery over the referent topic. In being able to craft and use a particularly clever and meaning-laden nonliteral utterance in a given, frequently negative situation, speakers can often demonstrate a degree of understanding of, unflappability toward, and creativity regarding the situation at hand (Colston & O'Brien, 2000a). This expression of control or mastery over a situation by how one talks might also tap into some gender differences in dominance-seeking or control-seeking behaviors or something similar that could also help explain gender differences in verbal irony use.

There is clearly much more work to be done to hone our explanations for the gender difference obtained on speakers' use of verbal irony. Future work should test these and other possible explanations, as well as possible combinations of the explanations (e.g., demonstrating mastery and willingness to risk misinterpretation constitute a form of aggressiveness, and demonstrating that mastery allows expression of socially acceptable emotions).

Another issue raised by the observed gender difference in verbal irony—an issue that is gaining importance in the overall investigation of nonliteral language—is the extent to which phenomena regarding nonliteral language (in this case, gender differences in reported usage) are universal to all forms of nonliteral language. Such effects may be relatively universal across all kinds of nonliteral language, or they may be germane to just one family of nonliteral language forms or just a single type. In terms of gender differences in use, the question is whether a gender difference holds for all nonliteral language use, as might be predicted by the attribution explanation just discussed (assuming one believes all nonliteral forms pose a higher risk of misinterpretation, something I and others have challenged; Colston, 2002b), or just for verbal irony, as would be predicted by some of the other explanations.

To initiate an investigation of this important question, I conducted a study that is analogous to my work with Sabrina Lee on gender differences in verbal irony. Now, however, the goal was to investigate gender differences in speakers' use of asyndeton, a relatively unexplored form of nonliteral language. If gender differences are also obtained here, this may support the attribution explanation and, in turn, the universality view.

GENDER DIFFERENCES IN ASYNDETON

Asyndeton is a kind of utterance in which all but the skeletal syntactic categories are dropped and a reduplicated phrase structure is used for the remaining words (e.g., "Been there, done that" and "I go, I work, I leave"). Asyndeton can be considered a form of indirect language because a speaker does not just say literally, albeit minimally, what he or she means. Instead, the speaker uses the minimal form to imply a great deal more than what is said. Moreover, the implied meaning in asyndeton goes beyond the meaning that would have been expressed by the utterance had it contained the omitted words. Speakers appear to use asyndeton to accomplish several pragmatic functions, including to express a negative attitude toward the referent topic (Colston, 2004a).

In six experiments conducted by myself and Virginia Lusch (Colston & Lusch, 2004), potential gender differences in asyndeton and two of their potential causes were studied. Experiment 1 presented participants with a series of short scenarios similar to those used in the Colston and Lee (2000, 2004) studies. The scenarios depicted characters in various generally neutral situations (e.g., a person is describing his or her summer job as a lifeguard). Neutral statements were used to enable comparison of asyndeton with direct positive and direct negative comments. No cues were given to assign gender to the characters (e.g., abstract symbols were used instead of character names, and the scenarios were designed to be gender neutral). One of the characters would then make a comment at the end of the scenario that was either literally positive, literally negative, or an asyndeton (e.g., "I love it," "I hate it," or "I go, I sweat, I leave"). Participants read the scenarios and the characters' comments and rated whether speakers using the comments were *most likely male* or *most likely female* on 7-point rating scales (as in the Colston and Lee study). The results of both male and female participants showed that verbal irony was considered more male-like than both kinds of literal remarks. In addition, both male and female participants indicated that negative remarks were more male-like than positive remarks. Thus, we have evidence for a gender difference in asyndeton use. Five subsequent experiments then evaluated the discourse goal match and risk attraction explanations already discussed.

Experiments 2 and 3 (Colston & Lusch, 2004) evaluated the possibility that the heightened risk of misunderstanding presented by asyndeton relative to literal comments would appeal to men. Experiment 2 presented a new set of participants with the scenarios from Experiment 1 and asked people to rate the degree of risk of misinterpretation of the comments. The results revealed that both men and women reported that asyndeton poses more of a risk for misinterpretation than do literal remarks. Both male and female participants indicated that negative remarks were more likely to be misinterpreted than positive remarks. Thus, we know that asyndeton use also involves some level of risk for a speaker that is noticeable to people.

Experiment 3, however, found no reported preference for use of asyndeton by male participants, as the risk attraction account would predict. Instead, both men and women reported they would be less likely to use asyndeton than literally positive remarks and equally likely to use asyndeton as literally negative remarks. Here, participants were given the scenarios from Experiment 1 with slight rewordings to make the participants be the speakers in the scenarios, and the participants were asked to imagine actually being present in these situations and to then rate the likelihood that they would actually use the remark that was presented.

This result was puzzling given the results of the first experiment. Contrary to results showing no gender differences in the likelihood of using asyndeton, why would people think that a speaker using asyndeton would likely be a man? To investigate, we (Colston & Lusch, 2004) conducted Experiment 4 which sought to test people's memory for having used asyndeton in the past. It could be possible that people have difficulty imagining using asyndeton in the situations we supplied, but they do recall having used asyndeton themselves in past situations.

In Experiment 4 we presented the same scenarios and comments as Experiment 3 to a new group of participants, who were asked to rate how often in the past they had used comments such as the ones they were reading, on 7-point rating scales ranging from *not at all often* and *somewhat often*. The results revealed an interesting pattern. Both men and women reported having used positive comments relatively frequently and having used asyndeton relatively infrequently. But for negative comments, women reported having used them more often than men. Thus, a gender difference of sorts is at work in reported use of asyndeton. If men wished to express some negative opinion, they reported having used asyndeton and directly negative comments roughly equally. If women wished to express a negative opinion, however, they reported using asyndeton less often than direct negative commentary. Thus, there is some support for the risk attraction account. Men are, in a way, reported to have used asyndeton more often than women—they used it as often as direct negative commentary, whereas women used it less often than direct negative remarks and asyndeton can risk misinterpretation.

We (Colston & Lusch, 2004) then conducted two final experiments to evaluate the discourse goal match explanation. Experiment 5 presented a new group of participants with the scenarios from Experiment 1 who were asked to rate how much the remarks in the scenarios would accomplish six of the functions that were evaluated in Colston and Lee (2000, 2004) on gender differences in verbal irony (i.e., to show negative emotion, to manage discourse, to deemphasize, to be rude, to insult, to imply, and to be humorous). We exchanged *to be unconventional* for *to clarify* for the Colston and Lusch (2004) study due to the relatively unconventional nature of asyndeton and because *to clarify* was the one function found to be performed to a greater degree by literal language than verbal irony in that previous study; thus, it was likely not something particularly suited to nonliteral language. Both male and female participants revealed that asyndeton is thought to be unconventional, to be humorous, and to deemphasize to a greater extent than both kinds of literal commentary.

In Experiment 6 participants were given the same situations as were presented in Experiment 3 (the ones in which the participants are the speakers of the comments), but no comments were presented. Participants were instead asked to rate the likelihood that they would wish to accomplish each of the pragmatic functions we had selected, in each of the particular scenarios that was presented. The results revealed that two of the three functions accomplished by asyndeton (to be unconventional and to be humorous) were more sought after by male participants than by female participants. The other function was equally sought by male and female participants. Thus, evidence supports the idea that men use asyndeton more often than women because the pragmatic functions of asyndeton particularly suit men's discourse goals.

Taken together, the results of this second study demonstrate that asyndeton is considered a more male-like than female-like form of communication because the particular pragmatic functions it accomplishes fit better with men's discourse goals than women's, and because the risk of misinterpretation inherent in asyndeton appeals to men's greater riskiness.

The results of these two studies have begun to tell us something about why one social/cultural variable, gender, has an effect on nonliteral language use. In both studies, gender differences in use of nonliteral language were obtained that cannot be attributed to gender differences in addressees, situational variables, or other factors. Clearly, something about differences in men and women underlies differences in their use of nonliteral language. Our studies raised at least six possible inherent gender differences that might underlie this nonliteral language usage difference—differences in aggression, mastery demonstration, attribution, discourse goals, riskiness, and emotional expression. Although these results are not conclusive, they do begin to suggest which one(s) of these explanations will hold up to future scrutiny.

Given that men have been measured to be more aggressive in some domains than women, it makes sense that men are more likely to use verbal irony because it is a relatively aggressive form of talking. But differences in aggression have a tougher time explaining men's greater likelihood of using asyndeton. This form is not typically an aggressive way of talking; thus, the aggressiveness explanation does not bode well in explaining asyndeton's greater usage by men.

Because many forms of nonliteral language, verbal irony and asyndeton included, can express a degree of mastery over a topic (something not reported here but for which some empirical support is emerging; see Colston & Izett, 2004), and given a general tendency for men to wish to demonstrate such a mastery, this explanation might be a contender. However, more work is still needed to find the direct link between a need or desire to demonstrate mastery and use of nonliteral language forms.

The attribution explanation also appears to hold up to the foregoing studies. Although not all forms of nonliteral language would necessarily pose a heightened risk for misinterpretation, the two forms here have been shown to pose such a risk. Thus, although attribution would likely not explain gender differences found on easily understood nonliteral forms, it does help to explain the gender differences obtained in Colston and Lee (2000, 2004) and Colston and Lusch (2004). Again, much more work is required to establish direct causal links.

The discourse goal match explanation did not hold up well under these studies. Although it helped account to a degree for men's greater likelihood of using asyndeton (recall that two of three of the functions that asyndeton performed were sought by men more than women), it did not explain men's greater usage of verbal irony (recall that three of five of the functions performed by verbal irony were more sought by women than men).

The risk explanation was supported by both Colston and Lee (2000, 2004) and Colston and Lusch (2004). Previous work has shown that men have a greater riskiness than women (Byrnes, Miller, & Schaper, 1999; Carlson & Cooper, 1974; Howland, Hingson, Mangione, & Bell, 1996). Verbal irony and asyndeton were shown to pose a greater risk of miscomprehension. And, men did show a greater likelihood of use of these nonliteral forms. Once again, the direct causal relationship between gender, risk and nonliteral language use remains to be investigated.

Finally, the emotion expression explanation did not receive much support in Colston and Lee (2000, 2004) and Colston and Lusch. Although the studies did not explicitly look at emotion expression of nonliteral language other than the *to express negative emotion* pragmatic function, no gender difference was obtained in these studies on prevalence of desiring to express negative emotion (but gender differences in the use of nonliteral language to express emotions were obtained by Link & Kreuz, see chap. 7, this book).

To summarize, it appears that the mastery, attribution and risk explanations were supported by the results. As already noted, it is also readily possible that these explanations can be combined in interesting ways. Researchers should consider this issue, determine direct causal links, and more strongly test these and other explanations. We consider our studies a first step in the process of explaining why gender differences are found in nonliteral language use, and welcome further explorations.

In terms of the universality issue—that is, whether phenomena or explanations for a particular form of nonliteral language generalizes to all forms of nonliteralism—the picture is also somewhat clearer but still incomplete. First, consider which explanations are consistent with the universality claim. The aggression, emotion, and discourse goal explanations would likely not be consistent with universality. Not all forms of nonliteral language are aggressive, express the same emotions, or perform the same pragmatic functions. Second, the risk and attribution explanations are also not likely consistent with universality if one agrees that not all forms of nonliteral language pose a heightened risk of miscomprehension. These explanations would be consistent, however, with a revised universality claim that gender differences would be obtained in all forms of nonliteral language that do pose a reasonably greater risk of miscomprehension. Finally, the mastery explanation does seem consistent with universality. I suspect that many if not most forms of nonliteral language would seem to perform this function, although this claim needs to be evaluated for a wide variety of nonliteral forms.

Thus, the explanations that Colston and Lee (2000, 2004) and Colston and Lusch (2004) supported seem to be the same ones that could be consistent with at least a revised universality claim that is restricted to nonliteral forms that do pose risks of miscomprehension. Once again, our analysis is not conclusive and many aspects of the phenomenon require confirmation, but our studies nevertheless suggest that limited universality might hold up to further examination. Our work also provides a blueprint for future testing of this issue.

The studies reported here, in addition to other works that have also looked into social/cultural variables on nonliteral language use, processing, and comprehension (some of which are reviewed by other chapters in this book), are beginning to establish the very important influence that social/cultural variables have on nonliteral language. I emphasize this important influence by describing a very recent study of mine (Colston, 2001, May) that not only shows the influence of a social/cultural variable on, in this instance, nonliteral language comprehension, but also illustrates the potential ramifications of such an influence. Essentially, social/cultural influences on nonliteral language comprehension may be a key component to intergroup conflict.

SOCIAL/CULTURAL VARIABLES, NONLITERAL LANGUAGE, AND INTERGROUP CONFLICT

Consider the following three, seemingly unrelated research domains in psycholinguistics, cognitive and social psychology: language comprehension, social tension, and cognitive load. Language comprehension involves a complex interaction of ascertaining the meaning of the language that speakers use and the intentions the particular speakers have in using that particular language in the given contexts. Research has demonstrated the necessity of this process most clearly for nonliteral forms including figurative language such as metaphor (e.g., "This weather is garbage" to refer to inclement weather) or verbal irony (e.g., "This weather is lovely"). Studies have also revealed this process in indirect language when, for instance, an utterance is said to one person but an intended meaning is directed at a third party (e.g., as in, "Some people think this is nice weather") or when an intended meaning is largely dependent on a listener's likely inference or response (e.g., as in, "How about this weather?"). Indeed, the process can be observed even in direct, literal language, which often is deceptively underdetermined (e.g., as in saying, "The weather is bad," but with no direct reference to the weather *here*). Although this process is reflected in many, and indeed arguably, all, kinds of language, it is arguably more obvious in the figurative forms.

This process of language and intention interdependence is also widely recognized by language scientists and theorists, as reflected in a wide variety of language comprehension theories. Notable among these are Gricean pragmatics, with its conversational maxims and conversational implicature mechanisms; relevance theory, with its system of computing elaborative contextual effects within reasonable processing constraints; the large body of inference literature, which shows that readers and listeners make a wide variety of coherence and elaborative inferences either online or shortly after encountering language; and, arguably, the direct access model, which claims that broad nonlinguistic contextual information is brought to bear during initial language comprehension.

A very different, but nonetheless large, cross-disciplinary literature has also reliably demonstrated an increase in tension (measured subjectively and objectively) as a product of factors like being in unfamiliar social- and cultural-group environments. This tension can be found in low-level measures normally outside of conscious control (e.g., Galvonic Skin Responses (GSRs)), as well as in subjective ratings. It also arises from a variety of sources such as being among a group of individuals of different gender, ethnicity, age, social status, and others. Phenomena along these lines have been studied in areas as diverse as adolescents' gender interaction development, personality trait work on shyness, and anxiety disorders in clinical psychology.

Last, still another large and cross-disciplinary literature has demonstrated a reliable breakdown in a variety of cognitive processes as a function of the presence of a diversity of stressors. Work on this phenomenon can be found in much of the research on divided and other forms of attention, from human factors research on topics like vigilance, and in much of the cognitive aging literature.

A recent new project of mine (Colston, 2001, May) sought to wed these research lines. The complexity of figurative language comprehension processes might make them vulnerable to the usual breakdowns from which intricate cognitive functions suffer (e.g., overload in short-term memory capacity hinders language inference processes). Social tension, as often occurs in diverse group interactions, may be one source of such processing breakdowns. Thus, I sought to determine if social tension is detrimental to complex, higher order language processing (e.g., comprehension of speaker intention in using figurative language) such that communicative misunderstandings ensue or increase. Moreover, I also sought to determine whether this mechanism is a component in group relations.

In two experiments, an affirmative answer to this research question was found. Participants rated subtle aspects of the intended meanings of tape-recorded speaker–actors who made comments in a variety of situations. *Group tension* in Experiment 1 was operationally defined as being in different-gender versus same-gender pairs when publicly making such evaluations, with different-gender pairs being the higher tension situation (norming data confirmed this definition).

Results showed a small but significant decrease, as a function of social tension, in the ability to comprehend sarcastic intent from a speaker's intonation. Essentially, people who were in same-gender groups were able to detect sarcastic intent based on the words and the intonation that the recorded speaker–actors used. This result was similar to earlier comparison studies that measured perceived sarcasm, humor, and pretense using the same recordings. But, people in different-gender groups were not able to use the speaker–actor's intonation to detect sarcasm.

Experiment 2 enhanced social tension by having people publicly make ratings in larger groups of one to three peers. Here, *high tension* was defined as having all other-gender members in the group, whereas *low tension* was defined as having at least one same-gender member in the group. This experiment replicated the first with a pointedly stronger effect size. The take-home message of these experiments is that when people are placed in unfamiliar social environments, based on gender, they lose the ability to use a speaker's intonation to detect sarcasm.

I have subsequently conducted an analogous study using ethnicity as the social/cultural variable instead of gender (Colston & Jones, 2004). To enable manipulation of ethnicity, I used videotaped scenarios. Each scenario first had a narrator describe a negative situation involving the participant and another person (e.g., "A classmate of yours is told to go up and speak in front of the class, something she (or he) hates doing. Before she (or he) gets up, she (or he) says to you"), which was followed by a comment by that other person. Half of the comments were literal (negative words, e.g., "I'm totally scared about this"), and the other half were sarcastic (positive words, e.g., "I'm totally thrilled about this"). Actor–confederates were hired to portray the speakers making these comments. Half of the confederates were African American, and the remaining confederates were European American. One half of each of the members of these ethnic groups was men. A videotape was then constructed that presented a series of these scenarios. A given scenario was preceded by 10 s of dead air, followed by the voice of the narrator describing the situation, and finally the audio and video recording of the confederate making his or her comment. The tape had an equal number of each kind of comment spoken by each type of confederate, which were presented in random order.

A set of 7-point rating scales ranging from *not at all sarcastic* (1) to *extremely sarcastic* (7) was used to measure participants' assessment of the degree of sarcasm in the speakers' comments. One group of the participants was randomly assigned to a low-stress condition in which they simply made their ratings with no additional instructions. The other group was told that the experimenters were additionally interested in the accuracy of their ratings. These participants were tested with the experimenter in the room, standing behind them, looking over their shoulders, and purportedly making accuracy ratings on each of their sarcasm ratings. This group was labeled the high-stress condition. Half of the participants were African Americans and half were European American, appropriately assigned to conditions for counterbalancing.

Analyses on the sarcasm ratings were conducted separately for the two ethnic groups. For the European-American speakers, the key finding was a three-way interaction between confederate ethnicity, language type, and stress. The pattern of the means was as follows: When rating their own ethnic group, no difference was observed in the magnitude of difference of ratings given for sarcastic and literal comments in the low-stress condition (literal = 1.86, sarcastic = 6.31) versus the high-stress condition (literal = 1.73, sarcastic = 6.23). But for ratings of African-American speakers, the magnitude of difference between sarcastic comments and literal comments dropped when moving from the low-stress (literal = 2.34, sarcastic = 6.18) to the high-stress condition (literal = 2.44, sarcastic = 5.35).

The pattern of ratings for the African-American participants interestingly did not reflect this pattern. Although the other general findings (e.g., that, all else being equal, sarcastic comments are rated as more sarcastic than literal comments) were mostly the same for African-American and European-American participants, the cross-ethnic comprehension degradation as a function of stress was not observed. Future research is required to determine the reason for the different pattern in African-American participants. Perhaps it has to do with the relative familiarity of African Americans to European Americans versus European-Americans to African Americans.

Essentially, what these results show is that, when placed in a high-stress situation, some people's ability to comprehend a dissimilar (based on ethnicity) speaker's nonliteral remark breaks down. These results support the hypothesis concerning the mechanism of intergroup conflict, at least for the majority (in the United States, European-American) participants. More research is required to explicitly link the remaining components of this mech-anism. Researchers should consider (a) that unfamiliar social/cultural encounters bring about the kind of stress shown here to affect comprehen-sion, (b) that degraded comprehension leads to misunderstandings, and (c) that misunderstandings can create or enhance intergroup conflicts, and so forth, but the straightforward nature of such links makes them highly plausi-ble, and they are consistent with the present data.

Thus, there is a very strong indication from this last line of research that social/cultural variables not only have an effect on nonliteral language com-prehension but that this effect is part of a larger mechanism that plays a sig-nificant role in intergroup relationships. Thus, it might behoove researchers to further investigate this phenomenon if for no other reason than that it might enable us to derive better solutions to intergroup conflicts.

CONCLUSION

I made arguments that social/cultural variables are on par with other kinds of contextual information in providing an influence on language use, com-prehension, and even processing—most notably for nonliteral language. I reviewed my and other scholars' work that has shown clear empirical evi-dence of such an influence at all of these levels of nonliteral language cogni-tion. Finally, I showed that such influences may underlie other broader phenomenon such as intergroup conflicts. I conclude by noting that, al-though the work discussed here has made important strides in recognizing the importance of social/cultural variables in language cognition, we have much further to go both in the continued work on nonliteral language and in work on more traditional literal language.

Mood, emotional state, physiological status, and a vast array of other heretofore psychological influences have been shown to have tremendous influences on many allegedly impenetrable cognitive, perceptual, and even sensory processes. Moreover, juxtapositions, sequences, and reinstantia-tions of these influences have their own set of ramifications that compound the influence on such cognitive processes. To consider just one, simple ex-ample, people's judgments of the magnitudes of quantities, a presumably straightforward sensory–perceptual–cognitive process, are influenced by all of the aforementioned factors. The amount of assigned work can seem greater if one is overwhelmed. The weight of something to be carried can seem lighter if one is happy. Even the sweetness of some substance can seem greater if one is hungry. Also, the shade of a color will seem darker when backdropped with bright light. The temperature of a liquid will seem colder after having felt something hot. Even a memory for some past experience is more likely to occur if the recaller is in the same emotional or other state as when the original experience first happened.

Many such straightforward cognitive, perceptual, or even sensory processes are thus influenced by very broad contextual and structural factors. And I considered just those influences on a given person's cognition, perception, and sensation of their world—for instance, I as an individual am influenced in my cognition, about the world by factors such as my emotional state, what has just come before this emotional state, and so on. When one looks at language cognition, the picture is even more complex—when I act as an interlocutor, empathic processes can make influences on the other person have an effect on me. The other person can manipulate these contextual and structural influences in the ways he or she acts or talks to have an influence on me. Indeed, moving to a social interlocutorial setting opens up its own enormous set of social influences that have been greatly explored in social psychology and other fields. Just my mere tendency to categorize people into in-groups and out-groups can have a tremendous influence on how I will comprehend, process them, and so on (e.g., an unusual form of dress will appear innovative on an ally but ridiculous on an enemy without my having to explicitly recognize that he or she is wearing a shirt).

Thus, in our continued exploration of how and what people comprehend and how and why they use nonliteral and indeed all kinds of language, we clearly have to pay much greater attention to these structural, social, and other kinds of broad influences in our consideration of heretofore very low-level, bottom-up language processes. For nonliteral language the need is perhaps more pronounced because of the somewhat greater importance of contextual information, but the influences are present for all language types. Nonliteral language researchers who have begun this consideration are thus to be applauded, but we need to do more, and our colleagues who study other arenas of language need to do more as well.

ACKNOWLEDGMENT

I thank Albert Katz for his comments on this chapter.

REFERENCES

Bloom, P. (2000). *How children learn the meaning of words*. Cambridge, MA: MIT Press.

Byrnes, J. P., Miller, D. C., & Schafer, W. D. (1999). Gender differences in risk taking: A meta analysis. *Psychological Bulletin, 125*(3), 367–383.

Carlson, K., & Cooper, R. E. (1974). A preliminary investigation of risk behavior in the real world. *Personality and Social Psychology Bulletin, 1*(1), 7–9.

Colston, H. L. (1997a). "I've never seen anything like it": Overstatement, understatement and irony. *Metaphor and Symbol, 12*, 43–58.

Colston, H. L. (1997b). Salting a wound or sugaring a pill: The pragmatic functions of ironic criticism. *Discourse Processes, 23*, 25–45.

Colston, H. L. (1999a). "Not good" is "bad," but "not bad" is not "good": An analysis of three accounts of negation asymmetry. *Discourse Processes, 28,* 237–256.

Colston, H. L. (1999b). The pragmatic functions of rebuttal analogy. *Metaphor and Symbol, 14,* 259–280.

Colston, H. L. (2000a). Comprehending speaker intent in rebuttal analogy use: The role of irony mapping, absurdity comparison and argumentative convention. *Language and Speech, 43*(4), 337–354.

Colston, H. L. (2000b). "Dewey defeats Truman": Interpreting ironic restatement. *Journal of Language and Social Psychology, 19*(1), 44–63.

Colston, H. L. (2001, May). *Figurative language comprehension processes and group relations.* Paper presented at the meeting of the Midwestern Psychological Association, Chicago, IL.

Colston, H. L. (2002a). Contrast and assimilation in verbal irony. *Journal of Pragmatics, 34,* 111–142.

Colston, H. L. (2002b). Pragmatic justifications for nonliteral gratitude acknowledgments: "Oh sure, anytime." *Metaphor and Symbol, 17,* 205–226.

Colston, H. L. (2004a). *The pragmatics of asyndeton.* Manuscript in preparation.

Colston, H. L. (2004b). *Seriality versus complexity in verbal irony comprehension.* Manuscript submitted for publication.

Colston, H. L., & Gibbs, R. W., Jr. (1998). Analogy and irony: Rebuttal to "Rebuttal Analogy." *Metaphor and Symbol, 13,* 69–75.

Colston, H. L., & Gibbs, R. W., Jr. (2002). Are irony and metaphor understood differently? *Metaphor and Symbol, 17,* 57–80.

Colston, H. L, & Izett, C. (2004). *Figurative language in social status management.* Manuscript submitted for publication.

Colston, H. L., & Jones, C. Q. (2004). *Indirect language comprehension and social tension: Implications for group relations.* Manuscript in preparation.

Colston, H. L., & Keller, S. B. (1998). You'll never believe this: Irony and hyperbole in expressing surprise. *Journal of Psycholinguistic Research, 27*(4), 499–513.

Colston, H. L., & Lee, S. Y. (2000, May). *On gender differences in verbal irony.* Paper presented at the meeting of the International Gender and Language Association, Stanford University, Palo Alto, CA.

Colston, H. L., & Lee, S. Y. (2004). *Gender differences in verbal irony use.* Manuscript submitted for publication.

Colston, H. L., & Lusch, V. (2004). *A gender difference in indirect language: The case of asyndeton.* Manuscript submitted for publication.

Colston, H. L., & O'Brien, J. (2000a). Contrast and pragmatics in figurative language: Anything understatement can do, irony can do better. *Journal of Pragmatics, 32,* 1557–1583.

Colston, H. L., & O'Brien, J. (2000b). Contrast of kind versus contrast of magnitude: The pragmatic accomplishments of irony and hyperbole. *Discourse Processes, 30,* 179–199.

Dews, S., Kaplan, J., & Winner, E. (1995). Why not say it directly? The social functions of irony. *Discourse Processes, 19,* 347–367.

Dews, S., & Winner, E. (1995). Muting the meaning: A social function of irony. *Metaphor and Symbolic Activity, 10,* 3–19.

Dews, S., & Winner, E. (1999). Obligatory processing of literal and nonliteral meanings in verbal irony. *Journal of Pragmatics, 31*(12), 1579–1599.

Gibbs, R. W., Jr. (1986). What makes some indirect speech acts conventional? *Journal of Memory and Language, 25*(2), 181–196.

Gibbs, R. W., Jr. (1987). Memory for requests in conversation revisited. *American Journal of Psychology, 100*(2), 179–191.

Gibbs, R. W., Jr. (2000). Irony in talk among friends. *Metaphor and Symbol, 15*, 5–27.

Gibbs, R. W., Jr., O'Brien, J. E., & Doolittle, S. (1995). Inferring meanings that are not intended: Speakers' intentions and irony comprehension. *Discourse Processes, 20*, 187–203.

Giora, R. (1995). On irony and negation. *Discourse Processes, 19*, 239–264

Giora, R. (1997). Understanding figurative and literal language: The graded salience hypothesis. *Cognitive Linguistics, 7*, 183–206.

Giora, R., Fein, O., & Schwartz, T. (1998). Irony: Graded salience and indirect negation. *Metaphor and Symbol, 13*, 83–101.

Holtgraves, T. (1992). Interpersonal underpinnings of request strategies: General principles and differences due to culture and gender. *Journal of Personality and Social Psychology, 62*, 246–256.

Holtgraves, T. (1997a). Politeness and memory for wording of remarks. *Memory and Cognition, 25*, 106–116.

Holtgraves, T. (1997b). Styles of language use: Individual and cultural variability in conversational indirectness. *Journal of Personality and Social Psychology, 73*, 624–637.

Holtgraves, T. (1991). Interpreting questions and replies: Effects of face-threat, question from, and gender. *Social Psychology Quarterly, 54*, 15–24.

Howland, J., Hingson, R., Mangione, T. W., & Bell, N. (1996). Why are most drowning victims men? Sex differences in aquatic skills and behaviors. *American Journal of Public Health, 86*(1), 93–96.

Jorgensen, J. (1996). The functions of sarcastic irony in speech. *Journal of Pragmatics, 26*, 613–634.

Katz, A., & Lee, C. (1993). The role of authorial intent in determining verbal irony and metaphor. *Metaphor and Symbolic Activity, 8*, 257–279.

Katz, A., & Pexman, P. (1997). Interpreting figurative statements: Speaker occupation can change metaphor to irony. *Metaphor and Symbol, 12*, 19–41.

Katz, A., Piasecka, I., & Toplak, M. (2001, November). *Comprehending the sarcastic comments of males and females.* Poster session presented at the 42nd annual meeting of the Psychonomic Society, Orlando, FL.

Kemper, S., & Thissen, D. (1981). Memory for the dimensions of requests. *Journal of Verbal Learning and Verbal Behavior, 20*(5), 552–563.

Kreuz, R. J. (1996). The use of verbal irony: Cues and constraints. In J. S. Mio & A. N. Katz (Eds.), *Metaphor: Implications and applications* (pp. 23–38). Mahwah, NJ: Lawrence Erlbaum Associates.

Kreuz, R. J. (2000). The production and processing of verbal irony. *Metaphor and Symbol, 15*, 99–107.

Kreuz, R. J., Kassler, M., Coppenrath, L., & McLain, A. (1999). Tag questions and common ground effects in the perception of verbal irony. *Journal of Pragmatics, 31*(12), 1685–1700.

Kreuz, R. J., & Link, K. E. (2002). Asymmetries in the use of verbal irony. *Journal of Language and Social Psychology, 21*(2), 127–143.

Kreuz, R. J., Long, D. L., & Church, M. B. (1991). On being ironic: Pragmatic and mnemonic implications. *Metaphor and Symbolic Activity, 6*, 149–162.

Lee, C., & Katz, A. (1998). The differential role of ridicule in sarcasm and irony. *Metaphor and Symbol, 13*, 1–5.

Leggitt, J., & Gibbs, R. W., Jr. (2000). Emotional reactions to verbal irony. *Discourse Processes, 29*, 1–24.

Okamoto, S. (2002). Politeness and the perception of irony: Honorifics in Japanese. *Metaphor and Symbol, 17*, 119–139.

Pexman, P. M., Ferretti, T., & Katz, A. (2000). Discourse factors that influence on-line reading of metaphor and irony. *Discourse Processes, 29*, 201–222.

Pexman, P. M., & Olineck, K. M. (2002). Understanding irony: How do stereotypes cue speaker intent? *Journal of Language and Social Psychology, 21*, 245–274.

Roberts, R. M., & Kreuz, R. J. (1994). Why do people use figurative language? *Psychological Science, 5*(4), 159–163.

Schwoebel, J., Dews, S., Winner, E., & Srinivas, K. (2000). Obligatory processing of the literal meaning of ironic utterances: Further evidence. *Metaphor and Symbol, 15*, 47–61.

Tomasello, M., & Akhtar, N. (1995). Two-year-olds use pragmatic cues to differentiate reference to objects and actions. *Cognitive Development, 10*, 201–224.

Toplak, M. & Katz, A. N. (2000). On the uses of sarcastic irony. *Journal of Pragmatics, 32*, 1476–1488.

Whaley, B. B., & Holloway, R. L. (1996). "Rebuttal" analogy: A theoretical note. *Metaphor and Symbolic Activity, 11*, 161–167.

Wiederman, M. W. (1997). The truth must be in here somewhere: Examining the gender discrepancy in self-reported lifetime number of sex partners. *Journal of Sex Research, 34*(4), 375–386.

Winner, E., & Gardner, H. (1993). Metaphor and irony: Two levels of understanding. In A. Ortony (Ed.), *Metaphor and thought* (2nd ed., pp. 425–443). New York: Cambridge University Press.

6

Irony as Persuasive Communication

Raymond W. Gibbs Jr.
Christin D. Izett
University of California, Santa Cruz

Persuading others to think or act in certain ways can be very difficult to accomplish. For example, how would you persuade teenagers not to smoke cigarettes? Many people suggest that the best way to convince others not to engage in this risky behavior is to have a serious, somber conversation in which the facts about the effects of smoking on health and life expectancy are described and discussed. This kind of plain talk may be impressive to some adults, but do such arguments convince teenagers?

A way to persuade teenagers is through the use of special rhetorical devices that may catch their attention and possibly seduce them to adopt some belief. One widely employed figure of speech in advertising that may nicely serve this function is irony. Consider the following radio advertisement, sponsored by the California Department of Health Services, played in May 1998 on California radio stations. The radio spot is spoken in the voice of a 60-year-old man in a very sincere tone (California Department of Health Services):

We the Tobacco Industry, would like to take this opportunity to thank you, the young people of America, who continue to smoke our cigarettes despite Surgeon General warnings that smoking causes lung cancer, emphysema, and heart disease. Your ignorance is astounding, and should be applauded. Our tobacco products kill 420,000 of your parents and grandparents every year. And yet, you've stuck by us. That kind of blind allegiance is hard to find. In fact, 3,000 of you start smoking everyday because we tobacco folks tell you it's cool. [Starts to get carried away.] Remember, you're rebels! Individuals! And besides, you impressionable little kids are makin' us tobacco guys rich!! Heck, we're billionaires!! [Clears throat/composes himself.]. In conclusion, we the tobacco conglomerates of America, owe a debt of gratitude to all teens for their continued support of our tobacco products despite the unfortunate disease and death they cause. Thank you for your understanding. Thank you for smoking. Yours truly, The Tobacco Industry.

Listeners likely have different reactions to this radio message. Many adults who decry the way the tobacco industry seduces children to smoke see great humor in the speaker's irony (e.g., "That kind of blind allegiance is hard to find"). Others may not get the point of this ad despite its heavy-handed use of irony throughout the speaker's heartfelt expression of gratitude. But most people certainly pay attention to the ad, precisely because it adopts a perspective that seems so incongruous (e.g., thanking people for engaging in a behavior that may likely end up killing them). We do not know whether this specific ad is persuasive to teenagers and gets them to not smoke. Yet, it is clear that advertisers see irony as a special weapon in their attempt to capture people's attention and persuade them to act in certain ways.

This chapter describes the role that irony plays in persuasive communication. We argue that irony has several special features that make it a wonderful tool for persuasion, especially the ability to highlight the contrast between expectation and reality. Irony works to create ad hoc intellectual communities that lead audiences to view themselves, even temporarily, as "conspirators" in accepting the values to which irony indirectly alludes. We describe several instances of this thesis in various applied contexts (e.g., advertisements, personal arguments, political debates, intellectual discussions, and literature) and suggest how contemporary research in cognitive and social psychology provides good evidence for why irony is employed so frequently in persuasive communication.

WHY USE IRONY?

Irony can be fraught with perils, enough so that one may reasonably ask why any person should ever use irony. Irony divides its audience in two different ways (Kaufer, 1977). First, there is the distinction between those who recognize the irony and those who do not. Those who recognize the irony understand what the speaker–author intends to say; because of their wisdom they may be called *wolves*. Those who fail to recognize the irony mistake what the speaker–author appears to say for what he or she intends to say. For their gullibility, these people may be called *sheep*.

Another difference in audiences is between those who agree with the speaker–author's intended meaning and those that do not. Supporters of irony are *confederates*; those that disagree are *victims*. These two groups are not the same as wolves and sheep, because understanding what the speaker–author intends to say and agreeing with it are distinct aspects of communication (Kaufer, 1977).

Employing irony, therefore, divides the audience into four groups (Kaufer, 1977). First, there are those who recognize the irony and agree with the author's intended message (i.e., wolf–confederates). For example, a speaker says "President Bush is such a humanitarian" and the addressee understands this statement as a sarcastic comment about President Bush and agrees with the speaker's opinion. A second group includes people who recognize the irony but disagree with the author's intended message (i.e., wolf–victims). Thus, an addressee may hear the speaker's sarcastic comment about President Bush, understands the speaker ironic meaning, but disagrees with the speaker's assessment. A third group includes those who do not recognize the irony but would agree with the author's message if they had correctly understood it (i.e., sheep-confederates). For example, a listener may not recognize the speaker's intended irony in saying "President Bush is a humanitarian" but would agree with the speaker's assessment if he or she had understood it correctly. Finally, there is a group that does not recognize the irony and would not accept the author's communicative message (i.e., sheep–victims).

One proposal suggests that the main job of an ironic speaker–author is to create as many wolf–confederates as possible and minimize the number of sheep–confederates who wrongly believe themselves opposed to the creator's position (Kaufer, 1977). For example, in the antismoking ad just presented, there are sufficient cues to the ad's ironic message (e.g., obvious incongruity, statements like "Your ignorance is outstanding," and dramatic tones of voice) for listeners to readily understand the ad and agree with its underlying message (i.e., wolf–confederate). Of course, there may be some, like the Tobacco Industry, who recognize the irony but are not persuaded by its urgent appeal for young people not to smoke (i.e., wolf-victim). Yet, the California Department of Health Services may specifically intend to mock these wolf–victims as part of their message. In fact, teenagers may be more likely persuaded to not smoke by realizing that they are part of a special group of individuals who are smart enough to make fun of the Tobacco Industry for its continued efforts at promoting cigarette smoking.

In addition to these rhetorical complexities, irony it is often regarded as special because it represents a mode of intellectual deattachment. "Irony engages the intellect rather than the emotions" (Walker, p. 24) and sits on "the cutting edge of not caring" (Austin-Smith, p. 51). Commentators since Aristotle have seen irony in speaking or writing as a sign of sophistication, at the very least in the use and understanding of language. Irony is inherently elitist in setting apart an elite (one who understands and employs irony) from the masses (those who neither use nor understand irony). This elitism accounts in part for irony's reputation since the time of Cicero as a gentlemanly form of discourse. Academic scholars and cultural critics have frequently characterized the late 20th-century as the Age of Irony. Many Americans enjoyed the pleasures of ironic detachment—skepticism, satirical humor, and, at times, a downright lack of caring—when it came to both private and public affairs. Younger people, particularly those of Generation X (i.e., born in the 1970s and later), employed irony as their dominant discourse style. Popular culture, for better or worse, has been dripping with irony, as books, films, television, magazines, and music all indulged in various forms of irony to highlight the great divide between expectations and reality. The antismoking ad is a perfect illustration of this.

But psychological research suggests that irony does not necessarily reflect or promote detachment or lead to apathy. People use irony to achieve a complex set of social and communicative goals (Colston, 1997; Dews & Winner, 1995; Kumon-Nakamura, Glucksberg, & Brown, 1995; Lee & Kutz, 1998; Roberts & Kreuz, 1994), including being humorous, acting aggressively, achieving emotional control, elevating one's social status, expressing attitudes, provoking reactions, mocking others, and muting the force of one's meaning. Some scholars have maintained that one form of irony, ironic criticism, automatically reduces the amount of condemnation that listener's experience (Dews & Winner, 1995). By stating literally positive words in an ironic criticism (e.g., "A fine friend you are!"), the speaker ensures that listeners will interpret what is said in a more positive manner. The results of several studies show that critical ironic statements are rated as less severe than literal ones (Dews & Winner, 1995). Studies like Dew and Winters' support the idea that irony can work to reduce the personal impact of a speaker's message.

However, other studies demonstrate that ironic criticism actually enhances, rather than dilutes, condemnation and criticism (Colston, 1997). Thus, the positive direct meaning of an ironic utterance, such as "How pleasing!" increases the degree of criticism listeners perceive, compared to when they hear direct literal remarks, such as "How disgusting!" The contrast between the actual situation and the speaker's positive remark, again relative to the literal comment, gives rise to an enhanced sense of criticism (Colston, 1997).

Irony's ability to mock, attack, and ridicule, provoking embarrassment, humiliation, even anger, suggests that it may, in many circumstances, work to evoke strong emotional reactions in an audience. Part of the appeal of the antismoking ad is that it clearly makes listeners feel something, regardless of whether that emotion is interpreted positively (e.g., "I am sure glad that I'm not one of those ignorant persons who smoke") or negatively (e.g., "I feel guilty because I smoke"). Research shows that different forms of irony evoke different kinds of emotional reactions, especially when compared to plain, literal talk (Leggitt & Gibbs, 2000).

Imagine yourself in the following situation: One day while parking your car at work Mary is splashed with mud. Mary walks over to your car while you are getting out. You look at Mary and ask why her clothes are such a mess. Mary looks back at the mud puddle in the road and answers: "You splashed mud on me with your car." Mary's utterance might very well make you feel guilty for doing what you, perhaps unintentionally, did to dirty her clothes. However, Mary's comment, although quite factual, does not convey much about her own attitude or emotion in regard to your act. She might simply be calling attention to what you did while forgiving your actions, or she might actually be displeased or quite angry with you.

Suppose, instead, that Mary actually uttered the sarcastic remark, "Thanks a lot for giving me a bath." Once again, you might feel guilty upon being alerted to your misdeed. Yet, by virtue of informing you about what you did in a sarcastic manner, you are likely to recognize that Mary appears rather angry. Sarcasm is considered especially appropriate for conveying a person's hostile attitude toward or ridicule of some other individual, usually the addressee (Gibbs, 1994; Lee & Katz, 1998). Consequently, being the object of another person's sarcasm might provoke intense emotional reactions. People may, for example, feel angry when they are the victims of sarcastic comments, because they resent the mocking style of the speaker's implied criticism. Moreover, speaking sarcastically may signal quite a different conceptualization of some event than if someone made literal comments, such as if Mary, in the aforementioned scenario, said "You have splashed mud on me" or "What you did makes me angry."

Leggitt and Gibbs (2000) demonstrated that people experience different emotional reactions to various ironic statements than to literal ones and feel more intense emotions having heard ironic remarks than literal ones. For instance, sarcasm, rhetorical questions, and overstatement all evoked similar and quite negative reactions, whereas understatement and satire evoked relatively neutral reactions. In general, a person's emotional reaction to an ironic statement depends on the degree to which the speaker directly challenges an addressee or makes a big deal of an issue. Listeners' evaluations of what ironic speakers must be feeling also differ depending on the type of ironic language employed. Speakers of sarcasm and rhetorical questions appeared to feel a wide range of negative emotions, but speakers of overstatements appeared to feel relatively neutral emotions. Moreover, speakers of satire were seen to feel more positive emotions and a lower degree of hostile emotions, and speakers of understatements were seen to feel relatively neutral emotions. These complexities in people's emotional reactions to different forms of irony highlight the pleasures and pitfalls associated with ironic communication. Speaking ironically may evoke strong emotions, yet these may not always be experienced as positive feelings.

People often use irony not to disparage others but to remind each other of the bonds that tie them together. Consider the following exchange between two college students (from the data described in Gibbs, 2000, p. 7). Melissa and a friend are in the kitchen of Melissa's apartment talking about the previous night. As they were talking, Melissa's housemate Jeanette, who was in her own bedroom, heard her name being mentioned:

Jeannette:	(yelling from her room) Are you talking about me again?
Melissa:	I have no life Jeannette. All I do is talk about you. All the time.
Jeannette:	(laughing) Get a life!

The housemates' interaction here is jocular, rather than sarcastic, in that each speaker was not entirely serious about the impact of what they were saying. Both speakers clearly enjoyed the exchange and found some humor in what each other said. But this minor exchange reflects one way that irony helps persuade others. When Jeannette, perhaps glibly, accuses Melissa of talking or gossiping about her, Melissa's jocular retort works to reassure Jeannette that she is not the constant topic of conversation or gossip. This slight instance of reassurance is persuasive in the sense that it reminds the two women of the good-natured friendship they have, precisely because they can speak jocularly without significant risk of having their intentions be misunderstood.

Irony is, in this way, a particularly compelling means of reaffirming presuppositions common to both the speaker–author and the audience. Thus, irony involves foregrounding the normative standards that make possible the correct interpretation of ironic statements. Summoning common norms and reinforcing them by apparently violating them is another way by which an ironic speaker–author can establish an implicit solidarity with the audience and persuade to adopt, or be reminded of, a certain belief.

Ironic language also enables speakers to establish bonds by marking who is part of the "in-group" and who is not. Consider the following conversation in which a group of college students disparage another person. This exchange took place outside a campus coffee shop (Gibbs, 2000, p. 8):

Kayla:	How are you doing?
Cherie:	Um … good, we're going to study Latin but the coffee shop is just packed.
David:	It's rockin'

Sarah:	I ... study Latin ... Latin language?
Kayla:	It's wet out here.
Sarah:	You guys are taking Latin? (laughs)
Cherie:	Yeah ... (laughs)
Kayla:	(whiny tone of voice) But that's a dead language (everyone laughs) I'm just kidding is that not what everyone tells you?
Cherie:	It's true and we don't really know how to pronounce everything.
David:	It's really hard.
Cherie:	Yeah, but it's only a year long program.
David:	So, you're fluent in Latin after a year. (everyone laughs)
Kayla:	Right ... right.
David:	It's true. (everyone laughs)
Sarah:	You read all those ancient texts, that's cool. (laughs)
Cherie:	Why you guys dissin' on Latin?
David:	(mocking tone) What, wo-ah, you're dissin' my Latin.
Kayla:	Actually, Latin helps because, doesn't it, it helps with etymology it help with words, breaking words down.
David:	totally ... yeah, yeah, she got it ... yeah.
Cherie:	structure, parts of speech, yeah.
David:	I'm a changed person since the last couple of weeks of Latin.

Teasing and jocularity, like that seen in this dialogue, offer gentle, indirect ways of pointing out people's deviation from social standards and is central to socialization practices between parents and children, friends, and romantic partners. By ironically noting the discrepancy between the reality of Cherie and David studying Latin and the expectation or belief that Latin is nothing more than a dead language, Kayla and Sarah aim to persuade the others of their beliefs about what is "hip" and what is not. The content of an ironic message can solidify the bond between ironist and audience, which also enhances the persuasive impact of an ironic argument. Yet, ironic arguments also communicate to an audience that the ironist shares certain beliefs and values (i.e., conspirators) that others, to their detriment, do not (i.e., victims).

A more blatant example of how noting the discrepancy between expectation and reality works to persuade is found in Swift's (1729/1996) *A Modest*

Proposal. Readers are forced to recognize the desperate poverty of the Irish people by the ironic solution of infanticide and cannibalism. Swift's purpose was to enrage his readers against the policies that had allowed the situation in Ireland to deteriorate to the point where a scheme to sell children as food was no more than a "modest proposal." Our understanding of Swift's ironic message creates an ad hoc community of those who share Swift's beliefs and values. The pleasure derived from the recognition of irony is compounded by our awareness of our own competence as its audience.

Various empirical research, in fact, demonstrates that irony is especially useful for highlighting the contrast between what was expected and what ensued. Experimental findings suggest that irony creates more contrast between expectations and resulting events than does understatement, whereas both forms of irony create more contrast than do literal statements (Colston & O'Brien, 2000b). Furthermore, the degree of contrast between expectation and reality also affects listeners' judgments of how humorous, how condescending, how expressive of surprise, and how protective of a speaker any ironic remark appears to be (Colston & Keller, 1998; Colston & O'Brien, 2000a). Other studies show that when a speaker restates another person's inaccurate remark (e.g., "Sure, Ronald Reagan was the president during the 1970s"), the ironic message works better than either refutation or correction to communicate the idea that the first speaker should have known better (Colston, 2000c). This body of work indicates that people employ irony to specifically and succinctly comment on the disparity between expectations or beliefs and what is actually happening.

WHY IS IRONY PERSUASIVE? SOCIAL PSYCHOLOGICAL EVIDENCE

Social psychology research supports our contention that irony may be especially effective in persuasive communication because it highlights the contrast between expectation and reality. For instance, the *contrast principle* of human perception describes how people view the difference between two options that are presented in succession. The basic premise of the contrast principle is that if the second item presented is distinctly different than the first, we will perceive it as being more different than it is in actuality. Consider the following example: If you lift a light item first, and then a heavy item, you will estimate that the second item is heavier than it actually is. Conversely, if a heavy item is lifted first, lifting a lighter item in turn will appear to be almost effortless in contrast to the heavy item.

The contrast principle is well established in the field of psychophysics and has been applied in a variety of social influence situations. Sales organizations and marketing executives worldwide make good use of the contrast principle in influencing consumers to purchase goods. Automobile dealers use the contrast principle to increase accessory sales. Dealers will wait until the price for the automobile is negotiated before they suggest one accessory option after another to the buyer, who in wake of a multithousand dollar purchase perceives a few extra hundred dollars as trivial in comparison. Home real estate agents utilize the contrast principle in increasing the dollar amount of properties that they sell. When showing a potential buyer a set of properties, an agent will almost always start by showing a couple of undesirable properties. Real estate companies call these homes *set-up properties*. Essentially, the companies maintain a few properties at inflated prices on its lists. These homes are not intended to be sold to buyers, but are used as a comparison to the genuine properties to increase the likelihood that they are sold. After looking at a few run-down and high-priced properties, the genuine properties, although more expensive, appear to be the deal of a lifetime (Cialdini, 1975). The main point of the contrast principle is that any element of human perception can be made to appear very different than it really is, depending on the nature of the event that precedes it.

A wonderful example of the contrast principle at work is seen in the following letter that a college student wrote to her parents (Cialdini, 1984, pp. 15–16):

Dear Mother and Dad:

Since I left for college, I have been remiss in writing and am sorry for my thoughtlessness in not having written before. I will bring you up to date now, but before you read on, please sit down. You are not to read any further unless you are sitting down, okay? Well, then, I am getting along pretty well now. The skull fracture and the concussion I got when I jumped out the window of my dormitory when it caught on fire shortly after my arrival here is pretty well healed now.

I only spent two weeks in the hospital and now I can almost see normally and only get those sick headaches once a day. Fortunately, the fire in the dormitory, and my jump, were witnessed by an attendant at the gas station near the dorm, and he was the one who called the fire department and the ambulance. He also visited me in the hospital and since I had nowhere to live because of the burnout dormitory, he was kind enough to invite me to share his apartment with him. It's really as basement room, but it's kind of cute. He's a very fine boy and we have fallen deeply in love and are planning to get married. We haven't got the exact date yet, but it will be before my pregnancy begins to show.

Yes, Mother and Dad, I am pregnant. I know how much you are looking forward to being grandparents and I know you will welcome the baby and give it the same love, devotion and tender care you gave to me when I was a child. The reason for the delay in our marriage is that my boyfriend has a minor infection, which prevents us from passing our premarital blood tests and I carelessly caught it from him.

Now that I have brought you up to date, I want to tell you that there is no dormitory fire, I did not have a concussion or a skull fracture, I was not in the hospital, I am not pregnant, I am not engaged, I am not infected and there is no boyfriend. I am getting a "D" in American History and an "F" in chemistry and I want you to see those marks in their proper perspective.

Your loving daughter, Sharon

By getting her parents to believe one set of events, the reality of Sharon's poor grades seems almost insignificant. In this way, Sharon has used the contrast principle to persuade others of her point of view. Irony often works to persuade others through the contrast principle. A good place to find examples of this is in advertisements. Consider the headline for the Range Rover: "The British have always driven on the wrong side of the road," accompanied by a picture of the automobile driven on a steep slope off to one side of the road. Understanding this headlines requires that observers be aware that the British drive on the left side of the road, and that the left side is the correct side in Britain, although it seems wrong to those accustomed to the alternative. An observer may thus reflect that for a 4-wheel drive vehicle, the wrong side of the road (i.e., off the road altogether) is the right side. Yet, people may readily infer that it may be wrong for an auto to leave the road but right (pleasurable and advantageous) not to be bound by the road. Not all observers will necessarily draw these complex inferences, but the advertisers' choice of an ironic message destabilizes one's understanding of what is right or wrong which liberates the observer's thoughts; perhaps he or she sees the beauty or even the necessity of driving or owning a Range Rover.

A different form of contrast is seen in a Kodak ad stating "This picture was taken by someone who didn't bring a camera." This message is self-contradictory and ironically destabilizes the idea that taking pictures requires a camera, and it leads observers to the possibility of buying a disposable camera (made by Kodak) on the spot. Thus, one's conventional assumption of bringing along a camera to take photographs has been ironically upended.

Consider one final ad to demonstrate irony's potential effectiveness in persuading by extreme contrast. In an effort to persuade people to devote their valuable time to a volunteer effort (to increase literacy by helping the illiterate learn how to read), an ad agency based in San Diego launched a creative campaign that employs the heavy use of sarcasm, guilt, and humor as persuasive devices. They describe this approach as a form of reverse psychology. Previous campaigns utilized a more traditional approach to persuasion whereby potential volunteer recruits where told that increasing literacy among fellow citizens is simply "the right thing to do." The sarcasm campaign employs a very different approach.

Here are some examples of their campaign ads: "Keep America Stupid!" and "Fight Literacy!" and "This country has enough smart people, what we need are more stupid people!" The ads then urge message recipients not to call the associated toll-free number to enlist as a volunteer. Within the first 2 days of the campaign launch, 60 people contacted the San Diego Council on Literacy to express an interest in volunteering. This number is staggering in contrast to the negligible number of volunteers recruited by ads emphasizing that volunteering simply is the right thing to do. The sarcasm campaign is being expanded nationwide due to its initial effectiveness (Stewart, 2000).

The *norm of reciprocity* is another well-known social psychological concept that utilizes the contrast principle to increase compliance and influence. A norm is a specific guide to conduct. Breaking a norm will most likely lead to some form of social sanction, and being put in a position of transgressing a norm causes even small children tremendous anxiety. To avoid feeling anxious or being disapproved of, most people comply with social norms without question. The norm of reciprocity is a good of example of a social norm in American culture: If I do something for you, you are then obligated to return the favor and do something for me (Cialdini, 1978).

One example of the norm of reciprocity working with the contrast principle to enhance social influence is the *door-in-the-face technique*. This technique increases compliance by operating as a type of perceptual hyperbole (creating a large contrast). First, a person is asked for a very extreme favor. The favor must be something to which almost no one would comply. Second, the requester makes a concession, thus invoking the norm of reciprocity, and asks for a much smaller favor. The implicit message by the requester is that "because I made a concession and am compromising now it is your turn to reciprocate my concession and grant me this favor."

For instance, Cialdini and Ascani (1976) asked university passersby to donate either a unit of blood sometime tomorrow or donate a unit of blood once every 2 months for a period of 2 years. When this extreme favor was inevitably rejected, the passersby were asked to simply donate a unit of blood sometime tomorrow. Results of this study showed that people not only agreed to give more blood but actually followed through on their agreement when they received the more extreme request first.

The contrast principle and the norm of reciprocity together make certain forms of irony especially persuasive. Consider a situation in which one friend asks another for a loan by saying "I need to borrow ten thousand dollars to pay my mortgage, which is way overdue, and to send in my son's college tuition, and to keep my car from being impounded." Listeners, especially friends, may react sympathetically to this appeal, despite its extreme nature, because of their desire to do the right thing and be helpful to a friend in need.

Of course, $10,000 is a great deal of money to most people, and this request would be almost impossible to fulfill. But if the speaker then said, "Okay, I really just need fifty bucks to pay my phone bill," then the listeners will experience a great sense of relief given the contrast to the original request. Consequently, the listener will be more likely lend the $50 than would be the case if the speaker had simply come out with this request in the first place. The norm of reciprocity, along with the contrast principle, makes hyperbole (one form of irony) especially useful in persuading others to comply with one's wishes.

Because ironic statements or arguments by nature use contrast to highlight the discrepancy between expectation and reality, irony appears to be an excellent example of utilizing the contrast principle to increase persuasion. Also, ironic statements act to destabilize the listener by presenting messages that appear contradictory to their previous beliefs or the reality of the situation. This destabilization forces listeners to acknowledge their beliefs, see if they are consistent with the present situation, and then reevaluate their position in light of the ironic statement or ad. In this way the destabilizing force of irony opens up listeners or observers to potentially adopting new beliefs, or at least seriously questioning their old ones. Once in this position, listeners or observers are more vulnerable to being persuaded or influenced by the speaker or ad.

By highlighting the discrepancy between expectation and reality, irony often produces a state of cognitive dissonance whereby an individual simultaneously holds to cognitions (ideas, attitudes, beliefs, and opinions) that are discrepant or psychologically inconsistent. This discrepancy produces a state of tension that can be very uncomfortable, and people become highly motivated to reduce it. Reducing cognitive dissonance involves changing one or both cognitions in such a way as to render them more compatible (more consonant) with each other or adding more cognitions to act as a bridge to the original cognitions (Festinger, 1957).

Consider the following example: A man who smokes cigarettes reads a report citing medical evidence linking cigarette smoking to cancer, lung disease, and premature death. The cognition "I am a smoker" is dissonant with the cognition "smoking will kill me." In an effort to reduce dissonance, a smoker may try to quit smoking. When he finds this task too challenging he may try to change the cognition "smoking will kill me." He may convince himself that the evidence that smoking kills is inconclusive. He may switch to a filtered brand, convinced that the filter will block the cancer-causing materials from entering his lungs. He may convince himself that he needs cigarettes to relax and ultimately to be happy and, therefore, conclude he would rather live a shorter, happier life. Reducing dissonance in any of these ways helps stabilize listeners by decreasing the discrepancy they experience between expectation and reality.

The antismoking ad discussed at the beginning of the chapter offers an excellent example of a commercial that produces cognitive dissonance. This ad highlights the two psychologically inconsistent cognitions: "I am a smoker" and "smoking cigarettes will kill me." The ad then uses irony to eliminate the possibility of changing the cognition "smoking will kill me" by making sarcastic remarks about possible dissonance reducing cognitions, such as "you are a rebel!" or "you are an individual!" The listener's only option is to change the cognition "I am a smoker."

A famous example of how ironic images provoke cognitive dissonance is seen in Margaret Bourke-White's photograph of a breadline during the American Depression of the 1930s. The photograph shows a group of impoverished African Americans waiting in line for a handout. Above them is a billboard with a picture of a White family of four driving happily in a car. The caption in the billboard reads "World's Highest Standard of Living. There's No Way Like the American Way!" Bourke-White invites us to experience a heightened sense of dissonance from the recognition of the contrast between expectation and reality and by threatening ones self-image as a caring, generous person. Part of this dissonance arises from observers' appreciation of the hypocrisy in the American ideal of us being a kind and prosperous nation that ignores the plight of the poor. In general, when presented with a communication or image that produces dissonance, the listener or viewer is very vulnerable to influence. By setting the decision-making criteria to include options that are desirable outcomes for the speaker or ad and will reduce dissonance for the listener or viewer, the ultimate resolution will benefit both parties (i.e., the listener or viewer is persuaded to comply to the request of the speaker or ad and listener or viewer reduces dissonance and reestablishes a positive self-image).

Another example of how irony can lead to dissonance and persuasion is seen in a study on decreasing HIV transmission (Aronson, Fried, & Stone, 1991; Stone, Aronson, Crain, Winslow, & Fried, 1994). One group of college students was asked to deliver a compelling speech to their peers about the benefits of using condoms and the dangers of HIV and disease transmission. The speech was videotaped, and the students were told that the tape would be shown to younger (i.e., more impressionable) high school students as part of a sexual education course. The students were then asked to recollect instances from their daily lives when they found it difficult, if not impossible, to use condoms during intercourse.

The experimenters set up a situation whereby the college students, who were more than likely not practicing safe sex, were made to be cognizant of their own actions and the action that they were advocating in their speech. Through the use of irony, hypocrites were confronted with their own hypocrisy. This irony produced a state of cognitive dissonance; to reduce dissonance and reestablish integrity, college students resolved to change their actual actions to be consonant with the actions they endorsed in their speech. Indeed, compared to college students who simply produced videotapes promoting condom use but were not asked to recall instances of not practicing safe sex (i.e., not made mindful of their own hypocrisy), students who were made to feel like hypocrites purchased far more condoms at the end of the study. Moreover, in a phone interview conducted 3 months later, 2% of these students reported using condoms regularly, more than twice as many as reported by hypocritical students who were not confronted with their own hypocrisy. Making people aware of their own ironic or hypocritical attitudes seems to be a very effective way of influencing human behavior. Advertisers may be well aware of this fact and use it to their profitable advantage.

Finally, social psychological research suggests another reason why ironic messages may be especially persuasive. A popular theory of social influence claims that attitude change arises from two sources (Petty & Cacioppo, 1986). The central route to persuasive communication relies on solid arguments, logic, and essential facts and figures. Listeners carefully scrutinize all the information presented and think carefully about the issue at hand. Conversely, the peripheral route to persuasion does not rely on engaging a person's thinking, but rather it relies on providing distracting cues that stimulate the acceptance of an argument with little or no thought. Irony may be especially persuasive because it works on both the central and peripheral routes for attitude change. For example, in the California antismoking campaign, people are persuaded by central arguments such as the fact that smoking kills 420,000 people per year and by peripheral cues such as humor and the speaker's mocking tone of voice. Thus, irony probes people to think about some matter by highlighting the contrast between expectation and reality, simultaneously evoking more extreme emotional reactions than typically felt when hearing literal statements.

IRONY IN INTELLECTUAL DEBATES

Our claim that irony is persuasive because of its special ability to highlight contrast and evoke cognitive dissonance is supported by other work on irony in intellectual debates. Whaley and Holloway (1996) argued, for example, that certain kinds of rebuttal analogies are especially effective in argumentation. For instance, one economist may use the analogy "Giving tax breaks to the rich is like putting sprinklers in the rainforest" when arguing with economists favoring tax cuts for wealthy Americans to stimulate the economy. Colston and Gibbs (1998) claimed that irony is a central element in rebuttal analogies. Quite specifically, in rebuttal analogy, a seemingly nonironic, unseen-as-ironic, or simply less ironic target domain is paired with a clearly ironic base domain, which highlights via irony the widely contrasting relations between the base and target. Consider the following two examples of ironic rebuttal analogies (Colston & Gibbs, 1998, p. 72):

> The White House trotted out Dick Darman, the budget director, to blast Governor Clinton's deficit reduction. This is a man who's run $1 trillion 238 million of deficits. Isn't that a little like the Boston Strangler criticizing street crime? (Cable News Network, 1992)

Base: The Boston Strangler criticizing street crime.

Target: A person who ran huge deficits criticizing overspending.

Irony: It is ironic for a criminal to condemn crime because crime is the behavior in which a criminal engages. It is analogously ironic for a person guilty of overspending to criticize that very behavior.

An inexperienced Secretary of Defense getting "on-the-job-training" is like taking your first drink of water from a fire hose. (National Public Radio, 1989)

Base: Taking your first drink of water.

Target: An inexperienced Secretary of Defense getting "on-the-job-training."

Irony: Taking one's first drink of water from a first hose is ironic because one cannot expect to get nourishment, especially for the first time, at the delicate task of drinking water will be forthcoming with enough pressure to knock a person down. It is equally ironic for a person to expect to gain job experience by taking on the enormously important task of managing the world's most powerful armed forces.

These examples illustrate how irony is a fundamental element of rebuttal analogies and may be especially effective as persuasive devices by pointing out the incompatibility of what is expected and what is presented. A recent set of studies confirmed this claim (Colston, 2000a). Analogies with ironic bases (e.g., "Doubling the defense budget to intimidate North Korea is like using a chainsaw to file your nails") were perceived by participants to be more argumentative, and more attacking than were analogies with absurd and nonironic bases. These findings support the idea that listeners' recognition of the ironic structure between base and target is more central to their understanding of rebuttal analogies than is absurdity comparison or argumentative conventions. Another study showed, however, that speakers who use rebuttal analogies were unfavorably perceived by listeners (Whaley &

Wagner, 2000). Thus, ironic rebuttal analogies may be persuasive in arguments, even if speakers may not always be positively perceived for using these devices.

Academic writing, although generally seen as containing few instances of irony and humor, actually contains many examples in which writers express certain ideas by ironically highlighting the contrast between other people's beliefs or expectations and some reality. One way this is accomplished is through a writer simply quoting someone else's previous work without comment, with the irony resulting from juxtaposition of the quoted passage with some other passage in the text. For instance, in one debate between some linguistics and computer scientists, Dresher and Hornstein (1976) in a footnote quoted without comment text from Winograd (1974), one of the people whose work they were attacking, in their discussion of practical issues in building computational models of natural language understanding. Dresher and Hornstein wrote, (1976:330) Thus, one could start with fairly simple components (a small number of syntactic components, a small lexicon, etc.) which could be improved indefinitely (by adding more syntactic patterns, more lexical items) according to practical considerations such as time, money and computer space. The quotation they cited from Winograd (1974, p. 93) was as follows: If someone is trying to build the best robot which can be completed by the next year, he will avoid any really hard problems that come up, rather than accepting them as a challenge to look at a new area. There will be pressure from the organization of the projects and funding agencies to get results at the expense of avoiding hard problems.

By quoting him directly, Dresher and Hornstein (1977) used Winograd's (1974) own words to support their contention about the implausibility of artificial intelligence models given the practical limitations faced by computer scientists. Again, simply quoting someone else's words allows writers to convey ironic intentions about the quoted work and author(s). How people come to process these quoted statement as ironic must be complex, as readers do not simply establish ironic intentions by recognizing certain textual features that conventionally mark irony. Instead, readers enter texts uncertain and use several possible relations among the reader, the writer, and another writer to establish several intentions, some of which might be ironic. Readers look for intentions consistent with the new incongruent relations proposed among the reader, the ironic writer, and the victimized writer. We assume that the quoted writers believe their original assertions as they are quoted. Irony arises, however, because we assume that the statement was made with a different intention in the original text. Scholars see these ironic mentions of other people's words as an effective device to persuade others of their own beliefs (see Colston, 2000b).

IRONY IN LITERATURE

People do not usually read literature to be persuaded by writers in the way they may when reading expository essays. But literature may indeed work to persuade readers of particular ideas and beliefs through the use of ironic contrast. An excellent example of this is seen in the work of the 20th-century British author Evelyn Waugh (Beaty, 1992). Waugh was a master at using irony as a way of perceiving life, and as an aesthetic device for reporting its unresolved paradoxes. For Waugh, irony was the most congenial aesthetic means of displaying the existential dilemmas of 20th-century man. Many of Waugh's earlier novels—*Decline and Fall, Vile Bodies, Black Mischief, A Handful of Dust,* and *Scoop*—illustrate his distinctive style to comment on the often chaotic environments that his characters inhabit yet allow him as author to remain somewhat disengaged from other people and events. The early novels convey the strong sense of Waugh's understanding of the absurdities of life that he clearly took great pleasure in writing about. Whether he was dealing with life in public schools and universities, religion, the shenanigans and hypocrisy of the upper class, or British history and politics, Waugh's purpose was not only to amuse readers but also to persuade them of his own critical assessment. In fact, some of Waugh's nonfictional essays expressed his strong belief in the importance of style in the art of persuasion. Irony was surely one of his greatest tools.

Irony also provided Waugh with the semblance of open mindedness, a feature that likely attracted readers, and offered him the tools for describing his very definite perceptions of reality. This detachment is a hallmark of most ironic literature, with Waugh's light style still coming across as relevant to very serious matters. We consider just two brief excerpts of Waugh's writing to illustrate how irony informed his imaginative creations.

Waugh's (1932) *Black Mischief* was perhaps his finest example of using irony to invite readers to discover with the narrator the complexities of life's incongruities. By using language inappropriate in context that highlights incongruities between appearance and reality, Waugh indirectly disclosed his own thoughts but also aimed to elicit similar reactions for a morally responsible audience. An example of this is seen in the one character's tribute to a slain comrade at his funeral. In this eulogy, the speaker attributes many qualities that were clearly not the case in real life: "Thousands fell by his right hand. The words of his mouth were like thunder in the hills. Weep, woman of Azania, for your royal lover is torn from your arms. His virility was inexhaustible, his progeny numerous beyond human computation .... When he led you to battle there was no retreating. In council the more guileful, in justice the most terrible, Seth the magnificent is dead" (p. 299).

Waugh's (1932) aim here was to blatantly mock the dead man's pretensions about his effectiveness as a loyal British subject serving the colonial empire in Africa. The speaker cannot be accused of speaking ill of the dead given the words he uses. But the incongruity of the words with people's recognition of the dead man's real-life attributes and accomplishments gives rise to a wonderful ironic feel that is both pleasurable and persuasive.

In *The Loved Ones*, Waugh (1948) also mocked the pretensions of a character, Aime, for hyperextensive preparations for a romantic evening:

> With a steady hand Aimee fulfilled the prescribed rites of an American girl preparing to meet her lover—dabbed herself under the arms with a preparation designed to seal the sweat glands, gargled another to sweeten the breath, and brushed into her hair some odorous drops from a bottle labeled "Jungle Venom"—(advertised as coming) "From the depth of a fever-ridden swamp, with the remorseless stealth of the hunting cannibal." Thus fully equipped for a domestic evening ... she was all set to accept her manifest destiny. (p. 111)

Waugh's (1948) exaggerated diction highlighted how Aimee's preparations were ridiculous and that she took herself way too seriously with thoughts of her romantic fate as "manifest destiny." The exaggeration here also marks the incongruity with Aimee's self-concept as a highly ethical person yet one that readily uses an arsenal of drugstore products to enable her own seduction, one that never happens despite her expansive efforts and supreme confidence.

Literature contains many examples like these in which authors try to instill a set of beliefs or attitudes through the characters' words and deeds. This kind of persuasion can be quite subtle yet surprisingly effective in seducing readers to think in particular ways while experiencing the pleasures of narrative worlds.

CONCLUSION

There are many ways to persuade people to think or act in particular ways. Speakers and writers employ many rhetorical devices in their attempt to get others to adopt their respective points of view. Our claim is that irony has special features that make it a highly useful tool or weapon in persuasive communication. Irony succinctly acts to emphasize the incongruity between some expectations or beliefs and the reality of a situation. Of course, speakers and writers can point out incongruous, inconsistent, even hypocritical thinking using literal language. But irony often seduces listeners to think hard about a speaker's message because of the highlighted incongruity and the emotions that arise from recognizing this disparity between expectation and reality.

There are clear risks to using irony for persuasion. History offers us many lessons of the negative consequences of using irony and failing to get one's message across. The songwriter Randy Newman experienced some of these perils in his 1982 song "Short People" which mocked short people for all their deficiencies, with the indirect aim of undercutting people's silly prejudices against others. Radio stations refused to play the song, and one state legislature even passed a resolution against the song. Like Jonathan Swift experienced in the 17th-century with his classic, A Modest Proposal and the contemporary singer Eminen with some of his ironic messages on homosexuals and others, any person trying to persuade others of some belief using irony risks failing to be understood. Yet, these perils are often counterbalanced by the positive persuasive effects that speakers achieve when trying to maximize the number of wolf–confederates and minimize the number of sheep–confederates (Kaufer, 1977). The prominence of irony in many social influence situations, ranging from personal conversations to political debates, is testimony to the widely held, but not universal, belief that irony is well worth the risks it sometimes entails.

Part of the reason why irony is a popular persuasive device is that listeners often feel differently about themselves and the speaker as a result of successfully interpreting ironic messages. First, recognizing incongruity can lead to a pleasurable feeling of arousal (Berlyne, 1971). This aesthetic reaction to irony makes it a joy to use in commenting on life's events and in understanding other's recognition of ironic situations. Simply detecting the irony in some situation can lead to a positive feeling about one's own abilities to recognize the complexities in life. But people experience additional aesthetic and emotional pleasures in knowing that they share ironic perceptions with others. As is often stated about metaphor (Gibbs, 1994), irony works to create a sense of intimacy between those who use and those who understand it. The feeling that one is part of a conspiracy in seeing irony is a strong reason why it is so frequently observed in persuasive communication. This heightened degree of arousal may also suggest one reason why ironic language is often more memorable than corresponding literal language (either literal uses of the same words or nonironic paraphrases; Gibbs, 1986). Not surprisingly, empirical research demonstrates that college students find ironic ads (reversals plus destabilization) more artful and cleaver than ads that express simple poetic figures (i.e., repetition plus substitution; McQuarrie & Mick, 1996).

Our arguments on irony's persuasive effects must be softened by the recognition of the complexities of ironic language and artwork. Similar to metaphor, irony has many linguistic and pragmatic features, each of which need not leads to enhanced persuasion.

For instance, irony is really a global term for a variety of figurative forms, such as sarcasm, jocularity, rhetorical questions, understatements, and hyperbole. Leggitt and Gibbs (2000) showed these varying types of irony many evoke different emotional reactions, as well as different beliefs about a

speaker's emotional state. Moreover, different forms of irony may work differently in emphasizing the contrast between expectations and reality (Colston
& O'Brien, 2000a, 2000b). Thus, we resist making any blanket statement
about whether all forms of irony are equally effective in persuasive communication. We also note that related cousins to irony, such as parody and satire,
make frequent appearances in persuasive discourse and advertisements. Our
suspicion is that these related figurative schemes share similarities to irony in
highlighting discrepancies between expectation and reality. Yet, there may be
important differences too in how this cluster of tropes function to seduce and
persuade. We are enthusiastic about blending ideas from social psychology
with research methods from psycholinguistics to empirically explore more of
the social, interpersonal dimensions of ironic talk.

REFERENCES

Aronson, E., Fried, C., & Stone, J. (1991). Overcoming denial and increasing the
    intention to use condoms through the induction of hypocrisy. *American Journal of
    Public Health, 81,* 1636–1638.
Austin-Smith, B. (1990). Into the beast of irony. *Dimension, 27,* 51–52.
Beaty, F. (1992). *The ironic world of Evelyn Waugh.* DeKalb, IL: Northern Illinois Press.
Berlyne, D. (1971). *Aesthetics and psychobiology.* New York: Appleton.
Cialdini, R. B. (1975). Reciprocal concessions procedure for inducing compliance:
    The door-in-the-face technique. *Journal of personality and Social Psychology, 31,*
    206–215.
Cialdini, R. B. (1978). The lowball procedure for producing compliance: Commit-
    ment, then cost. *Journal of Personality and Social Psychology, 36,* 463–476.
Cialdini, R. B. (1984). *Influence: The psychology of persuasion.* New York: Morrow.
Cialdini, R. B., & Ascani, K. (1975). The test of concession procedure for inducing
    verbal, behavioral and further compliance with a request to give blood. *Journal of
    Applied Psychology, 61,* 296–300.
Colston, H. L. (1997). Salting a wound or sugaring a pill: The pragmatic functions of
    ironic criticism. *Discourse Processes, 23,* 25–45.
Colston, H. L. (2000a). Comprehending speaker intent in rebuttal analogy use: The
    role of irony mapping, absurdity comparison and argumentative convention.
    Language and Speech, 43, 337–354.
Colston, H. L. (2000b). "Dewey defeats Truman": Interpreting ironic restatement.
    Journal of Language and Social Psychology, 19, 44–63.
Colston, H. L. (2000c). On necessary conditions for verbal irony comprehension.
    Pragmatics & Cognition, 8, 277–324.
Colston, H., & Gibbs, R. W., Jr. (1998). Analogy and irony: Rebuttal to "Rebuttal
    analogy." *Metaphor and Symbol, 13,* 69–76.
Colston, H., & Keller, S. (1998). You'll never believe this: Irony and hyperbole in
    surprise. *Journal of Psycholinguistic Research, 27,* 49–513.
Colston, H. L., & O'Brien, J. (2000a). Contrast and pragmatics in figurative language:
    Anything understatement can do, irony can do better. *Journal of Pragmatics, 32,*
    1557–1583.

Colston, H. L., & O'Brien, J. (2000b). Contrast of kind vs. contrast of magnitude: The pragmatic accomplishments of irony and hyperbole. *Discourse Processes, 30*, 179–199.

Dews, S., & Winner, E. (1995). Mutiny to meaning: A social function of irony. *Discourse Processes, 19*, 3–19.

Dresher, E., & Hornstein, N. (1976). On some supposed contributions of artificial intelligence to the scientific study of language. *Cognition, 4*, 321–398.

Festinger, L. (1957). *A theory of cognitive dissonance*. Stanford, CA: Stanford University Press.

Gibbs, R. W., Jr. (1986). On the psycholinguistics of sarcasm. *Journal of Experimental Psychology: General, 115*, 3–15.

Gibbs, R. W., Jr. (1994). *The poetics of mind: Figurative thought, language, and understanding*. New York: Cambridge University Press.

Gibbs, R. W., Jr. (2000). Irony in talk among friends. *Metaphor and Symbol, 15*, 5–27.

Kaufer, D. (1977). Irony and rhetorical strategy. *Philosophy and Rhetoric, 10*, 94–98.

Kumon-Nakamura, S., Glucksberg, S., & Brown, M. (1995). How about another piece of pie: The allusional pretense theory of discourse irony. *Journal of Experimental Psychology: General, 124*, 3–121.

Lee, C., & Katz, A. (1998). The differential role of ridicule in sarcasm and irony. *Metaphor and Symbol, 13*, 1–15.

Leggitt, J., & Gibbs, R. W., Jr. (2000). Emotional reactions to verbal irony. *Discourse Processes, 29*, 1–24.

McQuarrie, E., & Mick, D. (1996). On resonances: A critical pluralistic inquiry into advertising rhetoric. Journal of Consumer Research, 19, 180–197.

Petty, R. E., & Cacciopo, J. T. (1986). *Communication and persuasion: Central and peripheral routes to attitude change*. New York: Springer-Verlag.

Roberts, R., & Kreuz, R. (1994). Why people use figurative language? *Psychological Science, 5*, 159–163.

Stewart, A. (2000, February). Mathews/Mark's anti-crusade. *Adweek, 50*, 7.

Stone, J., Aronson, E., Crain, A. L., Winslow, M. P., & Fried, C. B. (1994). Inducing hypocrisy as a means of encouraging young adults to use condoms. *Personality and Social Psychology Bulletin, 20*, 116–126.

Switt, J. (1996). *A modest proposal and other satirical works*. New York: Dover.

Walker, N. (1990). *Feminist alternatives: Irony and fantasy in contemporary novels by women*. Jackson: University of Mississippi Press.

Waugh, E. (1932). *Black mischief*. Boston: Little.

Waugh, E. (1948). *The loved one: An Anglo-American tragedy*. Boston: Little.

Waugh, E. (1930). *Vile bodies*. Boston: Little.

Waugh, E. (1938). *Scoop*. Boston: Little.

Whaley, B., & Holloway, R. (1996). Rebuttal analogy: A theoretical note. *Metaphor and Symbol, 11*, 161–167.

Whaley, B., & Wagner, L. (2000). Rebuttal analogy in persuasive messages: Communicator likeability and cognitive responses. *Journal of Language and Social Psychology, 19*, 66–84.

Winograd, T. (1974). *Five lectures on artificial intelligence* (Memo AIM No. 246). Stanford, CA: Stanford University, Artificial Intelligence Laboratory.

7

Do Men and Women Differ in Their Use of Nonliteral Language When They Talk About Emotions?

Kristen E. Link
State University of New York College at Oswego

Roger J. Kreuz
The University of Memphis

The goal of our research was to determine whether there are gender differences in nonliteral language use when people communicate about emotions. In Experiments 1 and 2, participants watched characters in film clips experience emotional events. In Experiment 3, participants read narratives that were analogous to the film clips. Later, they wrote a description of the character's emotion or a description of how they would have felt in the same situation. There was no correlation between the perceived intensity of the emotion and the amount of nonliteral language in the participants' descriptions, which is problematic for Ortony's (1975) vividness hypothesis. Men used more nonliteral language in descriptions of negative emotions than positive emotions, whereas no difference was found for women. Finally, men tended to use more nonliteral language in descriptions of others' emotions, whereas women tended to use more in descriptions of their own emotions. These findings suggest that men and women do use nonliteral language differently, at least in the context of emotional communication.

153

The communication of emotion can be accomplished in a variety of ways. For example, emotion can be expressed through nonverbal means (e.g., Ekman, Friesan, & Ellsworth, 1972; Izard, 1971) and through language (Rimé, Mesquita, Philippot, & Boca, 1991; Shimanoff, 1985a). This research has documented the characteristics of emotional language, such as which emotions are expressed and to whom they are disclosed. For example, Rimé et al. illustrated that shame is less likely to be discussed than other emotions, and they noted that emotions are typically expressed to a close friend, spouse or partner, or family member.

A great deal of this research has investigated the claim that men and women talk about emotions in different ways. For the most part, this work has not focused on the role of nonliteral, or figurative, language in emotional communication. The purpose of the research presented in this chapter is to explore whether men and women use nonliteral language differently when they are asked to describe emotions. We review the relevant research on gender, emotion, and nonliteral language, and report the results from a series of experiments that were designed to explore whether gender differences exist.

GENDER AND EMOTIONAL LANGUAGE

The research on gender and emotional expression through language has not yet produced a consistent picture. A number of studies have documented gender effects, but they are difficult to summarize simply due to differences in methodology and subject populations.

First, results have varied depending on whether direct or indirect self-report measures were used (LaFrance & Banaji, 1992). With direct self-report measures, participants rate their subjective emotional states or expression. For example, Snell, Miller, and Belk (1988) developed the Emotional Self-Disclosure Scale that measures individual's willingness to disclose eight different emotions to specific individuals (e.g., female friend, spouse or partner, etc.). An investigation of gender differences utilizing this scale have illustrated overall gender differences, with women reporting a greater willingness to disclose their emotions than men (Snell, Miller, Belk, Garcia-Falconi, & Hernandez-Sanchez, 1989). However, Stein and Brodsky (1995) found this difference only when the participants experienced an unpleasant emotion before they filled out the questionnaire. Rimé et al. (1991) also used a direct measure, in which participants recalled emotional experiences and described how the emotions were expressed. These authors found no gender differences regarding how often participants chose to talk about their emotional experiences with others. These results might differ from those reported by Snell et al. (1989) because these participants recalled specific experiences, whereas those in

Snell et al. (1989) had to make a judgment based on their memories of several experiences with a particular emotion. However, both direct measures discussed thus far required that participants rely on their memories to indicate their emotional expressiveness. Feldman Barrett, Robin, Peitromonaco, and Eyssell (1998) used a diary technique in which participants indicated how much they expressed their emotions immediately after every interaction. In this case, women reported that they expressed their emotions more often than men. LaFrance and Banaji (also see Shimanoff, 1985b) suggested that when individuals must make a general rating of their emotionality based on their memories, they are likely to rely on the own gender-based stereotypes of emotional expressiveness.

With indirect self-report measures, individuals' verbalizations are coded for emotion content and scores are derived from this analysis (LaFrance & Banaji, 1992). For example, in Shimanoff (1983, 1985a), participants tape-recorded their conversations outside of the laboratory, and segments of these conversations were analyzed for their emotional content. No overall gender differences were found in terms of the number of affect words (e.g., *angry*, *happy*, and *sad*) used. A similar result was reported by Banaji and LaFrance (1989; cited in LaFrance & Banaji, 1992). Leaper, Carson, Baker, Holliday, and Myers (1995) tape-recorded 5-min conversations between friends in the laboratory. In this case, however, men were found to disclose significantly more private facts and personal thoughts and feelings than women. However, the authors did not distinguish emotional disclosures from other types of disclosures in their analyses. In addition, they did not consider whether men talked more in the conversations in general, allowing for a greater number of disclosures. There is the possibility that a higher proportion of the women's conversation included references to emotion.

Fussell and Moss (1998) used a somewhat different indirect procedure. Film clips were shown to participants who were then asked to describe the emotions in the clips. Results suggest that men and women used the same number of words in their descriptions of emotion. The results of the studies reviewed so far suggest that when participants are asked to estimate how frequently they talk about their emotions in general, greater gender differences are observed than when more objective measures are used (see LaFrance & Banaji, 1992).

In addition, investigations of gender differences in talk about emotions have varied depending on the relationship between the research participants. Researchers have studied the emotional communication of different subject populations, and some have focused on how husbands and wives communicate with one another. Shimanoff (1985b) found that wives reported disclosing significantly more emotions than their husbands. In addition, wives had a more positive attitude toward disclosing vulnerable, hostile, and regret emotions than their husbands. However, when she analyzed their tape-recorded conversations, Shimanoff found no differences in the number of affect words husbands and wives used. However, Notarius and Johnson (1982) found that wives expressed more neutral and negative emotions than their husbands. Consistent findings were reported by Snell et al. (1988) using a direct self-report measure, in which men reported less willingness to disclose negative emotions such as depression, anxiety, anger, and fear to their spouses or partners than women. Other studies have found similar gender differences when couples interact in conflict situations (e.g., Christensen & Heavey, 1990; Kelley et al., 1978; Noller, 1993).

However, studies that did not employ married couples are typically less consistent in terms of the valence of the emotion. For example, Feldman Barrett et al. (1998) reported that women expressed their emotions more than men regardless of the emotion. Similar results were reported by Snell et al. (1989); women reported more willingness to disclose feelings of depression, happiness, anger, calmness, and fear. Men and women were equally willing to disclose jealously, anxiety, and apathy. Somewhat different results were indicated by Brody and Hall (1993), whose review of several studies revealed that women were more likely to express their emotions than men except for anger.

Studies investigating dyads composed of friends or strangers reveal different patterns. Specifically, in a meta-analysis, Dindia and Allen (1992) found greater gender differences in self-disclosure (with women self-disclosing more than men) when the dyads were in relationships than when they were strangers. This suggests that several factors are important when considering the effect of gender on emotional expression. Some of the inconsistencies in the literature may be clarified if the particular type of language that is used in self-disclosures is investigated. That is, research on gender and emotional communication has not specifically focused on the use of nonliteral language. Nonliteral language is used to describe emotion, and this issue is addressed in the next section.

NONLITERAL LANGUAGE AND EMOTION

A consistent finding in the literature is that people find it difficult to express their emotions via literal language (e.g., Bowers, Metts, & Duncanson, 1985) and that nonliteral language may be used for this purpose (e.g., Fainsilber & Ortony, 1987; Gibbs & Nascimento, 1996; Leggitt & Gibbs, 2000; McMullen & Conway, 1996). Examples of nonliteral language include *metaphor* (e.g., "His anger was a wild animal"), *simile* (e.g., "She was like a kid in a candy store"), *idiom* (e.g., "He blew his top"), and *hyperbole* (e.g., "She was as high as the clouds"). Some of these forms of nonliteral language (e.g., metaphor and simile) are often used to express abstract ideas, like emotions, that are difficult to convey using literal language. In addition, nonliteral language might be more useful to distinguish different intensities of the same emotion. For example, the simile "She was like a kid in a candy store" better captures the degree of happiness than the literal expression "She was really happy." These and other types of nonliteral language have been explored in the psychological literature (for a review, see Gibbs, 1994).

Ortony (1975, p. 45) suggested that metaphor and simile may be used to communicate ideas that are difficult to verbalize using literal language (i.e., the *inexpressibility hypothesis*), and they may help communicate one's subjective experience more vividly (i.e., the *vividness hypothesis*). To test these ideas, Fainsilber and Ortony (1987) had participants describe their actions and feelings for mild and intense experiences of positive and negative emotions. The authors found that more metaphors were used in descriptions of feelings than in descriptions of actions, supporting the inexpressibility hypothesis. In addition, more metaphors were used in descriptions of intense emotional experiences than mild ones, supporting the vividness hypothesis. Anderson and Leaper (1998) provided additional evidence that could support the inexpressibility hypothesis. In their study, direct and indirect references to emotion were coded in tape-recorded conversations between pairs of friends. Direct references were defined as specific emotion terms (e.g., *angry*, *scared*, and *happy*), whereas indirect references included words or phrases that "substituted for, or related to, an emotion term," including *annoyed*, *bummed*, and "other phrases and metaphors that referred to emotion terms" (p. 428). Indirect references, although not exclusively nonliteral, were more common than direct references, particularly for negative emotions. It is clear from these studies that nonliteral language is very commonly employed to describe affective states.

MOTIVATION AND DESIGN

The purpose of our research was to further explore how nonliteral language is used in the context of emotional expression. Experiment 1 was designed to test Ortony's (1975) vividness hypothesis, using a different methodology and procedure to assess the generalizability of this effect. In addition, materials for later experiments were selected in this experiment. Experiments 2 and 3 were designed to examine whether men and women use nonliteral language in emotional communication in different ways. We showed that there are many inconsistencies in the gender and emotional expression literature, many of which are explained by factors such as the relationship between the conversation partners and the gender makeup of the dyad. However, perhaps these inconsistencies also result from not considering the use of nonliteral language in emotional disclosures. In this study we examined whether nonliteral language plays a differential role in how men and women express their emotion through language; the particular emotional experience being described and the individual to whom it is described were held constant.

Experiments on gender differences in emotional expression via nonliteral language are needed due to limitations in previous research. For example, Shimanoff (1983, 1985a, 1985b) explicitly removed nonliteral language from her analysis of emotional communication in conversations. In Anderson and Leaper's (1998) analysis of direct and indirect references, nonliteral language was included, but it was collapsed with other indirect, but literal forms. Other researchers who have examined the role of nonliteral language in emotional expression have looked only at metaphor (Fainsilber & Ortony, 1987; Gibbs & Nascimento, 1996; Williams-Whitney, Mio, & Whitney, 1992). In addition, researchers who have examined nonliteral language more generally have not included analyses of different types of nonliteral expressions (Fussell & Moss, 1998). The possibility that certain forms of nonliteral language are used more often than others to express emotion has not been examined.

Because gender effects may be manifested in different ways, we chose to manipulate both perspective and valence in Experiments 2 and 3. *Perspective* refers to whether a person is reporting his or her emotional experience or the experience of someone else. Perspective was manipulated by Williams-Whitney et al. (1992) and was shown to affect the amount of nonliteral language that participants used. Specifically, nonexpert writers used more nonliteral language when describing their own emotions than others' emotions. Shimanoff (1983) also examined the role of perspective and found that it interacted with gender: Men talked more about their own emotion than others' emotions, whereas there was no difference for women.

Valence refers to whether an emotion is positive or negative. It, too, has been shown to affect emotional communication. Fussell and Moss (1998) found that participants used more nonliteral language in their descriptions of negative emotions, and Anderson and Leaper (1998) found that negative emotions were particularly likely to be referenced indirectly. Other researchers (Notarius & Johnson, 1982; Shimanoff, 1983, 1985b) have found that women expressed more negative emotions than men, but only when the participants were married couples.

Finally, participants' verbal ability was measured in Experiments 2 and 3. This individual difference has been used as a control in some previous work on nonliteral language (e.g., Trick & Katz, 1986). We controlled for verbal ability for two reasons. First, individuals with high verbal ability may be more likely to use nonliteral language than individuals with low verbal ability. In addition, there is a possible confound with gender. For example, if women used more nonliteral language in their descriptions, then it might be a true gender effect or simply a reflection of higher verbal ability, an effect that has been repeatedly demonstrated (e.g., Hyde & Linn, 1988).

We chose to use film clips to elicit descriptions of emotions in Experiments 1 and 2. This is similar to the approach used by Fussell and Moss (1998) who argued that these more objective stimuli avoid the variability inherent in autobiographical experiences of emotions. We also chose to elicit descriptions of emotions using narrative descriptions of the film clips in Experiment 3. Text-based stimuli have been used previously to elicit nonliteral language. Gibbs and Nascimento (1996, Experiment 4) used love poetry to elicit conceptual metaphors, and Williams-Whitney et al. (1992) employed short scenarios to elicit descriptions of emotions.

It may be that individuals process films and texts in different ways. On the one hand, films can provide a very rich sensory experience. On the other hand, texts can provide an equally rich experience if the reader creates a fleshed-out situation model (Kintsch, 1998). These differences between films and texts may affect how people process them. Evidence for such differences has been reported by Pezdek and her colleagues (Pezdek, Lehrer, & Simon, 1984; Pezdek, Simon, Stoeckert, & Kiely, 1987). They reported that the comprehension processes involved in watching television differ from those involved in reading narrative texts. We hypothesize that these processing differences may influence the language people use to describe these experiences. Therefore, both film clips and narratives were utilized in our research to assess the existence of any gender effects.

It is difficult to derive predictions about men's and women's use of nonliteral language in their expression of emotion because of the lack of empirical research on the topic. However, two opposing hypotheses can be generated. First, because women experience emotions more intensely (e.g., Brody & Hall, 1993) and descriptions of intense emotions are more likely to contain nonliteral language (Fainsilber & Ortony, 1987), one might conclude that women's linguistic expressions of emotion will contain more nonliteral language. Second, because there is a sex-role expectation for men to control their emotional expression (except for anger; see Brody & Hall, 1993, for a review), they may be more likely to use indirect methods of expression, including nonliteral language. To the degree that the discomfort involved with men's expression of emotion is face threatening, the use of an off-record speech act might be warranted. Brown and Levinson (1987) described several off-record strategies that employ nonliteral language (e.g., metaphor and hyperbole). Men may resort to using nonliteral language in such cases, particularly in descriptions of their own emotions.

EXPERIMENT 1

This experiment was designed to test Ortony's (1975) vividness hypothesis and to select materials for later experiments. Thirty-two undergraduate introductory psychology students from the University of Memphis participated for course credit. Seventeen excerpts from 17 different films were used. The films were contemporary English-language productions (e.g., *Steel Magnolias*, Stark & Ross, 1998, and *The Shawshank Redemption*, Glotzer, Lester, Marvin, & Dourabont, 1994) and were chosen from a variety of genres. The films were chosen based on suggestions made by colleagues of the authors and the authors themselves, who recalled particularly emotional scenes in movies. The length of the films clips ranged from 35 s to 4 min (M = 2 min 16 s, SD = 55 s). The clips contained characters experiencing a variety of emotions. The length of each clip and the emotion represented by each clip appears in Appendix A.

Participants watched the film clips in small groups. After each clip was presented, they provided a written description of the emotion that was being experienced by the specified character in the clip. Participants then wrote down the name of the emotion that they perceived the character was experiencing. Next, they rated, on a 6-point Likert scale, the intensity of the emotion and the genuineness of the emotional display. Finally, participants indicated whether they had previously seen the film from which the clip was drawn.

Test of the Vividness Hypothesis

For the purposes of determining reliability, the participants' descriptions were divided into sentences. In most cases, sentences were defined by terminal punctuation (i.e., periods, question marks, and exclamation points). However, when participants did not use proper punctuation, their contributions were divided into sentence units by two judges based on the following criteria: (a) a topic shift and/or (b) a capitalized first word in the absence of punctuation. In these cases, divisions were made conservatively rather than marking all possible sentences.

We identified the metaphors and similes in participants' descriptions to evaluate Ortony's (1975) vividness hypothesis, which predicts that metaphors and similes should be used more frequently to describe emotionally intense experiences. Two independent judges identified the metaphors and similes in each sentence. Nonliteral expressions that were repetitions of characters' statements were not coded. The judges agreed 86% of the time on the number of nonliteral expressions in each sentence. The correlation between the coders was 0.53, indicating a modest level of agreement (Bakeman & Gottman, 1986). However, the judges discussed all disagreements until 100% agreement was reached, and only those expressions that were agreed upon as being nonliteral were included in the analyses. A total of 234 metaphors and 58 similes were identified. The mean number of metaphors and similes per 100 words was 1.75 (SD = 2.96).

The number of metaphors and similes per 100 words used by each participant for each clip was calculated. This metric of nonliteral language use was chosen to be used in this and further analyses because it controlled for the number of words in participants' descriptions, and it was deemed meaningful and easily interpretable. The vividness hypothesis predicts a positive correlation between the proportion of metaphors and similes produced and the perceived intensity of each clip, irrespective of the valence of the emotion. Such a relationship was not supported by these data, $r(544) = -0.06$, ns.

The film clips used in this experiment contained emotional experiences that varied in perceived intensity. However, essentially no relationship was found between the intensity of the emotion and the amount of nonliteral language used to describe it. This lack of correlation is probably not due to a restriction of range because participants used the entire intensity scale ($M = 4.62$, $SD = 1.35$) and varied greatly in the number of metaphors and similes they employed. Therefore, a strong form of the vividness hypothesis, which predicts more nonliteral language with increasing emotional intensity, was not supported.

Selection of Materials for Experiment 2

Another goal of this experiment was to select 8 film clips (4 positive and 4 negative) from this set of 17 to be used in Experiment 2 by measuring the nonliteral language produced by the participants and examining the ratings of the clips.

The nonliteral expressions in participants' descriptions were identified by one judge using a taxonomy developed by Kreuz, Roberts, Johnson, and Bertus (1996). Eight forms of nonliteral language were identified: hyperbole, idiom, indirect request, irony, metaphor, rhetorical question, simile, and understatement. Examples and definitions of these eight forms appear in Table 7.1. The mean number of nonliteral expressions per 100 words was 1.72 ($SD = 2.89$). Mean genuineness ($M = 4.84$, $SD = 1.20$) and intensity ($M = 4.62$, $SD = 1.35$) ratings were also calculated across all film clips and participants.

To determine whether participants interpreted the emotional experiences of the characters in the clips uniformly, the most common emotion label (e.g., *happiness*) for each clip was determined. The percentage of participants who provided this label was averaged across the clips ($M = 63.53$, $SD = 19.90$). Because two thirds of the participants agreed on each label, it seems likely that the emotions in these clips were highly interpretable.

Previous exposure to the films may be a confound in the data provided by the participants. It may be that individuals who have seen the films can draw on a richer context for their descriptions than subjects who saw only clips from these films. For example, genuineness ratings might be inflated for participants who had seen the entire film from which a clip was drawn. Therefore, we conducted analyses to determine whether this problem exists.

TABLE 7.1
Examples and Definitions of Nonliteral Language Types

Figure	Definition	Example
Hyperbole	Deliberate overemphasis	"It takes *all of his strength* to write his letter."
Idiom	Conventionalized expression	"He doesn't think sorry will *cut it*."
Indirect request	Requests stated as questions about ability	*Do you have the time?*
Irony	Opposite meaning expressed	*Thanks for all your help!*
Metaphor	Implicit comparison	"Through all of it I would be *empty*."
Rhetorical question	Assertions framed as questions	"*What did I do wrong?*"
Simile	Explicit comparison	"I would feel *like my heart will just jump out of my chest* ..."
Understatement	Deliberate underemphasis	"He clearly has *issues*." [Written about a suicidal character]

Note. Examples within quotations were taken from Experiments 2 and 3. Nonliteral expressions are italicized.

A 17 (film) × 2 (seen previously vs. not seen) analysis of variance (ANOVA) was performed for each dependent measure, with the seen versus not seen variable nested within each film. Therefore, a subject might have been in the seen condition for one film but in the not seen condition for another film. Participants who had previously seen a film rated the clip from that film as being more intense ($M = 4.86$, $SD = 1.31$) than participants who had not seen the film ($M = 4.56$, $SD = 1.36$), and the difference was significant, $F(1, 507) = 5.97$, $p < .05$.[1] Participants who had previously seen a film also rated the clip from that film as being more genuine ($M = 5.20$, $SD = 1.05$) than participants who had not ($M = 4.65$, $SD = 1.27$); once again, the difference was significant, $F(1, 507) = 18.99$, $p < .001$. A lack of an interaction in both analyses ($Fs < 1$) indicates that films clips rated as more intense and genuine by participants who had seen the films were also rated as more intense and genuine by participants who had not seen the films.

Separate mean nonliteral language scores were calculated for participants who had seen the films ($M = 1.72$, $SD = 2.91$) and for participants who had not seen the films ($M = 1.73$, $SD = 2.89$). A 17 × 2 ANOVA revealed no main effect of having previously seen the films, $F(1, 507) = 1.28$,

[1]Large degrees of freedom resulted from subjects being nested within each film.

ns, and no interaction, $F(16, 507) = 1.16$, *ns*. These results indicate that whether participants had previously seen the films did not affect the amount of nonliteral language that they produced.

Mean genuineness and intensity ratings, as well as amount of nonliteral language, were calculated for each clip. Because the two ratings were relatively high and correlated, $r(17) = 0.77$, the selection of clips for later experiments was based on two other criteria: the amount of nonliteral language the clips elicited and the amount of nonliteral language within the clips themselves. Clips that contained a significant amount of nonliteral language were eliminated. We then selected the four positive emotion clips that had elicited the most nonliteral language from the participants so that they would be likely to elicit nonliteral expressions in Experiment 2. The emotions depicted in these clips were *happiness* and *love*. In a similar way, four negative emotion clips, depicting *sadness* and *anxiety*, were chosen.

EXPERIMENT 2

We addressed the question of whether men and women differ in their use of nonliteral language when describing positive and negative emotions from different perspectives in Experiment 2. Participants were presented with depictions of emotional experiences in film clips selected from Experiment 1. They were asked to describe the emotions as experienced by the character or as the participants would have experienced them. These descriptions were analyzed to determine the effects of gender, valence, and perspective on the use of nonliteral language in descriptions of emotion.

Participants were 20 male and 20 female undergraduate students from The University of Memphis taking an introductory psychology course and participating for course credit. The eight film clips selected from Experiment 1 were used. The clips ranged in length from 1 min 21 s to 4 min ($M = 2$ min 52 s, $SD = 53$ s). (See Appendix A for additional information.) Four different random orders of the film clips were recorded onto videotape. A practice clip (i.e., *The Shining*, Fryer et al., 1980) was placed at the beginning of each tape.

Participants were tested in small groups. They first received the Author Recognition Test (ART; Stanovich & West, 1989), which is a measure of exposure to print. The ART has been shown to correlate significantly with measures of verbal ability (Stanovich & Cunningham, 1992). For example, the correlations between the ART and two measures of verbal ability—the Nelson–Denny vocabulary subtest and a verbal fluency task in which participants wrote down as many words as they could in a given category—were 0.60 and 0.40, respectively. We used the ART to control for individual and possible gender differences in verbal ability.

Participants viewed the practice clip and wrote a description of how the specified character was feeling. The experimenter checked each participant's description to ensure that they were following directions, and not simply describing the depicted events. The participants then watched the eight film clips. After each clip, participants were given 5 min to (a) write a description of the emotional experience of the character in the film clip (the other condition) or (b) imagine themselves in the same situation, and write a description of how they would feel (the self condition). Across the four tapes, each clip appeared equally often in each condition. Each participant responded with a self description for two positive and two negative clips and with an other description for two positive and two negative clips.

The design was a 2 × 2 × 2 mixed design with gender (male vs. female) as the between-subject factor and valence of the emotion (positive vs. negative) and perspective (self vs. other) as the two within-subjects factors.

The mean ART score was 8.95 ($SD = 6.52$). Men's ($M = 9.65, SD = 7.41$) and women's ($M = 8.25, SD = 5.58$) scores on the ART did not differ significantly, $t(38) = 0.68$, ns. However, ART scores were included as a covariate in later analyses to control for individual differences in verbal ability.

As in Experiment 1, eight forms of nonliteral language were coded by two independent judges. The judges agreed with each other 72% of the time on the number of nonliteral expressions in each sentence. The correlation between the judges was modest ($r = 0.57$). However, the judges discussed all disagreements until 99.7% agreement was reached. Only two instances of disagreement were left unresolved, and these were not included in the analyses. A total of 899 nonliteral expressions were identified.

Participants indicated whether they had previously seen the films so that we could assess whether this factor affected their written descriptions. The amount of nonliteral language produced in each description was calculated as in Experiment 1 (i.e., mean number of nonliteral expressions per 100 words). Separate mean nonliteral language scores were calculated for participants who had seen the films ($M = 3.69, SD = 4.40$) and for participants who had not seen the films ($M = 3.82, SD = 3.63$). An 8 (film) × 2 (seen previously vs. not seen) ANOVA revealed no significant main effect of prior viewing, $F(1, 303) < 1$, and no significant interaction, $F(7, 303) = 1.49$, ns.

A similar analysis was performed to determine whether having previously seen the films influenced the number of words participants used in their descriptions. The analysis revealed a significant main effect of having previously seen the films, $F(1, 302) = 15.32, p < .001$. That is, participants who had seen the films used significantly more words ($M = 82.25, SD = 45.86$) in their descriptions than participants who had not seen the films ($M = 67.83, SD = 29.57$). However, upon inspection of the data, an outlier was identified who had seen seven of the eight films and whose shortest description (232 words) was 101 words longer than the longest description of any other participant. In addition, this participant used a mean of 264.13 words ($SD = 20.99$) per description, compared to the remaining participants' mean of 69.88 (SD = 24.27). When the outlier was removed from the analysis, the mean number of words used by participants who saw the films was 72.40 (SD = 22.51), and the mean number of words used by participants who did not see the films was 67.56 (SD = 25.62). This difference was not significant, $F(1, 294)$ = 2.57, ns. Therefore, whether participants previously saw the film was not included in the remaining analyses in which repeated measures analyses could be performed (and each participant could act as his or her own control).

The amount of nonliteral language produced was analyzed with a 2 (gender) × 2 (valence) × 2 (perspective) mixed-design analysis of covariance (ANCOVA), with ART scores as the covariate. The analysis was performed with both subjects (F_1) and items (i.e., the film clips; F_2) as random factors (Clark, 1973). There was a significant gender × valence interaction, $F_1(1, 37)$ = 7.66, $p < .01$ (see Fig. 7.1), which was marginally significant in the item analysis, $F_2(1, 6)$ = 5.39, $p = .059$. Follow-up tests performed by subjects indicated that men used significantly more nonliteral language when describing negative emotions (M = 4.81, SD = 2.40) than positive emotions (M = 2.60, SD = 2.19), $F_1(1, 38)$ = 25.09, $p < .001$. Women, however, did not differ in the amount of nonliteral language used in descriptions of negative (M = 4.02, SD = 2.59) and positive (M = 3.61, SD = 3.20) emotions, $F_1(1, 38)$ < 1. Men and women did not differ significantly in the amount of nonliteral language used to describe either positive, $F(1, 37)$ = 1.03, ns or negative emotions, $F(1, 37)$ < 1.

The number of words used in each participant's description was analyzed with a 2 (gender) × 2 (valence) × 2 (perspective) mixed-design ANCOVA, with ART scores as the covariate. There were no significant effects in the subject analysis. Note that men and women did not differ in the number of words they used to describe emotions. This is consistent with many of the studies reviewed by James and Drakich (1993). However, there was a main effect of gender in the item analysis, $F_2(1, 6)$ = 148.83, $p < .001$, with women using more words (M = 82.89, SD = 47.00) in their descriptions than men (M = 66.59, SD = 17.59). This may be due to the fact that the ART scores could not be used as a covariate in the item analysis because the items (i.e., the film clips) were the cases rather than the participants. Therefore, individual differences in verbal ability were not controlled. For example, the outlier discussed earlier may be driving this effect; she wrote a large amount for each clip, which inflated the mean for the women, but we could not control for her verbal ability in the item analysis, which also may have been higher than average. Whatever the reason for the effect, this finding was only significant in the item analysis and, therefore, may not generalize to other participant populations.

Experiment 2 revealed that men are more likely to use nonliteral language when describing negative than positive emotional experiences. This is consistent with the idea that men are less comfortable when they describe

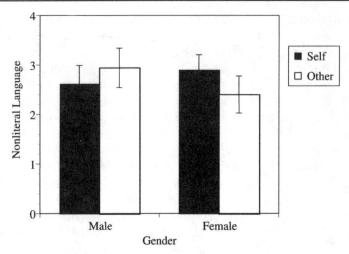

FIG. 7.1 Mean number of nonliteral expressions per 100 words for men and women when describing positive and negative emotions. Error bars are standard errors.

negative emotions (e.g., Shimanoff, 1985b). As a result, men may resort to using nonliteral language in such cases. Our findings support the notion that nonliteral language is used in descriptions of emotion as a means of being indirect.

EXPERIMENT 3

Given that films differ from other types of aesthetic experience, it is worth exploring the nonliteral language elicited by narrative descriptions of emotional experiences. As mentioned earlier, the processing of films and texts may lead to different representations, and it may cause people to talk about them in different ways. Experiment 3 was designed to explore whether text versions of the film clips would elicit descriptions in the same way or whether differences between text and film would lead to a different pattern of results.

Participants were 20 male and 20 female undergraduates from the University of Memphis taking an introductory psychology course and participating for course credit. A narrative was created for each film clip in Experiment 2. The narratives, containing verbatim dialogue, actions, and descriptions of the scene, served as stimuli. The narratives ranged from 335 to 845 words ($M = 582.63$, $SD = 200.59$). A pilot study was conducted to ensure that the narratives closely corresponded to the film clips. Twenty-four individuals from the same population that participated in the experiments rated how well the narratives represented the film clips. On a six-point scale ranging from 1 (*low match*) to 6 (*perfect match*), the mean correspondence rating was 5.48 ($SD = 0.77$). A sample narrative appears in Appendix B. Four different random orders of the narratives were prepared, and a practice narrative began each set.

Participants were tested in small groups. They first received the ART. Participants then read the practice narrative and wrote a description of how the specified character was feeling. The experimenter checked each participant's description to ensure that they were following directions. The participants then read the eight narratives. They were given 1 min, 30 sec to read each page of the narratives. After each narrative, participants were given 5 min to write a description in either the self or other condition. Across the four different random orders, each narrative appeared equally often in each condition such that each participant responded with a self description for two positive and two negative clips and with an other description for two positive and two negative clips.

The mean ART score was 9.28 ($SD = 5.19$). As in Experiment 2, men's ($M = 9.55, SD = 5.72$) and women's ($M = 9.00, SD = 4.75$) scores on the ART did not differ significantly, $t(38) = 0.331$, *ns*.

The eight types of nonliteral language were coded by the same judges as in Experiments 1 and 2. The judges agreed with each other 82% of the time on the number of nonliteral expressions in each sentence. The correlation between the judges was 0.68. As before, the judges discussed all disagreements until 100% agreement was reached. A total of 595 nonliteral expressions were identified.

The same procedure as in Experiment 2 was used to analyze the effect of having previously seen the films on which the narratives were based. The mean nonliteral language score and mean number of words used for participants who had seen the films ($M = 2.60, SD = 2.53; M = 67.71, SD = 23.9$; respectively) and for participants who had not seen the films ($M = 3.00$, $SD = 3.01; M = 68.94, SD = 27.80$; respectively) were compared. Separate 8 (film) × 2 (previously seen vs. not seen) ANOVAs revealed no main effects, $Fs < 1$, and no interactions, $Fs < 1$. Therefore, whether participants previously saw the film was not included in the analyses.

The amount of nonliteral language was calculated and analyzed as in Experiment 2. There was a marginally significant gender × perspective interaction, $F_1(1, 37) = 4.00, p = .053$ (see Fig. 7.2). This interaction was not significant in the item analysis, $F_2(1, 6) = 2.77$, *ns*. Follow-up tests produced no significant simple effects. However, it appears that, although men tend to use more nonliteral language to describe others' emotions ($M = 2.95$, $SD = 1.78$) than their own emotions ($M = 2.66, SD = 1.65$), women tend to use more nonliteral language to describe their own emotions ($M = 2.87$, $SD = 1.37$) than others' emotions ($M = 2.39, SD = 1.68$). In addition, an item analysis revealed a significant main effect of valence, $F_2(1, 6) = 9.18$,

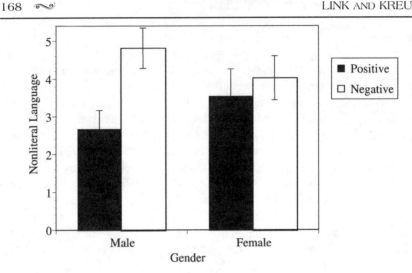

FIG. 7.2 Mean number of nonliteral expressions per 100 words for men and women when describing their own and others' emotions. Error bars are standard errors.

$p < .05$ in which more nonliteral language was used in descriptions of negative emotions ($M = 3.21$, $SD = 2.02$) than positive emotions ($M = 2.22$, $SD = 1.54$). This finding is consistent with that of Fussell and Moss (1998).

The number of words used in each participant's description was calculated and analyzed with a 2 (gender) × 2 (valence) × 2 (perspective) mixed-design ANCOVA, with ART scores as the covariate. There were no significant effects in the subject analysis. However, the ART proved to be a significant predictor of the number of words participants used in their descriptions, $F(1, 37) = 5.02$, $p < .05$. The number of words used in descriptions of emotions increased as ART scores increased. There was a marginally significant gender × valence interaction in the item analysis, $F_2(1, 6) = 5.67$, $p = .055$; women used more words in their descriptions of negative emotions ($M = 70.94$, $SD = 28.07$) than men ($M = 65.34$, $SD = 21.35$), whereas the number of words used for describing positive emotions did not differ (Ms = 68.48 and 68.65, SDs = 27.78 and 26.25, respectively).

In participants' descriptions from both Experiments 2 and 3, six of the eight types of nonliteral expressions shown in Table 7.1 were identified: metaphor, hyperbole, idiom, simile, rhetorical question and understatement. The mean number of nonliteral expressions per 100 words was 3.76 ($SD = 4.01$) in Experiment 2 and 2.72 ($SD = 2.69$) in Experiment 3, and this difference is significant, $F(1, 75) = 5.31$, $p < .05$. This effect supports the idea that the film clips and narratives were processed differently, resulting in differential amounts of nonliteral language in the participants' descriptions.

The data from these two studies were collapsed to allow the relative frequencies of the smaller nonliteral language categories to be assessed. These frequencies appear in Fig. 7.3. A 5 (type of nonliteral expression) × 2 (gender) repeated measures ANCOVA with ART scores as the covariate was performed (the two instances of understatement were not included in the analysis). The analysis revealed significant differences among the nonliteral expressions in their rate of use, $F(2.1, 163.9) = 12.43, p < .001.$[2] Neither the main effect of gender nor the interaction was significant, $Fs < 1$.

Post hoc pairwise comparisons revealed that metaphors were used significantly more often than any other type of expression. The frequency of use for hyperbole, similes, and idioms did not differ, but each was used significantly more often than rhetorical questions. The relative frequencies of each type of nonliteral expression are similar to those found in another area of study. Specifically, Kreuz et al. (1996) found that, in a literary corpus, metaphor was used most frequently, followed by hyperbole, idiom, rhetorical questions, simile, irony, understatement, and indirect requests. There are, therefore, similarities in the use of nonliteral language in two very different domains.

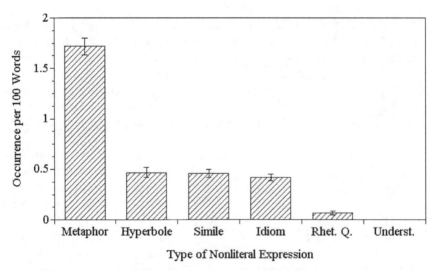

FIG. 7.3   Mean number of each type of nonliteral expressions per 100 words in Experiments 2 and 3. Error bars are standard errors.

---

[2]Degrees of freedom were adjusted using the Greenhouse-Geisser epsilon because the assumption of sphericity was not met.

DISCUSSION

The results from these experiments provide some evidence about how individuals use nonliteral language to describe emotions. One result that is surprising is the test of Ortony's (1975) vividness hypothesis in Experiment 1. We found essentially no relationship between the intensity of the emotion and the amount of nonliteral language used. However, Fainsilber and Ortony (1987) found support for the vividness hypothesis using autobiographical emotional experiences in which participants identified mild and intense experiences of a specific emotion and described them.

The results of the current study may differ from Fainsilber and Ortony's (1987) work because of differences in methodologies. Perhaps the effect of intensity on nonliteral language use only occurs in autobiographical emotional experiences. That is, in our experiment, participants described how another person was feeling, whereas in Fainsilber and Ortony's study, participants described their own feelings. One may argue, however, that more objective stimuli were used in Experiment 1 because the descriptions did not rely on idiosyncratic autobiographical memories (Fussell & Moss, 1998). Therefore, variations in intensity were more tightly controlled in our experiment, in that we did not rely on participant's intuitions of what constitutes a mild or an intense emotional experience.

Note that the amount of nonliteral language used by the participants was relatively high. In Experiments 2 and 3, the participants produced a figure of speech once every 31 words. This compares to a rate of one figure of speech per 37 words in a corpus of contemporary short stories (Kreuz et al., 1996). In other words, the college students used more nonliteral language than published authors. This counterintuitive finding can be explained by the task: The participants were specifically describing emotions, whereas authors must tell a complete story.

More important, our results shed light on several questions concerning nonliteral language, gender, and emotion. First, they illustrate that men and women, in general, do not use different amounts of nonliteral language, and men and women do not differ in their preference for a certain type of nonliteral expression. In addition, men and women did not differ in the number of words they used in their descriptions of emotion. This could be viewed as evidence against gender differences in emotional communication, at least when descriptions of emotions are obligatory. This result is consistent with Anderson and Leaper (1998), who suggested that their lack of gender differences in emotional expression might have been due to task demands. Specifically, "when people are placed in a situation where self-disclosure is expected, women and men self-disclose similarly" (p. 423). However, according to other researchers, if men tend to shun discussions of emotion (e.g., Gallois, 1993), they should say as little as possible even when obliged to describe emotions.

This lack of gender differences, however, must be qualified by the two interactions involving gender. Specifically, the results from Experiment 2 revealed that men produced more nonliteral language when they described negative emotions than when they described positive emotions. Women, however, used the same amount of nonliteral language when they described positive and negative emotions (see Fig. 7.1). This finding was obtained even when controlling for differences in verbal ability. Some of the previous studies that examined only literal language found that men and women (specifically, unmarried couples) in a natural setting talk about positive and negative emotions with equal frequency (e.g., Shimanoff, 1983), whereas others indicate that women are more likely to disclose negative emotions than men (e.g., Shimanoff, 1985b; Snell et al., 1989). Our results support those of the first group of researchers: Men and women did not differ in the number of words they used to describe positive and negative emotions. However, the analysis of nonliteral language revealed a different pattern; men used more figurative language in their descriptions of negative emotion, whereas this difference was not significant for women. It is possible that men's negative attitude toward disclosing negative emotions (Shimanoff, 1985b) makes them prefer to be less direct and, hence, use more nonliteral language in these cases. Alternatively, this difference in nonliteral language use might explain why some researchers find that women are more likely to disclose negative emotion. Because this research has typically disregarded nonliteral expressions, much of what a man says about negative emotions is disregarded. It may be, then, that men and women are more similar in the amount they talk about positive and negative emotions (as was found in this study with respect to the number of words used to describe emotions), but the difference lies in how they talk about these emotions.

Experiment 3 also revealed a marginally significant gender × perspective interaction. Men tended to use more nonliteral language when they described others' emotions while women tended to use more nonliteral language when they described their own emotions. With a similar population, Williams-Whitney et al. (1992) found that participants used more nonliteral language in descriptions of their own emotions than another person's emotions. This pattern was found only for the women in Experiment 3. This difference for men may be due to the specific emotions used in the two studies. Specifically, Williams-Whitney et al. used the emotions *pride* and *shame*, whereas Experiment 3 used emotions (e.g., *happiness* and *sadness*) that may have been perceived differently. This is particularly important given gender differences reported by Brody and Hall (1993) in which men were more likely than women to express outwardly directed emotions, such as pride, whereas women were more likely to express more inwardly directed emotions, such as shame. The effect of the particular emotion needs to be investigated more thoroughly in future research. However, a possible explanation for our finding is that women's tendency to use more nonliteral language in descriptions of their own emotions reflects their tendency to experience emotions more intensely.

Shimanoff (1983) found that men talked more about their own emotions in naturally occurring conversations. As previously noted, she did not analyze nonliteral language. Therefore, it could be that more of what men said about others' emotions was eliminated from her analysis than what women said about others' emotions. Therefore, a similar conclusion might be drawn: Men and women do not differ in the amount of talk about their own and others' emotions but in how they talk about their own and others' emotions. Specifically, men use more indirect, nonliteral forms of speech when they talk about others' emotions. Perhaps because of societal expectations, they do not feel like experts in the area of emotion, resulting in the tendency to talk indirectly about how others feel.

Therefore, both interactions, along with data from other experiments that show gender differences, seem to indicate that it is not the amount of emotional communication that differs, but the way in which men and women describe emotion. Perhaps the differences between men and women in the amount of emotional communication appear because indirect references to emotion have been disregarded in analyses of emotional communication, and these differences would disappear if both literal and nonliteral expressions were included. Of course, this conjecture needs to be tested empirically.

Finally, although the gender × valence and gender × perspective interactions were not found in both experiments, it is important to remember that the stimuli used in Experiments 2 and 3 were not the same. Specifically, participants in Experiment 2 saw and heard the actors experiencing emotions, whereas those in Experiment 3 simply read about these characters. Previous research has documented differences in how spoken and written language are processed (Ferreira & Anes, 1994; Pezdek et al., 1984; Pezdek et al., 1987). Perhaps such differences affected the participants' task of describing emotions. In addition, there are four cinematic devices that are available to film makers, which are not available to writers, that aid in conveying the events in a story (Magliano, Dijkstra, & Zwaan, 1996): *mise en scène* (i.e., setting design, costume and make-up, lighting, and direction of actors), montage (i.e., shots edited together), cinematography (i.e., aspects of filming including film stock, camera speed, and lens) and framing (i.e., placement and focus of camera); and sound (i.e., dialogue, external noises, and music). These devices may function to more readily portray emotion than a transcription of a film. Specifically, these devices include the use of music, facial expressions, and prosodic and paralinguistic cues that are not easily translated into the written word. Bourg (1996) stated that "in order to interpret the emotional states of others, one must first engage in the cognitive processes of perceiving and discriminating cues" (p. 243). Therefore, because these additional cues are present in the film clips, the task of inferring the characters' emotions and how intensely the character is experiencing the emotion becomes easier. For example, the film clips may have provided a richer sensory experience, and the intensity of the emotions may have come across more clearly, resulting in a greater reliance on nonliteral language use to describe these emotions. Evidence for this suggestion can be found in the differential amounts of nonliteral language produced in the two experiments. Participants who saw the film clips generated 28% more nonliteral expressions than participants who read the narratives.

These experiments provide some support for the existence of gender differences in emotional communication and the role that nonliteral language plays. Researchers need to consider linguistic emotional expression not only in terms of how frequently words describing affect are used, but also in terms of the nonliteral language that is used to describe emotions. It has been illustrated, both in our research and elsewhere (Fainsilber & Ortony, 1987; Gibbs & Nascimento, 1996; Ortony, 1975; Williams-Whitney et al., 1992), that nonliteral language is an important part of expressing one's emotions. The larger question of whether there are gender differences in the use of nonliteral language across different discourse contexts remains to be investigated. In the specific realm of describing emotional experiences, however, evidence has been provided that men and women do use nonliteral language differently.

Roberts and Kreuz (1994) suggested that different types of nonliteral expressions can be used to fulfill different discourse goals. One might expect that gender differences exist depending on both the discourse context and the discourse goals of the speaker. Men and women may have different discourse goals in the same discourse context. Specifically, men's use of nonliteral language may have depended on whether they wished to be more or less expressive about the emotion that they were describing. In other discourse contexts, gender differences may be present or absent depending on whether men's and women's discourse goals are similar or dissimilar. For example, Tannen's (1990) gender-as-culture hypothesis has implications for the way men and women approach conversations in general. According to this hypothesis, men are more likely than women "to manage the discourse," a discourse goal discussed by Roberts and Kreuz (p. 161). Because this discourse goal can be achieved through the use of rhetorical questions (Roberts & Kreuz), men might use rhetorical questions more often than women in conversations. Therefore, the question of gender differences in nonliteral language use might be addressed with future studies that integrate research on differences in men's and women's discourse goals and show how these goals are achieved using nonliteral language.

ACKNOWLEDGMENTS

We thank Craig Stewart for his assistance in nonliteral language coding and Katherine Kitzmann and Brent Olde for helpful comments on earlier versions of this chapter. This research was supported by a Center of Excellence grant to the Department of Psychology at the University of Memphis by the state of Tennessee.

Correspondence concerning this chapter should be addressed to Kristen E. Link, Department of Psychology, State University of New York College at Oswego, Oswego, NY 13126. E-mail: klink@oswego.edu

REFERENCES

Anderson, K. J., & Leaper, C. (1998). Emotion talk between same- and mixed-gender friends: Form and function. *Journal of Language and Social Psychology, 17,* 419–448.

Bakeman, R., & Gottman, J. M. (1986). *Observing interaction: An introduction to sequential analysis.* Cambridge, England: Cambridge University Press.

Banaji, M., & LaFrance, M. (1989, May). *Gender differences and emotionality: Differences in verbal expression and similarities in rated intensity.* Paper presented at the meeting of the Eastern Psychological Association, Boston.

Bourg, T. (1996). The role of emotion, empathy, and text structure in children's and adult's narrative text comprehension. In R. J. Kreuz & M. S. MacNealy (Eds.), *Empirical approaches to literature and aesthetics* (pp. 241–260). Norwood, NJ: Ablex.

Bowers, J. W., Metts, S. M., & Duncanson, W. T. (1985). Emotion and interpersonal communication. In M. L. Knapp & G. R. Miller (Eds.), *Handbook of interpersonal communication* (pp. 500–550). Beverly Hills, CA: Sage.

Brody, L. R., & Hall, J. A. (1993). Gender and emotion. In M. Lewis & J. M. Haviland (Eds.), *Handbook of emotion* (pp. 447–460). New York: Guilford.

Brown, P., & Levinson, S. (1987). *Politeness: Some universals in language usage.* Cambridge, England: Cambridge University Press.

Christensen, A., & Heavey, C. L. (1990). Gender and social structure in the demand/withdrawal pattern of marital conflict. *Journal of Personality and Social Psychology, 59,* 73–81.

Clark, H. H. (1973). The language-as-fixed-effect fallacy: A critique of language statistics in psychological research. *Journal of Verbal Learning and Verbal Behavior, 12,* 335–359.

Dindia, K., & Allen, M. (1992). Sex differences in self-disclosure: A meta-analysis. *Psychological Bulletin, 112,* 106–124.

Ekman, P., Friesan, W. V., & Ellsworth, P. (1972). *Emotion in the human face.* New York: Pergamon.

Fainsilber, L., & Ortony, A. (1987). Metaphorical uses of language in the expression of emotions. *Metaphor and Symbolic Activity, 2*, 239–250.

Feldman Barrett, L., Robin, L., Pietromonaco, P. R., & Eyssell, K. M. (1998). Are women the "more emotional" sex? Evidence from emotional experiences in social context. *Cognition and Emotion, 12*, 555–578.

Ferreira, F., & Anes, M. (1994). Why study spoken language? In M. A. Gernsbacher (Ed.), *Handbook of psycholinguistics* (pp. 33–56). New York: Academic Press.

Fryer, R., Harlan, J., Johnson, M. L., Kubrick, S., Richards, M. (Producers), Kubric, S. (Director). (1980). *The Shining* [Motion picture]. United States: Warner Bros.

Fussell, S. R., & Moss, M. M. (1998). Figurative language in emotional communication. In S. R. Fussell & R. J. Kreuz (Eds.), *Social and cognitive approaches to interpersonal communication* (pp. 113–141). Mahwah, NJ: Lawrence Erlbaum Associates.

Gallois, C. (1993). The language and communication of emotion: Universal, interpersonal, or intergroup? *American Behaviorist, 36*, 309–338.

Gibbs, R. W., Jr. (1994). *The poetics of mind.* New York: Cambridge University Press.

Gibbs, R. W., Jr., & Nascimento, S. B. (1996). How we talk when we talk about love: Metaphorical concepts and understanding love poetry. In R. J. Kreuz & M. S. MacNealy (Eds.), *Empirical approaches to literature and aesthetics* (pp. 291–307). Norwood, NJ: Ablex.

Glotzer, L., Lester, D., Marvin, N. (Producers), & Dourabont, F. (Director). (1994). *The shawshank redemption* [Motion picture]. United States: Columbia Pictures.

Hyde, J. S., & Linn, M. C. (1988). Gender differences in verbal ability: A meta-analysis. *Psychological Bulletin, 104*, 53–69.

Izard, C. E. (1971). *The face of emotion.* New York: Appleton-Century-Crofts.

James, D., & Drakich, J. (1993). Understanding gender differences in amount of talk: A critical review of research. In D. Tannen (Ed.), *Gender and conversational interaction* (pp. 281–312). Oxford, England: Oxford University Press.

Karsch, A. S. (Producer), & Streisand, B. (Producer & Director). (1991). *The prince of tides* [Motion picture]. United States: Columbia Pictures.

Kelley, H. H., Cunningham, J. D., Grisham, J. A., Lefebvre, L. M., Sink, C. R., & Yablon, G. (1978). Sex differences in comments made during conflict within close heterosexual pairs. *Sex Roles, 4*, 473–489.

Kintsch, W. (1998). *Comprehension: A paradigm for cognition.* Cambridge, England: Cambridge University Press.

Kreuz, R. J., Roberts, R. M., Johnson, B. K., & Bertus, E. L. (1996). Figurative language occurrence and co-occurrence in contemporary literature. In R. J. Kreuz & M. S. MacNealy (Eds.), *Empirical approaches to literature and aesthetics* (pp. 83–97). Norwood, NJ: Ablex.

LaFrance, M., & Banaji, M. (1992). Toward a reconsideration of the gender–emotion relationship. In M. S. Clark (Ed.), *Emotion and social behavior: Review of personality and social psychology* (Vol. 14, pp. 178–201). Newbury Park, CA: Sage.

Leaper, C., Carson, M., Baker, C., Holliday, H., & Myers, S. (1995). Self-disclosure and listener verbal support in same-gender and cross-gender friends' conversations. *Sex Roles, 33*, 387–404.

Leggitt, J. S., & Gibbs, R. W., Jr. (2000). Emotional reactions to verbal irony. *Discourse Processes, 29*, 1–24.

Magliano, J. P., Dijkstra, K., & Zwaan, R. A. (1996). Generating predictive inferences while viewing a movie. *Discourse Processes, 22,* 199–224.

McMullen, L., & Conway, J. (1996). Conceptualizing the figurative expressions of psychotherapy clients. In J. S. Mio & A. N. Katz (Eds.), *Metaphor: Implications and applications* (pp. 59–71). Mahwah, NJ: Lawrence Erlbaum Associates.

Noller, P. (1993). Gender and emotional communication in marriage: Different cultures or differential social power? *Journal of Language and Social Psychology, 12,* 132–152.

Notarius, C. I., & Johnson, J. S. (1982). Emotional expression in husbands and wives. *Journal of Marriage and the Family, 44,* 483–489.

Ortony, A. (1975). Why metaphors are necessary and not just nice. *Educational Theory, 25,* 45–53.

Pezdek, K., Lehrer, A., & Simon, S. (1984). The relationship between reading and cognitive processing of television and radio. *Child Development, 55,* 2072–2082.

Pezdek, K., Simon, S., Stoeckert, J., & Kiely, J. (1987). Individual differences in television comprehension. *Memory & Cognition, 15,* 428–435.

Rimé, B., Mesquita, B., Philippot, P., & Boca, S. (1991). Beyond the emotional event: Six studies on the social sharing of emotion. *Cognition & Emotion, 5,* 435–465.

Roberts, R. M., & Kreuz, R. J. (1994). Why do people use figurative language? *Psychological Science, 5,* 159–163.

Shimanoff, S. B. (1983). The role of gender in linguistic references to emotive states. *Communication Quarterly, 31,* 174–179.

Shimanoff, S. B. (1985a). Expressing emotions in words: Verbal patterns of interaction. *Journal of Communication, 35,* 16–31.

Shimanoff, S. B. (1985b). Rules governing the verbal expression of emotions between married couples. *The Western Journal of Speech Communication, 49,* 147–165.

Snell, W. E., Jr., Miller, R. S., & Belk, S. S. (1988). Development of the Emotional Self-Disclosure Scale. *Sex Roles, 18,* 59–73.

Snell, W. E., Jr., Miller, R. S., Belk, S. S., Garcia-Falconi, R., & Hernadez-Sanchez, J. E. (1989). Men's and women's emotional disclosures: The impact of disclosure recipient, culture, and the masculine role. *Sex Roles, 21,* 467–486.

Stanovich, K. E., & Cunningham, A. E. (1992). Studying the consequences of literacy within a literate society: The cognitive correlates of print exposure. *Memory & Cognition, 20,* 51–68.

Stanovich, K. E., & West, R. F. (1989). Exposure to print and orthographic processing. *Reading Research Quarterly, 24,* 402–433.

Stark, R. (Producer), & Ross, H. (Director). (1989). *Steel Magnolias* [Motion picture]. United States: TriStar Pictures.

Stein, L. B., & Brodsky, S. L. (1995). When infants wail: Frustration and gender as variables in distress disclosure. *The Journal of General Psychology, 122,* 19–27.

Tannen, D. (1990). *You just don't understand: Women and men in conversation.* New York: Ballantine.

Trick, L., & Katz, A. N. (1986). The domain interaction approach to metaphor processing: Relating individual differences and metaphor characteristics. *Metaphor and Symbolic Activity, 1,* 185–213.

Williams-Whitney, D., Mio, J. S., & Whitney, P. (1992). Metaphor production in creative writing. *Journal of Psycholinguistic Research, 21,* 497–509.

Appendix A

INFORMATION ABOUT FILM CLIPS USED
IN EXPERIMENTS 1 AND 2

Film	Emotion	Length
The Bridges of Madison County	Sadness	0.09375
The Prince of Tides*	Sadness	0.166667
A Christmas Carol	Happiness	0.02431
The Princess Bride*	Love	0.154167
A Cry in the Dark	Anxiety	0.08125
Roxanne	Love	0.116667
Falling Down*	Anxiety	0.08194
The Shawshank Redemption*	Happiness	0.1125
A Few Good Men	Anger	0.127083
The Shining	Anxiety	0.07292
The Fisher King*	Sadness	0.08958
Steel Magnolias*	Sadness /anger	0.05625
Indiana Jones and the Last Crusade*	Happiness	0.104167
The Untouchables	Anxiety	0.03542
It's a Wonderful Life*	Happiness	0.126389
Vertigo	Anxiety	0.0625
An Officer and a Gentleman	Sadness	0.104167

Note. All films listed were used in Experiment 1. Clips used in Experiment 2 are marked with an asterisk.

Appendix B

From *The Prince of Tides* (adapted from Karsch & Streisand, 1991)

Sally is lying on her bed in her robe, holding the phone to her ear, with her other arm wrapped around herself. She is squirming uncomfortably as she tells the person at the other end, "Uh, Tom … I don't think it's a good idea for you to come home this weekend."

Tom, the man she is talking to, is standing by the refrigerator in his kitchen shuffling papers as he responds to Sally: "Why not?"

"Well, I'm not sure … I'm just not sure that I want to see you right now. I … uh … I have a lot to figure out."

As he walks out of the kitchen, Tom says doubtfully, "Uh-huh." He continues walking into a dim living room as Sally explains further.

"What's the point, Tom? I mean, let's face it. We don't make each other feel good anymore."

"Right," says Tom as he sits down on a couch and runs his hand through his hair.

Sally's voice begins to quiver as she continues. "Look. Um … I didn't want to tell you this over the telephone. I wanted to tell you before you left, but the way you left …." Sally pauses as she begins to cry. "There wasn't any time."

Tom, leaning forward intently, asks, "What'd you want to tell me, Sally?" There is a long pause while Tom waits and Sally cries. Tom becomes impatient and asks, "What's his name? … What's his *name*, Sally? The man *must* have a name!"

"Jack Cleveland."

Tom puts his head in his free hand and leans back against the couch say-ing, "Oh no, oh no!" He rubs his forehead as he continues, "Jesus, Sally." Tom now begins to get angry, stands up, and continues in a stronger voice, "Geez, Jack Cleveland?! You mean that aging pompous hippie from the hos-pital who still rides a motorcycle?!"

As Tom is screaming this at her, Sally rests the phone on her shoulder and shuts her eyes. He continues, asking, "Oh, for Christ's sake, Sally, why him?! Why him?!"

Sally is crying harder, now, with dark streaks of make-up underneath her eyes. She wipes her nose with a tissue, breathes deeply, and says, "Because he knows how he feels about me."

At this, Tom is more calm. He collapses wearily into a chair, clasps his hand to his forehead, and whispers, "Oh, Sally." Tom sighs and leans for-ward, with his head still being held up by his hand. "This is too difficult to talk about over the phone .... Um, just think about it carefully, 'kay?" His hand is nervously playing about his mouth.

"I hardly think about anything else .... Goodnight, Tom."

As she begins to hang up the phone, Tom stops her when he calls out, "Sally?" She brings the phone back up to her ear, shaking her head, and asks with annoyance, "What?"

"Are you *really* in love?" Tom asks.

Sally answers with a quivering voice, "I'm not sure. I might even be doing this to hurt you. I gotta go," and hangs up the phone.

Tom sits there, holding the phone for a few seconds more before hanging up, listening to the dial tone. He sighs and covers his face in his hands. He sits there wringing his hands for a moment, and glancing to the side, gets up and walks to a desk in the same room. He sits at the chair in front of it and turns on the desk lamp. He pulls out a sheet of stationery from a drawer in the desk, picks up a pen, and stares at it as he turns it in his hands. He begins to compose a letter to Sally in his head, and then starts to write: "Dear Sally, I wish the words 'I love you' weren't so difficult for me. I've missed you. I miss touching you. I don't know what keeps me at such a distance." Tom pauses, and looks up, with a pained expression on his face. He continues writing, "I'm sorry I disappoint you, Sally. But you're right to feel that way. How else could you react to half a man?" Tom sighs deeply. "How could you not be dis-appointed? Hell, I seem to disappoint anyone who tries to find the best in me." When he finishes writing, Tom slumps with exhaustion into the chair and leans his head back, clenching his eyes shut.

PART III

Sociocultural Processing Influences

8

Discourse and Sociocultural Factors in Understanding Nonliteral Language

Albert N. Katz
University of Western Ontario

There is a well-established tradition in linguistics and in certain fields of psycholinguistics that the study of language comprehension should employ sentences presented without discourse or social context (e.g., see Glucksberg, 2001). That is, participants presented with a target sentence such as, "The night sky was filled with drops of molten silver" (1), might be asked to rate whether the sentence is syntactically correct, semantically meaningful, easy to comprehend, or literally true. What is surprising about this tradition, at least from my perspective (see Katz 1996b), is that as natural language processors, humans never encounter sentences out of either discourse or cultural context. Discourse context refers to the characteristics about the language in which a sentence, such as (1), is embedded, cultural context refers to factors such as the shared beliefs between speaker and listener(s), conventions shared between writer and reader, or, in a more general sense, the beliefs that surround who the speaker is, who the listener is, and the environment in which Speaker X makes an utterance to Listener Y (see Clark, 1996).

In this chapter I discuss both discourse and cultural contexts usually in tasks in which a target sentence is read within a passage. Discourse factors that can be manipulated include variables such as whether the reader is warned in the passage that a given target is forthcoming by use of a marker, such as, "in a manner of speaking," "really," or "truly"; the number of plausible continuations invited by the discourse in which the statement is embedded, and so forth. Note that in these cases any influence on the understanding of the target is based on factors limited to our knowledge of language and language use.

Cultural or social factors are also presented within the confines of a passage presented for processing. Now, however, the information being accessed is knowledge (or beliefs) about the sociocultural world that goes beyond our knowledge of language use but reflects instead broad beliefs about our culture and various subgroups within that culture. Within an experiment, variables of interest might be whether the target sentence is uttered by a man or woman (and the gender of the audience), whether it is uttered by a priest versus a car salesman, or whether it is uttered by a boss speaking to a subordinate. Note that in these cases there is no logical necessity for the meaning of the utterance to be influenced by these factors; however, on pragmatic grounds the speaker and listener both might be tapping into accepted beliefs about the world; if this were the case, then such factors should be evident in how the target is processed. The interest here is whether sociocultural context (e.g., our beliefs about female speakers or car salesmen) is taken into account at the very earliest moments of comprehension and, if so, whether discourse factors moderate these effects. I discuss this matter both in terms of utterances in which the expressed meaning is the same or very similar to the intended meaning and in terms of utterances in which the expressed meaning differs considerably from the intended meaning, such as metaphor, irony, indirect requests, and proverbs.

ON CONTEXT

I begin with a simple mind experiment. Consider the sentence, "He certainly is Abelard to her Heloise" (2), and write down what that sentence means to you. When I have conducted this exercise informally, it is clear that people have intuitions about this sentence. They recognize that it is syntactically correct and usually recognize that Abelard and Heloise refer to people involved in some social interaction; but, if ignorant of the story of these two people, they can give us little more. Lacking knowledge about Abelard or Heloise, my respondents appear to base their inferences on the presented grammatical information alone. It is as if my respondents assume that "X (a person = He) certainly is Y (a person = Abelard) to her Z (a person = Heloise)" acts as a construction in construction grammar terms (see Kay, 1997), in which the construction is used to describe a limited number of types of interpersonal relationships with the exemplar (Y is to Z) being a prototype of each type (i.e., acts metaphorically).

Contrast sentence (2) with a similar construction in which the requisite context tends to be accessible to many in our culture: "He certainly is Romeo to her Juliet" (3). Now my respondents have little difficulty in coming up with an elaborated interpretation. Indeed, one can easily see how one could describe the interpretation that the phrase "Romeo and Juliet" serves as a prototype for a certain type of romantic relationship and that the interpretation of the statement would arise by classifying the topic (he) to the category suggested by the nominal vehicle represented by "Romeo and Juliet" (see, e.g., Glucksberg, 1991). That is, the interpretation is one in which the person being described is depicted in a passionate but tragically doomed relationship.

The point is that even when presumably out of context, the interpretation of a given statement is inextricably linked to the manner in which it is presented, and when an explicit context is not available, one is constructed from stored knowledge during the act of comprehension. Language use is never context free, despite the logic of many experiments that may suggest otherwise. In this chapter I do not make the pretense that language is context free; instead, I emphasize examining the comprehension of sentences such as those just presented when they are presented in a discourse or sociocultural context. For instance, consider if (3) was as follows: The priest said, "He certainly is Romeo to her Juliet" (4) versus the comedian said, "He certainly is Romeo to her Juliet" (5).

Would social stereotypes about priests and comedians come to the fore and influence how the target is understood, for instance as a metaphoric description on one hand and as an ironic or sarcastic commentary on the other? I present some data that indicates the answer is "yes."

Consider another aspect of a sociocultural context, one not based on stored declarative knowledge (as in the aforementioned examples) but on the ongoing sociocultural ecology that is active as the comment is being made. For instance, consider the scenario in which three people are in a conversation, but only two of these people know that a friend (John) has separated from another friend, Mary. If one of the people "in the know" states "John and Mary are acting like love birds these days" (6), the two recipients of this statement would inevitably draw different interpretations, because of what they know. Indeed the speaker might have framed the message in the way that he did on purpose: namely, to send one message to the other person in the know (who should recognize the irony intended by the speaker) and another message to the unaware communicant—a message intended to keep that person ignorant of the facts (Kierkegaard, 1996, argued that this is in fact one of the functions served by ironic usage).

Naturally, the sociocultural ecology described in (6) can also be made salient in ongoing discourse; moreover, discourse-based and declarative knowledge-based context can interact. Consider the following:

Speaker A: John can't stand Mary. You can't even have them in the same room anymore.

Speaker B: Yeah. He certainly is Romeo to her Juliet.

It is obvious that Speaker B is using the metaphor to be ironic or even sarcastic. That is, understanding the comment requires knowledge both of the metaphor and of the ironic spin made about it. Given the familiarity of the metaphoric base, the ironic spin should be quite transparent. Consider next the analogous conversation:

Speaker A: John can't stand Mary. You can't even have them in the same room anymore.

Speaker B: Yeah. He certainly is Abelard to her Heloise.

The situation is somewhat different because the ironic spin is not apparent given the relative unfamiliarity of the contrast. No doubt one could understand Speaker B: The syntax is not ambiguous and, assuming that Gricean principles are being followed, one can assume that Speaker B was following conversational maxims. But what should Speaker A make of the comment given this speaker's ignorance of the Abelard and Heloise story? Assuming a metaphoric default, it is quite possible that the ironic intent is lost completely, with Speaker A making the assumption that the example provided is of two people who typify an estranged couple.

The informal examples just presented are illustrative of the points I make in the rest of the chapter. I describe some research from my laboratory and from others that demonstrates the importance of the social environmental context in disambiguating speakers' intent that a nonliteral interpretation of an utterance is in order and that, in many instances, this contextual information occurs at the onset of processing.

The Nature of Nonliteral Language

The psycholinguistic literature on nonliteral language often ignores the difference between literal and figurative language versus familiar and unfamiliar expressions. Although literal use and the familiar expressions are doubtlessly correlated, it is important to make the distinction between them. Familiar or canonical language refers to language as it is most commonly used. Thus, familiarity and literality are orthogonal to one another. That is, there are instances of nonliteral language in which the dominant use of certain phrases are intended to express and are understood as expressing something different than what is being described by individual words. Examples abound in many types of nonliteral language: When one states that his or her car is a lemon or that the grass is greener on the other side of the fence or that Joe is acting as my best friend, it is generally understood that the car is deficient (and not a fruit), that envy is being expressed (and not a statement about fertilizers), and that Joe has acted as a jerk. In other cases the use is novel, such as when someone might compare their car to a banana or hear a proverb with which they are not familiar. This distinction between fixed or familiar use versus unfamiliar or novel use is expressed in many ways in the literature as, for instance, the distinction between frozen and novel metaphors, fixed expressions versus creative usage (see Moon, 1998), and familiar and unfamiliar tropes and is the basis for a general theory of language processing—namely, the graded salience hypothesis of (Giora, in press).

This distinction between familiar and literal use has certain implications. It does not permit one to generalize findings or their theoretical implications from studies that use conventional metaphor (or salient ironies) to the less canonical counterparts. Of more direct interest to the issue of context is the role played by familiar and less familiar tropes and by different types of tropes, such as irony versus metaphor. Assuming that the salient meaning comes to mind more readily than a nonsalient or noncanonical meaning, one can predict that familiar, fixed expressions, used in their usual way, should be understood more readily with minimal support because the expression has a well-established sense that transcends specific contexts. Unfamiliar tropes, by contrast, might require context to help disambiguate speakers' intent and, in general, would be more difficult to integrate into the ongoing discourse. That is, a syntactically acceptable string of words might be processed and integrated into ongoing discourse quite readily if this string was a fixed expression whose dominant meaning was nonliteral. Consider, however, what would happen if the canonical use is violated—that is, if a familiar proverb or metaphor is used in a manner that is inconsistent with the dominant sense, such as when one states that their car is a lemon, referring to how it is decorated as a float in a parade. Now, based on the same logic (i.e., that one has ready access to the dominant sense), one can predict that interpretative problems occur because the dominant sense has to be ignored for the contextually driven (and, in this case, the literal) sense to be derived.

There is another way in which our understanding of the role played by context has direct implications for understanding nonliteral language. The degree of contextual support required for comprehension differs for different forms of nonliteral language. This is in contrast with the usual approach (e.g., see the reviews presented in Gibbs, 1994; and Glucksberg, 2001; but also see Colston & Gibbs, 2002) which has implicitly argued for commonality of processing for all forms of nonliteral language but is consistent with the approach of, for instance, Winner (1988) who argued that comprehension of irony involves knowledge of social norms and expectations, which is not the case for the comprehension of metaphor. Thus, knowledge of who said what might be much more important in the processing of irony than, for example, the processing of metaphor. Ellen Winner (1988), in fact, noted that a child learns to recognize metaphor at an earlier age than he or she recognizes irony because understanding social conventions (on which irony is based) develops later than the cognitive skills required to understand metaphor. Colston and Gibbs (2002) made a complementary argument with the processing of metaphor and irony by adults based on the more complex metarepresentational reasoning required to infer ironic messages compared to metaphoric messages.

I argue that the distinctions made by Winner (1988) and by Colston and Gibbs (2002) represent the natural and basic reality of language processing and should not be shunted as peripheral or minor: What is recovered from the intent of a speaker is intimately tied to our knowledge and beliefs about the discourse and social environments in which language is used. Over the last few years, in my laboratory my colleagues and I have addressed the question of the roles played by discourse and social context in the processing of various forms of nonliteral language, employing both off-line and on-line methodologies. We showed that the effects of social factors can be quite subtle. For instance, in Lee and Katz (1998) we demonstrated that sarcasm, but not irony in general, involves the ridicule of a specific person or group of people. That is, social factors are more important in producing a sense of sarcasm than they are in producing a sense of irony.

It is a sad commentary on much of the experimental literature that social factors are not even considered in the construction of the experimental materials—let alone systematically manipulated. The experimental stimuli should reflect real-life contextual constraints. Gibbs (2000) reinforced the need for such care. He analyzed the conversation of university students and their friends for instances of ironic speech and noted that five distinct types of irony were frequently employed: teasing–jocularity, sarcasm, rhetorical questions, hyperbole, and understatement. Moreover, social factors were found to be important: Some types were more frequently used by men, others by women; and, most important, use of irony was often a collaborative social event, with an ironic comment being followed by ironic responses by others in the conversation. Presumably, to create experimental situations that simulate real-life conditions (and, hence, the contextual constraints that would be active in real-life language production and comprehension) experimenters should at least construct discourse contexts that reflect the social conditions in which various forms of language are employed. To date, this degree of care has not generally been observed, and, in fact, the even more modest attempt to ensure that the experimental stimuli are realistic is not the norm. Consider, for example, a study Maggie Toplak and I (Toplak & Katz, 2000) conducted to examine the reasons a person might use an indirect sarcastic statement rather than the direct criticism. We employed items taken from a seminal article on irony processing (Kreuz & Glucksberg, 1989) but normed these items to see if our sample could imagine themselves in the scenario being described and whether, in that scenario, they would have used the statement attributed to the speaker. To our surprise, only about one third of the items from that article met our relatively modest attempt to ensure ecologically realistic discourse contexts. Clearly much more work is required in the experimental preparation of the stimuli used to examine selected theoretical issues in the processing of language, especially nonliteral language.

Off-line Examination of Social Factors in the Use and Comprehension of Nonliteral Language

Much of the literature on social factors is nonexperimental and involves, for instance, trying to identify a unique form of woman's speech (e.g., Weatherall, 2002) or as a form of speech that changes with age (Ekert, 1997). These approaches are off-line in the sense that there is no monitoring of the moment-to-moment processing of the nonliteral use; some text is analyzed at some temporal distance from when it might have been originally produced or encountered. This tradition is also well-represented in experimental psycholinguistic work. Typically the psycholinguistic studies use *textoids*, a set of short passages in which some nonliteral use is presented and participants are asked to make some decision about the use, such as rating the degree to which sarcasm is expressed or the subsequent memory of the textoid. Experimental manipulations, when they occur, are produced by changing the context in which the target sentence is presented. I present some instances next.

Relationships Among the People in Communication.   The amount of literature is growing, which points to the importance of systematically examining the role played by different participants in a conversation. For instance, the use of sarcasm has been shown to vary as a function of the degree of relatedness of the speaker and the victim of the speaker's barb (Jorgensen, 1996; Kreuz, 1996). Toplak and Katz (2000) showed that different members in communication give somewhat different reasons why someone would make an indirect sarcastic statement. And, Kreuz, Kassler, Coppenrath, and McLain (1999) showed that the appropriateness of an ironic expression is associated with the amount of shared information between speaker and listener.

Katz and Lee (1993) manipulated contextual information based on whether or not members of a conversation shared background information (by virtue of being mutually present when some information was presented) or not (when the requisite information is presented when one member of the conversational group was not present). The manipulation occurred by varying the nature of various texts, which our respondents were asked to rate: Participants were presented a set of scenarios in which one person echoed an earlier statement made by someone else, with the echoic mention now being metaphoric is use. Two manipulations were important: (a) whether the context would lead a listener to believe that the speaker was endorsing the statement or was being pragmatically insincere and (b) whether the listener was present or not when the original mention of the statement had been made. This last manipulation would lead to two groups of listeners: a privileged audience that would share with the speaker the knowledge of the context in which the statement had been made originally and a nonprivileged audience that would not have access to this background contextual knowledge.

The findings, based on ratings given to authorial intent and degree of metaphoricity or ironicity, were very clear. If a listener thought the speaker was endorsing the truth value of the statement, then the comment was taken as a metaphoric description; but if the listener thought the speaker was actually rejecting the truth value of the statement, then it was taken as an ironic comment. Moreover, perception of the statement as being ironic varied as a function of audience privilege: An interpretation of irony was especially salient when the listener not only perceived a speaker to be making an incongruent (i.e., a rejecting) statement but also recognized that someone else in the conversation (the nonprivileged listener) was unaware that the speaker was not in fact endorsing the position he or she just espoused.

The Impact of Social Roles. The variables just noted could be thought of as contextual constraints engendered by the social dynamics of communicating with people of varying degrees of relatedness and shared knowledge. In addition, there are contextual constraints engendered by social convention. That is, one could argue that there are social conventions associated with gender, socioeconomic class, and power or status inequalities that could be used to disambiguate speaker's intent. An example of socioeconomic factors is evident in the use of indirect requests, such as when one asks: "Can you open the window?"; taken literally this is a question about ability but pragmatically is understood as a request to perform the act. Holtgraves (1997a) and Kemper and Thissen (1981) showed that statements differing in politeness effect our memory: Participants were more likely to remember the wording of statements that are incongruous with social status, such as when a low-status person talks in an impolite manner to a high-status person.

Effect of Gender. Analogous effects can be found with gender: Women are more likely than men to interpret statements as being indirect (e.g., Holtgraves, 1991); in addition, as a function of power relationships, closeness of relationship with the person to whom she or he is talking, and the size of the request being made, women differ from men in their use of polite language (Holtgraves, 1992). Gender differences have been noted especially with the use of irony and sarcasm. For instance, Gibbs (2000) found that men make sarcastic remarks almost twice as often as women, and in general agreement, Colston and Lee (2000) found that irony is considered a "male-like" trait by both men and women. Katz, Piasecka, and Toplak (2001) conducted an experimental study in which participants read a set of short textoids in which several constraints that might influence a statement as being sarcastic were manipulated. Of interest here was whether the actor in the textoid who made the comment was a man or a woman. After reading each scenario, participants were asked a set of questions about the intent of the speaker, such as whether the speaker was being sarcastic, ironic, humorous, aggressive, and so on. Gender effects emerged: When the comment was not obviously intended, men were perceived as more sarcastic, whereas when the comment was intended, women were rated as more sarcastic. There were no gender-related effects on the ratings of irony, indicating (consistent with Lee & Katz's 1998 study), that sarcasm involves a specified victim.

Effect of Occupational Stereotypes.   Taken together the data can be viewed as strong evidence for socially driven interpersonal factors in interpreting nonliteral and other forms of somewhat ambiguous statements. Penny Pexman and I (Katz & Pexman, 1997) asked whether we could demonstrate another socially driven effect on the comprehension of nonliteral language. In this case the social factor was beliefs (or stereotypes) regarding the occupation of a speaker. We wished to find out whether these stereotypes could change the interpretation of a statement from being treated as a metaphor to being treated as a sarcastic commentary on the metaphoric contrast. Moreover, we were interested to see whether any such effects would be moderated by the discourse context or the familiarity of the statement.

Our study (Katz & Pexman, 1997) was quite simple. To conduct this study we first had to demonstrate a difference in the perceptions of language usage for members of different occupations. We obtained norms that clearly showed some differences: For example, clergymen, doctors, and teachers were perceived as likely to use metaphor (and less likely to use irony) in everyday speech, whereas comedians, police and factory workers were perceived as more likely to use irony (but not metaphor; for a related matter, see Holtgraves, 1997b, who provided evidence of cross-cultural and individual differences in using indirect language).

Once we obtained these occupational differences, we constructed textoids. In one scenario a statement in the form of a nominal metaphor (e.g., "children are precious gems") was placed in a discourse that either brought out the metaphoric sense or an ironic usage or was neutral with respect to the metaphor versus ironic difference. The nominal metaphors were either highly familiar instances of basic conceptual metaphors or were novel instances. For each of the three contexts, the nominal metaphor would be uttered by a person who was perceived as a high metaphor user (e.g., clergyman) or high irony user (e.g., comedian). A fourth (control) condition was also constructed: This condition was the same as the neutral condition just described except that the speaker was not associated with any specific occupation. Naturally, passages were counterbalanced such that any one person only saw the target sentence in one context, which was uttered by a person from one occupation; but, across the study, all key passages were uttered by someone from each occupation (or, in the final control condition, by a person from no specified occupation).

Two types of dependent measures were taken. First, after each scenario, participants answered a set of questions regarding the intent of the speaker, two of which were especially relevant—namely, whether the speaker was sarcastic and whether the speaker was mocking someone else. Across studies we manipulated, in the rating questions themselves, whether the occupation of the speaker was made salient. Second, after all the scenarios were rated and after completing a distraction task, participants were asked to recall as many of the target sentences as possible.

The results were very clear. With respect to the rating data, the discourse contexts acted as one would expect: The key statement was perceived as more sarcastic when placed in a counterfactual context meant to bring out the ironic commentary. There was no difference between the neutral context and the context meant to bring out the metaphoric sense, suggesting that the default was to treat the comparison as a metaphor. Of greater interest here is the influence of speaker occupation. When the neutral conditions were compared (the two in which speaker occupation was mentioned and the one in which it was not), speakers from high-irony occupations were perceived as more sarcastic, at least for the highly familiar statements. When the occupation was made salient in the rating scale, the effects were even more general: Statements made by speakers of high-irony occupations were seen as being more sarcastic than the exact same statements made by high-metaphor speakers. Overall, familiar statements were perceived as especially sarcastic when uttered in a irony-inducing context or when uttered by a member of a high-irony occupation. The memory data confirmed the influence of speaker occupation: Statements uttered by members of high-irony occupations were better recalled than the same statements made by members of high-metaphor occupations. Because the statements and contexts were identical in every other way, these data suggest that occupation was coded somewhere in the process of comprehension.

Taken together, these findings indicate that the social role of the person who makes a statement plays an important role in our perception of a given statement as being a metaphor or a sarcastic commentary on that metaphor. Moreover, these effects interact with the familiarity of the statement itself. Our interpretation of these data was that the metaphoric content of a familiar statement would be available for use regardless of context. Thus, when the context is consistent with the metaphoric interpretation, one need not look for an alternative (ironic) usage. However, when the context is nonendorsing and suggests a sarcastic usage, the incongruity between the familiar metaphoric use and the ironic context is made especially salient, leading to a heightened sense of sarcasm. Incongruity is less marked with unfamiliar statements because those statements are not associated with metaphoric use. An analogous argument is made with respect to speaker occupation: In the neutral condition participants have little explanation of why the speaker made the comment. Participants provided with a highly familiar statement know that the statement is likely to be used as a metaphor, and it is made by a person associated with either metaphoric or ironic speech. Only in the latter case a sense of incongruity was obtained, and it is reflected in the sarcasm ratings. With unfamiliar items, however, the metaphoric content of the statement is much less salient, and the sense of incongruity does not arise.

Taken together, these data provide evidence that people are sensitive to the social roles of a speaker and that the influence of these roles interacts with constraints engendered by the discourse context and the salience of the statement itself. The interactive effects of speaker occupation, discourse context, and statement familiarity suggest that multiple sources of information are been weighed when one attempts to understand the intent behind the use of a given statement.

On-Line Processing and the Role of Contextual Constraints: A Constraint Satisfaction Approach

I already presented data from off-line studies that support my contention that social factors play an important role in helping us understand metaphor, irony, and indirect requests. The question of interest now is whether these contextual factors act on-line—that is, during the act of comprehending the text. In fact, there is a vigorous ongoing debate whether semantic and pragmatic factors come into play at the earliest stages of comprehension or whether they only come into play later, after some obligatory processing has occurred. The contrast between whether contextual constraints are primary and limit what interpretations occur to some verbal information during the act of reading that information and whether contextual constrains come into play after the fact is relevant not only to our understanding of nonliteral language comprehension per se, but to a larger set of issues in language processing. This controversy can be found from low-level activities such as at the level of word access (Giora, in press) and resolution of syntactic ambiguities (McRae, Spivey-Knowlton & Tanenhaus, 1998) to high-level activities such as the processing of metaphor (Glucksberg, 1991), sarcasm (Giora, Fein, & Schwartz, 1998), and proverbial language (Turner & Katz, 1997).

With respect to the debate on the processing of nonliteral language, the classic position (e.g., Searle, 1979) is that nonliteral meaning is not processed at the earliest moments. This position holds that one is obligated to initially process for the literal sense of a trope and only when that fails to provide a contextually adequate interpretation does one then go on and try to find a plausible (and nonliteral) interpretation. In contrast, there is by now a 25-year-old experimentally based position and the currently accepted received wisdom which claims that, with appropriate contextual support, the nonliteral meaning is made available as rapidly as the literal sense and that the access of the nonliteral interpretation is not dependent on a failure to achieve a plausible literal interpretation (see Katz, 1996a, for a review). In short, the alternative holds that at the earliest moments nonliteral language can be accessed directly but only if there is an appropriately rich supportive context.

My understanding of the literature is that the received wisdom in favor of the direct-access approach has been best demonstrated with familiar tropes and, in line with the classic notion supporting obligatory processing of literal meaning, that less familiar nonliteral meaning might still involve the initial processing of either literal meaning (see Turner & Katz, 1997) or *salient meaning*—that is, coded meaning such as occurs when the nonliteral sense is the most familiar usage of the item (see Giora, in press; Giora et al., 1998). In Giora's graded salience hypothesis, there is an obligatory activation of the dominant sense of an item regardless of context; context can boost the activation level of nonsalient meaning but will never do so at a cost to the activation level of the dominant or salient meaning. Thus, in general, the salient sense is context independent (i.e., it is always activated regardless of context), whereas the initial activation of nonsalient meaning is context dependent. One implication of this position is that the critical variable is saliency, not the literalness of the trope: If the most familiar usage is nonliteral, then that would be activated at the earliest moments of comprehension; in fact, the literal sense of such items would only occur later (if at all) in processing.

Naturally, the opposing position is that context determines what becomes aroused at the earliest moments of processing and, consequently, does not give a processing priority to either a salient or a literal sense of an item. Rather, with an appropriate context one should be able to find early activation of either literal or nonliteral meaning. From my perspective, however, this approach is underspecified and it is not clear what constitutes contextual support that would encourage either a literal or nonliteral understanding of a message. The argument that I will make presently is that a constraint satisfaction perspective permits the necessary specification.

Examination of these issues and testing of the contrasting theoretical positions requires measures that are sensitive to the moment-to-moment processing that occurs as one reads or hears the critical information. For instance, consider again statements such as:. "John and Mary really seem to hate each other. You can't even leave them alone in the same room anymore. You can say that he is certainly Romeo to her Juliet." Compare these statements to the following: "John and Mary really seem to love each other. You can't even leave them alone in the same room anymore. You can say that he is certainly Romeo to her Juliet." Assuming familiarity with the contrast, the former usage is ironic whereas the latter one is metaphoric. We already discussed how familiarity, the nature of the discourse context, and social factors (e.g., the person who would make such a comment) all play a role in helping us realize the ironic intent. The issues of interest are (a) whether the ironic sense would emerge as rapidly as the metaphoric sense if the context was such that discourse and social factors were both consistent with either the metaphoric or ironic usage and (b) whether, during the processing of target items such as in the Romeo and Juliet example, there is evidence that the metaphoric or ironic meaning arises very early or more slowly, well after the target is no longer being read or heard.

There are a limited number of relevant on-line studies. Using a cross-modal priming procedure, Blasko and Connine (1993) demonstrated that the nonliteral meaning of familiar and apt metaphors is accessed early in the processing sequence. Using measures of brain activity, Pynte, Besson, Robichon, and Poli (1996) indicated that, when contextually relevant, the metaphorical meaning of a sentence is the only one accessed. Both of these studies are consistent with the received wisdom that, when contextually supported, the metaphoric meaning is processed early in the sequence and, hence, unlikely to be dependent on a prior (and obligatory) processing of literal meaning.

The evidence with sarcastic statements is less clear: Gibbs (1986) showed that the sarcastic sense is processed as rapidly as the literal sense (and thus occurs early in the processing sequence and is constrained by context), whereas Giora et al. (1998) provided evidence (supporting her graded saliency position) that the ironic sense of a statement takes longer to develop than the literal sense (and thus occurs later in processing; for nonsalient items, context does not constrain which meaning is accessed; see Giora et al., 1998 for details).

Although these studies were well executed, neither Giora et al. (1998) nor Gibbs (1986) study took into account (a) the richness of contextual constraints that are available to aid comprehension; (b) the multiplicity of contextual constraints that are, in principle, available for use; or (c) the notion that social factors might be especially important in inviting an ironic but not a metaphoric interpretation. As such, the differences between Giora et al. and Gibbs' findings may merely represent differences in the contextual constraints available and differences in when a constraint might come into play: Perhaps some constraints are more likely to work early in processing, whereas others develop more slowly and thus only work later in the processing sequence.

The emphasis on constraints has led me to consider an alternative theoretical account of nonliteral language processing—multiple sources of information are evaluated and integrated continuously. Constraint satisfaction models, the name typically assigned to such a theoretical approach, have been quite successful in explaining much of the variability in linguistic ambiguity resolution, such as that found in syntax (see McRae et al., 1998). We argue that, in principle, these models should be applicable to resolving the ambiguity inherent in the processing of nonliteral language.

The logic of constraint satisfaction is that the understanding of text involves constructing an interpretation that fits the available information better than plausible alternative interpretations. Such models assume that different sources of information (i.e., constraints) provide immediate probabilistic support for competing interpretations in parallel over time (e.g., literal vs. nonliteral or metaphoric vs. ironic interpretation) and, as such, do not posit modular obligatory processing priorities, such as suggested by models that assume one is obligated to process for literal or salient meaning. In general, competition duration (and thus reading time) is itself a function of the strength of the various alternatives: If the constraints all point to the same interpretation, then competition is resolved rapidly, whereas settling on an interpretation is delayed as support for different alternatives become more equal.

I argued (e.g., Katz & Ferretti, 2001) that constraint satisfaction might prove to be a useful way to resolve some of the issues in the time taken to comprehend a statement used either literally or in its nonliteral, figurative sense. Among the constraints of importance would be the context itself (the extent to which it supports a literal or a nonliteral reading) and the nature of fixed expressions (the reading of the initial words of a familiar fixed expressions, e.g., as a proverb, idiom, or frozen metaphor, might trigger the rest of the expression). I argue that additional discourse contexts, such as explicit markers to usage and, by extension, sociocultural context, should also act as constraints favoring one or another interpretation.

We (Katz & Ferretti, 2001) began to test this approach in a series of reading studies involving familiar and unfamiliar proverbs placed in contexts constructed to support either the nonliteral (i.e., proverbial) or literal (i.e., nonproverbial) sense of the item. We also employed proverbs that were rated as highly familiar or unfamiliar by our population because, by manipulating proverb familiarity and whether the context supports the literal or nonliteral sense of the item, we could disentangle effects of literality from saliency. In Katz and Ferretti (2001), we took just those two constraints into account—that is, the extent to which the context was biased toward a literal or nonliteral use—and whether the trope was familiar or not.

Our task employed a self-paced moving window procedure in which readers advance a text word-by-word across a computer screen at their own pace. This procedure mimics the eye movements found in normal reading; removes spurious strategies adopted by readers forced to read at an uncomfortable and, for them, unusual pace; and permits the computation of reading latencies (or reading times, RTs) for each word in a text. Thus, we got a measure of how long a person lingered over each word, and the amount of time taken to go from one sentence to the next.

We found that familiar proverbs were read more rapidly that nonfamiliar proverbs and that this familiarity effect emerged very early—by the second word of the proverb. We also observed that, for familiar proverbs, there was no difference in RT by the end of the proverb regardless of context. That is, the proverbial meaning was as easily integrated into the discourse on-line whether used in its familiar (proverbial) or less familiar (literal) sense. With unfamiliar proverbs, relative to the literal biasing context, there was a slowing of reading when the item was placed in a context that brought out its nonliteral (proverbial) sense—an effect that began to emerge about midway through the reading of the proverb. This difference was very noticeable at the last word of the proverb, and it extended into the reading of the sentence following the proverb. Thus, the resolution or integration of the nonliteral sense into the discourse was not completed until some time after the proverb itself was no longer being read.

Without going into detail, these data do not support models that do not emphasize the context in which nonliteral language is embedded, and they do not clearly support either those models that posit an obligatory initial processing of literal or salient meaning or those models that argue that, with an elaborated context, literal and nonliteral meaning are equally easy to integrate into discourse. But they are more compatible with a constraint satisfaction approach. Thus, we argued that the more rapid reading of the familiar (vs. unfamiliar) proverbs and for unfamiliar proverbs placed in a literal biasing (compared to a nonliteral biasing) context was due to the fact that there is less competition between the various sources of information being evaluated in those conditions. Although the two constraints that we examined could explain much of the data, another prediction that would be made by a constraint satisfaction perspective was not observed—namely, the prediction that a familiar proverb used literally should be more readily integrated than the same proverb used nonliterally because, in literal usage, there are two sources of information (i.e., the expressed literal and the nonliteral or salient sense) providing information consistent with the literal interpretation. We did not find this pattern possibly because the constraints pointing toward a literal interpretation were not very strong. Moreover, by an analogous argument, the constraint satisfaction approach would predict that differences in processing unfamiliar proverbs used literally and nonliterally should be resolved much earlier in processing if there was a constraint that signaled that an item was to be read as a proverb.

To test this possibility, we directly manipulated what some linguists would label as *introductory formulae*, explicit markers that are the standard ways of signaling that the receiver will be presented with a proverb (Katz & Ferretti, in press). Toward this end, we chose to examine the markers "Proverbially speaking," "In a manner of speaking," and "Literally speaking" because they disambiguate the intended meanings of proverbs and are consistent with the types of markers typically used in introducing proverbial (see Mieder, 1982, 1990) and nonliteral usages (Moon, 1998). Thus, we replicated Katz and Ferretti's (2001) study but added one or another explicit discourse marker.

The findings were clear and striking. Warning the reader about the proverbial nature of the upcoming statement appears to allow for the comprehension and integration of unfamiliar proverbs used nonliterally by the end of the statements. That is, with the appropriate constraint—the marker, "proverbially speaking"—we eliminated, for unfamiliar proverbs used proverbially, the difference in RT between a literal and nonliteral usage on-line, as predicted by the constraint satisfaction approach. Moreover, for the first time, we found evidence that familiar proverbs were integrated more easily when presented in a literal than nonliteral (proverbial) biasing context— namely, the first word of the sentence following the familiar proverb was read more rapidly in the literal inviting context. Thus, as predicted again from the constraint satisfaction perspective, the dominant tendency toward a specific interpretation can be overridden if there is sufficient support toward an alternative (in this case, literal) interpretation.

Thus, overall we found encouraging support for a constraint satisfaction approach for understanding the processing of nonliteral language. To date, the explicit tests of this theoretical position have been based on manipulations of discourse context. But, as already reviewed, we have off-line evidence that sociocultural context also plays a role in how we interpret and understand nonliteral language; in principle, these factors can also act in a constraint satisfaction manner. In fact, there is a growing body of evidence that, as predicted by a constraint satisfaction perspective, sociocultural context comes into play early in processing.

Occupational Stereotypes. As a first step at examining the role of sociocultural contextual constraints, Penny Pexman, Todd Ferretti, and I (Pexman, Ferretti, & Katz, 2000) examined the role of the three constraints that were examined in Katz and Pexman (1997). Recall that in the earlier study we presented target items in the form of a nominal metaphor—namely, "An A is (does) B." These items were either familiar or unfamiliar instantiations of basic conceptual metaphors, and they were always presented in short passages, being uttered by one of the characters in the story. Thus, the first constraint we examined was the role that expressed familiarity played on disambiguating the meaning intended by the character who uttered the statement. The second constraint was the nature of the discourse that preceded the target item: The discourse either suggested the target statement was an endorsement and hence being used as a metaphor (the metaphor-inviting condition) or suggested that the speaker was rejecting the truth value of the statement and hence using the metaphor to make a sarcastic commentary (the sarcasm-inviting condition) or was neutral with respect to endorsement rejection. The third constraint was a social factor—the occupation of the person who made the statement (either high-irony speaker, high-metaphor speaker, or a control condition in which the speaker's occupation was not presented)—which was manipulated. The findings of this earlier study were clear using off-line dependent measures (either recall or ratings of sarcasm and mocking): Each of these constraints helped to disambiguate the metaphoric or sarcastic intent of the speaker, which often acted interactively.

We wished to see whether any of these three constraints acted on-line during the reading of the target item or whether effects only occurred later in the processing sequence. The latter point is especially important because it allows us to determine when each of the contextual constraints exerts its influence on the target sentence. Moreover, we eliminated the possibility that our sample adopted special metaphor or sarcasm reading strategies (see Steen, 1993) by intermixing the critical experimental passages among a large number of filler passages. The critical experimental passages were very similar to those employed in Katz and Pexman (1997) with the major alteration being the addition of text after the target statement, allowing us to investigate contextual effects that arise after the target has been read.

The RT data were very clear. Averaged over all conditions, there was little variability in reading the target sentence until the last word, which was read 170 ms. more slowly than the preceding words. This increase in RT at sentence end is a standard finding and is known as sentence wrap-up in the language processing literature, which indicates "A search for referents that have not been assigned, the construction of inter-clause relations ... and an attempt to handle any inconsistencies that could not be resolved within the sentence" (Just & Carpenter, 1980, p. 345). Given that most theories of metaphor processing put the processing load for comprehension with the vehicle (in our case, the last word), variability in RT for the last word in the sentence should depend on how readily the last word is integrated into the representation of text. If the processing of a metaphor in context occurs directly, it should be expected that the resolution of any ambiguity would be completed by sentence end and not spill over to the RTs taken downstream (as evidenced by longer RTs taken to start reading the sentence following the target or even the first few words of the following sentence). Thus, we wished to see if spill over occurred and if such an occurrence varied with the contextual constraints.

There was clear evidence that the constraints came into play quite early in the processing sequence. First, on comparing the two neutral conditions in which speaker's occupation (high-metaphor or high-irony) was mentioned with that for which there was no mention of occupation, we found reliably longer RTs for the last word of the ambiguous statement in the two conditions involving occupational mention; this effect was most evident for statements that were unfamiliar. Taken together, these data indicate that the effect of a social constraint and the indicator of speaker's intent is available no later than the end of the utterance—that is, at an early stage of statement processing. The familiarity effect suggests that at these early stages of processing the cue is mainly useful in the comprehension of unfamiliar statements, presumably those without a well-established canonical (or salient) meaning.

Second, there were clear effects based on the nature of the discourse that preceded the target statement. Targets that were embedded in the metaphor-inviting context produced much less spillover to locations downstream than the same items placed in a sarcasm-inviting condition. In fact, the RTs in the two conditions were the same at the last word in the target location, suggesting that, regardless of the nature of the context, the metaphoric interpretation of the statement was largely completed by statement's end. However, the time taken to proceed to the first word of the sentence following the target was slower (by 54 ms) in the sarcasm-inviting condition. These data suggest that although the metaphoric content of the statement might be available early, the recognition of the sarcastic commentary takes longer to develop.

Third, there was an interactive effect of discourse context and occupational mention: When the target statement was uttered by a person from a high-metaphor occupation, RTs at the last word in the statement were substantially slower in the neutral condition (by over 100 ms) than either the irony-inviting or metaphor-inviting contexts, which did not differ from one another. When the target is uttered by a person from a high-irony occupation, once again we find slower RTs in the neutral condition relative to the other two conditions. However, now there are additional effects, with differences found in RTs beyond the statement itself: The time taken to proceed to the next sentence is faster in the metaphor-inviting condition but slower in the irony-inviting condition, a difference of over 100 ms.

Taken together, the effects show that providing enriched context leads to some resolution of meaning of an ambiguous statement by the last word of that statement. Given that in our case the statements are in the canonical form of a nominal metaphor, these data are consistent with the claim that, first, with contextual support, metaphoric meaning is available very early in the processing sequence. Second, when the statement is uttered by a person typically understood as a high-metaphor user, further analysis of the statement does not appear to occur (as evidenced by a failure to find marked spillover effects in RT beyond the sentence itself). Third, when the speaker is typically understood as a high-irony user, additional processing occurs downstream, almost immediately when the discourse context invites an ironic interpretation and more slowly when the context just supports the default metaphoric interpretation. Thus, it appears that at least one social factor (speaker's occupation) plays an important role in the on-line reading of nonliteral language. When the discourse context is sarcastic, interpretation of the speaker is assessed early and aids in the integration of the target statement's meaning very shortly after the statement has been read; when there is an incongruity between the sarcastic nature of the speaker and a context that invited a nonsarcastic interpretation, this incongruity appears to be initially ignored but is noted by the beginning of the next sentence. Although we did not discuss it in these terms in Pexman et al. (2000), these data are completely consistent with a constraint satisfaction perspective.

Gender Effects. As noted earlier, sociolinguistic and off-line psycholinguistic work implicates gender as an important factor in the processing of sarcasm. In my laboratory, we (Katz et al., 2001) started to examine the on-line role of gender using the moving windows methodology. We asked participants to read a set of passages as in the studies already described. The critical passages were pretested to ensure that the speaker was being sarcastic. Of most interest was our manipulation—namely, the gender of speaker and listener—which we orthogonally varied in a 2 (male or female speaker) × 2 (male or female listener) design. The passages were exactly the same except for the gender assigned to speaker and listener (as operationalized by gender-specific names). The results were intriguing: First, overall passages were read more quickly by a male rather than a female speaker; this effect was most noted for the last two words of the utterance made by the speaker. That is, gender effects emerged during the act of reading the critical sarcastic statement, once again supporting the argument that social constraints come into play very early in the process of comprehension—an interpretation that is supported by other lines of emerging research (Garnham, Oakhill, & Reynolds, 2002). One can speculate that the slowdown in reading for the female-speaker condition suggests that it is more difficult to settle on an interpretation of a possible sarcastic comment when the statement is uttered by a women, perhaps because sarcasm is less likely to be associated with women. The effect just noted was modified by the gender of the listener. The effect emerged, once again, for the last two words of the possibly sarcastic comment. That is, the slower reading of comments made by female speakers is found most notably when the comment is directed at another woman, once again supporting the notion that, because sarcasm is more likely to be associated with men, noncanonical usage is delayed as people attempt to integrate what they are reading with both the text and their stored knowledge of the world. And this occurs on-line during the act of reading.

SUMMARY AND CONCLUSIONS

Based on the data presented, I draw the following conclusions and take the liberty to speculate freely. First, I argue that social constraints are a ubiquitous force in the disambiguating of speakers intent. In the aforementioned review, I limited myself to certain linguistic forms in which what a speaker expresses differs from what he or she intended to convey: metaphor, sarcasm, and, to a lesser extent, indirect requests. And I limited most of the discussion here to two such social constraints: occupational status and gender. In principle, however, any of a number of linguistic forms could be considered and a host of additional sociocultural factors examined, such as age or ethnicity or whether the people interacting in a passage are related in some way. Second, the effects of these social constraints are found not only in off-line tasks, but also (from my perspective, even more provocatively), in on-line tasks. Social constraints come into play almost immediately during the act of comprehension. Third, the effects of social constraints appear to interact with a host of other variables, such as the familiarity of the expression being used by the speaker; although the evidence for this is most clearly seen in the off-line studies, it also is observed in some of the on-line data.

These data have direct implications for the type of processing models that are suitable for explaining language comprehension in general and nonliteral language comprehension more specifically. The standard theoretical contrast, in both cases, has been between two classes of models. In one case, the extraction of some information is obligatory and in which the effects of context (however it is defined) limits comprehension to one (or, at most, a very few) context-appropriate meanings. The second and contrasting theoretical approach does not put an emphasis on the processing of obligatory information but instead considers that context plays a central and immediate role in the extraction of information.

Therefore, I favor the second set of models in which discourse is considered to play an immediate role in the ongoing extraction of meaning from language. But I especially favor a specific version of such models based on the finding that the interpretation that we make is based on a set of factors that interact with one another—namely, constraint satisfaction. Thus, a sociocultural factor, such as knowledge of a persons occupation, might invite a metaphoric or an ironic understanding of the same phrase, but this effect is moderated by the familiarity of the phrase itself. Generally, the effect of occupation, gender of the speaker, or whether one is speaking to a close friend by itself will not be sufficient enough to provide an unambiguous interpretation; in fact, these factors might only come into play when other factors are not present. For instance, occupational knowledge might be a strong constraint when other information in the context is not available for disambiguation to occur. As such, and in line with the evidence that I already reviewed, I favor an approach like that instantiated in constraint satisfaction models.

Note that in many ways the most recent version of the graded salience model is also compatible with much of the data discussed as supportive of constraint satisfaction (see Giora, in press). In this version the original theory has been modified such that Giora's original modular component (sensitive to salience) is now complemented by an additional context-sensitive mechanism. Giora posited that context can boost the activation of non-salient material but not at the cost of the activation of salient material. Although the addition of a second component often leads to similar predictions to those offered by constraint satisfaction models, the theoretical differences between the two positions should not be minimized. Constraint satisfaction models do not give processing priority to salient information; rather, these models view language processing as a function of the ongoing interaction of multiple sources of information, each of which will constrain the interpretation that will emerge to various degrees. Constraints that are very strong (e.g., item saliency) may appear to be obligatory because the other constraints present in the context are not strong enough to overcome the dominance of a very strong constraint. Moreover, and most important, constraint-based models hold that increasing the strength of opposing constraints can, in principle, lead to greater activation of less salient meanings than salient meanings and, in opposition to Giora's position, might even lead to the salient meaning not be activated at all (see Vu, Kellas, & Paul, 1998, for a demonstration of word access). Thus, in principle, constraint-based and the graded salience models can be empirically disentangled, although, given the dominance of salience, one might need a methodology more sensitive than the moving windows technique that I used. One possibility is to use event-related brain potentials that, because of the multidimensional nature of the data sets produced, have proven sensitive to subtle differences in the processing of language and other cognitive processes (see Osman, 1998, for a review).

In conclusion, there are two consequences that follow from adopting a constraint satisfaction approach. First, the standard approach taken in the nonliteral language processing literature wherein a researcher looks to see if in a given experiment some obligatory processing occurs or not (e.g., the extraction of literal meaning) is, from the constraint satisfaction approach, a fruitless enterprise because one would expect that literal meaning might in fact be extracted before nonliteral meaning if the constraints all point toward a literal interpretation but would not be extracted initially if the constraints point toward a figurative interpretation. The emphasis is thus neither on the characteristics of the target phrase per se nor, generally speaking, just on the discourse characteristics, but rather on the specific factors that appear in the presentational context and the meaning of those factors to the interpreter. The second point follows directly from the first. Given the importance of understanding the constraints available in the discourse, a major job for experimenters will be to systematically identify constraints and to quantify the strength of these constraints in different contexts. I argue further that central to this mission would be a systematic examination of social factors, such as gender, occupation, and social status. Research that identifies pragmatic sociocultural constraints include, but is not limited to, identifying (a) when a specific person might employ humor, sarcasm, or hyperbole, (b) socioeconomic knowledge about language use; and (c) gender-related effects. In essence, a constraint-based approach requires an in-depth examination of the reasons why a given expressions might be used (e.g., see Toplak & Katz, 2000, for sarcastic irony) and when it might be employed (e.g., see Drew & Holt, 1995, for a well-developed example with idioms).

ACKNOWLEDGMENT

This research was supported by a grant from the Natural Sciences and Engineering Research Council of Canada (Operating Grant No. 06P007040).

Correspondence concerning this chapter should be addressed to Albert Katz, Department of Psychology, The University of Western Ontario, London, Ontario, Canada, N6A 5C2. E-mail: katz@uwo.ca

REFERENCES

Blasko, D., & Connine, C. (1993). Effects of familiarity and aptness on metaphor processing. *Journal of Experimental Psychology: Learning, Memory, and Cognition, 19*, 295–308.

Clark, H. (1996). *Using language.* Cambridge, England: Cambridge University Press.

Colston, H., & Gibbs, R. W., Jr. (2002). Are irony and metaphor understood differently? *Metaphor and Symbol, 17*, 57–80.

Colston, H., & Lee, S. (2000, May). *On gender differences in verbal irony.* Paper presented at the meeting of the International Gender and language Association, Stanford University, Palo Alto, CA.

Drew, P., & Holt, E. (1995). Idiomatic expressions and their role in the organization of topic transition in conversation. In M. Everaert, E. J. van der Linden, A. Schenk, & R. Schreuder (Eds.), *Idioms: Structural and psychological perspectives* (pp. 117–132). Hillsdale, NJ: Lawrence Erlbaum Associates.

Ekert, P. (1997). Age as a sociolinguistic variable. In. F. Coulmas (Ed.), *The handbook of sociolinguistics* (pp. 151–167). Oxford, England: Blackwell.

Garnham, A., Oakhill, J., & Reynolds, D. (2002). Are inferences from stereotyped role names to characters' gender made elaboratively? *Memory and Cognition, 30*, 439–446.

Gibbs, R. W., Jr. (1986). On the psycholinguistics of sarcasm. *Journal of Experimental Psychology: General, 115*, 3–15

Gibbs, R. W., Jr. (1994). *The poetics of mind.* Cambridge, England: Cambridge University Press.

Gibbs, R. W., Jr. (2000). Irony in talk among friends. *Metaphor and Symbol, 15*, 5–27.

Giora, R. (2003). *On our mind: Salience, context and figurative language.* New York: Oxford University Press.

Giora, R., Fein, O., & Schwartz, T. (1998). Irony: Graded salience and indirect negation. *Metaphor and Symbol, 13*, 83–101.

Glucksberg, S. (1991). Beyond literal meanings: The psychology of allusion. *Psychological Science, 2*, 146–152.

Glucksberg, S. (2001). *Understanding figurative language: From metaphors to idioms.* New York: Oxford University Press.

Holtgraves, T. (1991). Interpreting questions and replies: Effects of face-threat, question form, and gender. *Social Psychology Quarterly, 54*, 15–24.

Holtgraves, T. (1992). Interpersonal underpinnings of request strategies: General principles and differences due to culture and gender. *Journal of Personality and Social Psychology, 62*, 246–256.

Holtgraves, T. (1997a). Politeness and memory for wording of remarks. *Memory & Cognition, 25*, 106–116.

Holtgraves, T. (1997b). Styles of language use: Individual and cultural variability in conversational indirectness. *Journal of Personality and Social Psychology, 73*, 624–637.

Jorgensen, J. (1996). The functions of sarcastic irony in speech. *Journal of Pragmatics, 26*, 613–634.

Just, M., & Carpenter, P. (1980). A theory of reading: From eye fixation to comprehension. *Psychological review, 87*, 329–354.

Katz, A. (1996a). Experimental psycholinguistics and figurative language: Circa 1995. *Metaphor and Symbolic Activity, 11*, 17–37.

Katz, A. (1996b). On interpreting statements as metaphor or irony: Contextual heuristics and cognitive consequences. In J. S. Mio & A. N. Katz (Eds.), *Metaphor: Implications and applications* (pp. 1–22). Mahwah, NJ: Lawrence Erlbaum Associates.

Katz, A., & Ferretti, T. (2001). Moment-by-moment comprehension of proverbs in discourse. *Metaphor and Symbol, 16*, 193–221.

Katz, A., & Ferretti, T. (2003). Reading proverbs in context: The role of explicit markers *Discourse Processes, 36*, 19–46.

Katz, A., & Lee, C. (1993). The role of authorial intent in determining verbal irony and metaphor. *Metaphor and Symbolic Activity, 8,* 257–279.

Katz, A., & Pexman, P. (1997). Interpreting figurative statements: Speaker occupation can change metaphor to irony. *Metaphor and Symbol, 12,* 19–41.

Katz, A., Piasecka, I., & Toplak, M. (2001). *Comprehending the sarcastic comments of males and females.* Paper presented at the 42nd annual meeting of the Psychonomic Society, Orlando, FL.

Kay, P. (1997). *Words and the grammar of context.* Stanford, CA: CSLI Publications.

Kemper, S., & Thissen, D. (1981). Memory for dimensions of requests. *Journal of Verbal Learning and Verbal Behavior, 20,* 552–563.

Kierkegaard, S. (1996). *The concept of irony, with constant reference to Socrates* (L. M. Caprl, Trans.). London: Collins.

Kreuz, R. J. (1996). The use of verbal irony: Cues and constraints. In J. S. Mio & A. N. Katz (Eds.), *Metaphor: Implications and applications* (pp. 23–38). Mahwah, NJ: Lawrence Erlbaum Associates.

Kreuz, R. J. & Glucksberg, S. (1989). How to be sarcastic: The echoic reminder theory of verbal irony. *Journal of Experimental Psychology: General, 118,* 374–386.

Kreuz, R. J., Kassler, M., Coppenrath, L., & McLain, A. B. (1999). Tag questions and common ground effects in the perception of verbal irony. *Journal of Pragmatics, 31,* 1685–1700.

Lee, C., & Katz, A. (1998). The differential role of ridicule in sarcasm and irony. *Metaphor and Symbol, 13,* 1–5.

McRae, K., Spivey-Knowlton, M., & Tanenhaus, M. (1998). Modeling the influence of thematic fit (and other constraints) in on-line sentence comprehension. *Journal of Memory and Language, 38,* 283–312.

Mieder, W. (1982). *International proverb scholarship: An annotated bibliography* (Vol. 1). New York: Garland.

Mieder, W. (1990). *International proverb scholarship: An annotated bibliography* (Vol. 2). New York: Garland.

Moon, R. (1998). *Fixed expressions and idioms in English; A corpus-based approach.* Oxford, England: Clarendon.

Osman, A. (1998). Brainwaves and mental processes: Electrical evidence of attention, perception and intention. In D. Scarborough & S. Sternberg (Eds.), *An invitation to cognitive science: Vol. 4. Methods, models and conceptual issues* (pp. 865–915). Cambridge, MA: MIT Press.

Pexman, P., Ferretti, T., & Katz, A. (2000). Discourse factors that influence on-line reading of metaphor and irony. *Discourse Processes, 29,* 201–222.

Pynte, J., Besson, M., Robichon, F.-H., & Poli, J. (1996). The time course of metaphor comprehension: An event-related potential study. *Brain and Language, 55,* 293–316.

Searle, J. (1979). Metaphor. In A. Ortony (Ed.), *Metaphor and thought* (pp. 92–123). Cambridge, England: Cambridge University Press.

Steen, G. (1993). *Metaphor and literary reception.* London: Longman.

Toplak, M., & Katz, A. (2000). On the uses of sarcastic irony. *Journal of Pragmatics, 32,* 1476–1488.

Turner, N., & Katz, A. (1997). The availability of conventional and of literal meaning during the comprehension of proverbs. *Pragmatics and Cognition, 5,* 199–133.

Vu, H., Kellas, G., & Paul, S. (1998). Sources of constraints on lexical ambiguity resolution. *Memory & cognition, 26,* 979–1001.

Weatherall, A. (2002). *Gender, language and discourse.* New York: Routledge.

Winner, E. (1988). *The point of words: Children's understanding of metaphor and irony.* Cambridge, MA: Harvard University Press.

9

Social Factors in the Interpretation of Verbal Irony: The Roles of Speaker and Listener Characteristics

Penny M. Pexman
University of Calgary

The topic of this chapter is the role of social factors in interpretation of ironic intent. To illustrate the type of factors that are discussed, imagine you are the addressee of the following remark: "You are so punctual." How will you interpret this remark? How will you determine what meaning the speaker intends? Your metalinguistic knowledge may indicate that although most remarks of this type are intended literally, some are intended ironically. In determining whether this remark is intended literally or ironically you may attend to clues in the situation in which the remark occurred: If you just arrived 20 min late for an important meeting, then the speaker likely has a negative attitude about your punctuality. Incongruity between the negative tone of the situation and the positive tone of the statement is a reliable cue to ironic intent (e.g., Colston & O'Brien, 2000a; Gerrig & Goldvarg, 2000; Katz & Lee, 1993; Katz & Pexman, 1997). Perhaps earlier in the day you made a positive claim to the speaker about your punctuality (e.g., "Don't worry, I'm really punctual. I'll make the meeting on time"). The fact that the speaker's remark echoed your claim could also be a cue to ironic intent (e.g., Colston, 2000; Gibbs, 1986; Jorgensen, Miller, & Sperber, 1984; Kreuz & Glucksberg, 1989; Kumon-Nakamura, Glucksberg, & Brown, 1995). Even if this claim had not been made, however, the fact that the remark echoes an implicit norm or social convention (that people should be punctual) could cue ironic intent. Another cue could be the speaker's use of the word *so* in the remark. The exaggeration implied by this word may be another hallmark of verbal irony (Colston & O'Brien, 2000a; Kreuz, 1996). Certainly, tone of voice can also signal irony, but ironic intent can be detected without tone of voice information (Kreuz & Roberts, 1995). In addition to these verbal cues, nonverbal cues like gesture and facial expression indicate irony. Much of the psychological research on verbal irony has focused on identifying these verbal and non-verbal cues to ironic intent. Less research has addressed the social cues that may be relevant. It seems likely that characteristics of the speaker would be considered: Is this someone who often speaks ironically? Does the speaker like the listener? It also seems possible that characteristics of listeners could influence their interpretation: Are some people (perhaps because they frequently speak ironically themselves) more prone to an ironic interpretation? I first summarize research on these issues, then consider how current theories of irony would (or would not) predict a role for social factors, and finally suggest ways in which these social factors might be relevant for interpreting other forms of figurative language.

SPEAKER CHARACTERISTICS

Past research has shown that certain characteristics are attributed to speakers making ironic statements. Compared to speakers who make nonironic remarks, speakers who make ironic remarks are perceived to be more angry, disgusted, and scornful (Leggitt & Gibbs, 2000), as well as ver-bally aggressive and offensive (Toplak & Katz, 2000). Colston (1997) re-ported that speakers who used ironic criticisms were perceived to be more condemning than speakers who used literal criticisms. Roberts and Kreuz (1994) found that irony was used to express negative emotion. It has also been argued, however, that irony does not serve only negative communi-cation goals. Kreuz, Long, and Church (1991; see also Colston & O'Brien 2000a, 2000b) reported that ironic statements were intended to mock someone but also to be funny. Dews and Winner (1995; Dews, Kaplan, & Winner, 1995) reported that speakers who made ironic criticisms were per-ceived to be less annoyed than speakers who made literal criticisms. Dews and Winner proposed the tinge hypothesis to explain these findings. Ac-cording to the tinge hypothesis, ironic criticisms are less critical than lit-eral criticisms because the positive surface meaning of an ironic statement tinges the listener's perception of the negative, ironic meaning. Thus, irony lessens the criticism conveyed.

Although Dews and Winner (1995) reported findings that supported the tinge hypothesis, Colston's (1997) results suggested a very different function for verbal irony: to enhance conveyed criticism. Colston noted that his procedure was somewhat different than Dews and Winner's. As is typical, Dews and Winner presented their stimuli to participants in written form (a target statement preceded by a context paragraph). In addition, and less typically, Dews and Winner gave participants tone of voice information for the statements in the form of a tape recording. Ironic criticisms were read in a nasal, mocking tone of voice, and literal criticisms were read in an angry tone of voice. As Colston pointed out, tone of voice information alone could have been used to perceive that speakers of ironic criticisms were less annoyed than speakers of literal criticisms. Colston did not present tone of voice information.

In a recent study, Kara Olineck and I (Pexman & Olineck, 2002a) presented some resolution to the debate over the tinge hypothesis. We argued that the social function of irony might depend on the perspective taken in interpretation. If one considers dimensions that tap perceived speaker intent by asking, for instance, whether the speaker was mocking the addressee, then ironic criticisms may be rated higher (more mocking) than literal criticisms. In contrast, if one considers dimensions that tap the general social impression created by the statement, such as whether the speaker is being impolite, then ironic criticisms may be rated lower (less impolite) than literal criticisms. This is precisely what we found. We concluded that the tinge hypothesis is relevant to the general social impression created by the ironic criticism (i.e., it is considered more polite than a literal criticism) but not necessarily to perceived speaker intent (i.e., it is perceived to be more mocking than a literal criticism).

Although there are clearly many different communication goals attributed to ironic speakers, the research reviewed thus far does not demonstrate that these attributes would necessarily function as cues to ironic intent. To demonstrate this, the attributes would need to be presented as speaker characteristics and be shown to increase the likelihood of an ironic interpretation. The attributes could be presented directly as traits (e.g., the speaker is labeled as a funny person) or could potentially be inferred from other types of social information (e.g., social categories). If these speaker characteristics were shown to influence attributions of speaker intent, then the controversial implication would be that communicative intentions are a perceived to be a function of both the situation and the person. That is, listeners consider factors like speaker personality traits to be relevant to communicative choices. In the following sections I describe research in which speaker attributes have been manipulated to examine their effects on interpretation of verbal irony. These attributes have included the nature of the speaker–addressee relationship, speaker occupation, speaker personality traits, and gender of the speaker.

Speaker–Addressee Relationship

Slugoski and Turnbull (1988) examined the influence of relationship variables on interpretation of potentially ironic remarks. That is, speakers and
addressees were identified as either close or distant and as either liking or
disliking each other. Results showed that relationship distance had little effect, but that liking had a strong effect. When the speaker and listener
clearly liked each other, literal insults were more likely to be interpreted as
ironic compliments (as compared to situations in which speaker and listener
disliked each other). In contrast, literal compliments were more likely to be
interpreted as ironic insults when the speaker and listener clearly disliked
each other. These findings suggested that listeners consider relationship
variables in the process of inferring speaker intent. Relationship affect, in
particular, seems to be a useful cue to ironic intent. This may be because it
reveals the speaker's attitude, which tends to be more positive for ironic
compliments than for literal insults, and more negative for ironic insults
than for literal compliments.

Speaker Occupation

Occupations are social categories that can be associated with particular
traits. Slusher and Anderson (1987) examined stereotypical traits of lawyers, artists, and clergymen. They found that participants characterized
these professions in the following ways: wealthy and aggressive lawyers, tem-
peramental and creative artists, and kind and friendly clergymen. Albert
Katz and I (Katz & Pexman, 1997) investigated whether occupation stereotypes extended to beliefs about language use. For 50 different occupations,
we asked participants to rate members of each occupation for (a) likelihood
of using irony and (b) likelihood of using metaphor. Results showed that participants had quite consistent perceptions about tendencies to use irony and
metaphor, such that members of certain occupations (e.g., comedian) were
reliably perceived as much more likely to use irony than were members of
other occupations (e.g., nurse). Similarly, there were large differences across
occupations in perceived likelihood of using metaphor, with members of certain occupations (e.g., English professor) rated as much more likely to use
metaphor than members of other occupations (e.g., factory worker).

   We further speculated that people's shared perceptions about language
use by members of different occupational categories might function as cues
to speaker intent. That is, if a speaker was described as a member of a
high-irony occupational category, then his or her remarks might be more
likely to be interpreted as ironic. To examine this issue, we devised stimuli
that were metaphors (e.g., "children are precious gems"). These stimuli
could be interpreted as positive metaphoric remarks but could also be interpreted as ironic remarks.

Our goal was to investigate whether speaker occupation cued ironic intent as a function of the incongruity of the statement with the discourse context and also the familiarity of the statement. As such, we presented participants with short context paragraphs followed by target metaphors. Speakers were identified as members of high-irony occupations, high-metaphor occupations, or no occupation was specified. Contexts were devised such that some were irony-inducing (a negative situation was described), some were metaphor-inducing (a positive situation was described), and some were neutral (outcome was not described as positive or negative). The target metaphors were all novel instantiations of root metaphors (Lakoff & Johnson, 1980) but were selected based on pilot study ratings such that half were relatively more familiar and half were relatively less familiar. Participants were asked to consider each context and target statement and rate speaker intent. Afterwards, they were given an unexpected free recall task for the target statements.

Results showed that speaker occupation did cue perceptions of speaker intent, because metaphoric statements made by members of high-irony occupations were considered to be more sarcastic than the same statements made by members of high-metaphor occupations. Also, in making the metaphoric statements, high-irony speakers were perceived to be more mocking than high-metaphor speakers, particularly when the statements were relatively less familiar. We argued that speaker occupation cued ironic intent through heightened incongruity. That is, the incongruity created when a highly ironic speaker made a positive metaphoric remark facilitated detection of ironic intent.

In addition, results of the free recall task indicated that statements made by members of high-irony occupations were remembered more accurately than statements made by members of high-metaphor occupations. We interpreted these memory data to mean that occupation was coded in the comprehension process. Left unresolved, however, was the issue of when in the comprehension process occupation information was activated and integrated. Was this an early or a late effect? Relatedly, in the Katz and Pexman (1997) study participants were required to make overt ratings of speaker intent, and it was possible that the occupation effects observed might be artifacts of this methodology.

In a subsequent study we investigated whether speaker occupation is activated and integrated in the comprehension process when participants are not required to make explicit decisions about speaker intent (Pexman, Ferretti, & Katz, 2000). We used the same stimuli as in Katz and Pexman (1997, Study 1), but we adopted a self-paced, moving windows reading task to assess processing. In the moving windows reading task stimuli were presented on a computer screen. Because participants advanced the moving window themselves, it was possible to measure reading time (RT) for each word in each context paragraph and each target statement. In moving windows experiments, processing for the target statement sometimes continues even after the last word in the statement has been read. To capture any spillover effects of this type, we added short wrap-up sentences to follow each target metaphor. Although participants answered a simple, factual comprehension question after each passage, they were never asked about speaker intent. As such, it was assumed that the task captured typical integrative processing.

Using this on-line procedure, results showed that for the last word in the target metaphor, RTs were significantly longer when speaker occupation had been mentioned in the context paragraph. In particular, RTs were almost 200 ms longer at the last word in the target when speaker occupation (either high-irony or high-metaphor) was mentioned for unfamiliar target metaphors, as compared to RTs for that location when no occupation was provided in the context paragraph. There were also interactive effects of speaker occupation and context incongruity slightly further downstream, at reading locations immediately after the target statement. For instance, when the speaker was a member of a high-irony occupation, and when the context suggested a nonironic interpretation, there was increased processing time at locations past the end of the target statement. These results suggested that participants coded speaker occupation information and integrated this information with other cues at the end of the target statement. Thus, speaker occupation information was activated and integrated fairly early in the processing of potentially ironic remarks. Note that participants used this cue even when they were not required to make overt ratings of speaker intent. We argued that these results supported a context-driven, interactive model of language processing. Relevant cues to ironic intent were activated quite rapidly and integrated to derive the best possible interpretation.

The results of the Katz and Pexman (1997) and Pexman et al. (2000) studies suggested that speaker occupation was a salient cue to ironic intent, but several issues were left unresolved. The investigations had, for instance, been limited to metaphoric stimuli, and the speaker occupations were either congruent with metaphoric speech (the high-metaphor occupations) or were incongruent with that type of speech (the high-irony occupations). The speaker occupation effects were attributed to this incongruity. It is also possible, however, that speaker occupation effects could be created not just by the incongruity of a high-irony speaker using a metaphor but also by the occupation cueing traits associated with ironic speakers. Those traits might cue an ironic interpretation even when the nonironic sense of the target statement itself was not obviously out of keeping with the speaker's conversational tendencies. This possibility was tested in a recent study by Kara Olineck and I (Pexman & Olineck,

2002b), in which the target statements were all nonmetaphors like "you are a wonderful friend."

In the Pexman and Olineck (2002b) study, we also addressed other unresolved issues with regard to speaker occupation effects. We assessed the impact of speaker occupation on interpretation of ironic criticisms but, unlike the previous Katz and Pexman (1997) and Pexman et al. (2000) studies, also included ironic compliments (e.g., "you are a terrible friend" said when your friend has just done something gracious). In everyday speech, ironic compliments are less common than ironic criticisms (Gibbs, 2000), and they may also be more difficult to interpret (Kreuz & Glucksberg, 1989). Because of this additional ambiguity for ironic compliments, we hypothesized that speaker occupation might be a particularly salient cue to ironic intent for these remarks.

The last unresolved issue that we addressed in the Pexman and Olineck (2002b) study was why speaker occupation cued ironic intent. Our expectation was that the occupational categories were associated with particular traits, but which traits were relevant in the context of potentially ironic speech?

In the Pexman and Olineck (2002b) study we conducted three experiments. The first two were ratings studies. In Experiment 1, participants were presented with short context paragraphs followed by positive or negative target statements like "you are a wonderful friend" or "you are a terrible friend." The context paragraphs described either a positive event or a negative event. In addition, these contexts were either strong (very positive or very negative) or weak (mildly positive or mildly negative). Finally, speaker occupation was manipulated. A pilot study was conducted to collect new occupation ratings. In the previous studies (Katz & Pexman, 1997; Pexman et al., 2000) my colleagues and I had used high-irony (and low-metaphor) or high-metaphor (and low-irony) occupations. In the Pexman and Olineck pilot study we asked participants to rate a set of occupations for likelihood that members of each occupation would use sarcasm. We suspected that participants would have clear ideas about sarcasm use but if asked to rate irony might confuse verbal irony with situational irony. Results showed that certain occupations were perceived to be very likely to use sarcasm (e.g., comedian, talk show host, movie critic, and cab driver) whereas other occupations were perceived as very unlikely to use sarcasm (e.g., accountant, doctor, clergyman, and scientist). Certainly, several of these occupations overlapped with the high-irony and high-metaphor occupations used in the previous studies.

For each target statement, participants were asked to make the following ratings: (a) Is the speaker being sarcastic? (b) Is the speaker saying something polite? (c) Is the speaker mocking someone? (d) How certain are you that you correctly interpreted the speaker's intent? They also completed an unexpected recall task.

The results of Experiment 1 showed that speaker occupation influenced ratings of the extent to which the speaker was mocking someone: Statements made by sarcastic speakers were perceived to be more mocking than statements made by nonsarcastic speakers. This effect interacted with context strength, such that the speaker occupation effect was stronger for statements presented in weak (as compared to strong) contexts. Although speaker occupation effects were observed in the mocking ratings, there were no significant effects in ratings of politeness, certainty, or, most important, sarcasm ratings. There were, however, effects of speaker occupation in the recall data. Recall tended to be highest for potentially sarcastic remarks, such as for positive statements made by sarcastic speakers, particularly when the remark was relatively more ambiguous, as in the weak context conditions or in situations in which the remark could be an ironic compliment (as compared to situations in which the remark could be an ironic criticism). Based on the results of Experiment 1, we concluded that speaker occupation information was coded in the comprehension process (hence, the recall effects) and influenced ratings of speaker intent (mocking ratings) but did not add significantly to perceived level of sarcasm. We hypothesized that the null occupation effects for sarcasm ratings could be explained by the presence of other cues: The contexts provided information about the positive or negative outcome of events, and the congruity or incongruity of this information with the obvious positive or negative tone of the target statements could have been a powerful (and sufficient) cue to ironic intent. Thus, speaker occupation, although coded in the comprehension process, would have been a redundant cue for level of perceived sarcasm.

In Experiment 2, we tested this hypothesis by modifying the context information. We removed all information in the context passages about whether the outcome of events had been positive or negative and thus created a neutral context condition. All target statements (both positive and negative) were presented in these neutral contexts. Speaker occupation information was, however, still provided. Under these conditions, when context incongruity was not signaled, there was a significant speaker occupation effect: Both positive and negative target statements were perceived to be more sarcastic when the speaker was a member of a sarcastic occupation. Speaker occupation effects were also observed for mocking ratings, politeness ratings, and certainty ratings. That is, participants were more certain that they had correctly interpreted speaker intent when the speaker was identified as a member of a sarcastic occupation.

These findings suggested that speaker occupation cues speaker intent, even for nonmetaphoric statements, particularly when other cues to speaker intent (e.g., context incongruity) are absent. The results of the previous studies (e.g., Katz & Pexman, 1997) had been taken to mean that speaker occupation effects are generated by incongruity between a speaker's perceived conversational tendencies (i.e., tendency not to use metaphor) and the type of utterance made (i.e., a metaphor). The more recent findings (Pexman & Olineck, 2002b) suggested that speaker occupation effects may also be generated by activating certain traits for the speaker, based on the occupational stereotype, that lead the listener to expect an ironic remark (or not). This type of effect would influence interpretation of many different types of utterances, even familiar, nonmetaphoric remarks, as was the case in the present study.

What are the traits that are perceived to predict ironic intent? To address this question, we asked participants to rate a set of occupations for particular traits (Pexman & Olineck, 2002b, Experiment 3). As noted, previous research had established that several traits are attributed to speakers who make ironic remarks, for instance, tendency to be humorous (e.g., Kreuz et al., 1991), tendency to criticize (e.g., Colston, 1997; Kreuz et al., 1991), tendency to be aggressive (e.g., Toplak & Katz, 2000), and social status or education level (Katz & Pexman, 1997). In addition, certain dimensions seem to be negatively associated with ironic speech, such as tendency to be sincere (e.g., Clark & Gerrig, 1984; Haverkate, 1990; Kumon-Nakamura et al., 1995) and tendency to have close relationships (Slugoski & Turnbull, 1988). We asked participants in Experiment 3 to rate 45 occupations on each of these dimensions. Recall that in the pilot study, we had asked a different set of participants to rate the same 45 occupations for likelihood of using sarcasm. In a regression analysis, we considered whether any of the trait ratings (collected in Experiment 3) predicted the sarcasm ratings (collected in the pilot study). Results showed that four of the trait dimensions had significant, unique relationships with sarcasm ratings: These were tendency to be humorous, tendency to criticize, tendency to be sincere, and education level. Of these four predictors, tendency to be humorous accounted for the largest proportion of variance in sarcasm ratings (28%). With all four of these predictors, the regression equation had an R^2 value of .74. The implication is that 74% of the variance in sarcasm ratings was explained by the combination of humor, criticism, sincerity, and education level. As such, we argued that these variables capture many of the critical components of occupational stereotypes in the context of potentially ironic speech. Certainly, there are other important factors such as stereotype strength and consistency that have not been captured in this analysis. Nonetheless, it seems reasonable to conclude that members of occupations that are associated with sarcastic speech are perceived to be funnier, more critical, less sincere, and to have lower education levels. This information, when integrated with the statement and other aspects of context, shapes perceptions of speaker intent. The on-line results reported in Pexman et al. (2000) suggested that this integration process is not merely a function of being asked to make explicit decisions about speaker intent. In the on-line study, in which participants were not required to make an explicit decision about speaker intent, there was evidence that participants integrated speaker occupation information relatively early in processing—as they read the last word in the target statement. It seems likely that the same type of processing occurred in this study.

Speaker Personality Traits

In the literature on speaker occupation effects (already reviewed), it is assumed that speaker traits are inferred from occupation stereotypes. It seems highly plausible that direct knowledge of a speaker's personality traits could also cue speaker intent. To my knowledge, this has only been tested in one study. This study was conducted in my laboratory and the participants were school-age children.

The developmental literature suggests that children begin to understand verbal irony around age 6 (e.g., Dews et al., 1996; Hancock, Dunham, & Purdy, 2000). The developmental literature also suggests that children begin to understand personality traits and to use those trait concepts to make nonobvious inferences even earlier, as young as age 4 (Heyman & Gelman, 1999). These ages mark early understanding of irony and personality traits, with children's concepts of verbal irony and traits becoming more complex as they mature.

In a recent study, my coauthors and I (Harris, Ivanko, Jungen, Hala, & Pexman, 2001) explored children's abilities to use speaker personality traits as cues to ironic intent. We investigated whether consistent personality trait information (a mean speaker making an ironic criticism) would facilitate detection of ironic intent and how children would interpret inconsistent personality trait information (a nice speaker making an ironic criticism). Literal compliments and ironic criticisms were presented to children in the context of short puppet shows with prerecorded narrative. Intonation was provided such that ironic criticisms were delivered with a slightly scornful tone of voice, whereas literal compliments were delivered with a more positive, earnest tone.

Before combining personality trait information with potentially ironic remarks, we first conducted a control experiment (Experiment 1) in which we tested 5- and 6-year-old children's understanding of personality traits separately from their understanding of potentially ironic remarks. In Experiment 1, participants were first asked to predict helping and sharing behavior of the mean and nice characters based on personality information alone. With a high degree of accuracy, the children predicted that the nice characters would be likely to help and share and that the mean characters would not. Separately, the children were also presented with the contexts and potentially ironic statements and were asked three questions devised to tap the children's understanding of speaker belief ("When Betty said 'you are so careful,' did she think Alex was careful or not careful?") and speaker intent ("When Betty said 'you are so careful,' was what she said nice or mean?" and "Now look at the faces and show me how nice or mean Betty was being"). The face scale depicted five faces, with expressions ranging from nice (broadly smiling face) to mean (scowling face).

Results of Experiment 1 showed that for statements presented in the positive contexts (literal compliments) the children responded correctly to the belief question in every case (100% correct) and were only slightly less accurate in their responses to the intent question (97% correct). For responses to statements presented in the negative contexts (ironic criticisms), the children were much less accurate on the belief question (55% correct), and they tended to be even less accurate in their responses to the intent question (45% correct). This difference in accuracy for speaker belief (attitude) and intent has been observed in other developmental studies (e.g., Ackerman, 1981, 1983; Hancock et al., 2000) and has been taken as evidence that detection of speaker attitude is a prerequisite for detection of speaker intent (Winner & Leekam, 1991).

We then combined the personality trait information with the contexts and statements in Experiments 2 and 3. The participants in Experiment 2 were again 5- and 6-year-old children. Speaker trait information did not influence performance on the speaker belief question, but it did affect accuracy on the speaker intent question. That is, in the negative context situations, in which the remark was intended to be an ironic criticism, the children tended to assess speaker intent more accurately when the speaker was a mean person (consistent trait information, 69% correct) than when the speaker was a nice person (inconsistent trait information, 50% correct). The same type of difference was observed in the positive context situations, in which the remark was intended to be a literal compliment: The children tended to assess speaker intent more accurately when the speaker was a nice person (consistent trait information, 88% correct) than when the speaker was a mean person (inconsistent trait information, 75%). These results suggested that young children used information about speaker personality traits to modify their interpretations of speaker intent for potentially ironic remarks.

The same procedure was used with older children (7- and 8-year-olds) in Experiment 3. These older children were generally more accurate in their interpretations of speaker belief and speaker intent. Their responses to the first intent question did not seem to be modified by speaker trait information (for literal compliments, 100% correct with nice speaker, 94% correct with mean speaker; for ironic criticisms, 87% correct with mean speaker, 81% correct with nice speaker). There was evidence, however, that the older children integrated the speaker trait information with the statements in their responses to the second intent question (face scale). Here, they rated ironic criticisms as somewhat less mean when the speaker was labeled as *nice* (as compared to their ratings for ironic criticisms made by mean speakers). In contrast, they considered all literal compliments to be very nice regardless of speaker traits.

There is an interesting developmental story in these findings. Younger children relied more heavily on trait information, and it biased their interpretations of both ironic and literal utterances. Older children had a stronger grasp on ironic intent and a more sophisticated understanding of personality traits. The older children seemed to realize that personality traits did not predict the essential intent behind ironic utterances (a person could be nice and still make a mean remark) but that the traits could be taken into consideration in determining how mean a remark is intended to be. Perhaps most surprising is the fact that both groups of children were able to deal with inconsistent or conflicting information and make decisions about speaker intent in very ambiguous contexts.

We think that this developmental work has some interesting implications for the issue of teasing and bullying. Sarcasm is often part of teasing behavior (Keltner, Capps, Kring, Young, & Heerey, 2001) because it allows a bully to simultaneously entertain bystanders and mock the target. Harris et al. (2001) suggested that children's detection of sarcasm is enhanced when they are told that the speaker is a mean person. This enhancement probably occurs because the trait provides the child with valuable information about the speaker's attitude and motive. The implication, albeit indirect, is that children's understanding of bullying behavior might be helped by explicit information about the motive and attitudes underlying that behavior.

Gender of the Speaker

The teasing literature has also provided some conflicting claims about gender differences and teasing. In research in which irony was considered to be one form of teasing, Lampert (1996) reported that men were more likely to tease than women. In contrast, Keltner et al. (2001) concluded that there was only weak support for gender differences in extent of teasing and found no evidence of gender differences in the style or manner of teasing. Gibbs (2000) reported that men were more likely to use sarcastic irony in conversation with friends.

Katz, Piasecka, and Toplak (2001) investigated whether gender, as a social category, could cue a speaker's tendency to use ironic language (or not). In a ratings task, Katz et al. found that men were perceived to be more sarcastic than women. Also, in an on-line reading task, there was evidence that gender of the speaker and gender of the addressee were processed as the sarcastic comment was read. As in the Pexman et al. (2000) study, the on-line data suggested that this social cue was integrated quite early in processing—as participants read the last word in the sarcastic statement.

The research just described suggests that speaker characteristics are coded in the comprehension process for verbal irony by adults and by children, and those characteristics can act as cues to speaker intent. These findings suggest that listeners perceive speaker intent to be a function of interacting situational and personality factors. As such, the participants in these experiments seem to share the view of some researchers in the field of communication—that personality traits are a significant predictor of communication behavior (e.g., McCroskey, Daly, Martin, & Beatty, 1998). According to this view, there should be individual differences in production of verbal irony: Some individuals should tend to use verbal irony more frequently than others. I consider this possibility next.

INDIVIDUAL DIFFERENCES

In a recent study in my laboratory (Ivanko, Pexman, & Olineck, 2003), we investigated individual differences and verbal irony. In particular, we tested the view that some individuals tend to use verbal irony more frequently than others. We also investigated the possibility that individual differences in irony production might be related to irony comprehension; that is, if a person tends to use irony quite often in their own speech, then they might be more likely to detect it in the speech of others. The issue of individual differences has received very little research attention in the irony literature.

In one of the few previous studies related to this issue, Jorgensen (1996) investigated gender differences in emotional reactions to verbal irony. She reported that men were more likely than women to perceive humor in sarcastic irony (Experiment 2). Also, Jorgensen found that women were more likely than men to be offended or angered by sarcastic remarks (Experiment 3). Given these findings, it seemed possible that gender might be one of the individual differences related to production and interpretation of verbal irony.

Another relevant characteristic might be captured by conversational indirectness. Holtgraves (1997) investigated individual differences in the production and comprehension of indirect requests (e.g., saying "it's cold in here" as a request for someone to close the door). He devised and validated the Conversational Indirectness Scale (CIS) to measure the extent to which individuals differ in their tendencies to express themselves indirectly and understand indirect meanings. The scale involves items that were designed to tap both interpretation (10 items) and production (9 items) of conversational indirectness. To the extent that verbal irony is an indirect form of speech, it seemed possible that the CIS might capture individual differences in production and comprehension of verbal irony.

To assess individual differences in use of verbal irony we devised a self-report measure in which participants were asked to rate their own tendencies to speak sarcastically in general (e.g., "How sarcastic are you?" and "How sarcastic would your friends say you are?") and in specific contexts (e.g., "How likely are you to make a sarcastic remark in an argument with your roommate over household chores?"). A large group of participants ($n =$ 251) completed this Sarcasm Self-Report Scale (SSS), and a principal components analysis of their responses produced four components. These components implicated several different functions for sarcasm: to gently criticize a close friend (general sarcasm component), to save face when delivering a compliment (face-saving component), to diffuse potential embarrassment in a very positive situation (embarrassment diffusion component, e.g., "just got engaged and telling friends" and "score winning point in final basketball game of the season"), or to diffuse frustration in a very negative situation (frustration diffusion component, e.g., "mile-long line at the grocery store" and "friend just locked your keys in car"). We also found significant gender differences for responses on the SSS, with male participants generally giving higher self-reports of sarcasm use than female participants. That is, male participants had higher scores than female participants for three of the SSS components (general sarcasm, face saving, and embarrassment diffusion); no gender difference was found for the fourth component (frustration diffusion).

It has been argued that men and women have different motives for using self-directed humor (Lampert, 1996): Men tend to use self-direct humor "in a self-protective manner to reduce social vulnerability, whereas for women, it worked more to increase social vulnerability and promote intimacy" (p. 585). Our findings seem consistent with these claims, because male participants reported that they were more likely to use sarcasm when it would decrease vulnerability (through face saving or embarrassment diffusion) but not when sarcasm would not decrease vulnerability (frustration diffusion). Explanations for these gender differences likely involve complex sociocultural factors (e.g., Tannen, 1993) beyond the scope of the present work.

Participants in the Ivanko et al. (2002) study also completed a production task (role playing) in which several situations were described. Half of the situations involved the speaker and a new acquaintance, and half of the situations involved the speaker and a best friend. Participants were asked to choose (from four options, including both literal and ironic utterances) the statement they would most likely make in each situation. We found that statement choices were predicted, to some degree, by SSS scores. In particular, individual scores for the face-saving component of the SSS were a significant predictor of statement choices for a situation involving a new acquaintance, and individual scores for the general sarcasm component were a significant predictor of statement choices for a situation involving a best friend. These results provided some validation for the SSS, because self-rated conversational tendencies were related to predicted communication behavior. These results also suggest that there are, indeed, individual differences in tendency to use sarcastic irony. We next tested whether those differences were related to differences in detection and interpretation of verbal irony.

Participants completed an interpretation task in which potentially ironic statements were presented. Participants were asked to rate various aspects of speaker intent: sarcasm, mocking, humor, and politeness. We examined whether any of the measured individual difference variables (SSS scores, CIS scores, and gender) predicted ratings on the interpretation task. Note that none of these individual difference variables predicted sarcasm ratings for ironic insults (e.g., saying "That sounds pretty exciting" in a conversation about a boring date). For ironic compliments (e.g., saying "That sounds pretty dull" in a conversation about an exciting date), however, gender was a significant predictor of perceived level of sarcasm, with women tending to perceive these statements as more sarcastic than men. We speculated that the gender difference observed in sarcasm ratings for ironic compliments was produced because the term *sarcasm* has a negative connotation and women's higher ratings to this dimension may reflect sensitivity to the negative tinge inherent in ironic compliments (e.g., Dews & Winner, 1995; Pexman & Olineck, 2002a). This conclusion is supported by the finding that women also rated ironic compliments as less polite than did men.

In addition, although the SSS and CIS did not predict sarcasm ratings in the interpretation task, they did predict ratings of the social impact of these statements. For instance, the perceived politeness of ironic criticisms was predicted, to some degree, by individuals' CIS–production scores (higher scores were associated with higher politeness ratings) and by their SSS–face-saving scores (a tendency to use sarcasm to save face was associated with lower politeness ratings). Thus, participants who rated themselves as likely to use indirect speech were less likely to perceive offense in ironic criticisms. Perhaps these participants were relatively more sensitive to the tinge function of ironic criticisms. In contrast, participants who rated themselves as likely to use sarcasm with new acquaintances or when complimenting others (face-saving component of the SSS) may have been more sensitive to the critical intent underlying these statements.

Ivanko et al.'s (2003) study also involved a processing task. This was a self-paced moving windows reading task in which literal and ironic statements were presented following short context paragraphs. We found that relative RTs for literal and ironic statements could be predicted by several individual difference variables. Participants who rated themselves as being more likely to use sarcasm in frustrating situations (SSS–frustration diffusion) or with new acquaintances (SSS–face saving) or to look for or use indirect speech (CIS–production and CIS–interpretation) tended to read the ironic statements faster than or in equivalent time to the literal statements. In contrast, older participants tended to read the ironic statements more slowly than the literal statements.

These results suggest that there are individual differences in verbal irony. These include differences in production, with some individuals tending to use sarcastic irony more than others. These differences in production depend, to some degree, on the situation. For instance, some individuals reported that they tend to use sarcasm with best friends but not with new acquaintances. Some use sarcasm in very positive situations, and others use sarcasm in very negative situations. These individual differences in production do have consequences for interpretation: influencing the perceived social impact of verbal irony and influencing the speed with which irony can be processed relative to literal language.

SUMMARY OF PREVIOUS FINDINGS

The research summarized in this chapter points to several conclusions. There is clear evidence that readers use social cues in the process of inferring speaker intent. They do this in laboratory tasks in which they are asked to make judgments of speaker intent, and they also do this in tasks in which no explicit judgments of speaker intent are required. They access these cues rapidly and integrate them with other available information in order to arrive at a coherent representation of the situation described. Although the evidence suggests that these cues are always coded in the comprehension process, they seem to influence judgments of ironic intent primarily when other verbal cues are minimal. One might wonder to what extent these social cues would be accessed in everyday interpersonal communication, in which the context is assumed to be richer, involving both verbal and nonverbal cues. On that issue, I first argue that there are many everyday situations in which verbal and nonverbal cues to speaker intent are few, as in e-mail and telephone conversations. Further, even in these everyday contexts in which nonverbal cues are absent, people still choose to speak ironically. In fact, Hancock and Dunham (2001) compared irony use in face-to-face conversations to irony use in computer-mediated communication and found that irony was actually produced more often in the computer-mediated context. In addition, despite the missing nonverbal cues, comprehension was just as good in the computer-mediated context as it was in the face-to-face context. The fact that participants in the studies reported here so readily used social cues to comprehend speaker intent even when not required to do so suggests that this is the normal procedure: I argue that these social cues are noted and considered in the context of everyday conversation.

This research also suggests that young school-age children are building theories of how personality traits are related to communicative intent. The data suggested that older children (7- and 8-year-olds) are beginning to understand that traits are not perfect predictors of behavior but that they are still relevant to deciding how mean a speaker intended to be in making an ironic criticism. Adult participants seem to have a similar perception: Speaker characteristics are relevant to decisions about, for instance, how mocking a speaker intends to be, but they are not the most reliable cues to irony. Speaker characteristics are, however, sufficiently reliable cues to irony to be relevant when the situation is relatively ambiguous, either because the statement is very unfamiliar or because the context is neutral with respect to outcome.

FITTING SOCIAL CUES AND INDIVIDUAL DIFFERENCES WITH THEORIES OF VERBAL IRONY

In the research described here it was demonstrated that social factors influence interpretation of ironic intent. These include characteristics of the speaker and characteristics of the listener. An important issue is the extent to which theories of verbal irony interpretation can account for such effects. Theories of irony do not make explicit predictions about the role of social cues, such as gender and speaker occupation, or about individual differences but for present purposes I attempted to derive predictions based on the general assumptions of each theory.

The *echoic mention theory* (Sperber & Wilson, 1981, 1986) holds that irony is made possible by an utterance that implicitly or explicitly echoes a previous event, expectation, or social norm. According to the *echoic reminder theory* (e.g., Kreuz & Glucksberg, 1989) the echoic nature of an ironic utterance reminds the listener of a failed expectation or violated social norm. As such, the ironic utterance expresses the speaker's negative attitude about the situation. According to these echoic theories, detection of irony should depend on the presence of an implicit or explicit antecedent. It is not obvious why speaker characteristics should influence the echoic aspect of ironic statements. One possibility, however, is that speaker characteristics cue particular expectations on the part of the speaker, and those expectations could be echoed in the statement. If that were the case, one would expect that ratings of irony would be higher when speakers were perceived to have strong expectations. These speakers would likely be the members of groups who are highly aware of social convention. Perhaps occupations like clergyman and doctor would fit this description. Yet, research shows these were actually the occupations that tended to generate lower ratings of irony (Katz & Pexman, 1997; Pexman et al., 2000; Pexman & Olineck, 2002b). The occupations that produced higher irony ratings (e.g., comedian and cab driver) do not seem candidates for highly conventional social expectations. The echoic theories would seem to have a difficult time explaining effects of social cues.

Echoic theories do, however, seem capable of explaining individual differences in processing. One could speculate that some individuals attend more than others to failed expectations. This type of difference could be related to a pessimistic or cynical outlook. This difference in outlook could mean those individuals have stronger expectations for an ironic statement; consequently, they process ironic statements more readily.

According to the *pretense models* (e.g., Clark & Gerrig, 1984), an ironic speaker pretends to be a very optimistic person, addressing an imaginary listener and assuming that the listener would interpret the utterance literally. Consequently, the ironic speaker expresses a negative attitude toward the situation, the imaginary listener, and the pretended optimist. Perhaps this theory would predict effects of social cues in terms of the consistency of the cues with this type of behavior. For instance, if a speaker's characteristics were consistent with jocularity or with insincerity, then a listener might be more likely to detect the speaker's pretense. This possibility is supported by our finding that humor and insincerity were two traits associated with the sarcastic occupation stereotype (Pexman & Olineck, 2002b). Similarly, if the listener was a funny and/or insincere person, then he or she might be more apt to detect the speaker's pretense.

The *allusional pretense theory* (Kumon-Nakamura et al., 1995) involves two main arguments: (a) ironic utterances allude to a failed expectation either by implicit or by explicit echo and (b) ironic utterances involve pragmatic insincerity (e.g., overpoliteness). As with pretense theory, it seems possible that social cues and individual differences affect perception of ironic intent by enhancing (or attenuating) the perception of pragmatic insincerity. Thus, there may be a mechanism by which this model predicts an influence for social cues in the perception of ironic intent.

Recently, Utsumi (2000) argued that none of these theories provides a complete account of verbal irony. Although echoic mention and pretense may be important factors in some instances of verbal irony, they are not necessary or sufficient conditions for irony (see also Colston, 2000). As an alternative, Utsumi proposed the *implicit display theory* of verbal irony, which involves three main assumptions. First, an ironic utterance assumes an "ironic environment" defined as "a situational setting which motivates verbal irony" (p. 1778). Second, an ironic utterance implicitly displays the ironic environment. Third, irony is characterized as a prototype-based category. As such, utterances with relatively more characteristics of implicit displays will be perceived as more ironic.

In elaborating on the notion of ironic environment, Utsumi (2000) specified that this environment involves a speaker having an expectation that is not met and having a negative emotional attitude toward the incongruity between expectation and outcome. Utsumi also noted that the speaker's negative attitude could be implicitly displayed by a host of cues, including verbal cues such as intonation and exaggeration and nonverbal cues such as gesture and facial expression. It seems possible that these cues might also include beliefs about the speaker. If the speaker's characteristics help to convey his or her negative attitude about the situation, then those characteristics might enhance detection of irony. This implicit display account holds that irony is understood more readily when the utterance is more similar to prototypical verbal irony. In other words, irony is subject to typicality effects. To the extent that speaker characteristics cue features involved in prototypical irony, they may make the utterance seem more similar to the prototype and thus enhance detection.

Therefore, it seems possible for implicit display theory to predict that social cues will influence interpretation of irony. It also seems that the model would have specific predictions about what types of characteristics should act as cues to irony. That is one would predict that effective cues would include characteristics that suggest a negative attitude, such as cynicism or a critical outlook. Further, the theory claims that the negative attitude must be conveyed indirectly, and so it would predict that characteristics such as insincerity and, perhaps, humor would also be effective cues. These predictions seem consistent with the results reported by Pexman and Olineck (2002b): Sarcastic speakers were perceived to be humorous, critical, insincere, and to have lower education or social status. The implicit display theory may even be able to explain this last, somewhat surprising association between sarcastic speech and lower education levels. Lower education levels (strongly correlated with lower social status) may signal a need to express criticism indirectly to lessen the risk of offending higher status others. Because the implicit display theory emphasizes indirect expression of negative attitude, it seems capable of explaining this result. As such, implicit display theory seems able to explain effects of social cues on interpretation of verbal irony.

The implicit display theory also gains a great deal of flexibility from the assumption that irony is a mental category that is subject to typicality effects. Through this assumption, the theory seems to be able to explain individual differences of the type we observed in Ivanko et al. (2003). The category of verbal irony could show effects of expertise, as other categories do (e.g., Tanaka & Taylor, 1991). Some individuals may have more experience with ironic utterances by virtue of using those utterances quite frequently. Consequently, they could have more knowledge of the types of situations in which those statements can be used and of the types of reactions with which those statements are met. This enhanced mental representation for verbal irony could facilitate processing of ironic statements relative to literal statements, as we observed.

Utsumi's (2000) theory is a good fit for the data reported in this chapter because it allows multiple sources of information to be considered in the process of interpretation and because it construes verbal irony as a mental category. Similar characteristics are described by Katz and Ferretti (2001) for the constraint satisfaction view of language processing. With this view, comprehension is achieved by a mechanism that taps all of the sources of information available to the comprehender. Different sources of information (lexical, conceptual, etc.) compete for activation. The interaction of these constraints provides probabilistic evidence for different interpretations until one alternative wins. The findings reviewed here suggest that these constraints also include characteristics of the speaker and characteristics of the listener. The constraint satisfaction view allows constraints to have different weights as a function of their reliability. That is, incongruity between the tone of the context situation and the tone of the statement is a strong and reliable cue to ironic intent. Speaker occupation is a less reliable cue (scientists can be sarcastic, but their perceived tendency is to be nonsarcastic). Thus, incongruity between context and statement can constrain interpretation so rapidly that less reliable or less strongly weighted constraints like speaker occupation or speaker gender, although coded by the comprehender, show little influence on interpretation. Similarly, my hunch is that individual differences constrain interpretation only when other constraints (like context and statement incongruity or lexicalized statement meaning) are weak. This hunch has yet to be tested.

Social Cues and Other Forms of Figurative Language

I argued that social cues and individual differences constrain the process of comprehending ironic speech. I suggest that this reflects the seamless integration of social, linguistic, and conceptual information that normally occurs in the course of language comprehension. Because the notion of constraint satisfaction is relevant to language comprehension in general, there seems little reason to believe that the influence of social cues would be unique to irony. Other forms of figurative language likely have distinct social functions, although those functions have received little research attention thus far (cf. previous research on indirect requests, e.g., Holtgraves, 1994, 1997, 1998). For instance, proverb (e.g., "strike while the iron is hot") and metaphor (e.g., "children are precious gems") can be used to convey wisdom, although they can certainly be used ironically, perhaps to mock those who would use them to convey wisdom. Idioms (e.g., "kick the bucket") allow us to communicate with others in our culture, but they seem to provide a means of excluding those with less shared knowledge. Metonymy (e.g., "the ham sandwich in the corner wants his bill") may also function as a type of cultural shorthand, allowing speakers to present themselves as witty and quick thinking. If these types of figurative language serve specific social functions, then inferences of speaker intent may be influenced by the extent to which social cues are consistent (or inconsistent) with this function.

There may also be widely held beliefs about the characteristics of people who use these forms of figurative language; however, as noted, there has been little research on this issue. For instance, it has been claimed that proverbs are particularly appropriate for conversation with older adults (Jackson, 1994). The implication is that there may be generational (cohort) effects in use and comprehension of proverbial statements. If so, speaker age could act as a constraint on proverb interpretation. Similarly, there may be a perception that speakers who offer metonymic statements tend to be cynical and humorous. Knowledge of these speaker characteristics could constrain interpretation of metonymy. As such, I predict that social cues constrain figurative language comprehension in general, but that different types of figurative language are cued by different social variables.

Gibbs (1999) suggested that in understanding language (and other human actions) we have a strong tendency to make inferences about intentionality. To the extent that social cues are tapped in the cognitive process of inferring intention, they should be relevant in almost every linguistic context. Research suggests that listeners consider social cues, such as characteristics of the speaker, to be relevant to inferences about intent. Thus, listeners have an implicit belief that individual traits and membership in particular social categories influence communicative behavior. The research summarized in this chapter provides evidence to support this implicit belief: Individual characteristics influence both interpretation and production of verbal irony.

REFERENCES

Ackerman, B. P. (1981). Young children's understanding of a speaker's intentional use of a false utterance. *Developmental Psychology, 17,* 472–480.

Ackerman, B. P. (1983). Form and function in children's understanding of ironic utterances. *Journal of Experimental Child Psychology, 35,* 487–508.

Clark, H. H., & Gerrig, R. J. (1984). On the pretense theory of irony. *Journal of Experimental Psychology: General, 113,* 121–126.

Colston, H. L. (1997). Salting a wound or sugaring a pill: The pragmatic functions of ironic criticisms. *Discourse Processes, 23,* 24–45.

Colston, H. L. (2000). On necessary conditions for verbal irony comprehension. *Pragmatics and Cognition, 8,* 277–324.

Colston, H. L., & O'Brien, J. (2000a). Contrast of kind versus contrast of magnitude: The pragmatic accomplishments of irony and hyperbole. *Discourse Processes, 30,* 179–199.

Colston, H. L., & O'Brien, J. (2000b). Contrast and pragmatics in figurative language: Anything understatement can do, irony can do better. *Journal of Pragmatics, 32,* 1557–1583.

Dews, S., Kaplan, J., & Winner, E. (1995). Why not say it directly? The social functions of irony. *Discourse Processes, 19,* 347–367.

Dews, S., & Winner, E. (1995). Muting the meaning: A social function of irony. *Metaphor and Symbolic Activity, 10,* 3–19.

Dews, S., Winner, E., Kaplan, J., Rosenblatt, E., Hunt, M., Lim, K., McGovern, A., Qualter, A., & Smarsh, B. (1996). Children's understanding of the meaning and functions of verbal irony. *Child Development, 67,* 3071–3085.

Gerrig, R. J., & Goldvarg, Y. (2000). Additive effects in the perception of sarcasm: Situational disparity and echoic mention. *Metaphor and Symbolic Activity, 15,* 197–208.

Gibbs, R. W., Jr. (1986). On the psycholinguistics of sarcasm. *Journal of Experimental Psychology: General, 115,* 3–15.

Gibbs, R. W., Jr. (1999). *Intentions in the experience of meaning.* Cambridge, England: Cambridge University Press.

Gibbs, R. W., Jr. (2000). Irony in talk among friends. *Metaphor and Symbolic Activity, 15,* 5–27.

Hancock, J. T., & Dunham, P. J. (2001, November). *Irony use in face-to-face and computer-mediated interactions.* Poster presented at the 42nd annual meeting of the Psychonomic Society, Orlando, FL.

Hancock, J. T., Dunham, P. J., & Purdy, K. (2000). Children's comprehension of critical and complimentary forms of verbal irony. *Journal of Cognition and Development, 1,* 227–248.

Harris, M., Ivanko, S., Jungen, S., Hala, S., & Pexman, P. (2001, October). *You're really nice: Children's understanding of sarcasm and personality traits.* Poster presented at the second biennial meeting of the Cognitive Development Society, Virginia Beach, VA.

Haverkate, H. (1990). A speech act analysis of irony. *Journal of Pragmatics, 14,* 77–109.

Heyman, G. D., & Gelman, S. A. (1999). The use of trait labels in making psychological inferences. *Child Development, 70,* 604–619.

Holtgraves, T. (1994). Communication in context: Effects of speaker status on the comprehension of indirect requests. *Journal of Experimental Psychology: Learning, Memory, and Cognition, 20,* 1205–1218.

Holtgraves, T. (1997). Styles of language use: Individual and cultural variability in conversational indirectness. *Journal of Personality and Social Psychology, 73,* 624–637.

Holtgraves, T. (1998). Interpersonal Foundations of Conversational Indirectness. In S. R. Fessell & R. J. Kreuz (Eds.), *Social and cognitive approaches to interpersonal communication* (pp. 71–89). Mahwah, NJ: Lawrence Erlbaum Associates.

Ivanko, S. L., Pexman, P. M., & Olineck, K. M. (2003, July). *How sarcastic are you?: Individual differences in the interpretation, production, and processing of verbal irony.* Poster presented at the 8th International Pragmatics Conference, Toronto, ON.

Jackson, V. R. (1994). Proverbs: A tool for work with older persons. *Activities, Adaptation, and Aging, 19,* 5–13.

Jorgensen, J. (1996). The functions of sarcastic irony in speech. *Journal of Pragmatics, 26,* 613–634.

Jorgensen, J., Miller, G. A., & Sperber, D. (1984). Test of the mention theory of irony. *Journal of Experimental Psychology: General, 113,* 112–120.

Katz, A. N., & Ferretti, T. R. (2001). Moment-by-moment reading of proverbs in literal and nonliteral contexts. *Metaphor and Symbol, 16,* 193–221.

Katz, A. N., & Lee, C. J. (1993). The role of authorial intent in determining verbal irony and metaphor. *Metaphor and Symbolic Activity, 8,* 257–279.

Katz, A. N., & Pexman, P. M. (1997). Interpreting figurative statements: Speaker occupation can change metaphor to irony. *Metaphor and Symbol, 12,* 19–41.

Katz, A. N., Piasecka, I., & Toplak, M. (2001, November). *Comprehending the sarcastic comments of males and females.* Poster presented at the 42nd annual meeting of the Psychonomic Society, Orlando, FL.

Keltner, D., Capps, L., Kring, A. M., Young, R. C., & Heerey, E. A. (2001). Just teasing: A conceptual analysis and empirical review. *Psychological Bulletin, 127,* 229–248.

Kreuz, R. J. (1996). The use of verbal irony: Cues and constraints. In J. S. Mio & A. N. Katz (Eds.), *Metaphor: Implications and applications* (pp. 23–38). Mahwah, NJ: Lawrence Erlbaum Associates.

Kreuz, R. J., & Glucksberg, S. (1989). How to be sarcastic: The echoic reminder theory of verbal irony. *Journal of Experimental Psychology: General, 118,* 374–386.

Kreuz, R. J., Long, D. J., & Church, M. B. (1991). On being ironic: Pragmatic and mnemonic implications. *Metaphor and Symbolic Activity, 6,* 149–162.

Kreuz, R. J., & Roberts, R. M. (1995). Two cues for verbal irony: Hyperbole and the ironic tone of voice. *Metaphor and Symbolic Activity, 10,* 21–31.

Kumon-Nakamura, S., Glucksberg, S., & Brown, M. (1995). How about another piece of pie: The allusional pretense theory of discourse irony. *Journal of Experimental Psychology: General, 124,* 3–21.

Lakoff, G., & Johnson, M. (1980). *Metaphors we live by.* Chicago: University of Chicago Press.

Lampert, M. (1996). Gender differences in conversational humor. In D. I. Slobin, J. Gerhardt, A. Kyratzis, & J. Guo (Eds.), *Social interaction, social context, and language* (pp. 579–596). Mahwah, NJ: Lawrence Erlbaum Associates.

Leggitt, J. S., & Gibbs, R. W., Jr. (2000). Emotional reactions to verbal irony. *Discourse Processes, 29,* 1–24.

McCroskey, J. C., Daly, J. A., Martin, M. A., & Beatty, M. J. (Eds.). (1998). *Communication and personality: Trait perspectives.* Creskill, NJ: Hampton.

Pexman, P. M., Ferretti, T. R., & Katz, A. N. (2000). Discourse factors that influence on-line reading of metaphor and irony. *Discourse Processes, 29,* 201–222.

Pexman, P. M., & Olineck, K. M. (2002a). Does sarcasm always sting? Investigating the impact of ironic insults and ironic compliments. *Discourse Processes, 33,* 199–217.

Pexman, P. M., & Olineck, K. M. (2002b). Understanding irony: How do stereotypes cue speaker intent? *Journal of Language and Social Psychology, 21,* 245–274.

Roberts, R. M., & Kreuz, R. J. (1994). Why do people use figurative language? *Psychological Science, 5,* 159–163.

Slugoski, B. R., & Turnbull, W. (1988). Cruel to be kind and kind to be cruel: Sarcasm, banter, and social relations. *Journal of Language and Social Psychology, 7,* 101–121.

Slusher, M. P., & Anderson, C. A. (1987). When reality monitoring fails: The role of imagination in stereotype maintenance. *Journal of Personality and Social Psychology, 52,* 653–662.

Sperber, D., & Wilson, D. (1981). Irony and the use-mention distinction. In P. Cole (Ed.), *Radical pragmatics* (pp. 296–318). New York: Academic Press.

Sperber, D., & Wilson, D. (1986). *Relevance: Communication and cognition.* Cambridge, MA: Harvard University Press.

Tanaka, J. W., & Taylor, M. (1991). Object categories and expertise: Is the basic level in the eye of the beholder? *Cognitive Psychology, 23,* 457–482.

Tannen, D. (Ed.). (1993). *Gender and conversational interaction.* New York: Oxford University Press.

Toplak, M. T., & Katz, A. N. (2000). On the uses of sarcastic irony. *Journal of Pragmatics, 32,* 1467–1488.

Utsumi, A. (2000). Verbal irony as implicit display of ironic environment: Distinguishing ironic utterances from nonirony. *Journal of Pragmatics, 32,* 1777–1806.

Winner, E., & Leekam, S. (1991). Distinguishing irony from deception: Understanding the speaker's second-order intention. *British Journal of Developmental Psychology, 9,* 257–270.

10

Negation as Positivity in Disguise

Rachel Giora
Tel Aviv University

Noga Balaban
Tel Aviv University

Ofer Fein
The Academic College of Tel Aviv

Inbar Alkabets
Tel Aviv University

Once there was a poor woman who had three or four little children, and she used to lock them up in her room when she went out to work, to keep them safe. One day when she was going away she said, "Now, my dears, don't let baby fall out of window, don't play with the matches, and don't put beans up your noses." Now the children had never dreamed of doing that last thing, but she put it into their heads, and the minute she was gone, they ran and stuffed their naughty little noses full of beans, just to see how it felt, and she found them all crying when she came home.

"Did it hurt?" asked Rob, with such intense interest that his mother hastily added a warning sequel, lest a new edition of the bean story should appear in her own family.

"Very much, as I know, for when *my* mother told me this story, I was so silly that I went and tried it myself ..."

—Alcott, (1962), 115–116[1]

INTRODUCTION: ON THE ROLE OF NEGATION

How explicit negation affects the representation in memory of negated concepts has been considered in recent empirical research into the discourse and cognitive functions of *negation markers* (*not* and *no*). The consensus among psycholinguists is that a negation marker is an instruction from a speaker to a hearer to suppress the negated information. Accordingly, a negation marker reduces the levels of activation of the negated concepts to the extent that eventually they are no more accessible than unrelated controls and significantly less accessible than equivalent positive concepts (Hasson, 2000; Kaup, 1997, 2001; Lea & Mulligan, 2002; MacDonald & Just, 1989; Mayo, Schul, & Burnstein, in press, Experiment 2). Folk wisdom, however, would have it otherwise (see the Alcott quote just cited). The belief here is that what is negated prevails, as the following exchange, taken from the Santa Barbara Spoken American Corpus, exemplifies:

(1) P: ... it was very clear. You know.
            ... She kept saying,
            ... prefacing everything with,
            ... you know, this is *not a personal attack.*
            ... This is *not a personal vendetta,*

    B: Yeah, yeah yeah yeah.
            Right Right.

    P: Which tells you, that it is.

    B: Yeah.

    P: That's immediately what it said.
            And that's what everybody perceived it.

    B: Yeah.
                    (Du Bois, 2000, italics added).

Adopting the same attitude, the following journalistic text suggests that it is how people conceive of negation that accounts for why, despite explicit denials, the person discussed, Kochi Mordechay, then wife of Itsik Mordechay (former Israeli Defense Minister convicted of sexual abuses), is taken to affirm what she denies (that she was a battered woman):

---

[1] We thank Dana Zimmerman for this citation.

(2) I think Kochi [Mordechay] was wrong in disputing the rumors in detail, focusing on their specifics .... Sometimes people are stupid, and
occasionally they would hear Kochi talking about "Itsik"
[Mordechay] and "beatings" but they wouldn't note the connectors
"there were no beatings, the rumors are vile." Now after she had been
specific, the story has become official kind of .... (Linor, 1999).

Admittedly, even a limited and random scan of how negation is used ren-
ders the suppression hypothesis suspect. In the following example (cited and
discussed in Jefferson, 2002), negation is used to provide for a supportive
and affiliative response, following a negative turn (line 6):

(3) 1 Maggie: .hh because I(c) (.) you know I told Mother what'd
                ha:ppened yesterday

2   there at the party,

3 Sorrell: [°Yeah.°]

4 Maggie: [a::]nd uh, .hhhhh (0.2) uh you know she asked me if
                it was

5   (–) because I'd had too much to dri:nk and I said no=

6 Sorrell: (–) =[N o ∷ ∷ .]

7 Maggie: =[because at the t]i:me I'd only ha:d,h you
                know that drink 'n a ha:lf

8   When we were going through the receiving line.

9 Sorrell: Ri:ght.

It is also quite apparent that the speaker of the following testimony does
not want us to deactivate the negated concepts:

(4) We suffer from shortage in medicines, milk for children, diapers.
There are no vegetables, no fruits, no meat and milk products. We
basically eat rice and what we grew in our yard. (Badra El-sha'ar, a
resident of Tko'a, a Palestinian village in the occupied territories, as
cited in ad by Betselem—the Israeli Center for Information of Human Rights, 2002).

Clearly, by publishing it, Betselem intended us to attend to rather than
dispense with the negated information about the elementary supplies the
Palestinians are in desperate need of as a result of the devastating destruction inflicted on them by the Israeli army and the siege and curfews that were
not lifted.
Similarly, when Naomi Klein (2002) entitled her recent book, *No Space,
No Choice, No Jobs, No Logo,* she by no means expected us to attenuate the

meanings of *space, choice, jobs,* or *logo.* Rather, she used these elements as objectives to be reclaimed by the people, by those entitled to them. The book laments the expulsion of the people from these public domains and deplores their exclusive control by corporations and governments (not, however, without indicating subversive ways to repossess them).

The following example (about a dozen bullets fired by an Israel Defense Forces soldier that pierced the windshield of a taxi in which the journalist, Gideon Levy, was traveling) further confirms that explicitly negated concepts are retainable (at least in the mind of the speaker):

(5)   NOTHING HAPPENED
      Nothing happened. Soldiers opened fire, no one was hurt. Not a
      thing happened. The soldiers evacuated the bullet-riddled taxi and
      its passengers from the zone of fire and no officer appeared: not to
      investigate, not to take testimony, not to explain, not to apologize,
      and above all not to show the soldiers that, after all, something did
      happen. (Levy, 2002).

The passage (as, in fact, the article throughout) is imbued with negated concepts. "Nothing happened" (literally "nothing didn't happen" in Hebrew) is actually an echoic (though negative) irony,[2] intending us to perceive that something did happen (which necessitates the retention of the meaning of *happen*). Similarly, the negations that follow ("**no** officer appeared: **not** to investigate, **not** to take testimony, **not** to explain, **not** to apologize, and above all **not** to show the soldiers that, after all, something did happen"; negations markers are in bold for convenience) do not dismiss the negated concepts but instead construct a set of expectations of what should have happened. Not only do the negation markers not obliterate these negated entities; in a way, they serve to bring them out and spell out the irresponsibility and indifference of the military (on the evaluative function of negation, see Labov, 1972). They all belong in the same class or ad hoc category of events that should have followed this shooting event—also in support of the retention-of-negated-concepts hypothesis (for a similar view on how a negated concept cannot be entirely eradicated, see Horn, 1989, pp. 50–51).

The following example is also illustrative of the retainability of negated concepts:

(6)   THE FACTS WERE IN ON ISRAEL'S ARABS
      Two statements by former Prime Minister Ehud Barak in his testi-
      mony before the Or Commission, which is investigating the events

---

[2]On the echoic mention view of irony see Sperber and Wilson (1986/1995).

of October 2000,[3] should raise an eyebrow. Or rather, raise hackles. One was, "There was **no** concrete intelligence assessment" of the possibility that disturbances of these dimensions would break out, and the other was that the reason **no** discussion had been held on the issue of the Arabs of Israel was "because in any case long-term problems would have come up in any such discussion."

[...]

A discussion of the question of the Arabs of Israel? Why wear ourselves out with it when all that could come up would be only long-term problems? Now, of all times, do we need to start dealing with the question of discrimination against Arabs? Or the fact that **no** Arab city has been established to date? Or perhaps of the NIS 4 billion that the government had allocated on paper to close the gaps? After all, what we have before us is an acute problem—Arabs are throwing stones at policemen and blocking roads. This is the only problem, and there is **nothing** more to it. **No** history of failings and **no** future of civil revolt. It began and ended in the month of October. Why should the prime minister deal with a problem like that? It's a problem for a squad commander, maximum a regional commander. (Bar'el, 2002).

The journalist is of course ironic. When writing "This is the only problem, and there is nothing more to it. No history of failings and no future of civil revolt. It began and ended in the month of October. Why should the prime minister deal with a problem like that?," he definitely intends us to entertain the possibility that "there is ... more to it," which necessitates its retention (see also Giora & Fein, 1999a, 1999b; Giora, Fein, & Schwartz, 1998). Indeed, assuming its accessibility allows the writer to immediately elaborate on it and go into details (of "history" and "future of civil revolt"). Only when the negated statement is retained we can make sense of the elaborations that follow (viewing them as members of "there is ... more to it" category). In the same way, the journalist does not intend us to reduce the possibility of "a history of failings" and of "a future of civil revolt." Rather, the availability of an ironic interpretation relies on the retention of these negated items.

Or take the following example from Kate Chopin's (1894/1976) *The Story of an Hour*, in which negated information allows us to draw a contrastive comparison between the heroine's reactions to the news about her husband's death and other women's reaction to such news:

---

[3]Following the breakout of the second Intifada (uprising) in the Palestinian Occupied Territories in September 2000, the Israeli Palestinians demonstrated against the Israeli occupation and were treated violently by the Israeli police who shot and killed 14 Arab demonstrators. The killing of Israeli citizens is called "the events of October 2000."

(7)   She did not hear the story as many women have heard the same,
      with a paralyzed inability to accept its significance. She wept at
      once, with sudden, wild abandonment.... (p. 198)

The use of a negated sentence ("she did **not** hear the story ...") highlights
the event in the foreground; it brings out and evaluates the heroine's unusual
reaction (cf. Labov, 1972). It also allows the specification of how women go or
should go about hearing such news. In contrast to expectations made explicit
by the negated phrase, the heroine is engulfed by a sense of relief:

(8)   There would be **no** one to live for during those coming years; she
      would live for herself. There would be **no** powerful will bending hers
      in that blind persistence with which men and women believe they
      have a right to impose a private will upon a fellow creature. (p. 199)

Here too the positive statements are evaluated by the negative statements that clarify and emphasize them, acquainting us with the heroine's
previous life experiences and that, therefore, cannot be assumed or expected to be suppressed.

But even evidence accumulated in the lab does not entirely support the
suppression hypothesis. For instance, findings show that jurors are influenced by information they have been instructed to disregard (Thompson,
Fong, & Rosenhan, 1981). Further, media audiences are influenced by news
they are told is untrue (Wegner, Wenzlaff, Kerker, & Beattie, 1981). When
asked not to think of a concept (e.g., pink elephants, white bear, or house),
subjects cannot suppress that concept;[4] at times, the to-be-suppressed concepts even gain in accessibility (Wegner, 1994; Wegner & Erber, 1992;
Wegner, Schneider, Carter, & White, 1987). Such findings contest the suppression hypothesis.

In this chapter we further question the suppression hypothesis and propose instead that suppression of negated items is not obligatory but op-
tional. The following pair of sentences (taken from Tottie, 1994, p. 414)
might illustrate the claim. They have identical initial clauses ("Fred didn't
see a cyclist") but different continuations, each necessitating the retention
of a different constituent from the previous identical clause, attesting that
suppression (following negation) cannot be obligatory and automatic but a
matter of deliberation, taking into consideration the scope of negation.
Thus, if (9) is acceptable, then *cyclist* should not be suppressed by the preceding negation marker but rather (if at all) *see*. Similarly, if (10) is acceptable then *see* should not be suppressed by the preceding negation marker
but rather *cyclist*:

---

[4]These concepts are not suppressed even when they are entirely irrelevant to an accessible context—to their stream of consciousness at the moment.

(9) Fred didn't see a cyclist who was coming down the hill and hit him.

(10) Fred didn't see a cyclist but a man on a horseback.

The evidence we present here supports the retention hypothesis. According to the retention hypothesis (Giora, 2003; Giora & Fein, 1999a, 1999b), suppression is not obligatory: An activated meaning need not be suppressed if it does not interfere with comprehension and might instead be instrumental in constructing the intended meaning. Accordingly, speakers' choice of a negated positive instead of an antonym ("the book is not interesting" vs. "the book is boring" and "the book is not boring" vs. "the book is interesting") can be viewed (among other things) as aimed at introducing information to the discourse (e.g., about expectations)[5] rather than eliminating it from the mental representation. Given the retention hypothesis, we propose that information introduced via negation would be retained and tinge the interpretation of the negated item so that the outcome is a mitigated product involving both the negativity of the negation marker and also the expressed meaning of the negated item (see also Givón, 1993; Jespersen, 1924/1976).

If indeed negation markers hedge information rather than discard it, they could convey social and pragmatic intentions and be used when, for instance, people wish to downplay information such as when they want to break bad news somewhat indirectly (see Experiment 4 below) or introduce new information in a nonconfrontational manner. Indeed, negation was found to be used when addressing controversial issues (Giora, 1994). Giora (1994) analyzed the use of negation in public addresses (e.g., the late Egyptian president Anwar Sadat's address to the Israeli Parliament). She showed that negation allows the speaker to make a claim without asserting it—to introduce new information nonassertively.[6]

ON THE ROLE OF NEGATION: EMPIRICAL FINDINGS

To reject the suppression hypothesis and support the retention hypothesis, we first have to show that negated meanings are indeed accessed, regardless of a prior negating context. Experiment 1 was designed to test this hypothe-

---

[5]Moxey and Sanford (2000) expressed a somewhat similar view: "It appears that 'not many' makes participants think that the speaker herself expected more, and that the speaker believed the listener expected more. In contrast, only the first of these holds for 'few' and 'very few' " (p. 245).

[6]We focus here on the hedging effect of explicit negation when negating is processed in a compositional manner. Familiar, fixed expressions and idioms involving a negation marker are excluded from the analysis because their pragmatic meanings are lexicalized and are not constructed on the fly.

sis. We aimed to tap initial processes and test the assumption that a negation marker (*not* as in not X) will not inhibit the access of salient meanings (of X) (as might also be deduced from Clark & Chase, 1972[7]). In Experiments 2, 3, and 4, we examined the effect of negation on later integrative processes. We wished to show that, contra the received view (e.g., Hasson, 2000, Experiment 3; Kaup, 2001; MacDonald & Just, 1989, Experiment 1), a negation marker will not suppress salient meanings activated initially but only modify them (for a similar view, see Horn, 1989, pp. 236–240). In Experiments 1 and 3 we used scalar adjectives (*sharp* and *rotten*). In Experiments 2 and 4 the negated elements were not necessarily adjectives, and they were not necessarily gradable ('fail'/'succeed'). In all the experiments, the participants, native speakers of Hebrew, were presented Hebrew items (translated here for convenience).

EXPERIMENT 1

According to the modular view (Fodor, 1983) and the graded salience hypothesis (Giora, 1997, 2003; Peleg, Giora, & Fein, 2001, in press), lexical access is invariant across contexts. Consequently, contexts containing both negated (not X) and nonnegated (X) constituents should initially facilitate salient (coded and prominent) responses related to X, whereas a context containing Y, which is the antonym of X, should not, because it does not involve an explicit mention of X or any of its salient features. Thus, if *piercing* is a salient feature of *sharp*, both (11) and (12) would prime it; (13) however, would not:

(11) This instrument is *sharp*.
(12) This instrument is *not sharp*.
(13) This instrument is *blunt*.

By measuring response times (RTs) to two types of probes (related and unrelated) in a nonnegated–positive condition, we first aimed to establish that the related probe (*piercing*) is indeed a salient meaning of the target (*sharp*) and would be facilitated compared to the unrelated probe. We predicted that the priming to be exhibited in a non-negated–positive (X) condition would be replicated in a negated–positive (not X) condition, but would not be replicated in an antonym (Y) condition. Specifically, RTs to salient (related) probes (*piercing*) follow-

---

[7]According to Clark and Chase (1972), the negation operator is dissociated from the message's core concepts and would, therefore, involve processing the core supposition and then negate it. Because the core supposition is processed as a cognitive unit, which is then marked with a negation tag, Mayo et al. (in press) terms this "the schema-plus-tag model."

ing a negated (positive) adjective ("This instrument is *not sharp*") would replicate those following a nonnegated (positive) adjective ("This instrument is *sharp*"). In contrast, the priming effect expected in the negated condition ("This instrument is *not sharp*") would not be replicated in an antonym condition ("This instrument is *blunt*"). Although, on the face of it, there seems to be a greater semantic affinity between a negated adjective (not X) and its antonym (*blunt* = *not sharp*) than between a negated and nonnegated adjective (*not sharp* ≠ *sharp*), the graded salience hypothesis would predict that, initially, the latter are much more alike. Both the negation (not X) and its positive opposite (X) share the same stimulus (X), whereas the antonym (Y) and its equivalent negation (not X) do not. Their processing, therefore, should involve different accessing routes.

Method

Design. A 3 × 2 factorial design was used with context type (positive, negative, and antonym) and probe type (related and unrelated) as within-subjects factors.

Participants. Participants were 36 graduate and undergraduate students of Tel Aviv University, between the ages of 19 and 33 (27 women and 9 men). All were native speakers of Hebrew.

Stimuli. Stimuli were 72 triplets, 36 of which were target triplets, each including a nonnegated–positive context (11), a negated–positive context (12), and an antonym context (13) (repeated in (14–16) for convenience), followed by two (related and unrelated) probes controlled for number of syllables (with antonym related probes not being conventionally associated with any item of the pairs as do direct opposites such as *black* and *white*, see Clark, 1970):

(14) This instrument is sharp.
(15) This instrument is not sharp.
(16) This instrument is blunt.

Probes: piercing (related); leaving (unrelated)

Of the 72 triplets, 36 were filler items (12 of which included a negation particle), followed by a nonword probe. In addition, 5 practice trials and 10 buffer trials were included.

Procedure. Participants were seated in front of a computer screen and were tested individually. They were first given oral and written instructions.[8] Reading of experimental sentences was self-paced: Participants pressed a key when they have read the sentence. Each participant saw one sentence of each of the triplets (e.g., one sentence of (14–16)). The interstimulus interval (ISI) between offset of each target sentence and onset of the probe was 100 ms. The probe was centrally displayed for 300 ms and the subjects had to make a lexical decision as to whether the probe was a word or a nonword. The participants responded by pressing one of two (yes or no) keys. The latency between the offset of the probe and the pressing of the key was measured by the computer and served as an RT. To guarantee an attentive reading of the experimental items, each lexical decision was followed by a yes or no comprehension question (that was, however, irrelevant to the target word). Interitem interval was 600 ms. Two subjects who did not respond correctly to a minimum of 80% of the comprehension questions were replaced.

Results

Means and standard deviations for the two conditions are presented in Table 10.1. In the nonnegated–positive (X) condition (e.g., (14)), there was a significant difference between the RTs to the related and unrelated probes (in the subject analysis), $ts(35) = 2.16, p < .01$; $ti(35) = 1.29, p = .1$. Similarly, as predicted, in the negated (not X) condition (e.g., (15)), there was also a significant difference between the RTs to the related and unrelated probes (in the subject analysis), $ts(35) = 2.13, p < .01$; $ti(35) = 1.5, p = .07$. In the antonym (Y) condition, the difference between the related and unrelated probes did not reach significance $ts(35) = 0.24, p = .4$; $ti(35) = 1.45, p = .07$. Responses to the yes/no questions that followed the different types of sentences did not vary significantly.

Discussion

Results of the subject analysis, which was backed by the same trend in the item analysis, support the graded salience and modular hypotheses accord-

---

[8]The first screen stated, "Thank you for participating in this experiment." The second screen stated, "A short sentence will be presented on the screen. Read it carefully and press the space bar when you are done. When you press the space bar, the sentence will disappear and a letter string will be displayed.

If the letter string makes up a word (e.g., *house*) press the 'L' key; if it does not make up a word (e.g., hois) press the 'S' key. Right after you have made the lexical decision, you will have to respond to a Yes/No question related to the sentence you have read. Press the 'L' key for 'Yes' and the 'S' key for 'No.' For practice press the space bar."

Then five practice trials followed.

The third screen stated, "Make your decision as fast as you can, without compromising precision. To start, press the space bar."

TABLE 10.1
RT (in ms) for Related and Unrelated Probes Following Positive,
Negative, and Antonym Contexts

	Nonnegated–Positive		Negated–Positive		Antonym	
Probe Type	Related	Unrelated	Related	Unrelated	Related	Unrelated
M	393	430	393	430	411	417
SD	195	199	178	193	208	167

ing to which lexical access is insensitive to contextual information. As predicted, a negating context did not inhibit access of salient meanings of target words. (For converging results, see Fischler, Bloom, Childres, Rocus, & Perry, 1983; Hasson, 2000, Experiments 1 and 2, which show that the affirmative meaning of negated metaphors are sustainable immediately and even after a 500-ms delay; MacDonald & Just's, 1989, reading times in all three experiments; and Mayo et al.'s (2002, pp. 10–16) Experiment 1). In contrast, an antonym did not facilitate the related probe, because its meaning was not made explicit in that context. Although a negation of X (*not sharp*) and its antonym Y (*blunt*) may be viewed as akin, initially they are less alike than a positive and a negative articulation of the same item (X/~X), which are commonly viewed as opposites (*sharp–not sharp*).

EXPERIMENT 2

Experiment 1 demonstrates that initial processing of negated and non-negated articulations of the same linguistic item (*sharp* and *not sharp*) prime the same concept(s). In spite of their semantic difference, both conditions facilitate the same salient meaning. Such findings demonstrate that a negation marker has no inhibitory effects on lexical access. They support the view that processing is initially insensitive to contextual information, as assumed by the graded salience hypothesis and the modular view.[9] The question, however, is whether a negation marker has postlexical suppressive effects. Would the meaning activated initially due to its salience be suppressed by the negation marker so as to allow for the contextually appropriate interpretation to be retrieved and exclusively integrate with prior context? Recall that according to the retention hypothesis (Giora, 2003; Giora & Fein, 1999a, 1999b), suppression is not obligatory. An activated meaning need not be suppressed if it may be functional in constructing the intended meaning. We, therefore, predict that the meaning activated ini-

---

[9]It also supports the ordered and reordered access views, see Rayner, Pacht, and Duffy (1994).

tially would be retained and tinge the interpretation of the negated element
so that the result is a mitigated product (for information on the tinge hypothesis, see Dews & Winner, 1995).

To test this hypothesis, we ran three off-line experiments. Off-line tasks
involve no time constraints and thus allow for suppression, which requires
extra processing time, to take place. However, if, following negation, suppression is not obligatory, we should find traces of the negated concepts. In
Experiment 2 we aimed to show that speakers retain at least some aspects of
the negated element (for a similar view, see Hegel, cited in Horn, 1989, p.
64).[10] Specifically, we wished to show that a negated item constrains the acceptability of the item that follows it. The assumption that, following negation, suppression is obligatory predicts that any element can follow a
negated item, because an entity that is not represented cannot constrain the
next discourse element. In contrast, assuming that negation does not eradicate all the features of the negated element (activated initially because of
their salience), the negated element should constrain the acceptability and
classifiability of the next constituent in the string (as would nonnegated elements). The retention hypothesis thus predicts that only elements classifiable as members of the category in which the negated item is a member can
follow that negated item (as would be the case with lists of nonnegated
items). (For information regarding how nonnegated items are classified into
ad hoc categories, see Barsalou, 1983.) We thus expected sentences such as
(17a and 18a) to be evaluated as more acceptable and appropriate than sentences such as (17b and 18b). Although in (17a and 18a), the two elements—the negated and the nonnegated items—can be grouped on the
basis of class membership, this does not hold for (17b and 18b):

(17) a. What I bought yesterday was not a bottle but a jug.
      b. What I bought yesterday was not a bottle but a closet.[11]
(18) a. I don't want coffee; I want tea.
      b. I don't want coffee; I want shoes.

Method

Participants. Participants were 40 students of Tel Aviv University,
who were between the ages of 20 and 40 (20 women and 20 men). They were
all native speakers of Hebrew.

---

[10]"For Hegel, a 'pure negative judgment' like *the rose is not red* suggests that a different
predicate from the same semantic class applies to the subject: 'To say that the rose is not red
implies that it is still coloured.' " (Hegel, 1892:306 as cited in Horn, 1989, p. 64)

[11]Only some of the sentences included *but* clauses. On the constraints of the *but* operator,
see Winter and Rimon (1994).

Stimuli.   Stimuli were 30 pairs of sentences such as (17) and (18) and 10 filler pairs.

Procedure.   Participants were asked to indicate which of the alternatives in each pair is a preferable, a more acceptable, or a more natural sentence in their language, given that they do not want to be funny or entertaining.

Results and Discussion

Results are straightforward. Ninety-six percent of the participants preferred the sentences in which the negated and nonnegated items are classifiable as members of the same category (17a and 18a), and a clear-cut dispreference (4%) for the sentences in which these items are less amenable to such categorization (17b and 18b). These results demonstrate that a negation marker does not eliminate the mental representation of the negated item altogether. Even when negated, the negated concept constrains the next discourse element; it determines which concepts can follow it and which ones cannot. This finding demonstrates that at least some of the aspects of the negated concept must be retained.

Taken together, the results of this experiment and the examples from naturally occurring discourses (1–8) testify to speakers' sensitivity to the retained aspects of items explicitly negated.

EXPERIMENT 3

To further test the retention hypothesis, we conducted another experiment in which we wanted to be more accurate about speakers' sensitivity to the tingeing or hedging effect of explicit negation. Therefore, here we asked participants to rate pairs of statements on a 7-point polarity scale (1 = X, 7 = Y). The target pairs included an item (X) and its negated antonym (not Y): "This instrument is *sharp*" and "This instrument is *not blunt*." The retention hypothesis predicts that the negated item (not Y) would be rated as distinct from (X) because of the difference between X and Y, despite the entailment relation obtaining between X and not Y, whereupon *sharp* entails *not blunt* (see, e.g., Bartsch & Vennemann, 1972; Brewer & Lichtenstein, 1975; Lyons, 1977).

The retention hypothesis further predicts that, when explicitly negated, both items with negative (*rotten*) and positive (*fresh*) associations would be similarly retained and tinged. This stands in contrast to the asymmetry assumed by Ducrot (1973) and Horn (1989). Ducrot (1973, as cited in Horn, 1989, p. 334) contended that negative and positive moral adjectives exhibit an asymmetry in that negating the positive (*not right*) implies the opposite (*wrong*); however, negating the negative (*not wrong*) does not imply the opposite (*right*), but a weaker version of it. This view was empirically supported by Colston (1999). Similarly, outside the moral sphere, Cornulier (1974, cited in Horn, 1989, p. 335) maintained that *not rich* is taken to implicate *poor* but *not poor* does not implicate *rich* (see also Brewer & Lichtenstein, 1975). (For a different view, see Clark & Chase, 1972; Fiedler, Walther, Armbruster, Fay, & Naumann, 1996; Johnson-Laird & Tridgell, 1972; Just & Carpenter, 1976; Wason, 1963.) We tested this assumption vis à vis the retention hypothesis.

Method

Participants.   Participants were 30 graduate and undergraduate students of Tel Aviv University, who were between the ages of 18 and 30 (19 women and 11 men). All were native speakers of Hebrew.

Stimuli.   Stimuli were comprised of 40 experimental pairs selected from Experiment 1 and 20 filler sentences. Of the experimental items, 10 contained nonnegated positive items coupled with their negated antonyms (e.g., "The vegetables looked *fresh*" and "The vegetables looked *not rotten*"). Another 10 repeated the positive item and its hedged antonym (e.g., "The vegetables looked *fresh*" and "The vegetables looked *fairly rotten*"). Another set of 10 items contained nonnegated negative items coupled with their negated (positive) antonym (e.g., "Sarit's dress was *ugly*" and "Sarit's dress was *not pretty*"). The matched set repeated the nonnegated negative items coupled with a hedged (positive) antonym (e.g., "Sarit's dress was *ugly*" and "Sarit's dress was *fairly pretty*"). The 20 fillers involved various hedges and intensifiers such as *really, fairly, entirely, little*, and so on.

Procedure.   Subjects were presented booklets containing pairs of sentences and were asked to rate each sentence of the pair on a 7-point polarity scale (e.g., sharp–blunt and fresh–rotten).[12]

---

[12]The instructions read as follows:

Dear Participant,

You will be presented with pairs of statements that express the impression two different people have of a certain object. Your task is to compare the expressions and to grade each of them on 1–7 scale. For example:

    a. This painting is terrible

    b. This painting is pretty good

    |__a_|__|__|__|__|__b_|__|

    1   7

    terrible   good

There are no right or wrong responses. We are interested in studying the way you understand the different expressions. Thank you for your cooperation!

Results

Results are presented in Tables 10.2 and 10.3 and Fig. 10.1. Ratings for the nonnegated positive items (*fresh*) differed significantly from their negated antonyms (*not rotten*), $t(14) = 17.07, p < .0001$, and from their hedged antonyms (*fairly rotten*), $t(14) = 28.55, p < .0001$. Likewise, ratings for the non-negated negative items (*ugly*) differed significantly from their negated antonyms (*not pretty*), $t(14) = 21.29, p < .0001$, and from their hedged antonyms (*fairly pretty*), $t(14) = 25.20, p < .0001$. As illustrated by Fig. 10.1, inverting the scale findings for the positive or negative adjectives shows that they act as a mirror image of each other.

Discussion

Results support the retention hypothesis, according to which salient meanings that might be instrumental in constructing the intended meaning should not be suppressed. Indeed, although a negation marker did not block salient meanings (*piercing*) of negated constituents (*not sharp*; cf. Experiment 1), it did not suppress them. The *bluntness* of *not blunt* or the "prettiness" of *not pretty* was not eradicated even when an off-line task allowed

TABLE 10.2
Mean Ratings of the Negative Adjectives
Relative to Negated and Hedged Positive Adjectives

Adjective Type	Negative (ugly)	Negated Positive (not pretty)	Hedged Positive (fairly pretty)	Positive (pretty)
	1.23 (0.26)	3.61 (0.43)		
	1.33 (0.32)		5.51 (0.39)	

Note. Items were rated on a 7-point scale (1 = *ugly* and 7 = *pretty*). Standard deviations are shown in parentheses.

TABLE 10.3
Mean Ratings of the Positive Adjectives Relative to Negated and
Hedged Negative Adjectives

Adjective Type	Negative (rotten)	Hedged Negative (fairly rotten)	Negated Negative (not rotten)	Positive Adjective (fresh)
		2.29 (0.34)		6.59 (0.32)
			4.23 (0.44)	6.64 (0.28)

Note. Items were rated on a 7-point scale (1 = *rotten* and 7 = *fresh*). Standard deviations are shown in parentheses.

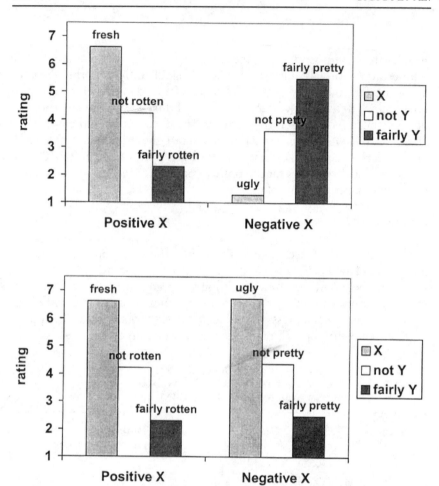

FIG. 10.1 Ratings of positive adjectives versus negated and hedged negative adjectives compared to ratings of negative adjectives versus negated and hedged positive adjectives (top panel). A mirror image of negative X appears in bottom panel.

subjects extra processing time during which suppression could have become effective. Instead, the "bluntness" of *blunt* or the "prettiness" of *pretty* tinged the meaning of *not blunt* and *not pretty* and made it distinctly different from *sharp* and *ugly*. Negation directed the modification of the negated concept towards the mid, neutral position on the scale.

Our results further show that negative (*ugly*) and positive (*fresh*) adjectives do not differ when compared with their negated opposites. The difference between negatives (*ugly*) and their negated positives (*not pretty*) is equivalent to that obtaining between positives (*fresh*) and their negated negatives (*not rotten*). Contra the asymmetry assumption (Colston, 1999; Horn, 1989), our findings demonstrate that the salient meanings of both negatives and positives affect interpretation similarly (psycholinguistically and partly semantically).

In sum, our findings concerning the tingeing effect allow us to classify negation markers within the category of modifiers rather than within the category of suppressors. Indeed, explicit negation is comparable to other modifiers such as *fairly*. Although *fairly* is a moderate modifier preserving the salient meaning of the modified adjective rather actively (*fairly rotten* is closer to *rotten* than *not rotten* and *fairly pretty* is closer to *pretty* than *not pretty*), *not* is a slightly (although distinctly) stronger modifier than *fairly*. Like *fairly*, however, it does not eradicate the salient meaning of the modified constituent (for more information on other modifiers sensitive to gradability, see Paradis, 2001).

EXPERIMENT 4

Are speakers aware of the tingeing effect involved in negation? Would they select a negated element when wishing to downplay unpleasant information? Experiment 4 was designed to test whether speakers are sensitive to the pragmatic functions of the negation marker *not*. Having shown that negation acts as a modifier rather than as a suppressor, allowing features of the negated item to infiltrate and affect the interpretation of the negative constituent (not Y), we aimed to show that speakers employ negated items when being polite.

Method

Participants. Participants were 30 graduate and undergraduate students of Tel Aviv University, between the ages of 21 and 36 (22 women and 8 men). All were native speakers of Hebrew.

Stimuli. Stimuli included 16 experimental pairs and 8 filler pairs. The experimental pairs comprised a sentence that contained a nonnegated negative item ("What you said was a *lie*") and a sentence that contained its antonym, which was marked for negation and conveyed the same semantic interpretation ("What you said was *not true*"). The fillers included two sentences with different semantic meanings ("The dinner you cooked for us was delicious" and "The dinner you cooked for us was filling"). The order of presentation of each of the items of the experimental pairs was randomized.

Procedure. Subjects were presented booklets containing these pairs and were asked to indicate which of the two sentences they would select if they wished to be polite or less offensive.

Results

To quantify the responses, a selection of a not X (*not true*) structure scored 1; a selection of an X (*a lie*) structure scored 0. The maximum score for a subject then would be 16. Results showed that indeed most of the subjects selected the sentences that contained a negated constituent. The mean score of all the responses was 14.27 (*SD* = 1.95).

Discussion

When speakers were aiming at politeness and were faced with two alternatives, they preferred a negated, semantically positive constituent (*not true*) to a nonnegated semantically negative constituent (*a lie*). This choice indicates that speakers are sensitive to the pragmatic function of negation, which often provides one with a mitigated, hedged version of the negated constituent. Such findings are consistent with the view that a negation marker (*not*) is not a strong suppressor, although it might reduce initial levels of activation (as shown by Hasson, 2000, Experiment 3 and Mayo et al., 2002, Experiment 2). Rather, it is a strong modifier.

GENERAL DISCUSSION

In this study, we tested the retention-of-negated-concepts hypothesis. Contrary to the received view, which assumes that suppression of negated concepts is obligatory, we adduced evidence showing that it is not. We showed that information introduced via negation is often retained rather than suppressed and tinges the negativity of the explicit negation. The interpretation of a negated item (*not pretty*) is therefore, more mitigated than its alternative opposite (*ugly*), which allows negation to be used when politeness or hedging is required. Findings in our lab as well as an analysis of naturally occurring discourses demonstrate that comprehenders neither block nor eliminate from mental representations salient meanings of negated concepts. As a result, speakers select negated positives as opposed to nonnegated negatives when they are after a polite or a low-key mode of expression and when they wish to hedge a positive expression.

In Experiment 1, we showed that negation does not have inhibitory effects. A negation marker (*not* in not-X) did not block access of the salient meanings of a target (X in not-X). Thus, *piercing* was primed following both *sharp* and *not sharp*. These results corroborate those of MacDonald and Just (1989) and Hasson (2000, Experiments 1 and 2). Although MacDonald and Just's findings may demonstrate some suppression effects, their reading time phase (in all their experiments), which is the only measure in their studies that could tap initial processes, shows no inhibition of salient meanings of concepts following negation. Similarly, in Hasson's study, tapping re-lated concepts immediately (150 ms and even 500 ms) after offset of the negated targets showed no inhibition effects.

How would comprehenders manage salient meanings of negated con-cepts, which are initially insensitive to negation effects? Would they sup-press them postlexically to allow the derivation of the appropriate meaning? Experiment 2 shows that salient meanings of negated concepts are not wiped out even when comprehenders are allowed extra processing time. Rather, they are retained and affect the ongoing discourse process-ing. Thus, lists including negated items were shown to behave like lists of nonnegated items; that is, they were viewed as acceptable only when categorizable in the same set. Specifically, subjects found "What I bought yesterday was not a bottle but a jug" acceptable. In contrast, "What I bought yesterday was not a bottle but a closet" was not acceptable. Such findings cannot be accounted for in terms of suppression. If a negation marker discards an entity altogether, the acceptability of the next item in the list should not be constrained by the prior occurrence of that entity. Experiment 2 thus suggests that at least some of the features of negated items are preserved and affect the classifiability of the next item in line.

Note that this is also true of negated items preceded by nonnegated el-ements. The following string (19), which describes the Israeli Chief of Staff, Ya'alon, is appropriate because the negated element can be classi-fied within the same category as the nonnegated item that precedes it, showing that the negated element must have preserved at least some of its properties:

(19) The word is that he is intelligent but not brilliant. Tough but not cruel, demanding but not macho. (Shavit, 2002)

This seems to be also true of the *neither–nor* construction. Although (20) is appropriate, (21) is not:

(20) The word is that he is neither tough nor cruel.
(21) The word is that he is neither tough nor thirsty.

Indeed (22) shows that such negation requires that the negated items make up a category (of predicates applicable to Sami Michael's—the new president of the Association for Civil Rights in Israel—identity):

(22) Michael says that ever since he came to this country [Israel] at the age of 22, he has not known what peace of mind is, neither as a Jew nor as an Israeli, nor as a person who believes in democracy and a just society. (Eldar, 2002)

Besides, it is quite obvious that double negation necessitates the retainability of the negated items. For instance, "I don't think this is implausible," approximately meaning "I think this is plausible," necessitates the retainability of both *think* and *plausible*.

Similarly, constructions such as X *if not* Y do not in fact suppress Y but rather mean "X and possibly Y," thus relying on the retainability of the affirmative meaning of Y:

(23) *Most if not all* of the remaining Gricean rules respond to the Speaker's Economy, either directly ... or indirectly .... (Horn, 1984, p. 12).

(24) Well yeah but you see that the trouble is they've been now *two if not three* pilot phases. (British National Corpus, 1993: H5E 929, http://sara.natcopr.ox.ac.uk/lookup.html).

(25) Unfortunately for such critics it has been found that acupuncture works *equally well, if not more effectively*, on animals. (British National Corpus, 1990: CB9 1459, http://sara.natcopr.ox.ac.uk/lookup.html).

If negation neither inhibits nor necessarily suppresses negated items, how does it eventually affect interpretation? Experiment 3 shows that a negation marker induces mitigation[13]: *Not pretty* is distinguishable from *ugly* (see also Clark & Clark, 1977: 426): It is perceived to be half way between *pretty* and *ugly*; that is, it is conceived of as "less than pretty." However, *not pretty* is also quite distinguishable from *fairly pretty*, which is rated as closer to *pretty*, which suggests that *not* is a stronger modifier than a more positive hedge (e.g., *fairly*) and would make *not pretty* less pretty than *fairly pretty* but also more *pretty* than *ugly*. No wonder the American administration, favoring the Israelis over the Palestinians, described the Israeli siege of Arafat as "unhelpful" (Sky News, 25 September 2002). "Unhelpful" certainly sounds less disastrous than *disastrous* or even *harmful*.

The following example illustrates this further. It shows that "not liquidate" does not mean "let be." Rather (the question of who will "not liquidate" Arafat set aside), "not liquidate" allows for a "less than liquidate" interpretation such as *neutralize* or *not be*:

(26) The Americans made it clear that they are not going to liquidate him, but that if the Palestinians want to see light at the end of the tunnel, they themselves should neutralize him. That is an unequivocal statement: Arafat will not be the decision-maker. He will not be. (Shavit, 2002)

---

[13]On other forms of mitigation see Caffi (1990, 2001).

Experiment 4 shows that speakers are sensitive to the modifying effect of explicit negation. Participants showed a clear-cut preference for negated items (*not succeeding*) that contained a negated positive (*succeeding*) over their antonym (*failing*) when they were asked to be polite. The negation marker, which failed to suppress the positivity of the negated concept, allowed this positivity to dilute the negativity of the negation marker and offer a more positive articulation of an undesirable state of affairs (failing).

In fact, a close look at some of the studies that assumed suppression reveals that they do not quite support a suppression hypothesis. For Instance, MacDonald and Just's (1989) third experiment, which uses related associates as probes, shows no suppression effects. It is only when participants had to make a decision as to whether a probe appeared or did not appear in the text that findings clearly supported the suppression hypothesis (MacDonald & Just, 1989, Experiment 1). However, as MacDonald and Just observed, it is quite possible that having to be positive and say "yes" about a target that appeared in a negated context (i.e., the target was preceded by *no*) involved some Stroop (1935) interference that slowed down responses to probes featuring negated targets. Using the same suspect methodology, Kaup (2001) replicated these results, but then it is possible that they, in fact, also testified to the accessibility of the negated concepts as negated concepts rather than to their inaccessibility as a result of a negative context.

Specifically, Kaup (2001) tried to support the view that accessibility or inaccessibility of concepts is a function of their representation in the situation model (Johnson-Laird, 1983; van Dijk & Kintsch, 1983; Zwaan, 1999). Thus, "Mary bakes bread but no cookies" should lead to a reduced accessibility of the negated concept (*cookies*), because it should not be kept in mind. (After all, no cookies came into being). In contrast, the negated concept (*photograph* in "Elizabeth burns the letters but not the photographs") should be included in the mental representation and should not be suppressed (because there must have been some photographs). Such an account, however, will not explain the speaker's expectation that the addressees (restaurant diners) retain the concept of "12% service" appearing on their bill (29) when paying it:

(27) The price does not include 12% service. Thanks!!![14]

Given that the price does not include 12% service, no mental representation of it is expected. According to Kaup, it should have been suppressed.

---

[14]We thank Mira Ariel (23–25 and 27).

However, it is quite obvious that the addressees were supposed to keep precisely this concept in mind and act upon it when tipping (for which they are even thanked in advance; also see the bean story in the epigraph).

Another example that stresses what is absent ("the real reasons why the United States has found itself under attack") is shown in (28). Although, according to Kaup (2001), what is absent should be suppressed (because it should not be represented in our mental model), here, what is absent is apparently what the journalist is after and is what he wants us to keep in mind:

(28) But the real lie in the President's speech—that which has dominated American political discourse since the crimes against humanity on 11 September last year—was the virtual absence of any attempt to explain the real reasons why the United States has found itself under attack.

      In his mendacious article in this newspaper last week, President Bush's Defense Secretary, Donald Rumsfeld, also attempted to mask this reality. The 11 September assault, he announced, was an attack on people "who believe in freedom, who practice tolerance and who defend the inalienable rights of man." **He made, as usual, absolutely no reference to the Middle East, to America's woeful, biased policies in that region, to its ruthless support for Arab dictators who do its bidding—for Saddam Hussein, for example, at a time when the head of Iraqi nuclear research was undergoing his Calvary—nor to America's military presence in the holiest of Muslim lands, nor to its unconditional support for Israel's occupation of Palestinian land in the West Bank and Gaza.** (Fisk, 2002)

Apparently, negation will not affect suppression in a question such as (29), no matter what the answer to that question is:

(29) Is this emphatically not true for our "postmodern" time? (Žižek, 2002).

A negation marker, then, might have different functions: It might indicate the absence of the negated entities (as when negating nouns), which either introduce the negated entities to the discourse (see Giora, 1994, and (4, 5, and 30)), or lead to similar alternatives (Experiment 4). It might hedge properties (as in the case of predicates, see Experiments 3 and 4). It is not entirely implausible that it might also suppress entities. Further research should investigate the conditions under which negation involves suppression. Our findings, however, argue against an obligatory view of suppression. They show that when exploitable, so-called irrelevant meanings partake in the interpretation process and affect speakers' linguistic choices vis à vis their social environments (for a similar view regarding irony and metaphor, see Giora, 2003; Giora & Fein, 1999a, 1999b).

ACKNOWLEDGMENTS

This research was supported by a grant from the Tel Aviv Basic Research Fund to the first author.

We thank Mira Ariel, Herb Colston, Jack Du Bois, Uri Hasson, Brooke Lea, Carita Paradis, Noa Shuval, and Aldo Savi for very helpful comments on an earlier draft.

REFERENCES

Alcott, L. M. (1962). Little Man; Life at Plumfield With Jo's Boys. New York: MacMillan Publishing Co. (Original work published 1871)
http://www.digital.library.upenn.edu/women/alcott/men/men.html

Bar'el, Z. (2002). The facts were in on Israel's Arabs. Ha'aretz in English. Retrieved 25 August 2002 from http://www.haaretz.vco.il

Barsalou, L. W. (1983). Ad hoc categories. Memory & Cognition, 11, 211–227.

Bartsch, R., & Vennemann, T. (1972). Semantic structures. Frankfurt: Anthenäum Verlag.

Brewer, W. F., & Lichtenstein, E. H. (1975). Recall of logical and pragmatic implications in sentences with dichotomous and continuous antonyms. Memory & Cognition, 3, 315–318.

British National Corpus. (1990). http://sara.natcorp.ox.ac.uk/lookup.html

British National Corpus. (1993). http://sara.natcorp.ox.ac.uk/lookup.html

Caffi, C. (1990). Modulazione, mitigazione e litote. In M.-E. Conte, P. Ramat, & A. Giaalone Ramat (Eds.), Diminsioni della linguistica (pp. 169–199). Milano: Angeli.

Chopin, K. (1976). The story of an hour. In B. H. Solomon (Ed.) The awakening and selected stories and Kate Chopin (pp. 198–200). New York: Signet. (Original work published 1894).

Clark, H. H. (1970). Word association and linguistic theory. In J. Lyons (Ed.), New horizons in linguistics (pp. 271–286). Baltimore: Penguin Books.

Clark, H. H., & Chase, W. G. (1972). On the process of comparing sentences against pictures. Cognitive Psychology, 3, 472–517.

Clark, H. H., & Clark, V. E. (1977). Psychology and language: An introduction to psycholinguistics. San Diego: Harcourt Brace Javanovich.

Colston, H. L. (1999). "Not good" is "bad," but "not bad" is not "good": An analysis of three accounts of negation asymmetry. Discourse Processes, 28, 237–256.

Cornulier, B., de. (1974). Remarques à propos de la negation (Notes on expected negation) anticipée. Le français moderne, 41, 43–57.

Dews, S., & Winner, E. (1995). Muting the meaning: A social function of irony. Metaphor and Symbolic Activity, 10, 3–19.

Du Bois, W. J. (200). *Santa Barbara corpus of spoken American English*. CD-ROM. Philadelphia: Linguistic Dat a Consortium [www.ldc.upenn.edu/Publications/ SBC/].

Ducrot, O. (1973). *La preuve et le dire* (The proof and the said). Paris: Herman.

Eldar, A. (2002, 16 September). Trumpeting a blast of despair. *Ha'aretz in English*.

Fiedler, K., Walther, E., Armbruster, T., Fay, D., & Naumann, U. (1996). Do you really know what you have seen? Intrusion errors and presuppositions effects on constructive memory. *Journal of Experimental Social Psychology, 32*, 484–511.

Fischler, I., Bloom, P. A., Childres, D. G., Rocus, S. E., & Perry, N. W. (1983). Brain potentials related to stages of sentence verification. *Psychophysiology, 20*, 400–409.

Fisk, R. (2002, 15 September). America's case for war is built on blindness, hypocrisy and lies. *The Independent*.

Fodor, J. (1983). *The modularity of mind*. Cambridge, MA: MIT Press.

Giora, R. (1994). On the political message: Pretending to communicate. In H. Parret (Ed.), *Pretending to communicate* (pp. 104–123). Berlin/New York: Walter de Gruyter Verlag (Communication and Cognition Series).

Giora, R. (1997). Understanding figurative and literal language: The graded salience hypothesis. *Cognitive Linguistics, 7*, 183–206.

Giora, R. (2003). *On our mind: Salience, context, and figurative language*. New York: Oxford University Press.

Giora, R., & Fein, O. (1999a). Irony: Context and salience. *Metaphor and Symbol, 14*, 241–257.

Giora, R., & Fein, O. (1999b). On understanding familiar and less-familiar figurative language. *Journal of Pragmatics, 31*, 1601–1618.

Giora, R., Fein O., & Schwartz, T. (1998). Irony: Graded salience and indirect negation. *Metaphor and Symbol, 13*, 83–101.

Givón, T. (1993) *English grammar: A function-based introduction, Vol. 1*. Amsterdam/Philadelphia: John Benjamins.

Hasson, U. (2000). *Comprehension of negation in negated metaphors*. Unpublished master's thesis, Princeton University, Priceton, NJ.

Hegel, G. W. F. (1892). *The logic of Hegel: Translated from the encyclopedia of the philosophical sciences*. W. Wallace, trans. 2nd ed. London: Oxford University Press.

Horn, L. R. (1984). A new taxonomy for pragmatic inference: Q-based and R-based implicatures. In D. Schiffrin (Ed.), *Meaning, form and use in context* (pp. 11–42). Washington DC: Georgetown University Press.

Horn, L. R. (1989). *A natural history of negation*. Chicago: University of Chicago Press.

Jefferson, G. (2002). Is "no" an acknowledgment token? Comparing American and British uses of (+)/(–) tokens. *Journal of Pragmatics, 34*, 1345–1383.

Jespersen, O. (1976). *The philosophy of grammar*. New York: Norton. (Original work published 1924).

Johnson-Laird, P. N. (1983). *Mental models*. Cambridge, MA: Harvard University Press.

Johnson-Laird, P. N., & Tridgell, J. M. (1972). When negation is easier than affirmation. *Quarterly Journal of Experimental Psychology, 24*, 87–91.

Just, M. A., & Carpenter, P. A. (1976). Eye fixations and cognitive processes. *Cognitive Psychology, 8,* 441–480.

Kaup, B. (1997). The processing of negatives during discourse comprehension. In M. G. Shafto & P. Langley (Eds.), *Proceedings of the nineteenth conference of the cognitive science society* (pp. 370–375). Mahwah, NJ: Lawrence Erlbaum Associates.

Kaup, B. (2001). Negation and its impact on the accessibility of text information. *Memory & Cognition, 29,* 960–967.

Klein, N. (2002). *No Logo.* New York: Picador.

Labov, W. (1972). The transformation of experience in narrative syntax. In *Language in the inner city* (pp. 354–395). Philadelphia: University of Pennsylvania Press.

Lea, B. R., & Mulligan, E. J. (2002). The effect of negation on deductive inferences. *Journal of Experimental Psychology: Learning, Memory, and Cognition, 28,* 303–317.

Levy, G. (2002). Nothing happened. *Ha'aretz Supplement in English.* Retrieved 16 August 2002 from http://www.haaretz.co.il

Linor, E. (1999). *Shiv'a Leilot, Yedi'ot Achronot* (A Hebrew daily, September 17, 1999).

Lyons, J. (1977). *Semantics.* Cambridge, England: Cambridge University Press.

MacDonald, M. C., & Just, M. A. (1989). Changes in activation levels with negation. *Journal of Experimental Psychology: Learning, Memory, and Cognition, 15,* 633–642.

Mayo, R., Schul, Y., & Burnstein, E. (in press). "I am not guilty" versus "I am innocent": The associative structure activated in processing negations. *Journal of Experimental Social Psychology.*

Moxey, L. M., & Sanford, A. J. (2000). Communicating quantities: A review of psycholinguistic evidence of how expressions determine perspective. *Applied Cognitive Psychology, 14,* 237–255.

Paradis, C. (2001). Adjectives and boundedness. *Cognitive Linguistics, 12,* 47–65.

Peleg, O., Giora, R., & Fein, O. (2001). Salience and context effects: Two are better than one. *Metaphor and Symbol, 16,* 173–192.

Peleg, O., Giora, R., & Fein, O. (in press). Contextual strength: The whens and hows of context effects. In I. Noveck & D. Sperber (Eds.), *Experimental pragmatics.* Basingstoke, England: Palgrave.

Rayner, K., Pacht, J. M., & Duffy, S. A. (1994). Effects of prior encounter and global discourse bias on the processing of lexically ambiguous words: Evidence from eye fixations. *Journal of Memory and Language, 33,* 527–544.

Shavit, A. (2002). The enemy within. *Ha'aretz Supplement in English.* Retrieved 30 August 2002 from http://www/haaretz/co/il

Sperber, D., & Wilson, D. (1986/1995). *Relevance: Communication and cognition.* Oxford, England: Blackwell.

Stroop, J. R. (1935). Studies of inference in serial verbal reactions. *Journal of Experimental Psychology, 18,* 643–662.

Thompson, W. C., Fong, G. T., & Rosenhan, D. L. (1981). Inadmissible evidence and juror verdicts. *Journal of Personality and Social Psychology, 40,* 453–463.

Tottie, G. (1994). Any as an indefinite determiner in non-assertive clauses: Evidence from present-day and early modern English. In D. Kastovsky (Ed.), *Studies in early modern English* (pp. 413–427). Berlin, Germany: Mouton de Gruyter.

van Dijk, T. A., & Kintsch, W. (1983). *Strategies of discourse comprehension.* New York: Academic Press.

Wason, P. C. (1963). The contexts of plausible denial. *Journal of Verbal Learning and Verbal Behavior, 4,* 7–11.

Wegner, D. (1994). The ironic processes of mental control. *Psychological Review, 101,* 34–52.

Wegner, D., & Erber, R. (1992). The hyperaccessibility of suppressed thoughts. *Journal of Personality and Social Psychology, 63,* 903–912.

Wegner, D., Schneider, D., Carter, S., & White, T. (1987). Paradoxical effects of thought suppression. *Journal of Personality and Social Psychology, 53,* 5–13.

Wegner, D., Wenzlaff, R., Kerker, R. M., & Beattie, A. E. (1981). Incrimination through innuendo: Can media questions become public answers? *Journal of Personality and Social Psychology, 40,* 822–832.

Winter, Y., & Rimon, M. (1994). Contrast and implication in natural language. *Journal of Semantics, 11,* 365–406.

Žižek, S. (2002). *Welcome to the desert of the real.* Retrieved October 17, 2002 from http://www.lacan.com/desertsymf.htm

Zwaan, R. A. (1999). Situation models: The mental leap into imagined worlds. *Current Directions in Psychological Science, 8,* 15–18.

PART IV

New Sociocultural Influences

11

Stereotype Processing and Nonliteral Language

Tracie L. Blumentritt
University of Wisconsin–La Crosse

Roberto R. Heredia
Texas A&M International University

Following the April 19, 1995, Oklahoma City bombing, news reports began circulating that the incident may have been the work of terrorists. The next day a Jordanian American was wrongfully detained and returned from London to the United States in connection with the terrorist attack. A few months later, the American Civil Liberties Union (ACLU) filed a claim against the United States on behalf of Abraham Ahmad. According to the ACLU's claim, "it [was] wrong to target someone in a criminal investigation based on cultural stereotypes … [and] Arab Americans have been subject[ed] to a great deal of prejudice and discrimination, both before and after the bombing" (ACLU, Freedom Network, 1995, p. 1). Unfortunately, the attacks on September 11, 2001 further reinforced and extended the stereotype that not only are all Arabs terrorists but also that all Muslims or people of the Islamic faith are terrorists. However, such generalizations are without foundation. No particular ethnic or cultural group holds an exclusive trademark for terrorism because other groups have been and are involved in such destructive acts (e.g., Anglo Americans, Europeans, and Latin Americans). In this chapter, the term *stereotype* describes the seemingly pervasive human tendency to perceive others not as individuals but as members of particular social groups with shared characteristics (Lippman, 1922). In other words, stereotypes are cognitive frameworks that consist of beliefs and generalizations about perceived typical characteristics for certain social groups. Thus, for some people, the term *terrorist* can be understood in terms of a dominant meaning, which typically includes acts of terrorism, such as bombing and gunfire, and a stereotype meaning that characterizes Arabs or Muslims as people who commit acts of terrorism. A vast amount of research has been conducted on stereotypes, the most recent of which involves examining stereotypes as a specific type of cognitive structure and discerning the processes by which these structures exert influence on behavior, attitudes, memory, social judgment, inferences, and various other perceptual processes (e.g., Banaji & Greenwald, 1995; Banaji, Hardin, & Rothman, 1993; Bodenhausen, 1988; Cohen, 1981; Darley & Gross, 1983; Kunda & Sherman-Williams, 1992; Synder, Tanke, & Berscheid, 1977). In short, when a stereotype is activated, practically all aspects of social information processing are affected. Clearly, the possession of a stereotype and its activation have extremely important implications for social life.

Within this chapter, we explore stereotype processing and the connection between stereotypes and language processing, and we propose that stereotypes can be construed as a special case of figurative language. For example, in the sentence (1) "It is important to assure that TERRORISTS do not access airports," it is possible to interpret the term *terrorist* in two ways. First, this term may trigger general information about things that denote acts of terrorism such as bombs, weapons, and highjackings. Second, when people listen to this term, they may retrieve information about a specific ethnic group that is associated with such terrorists attacks. This stereotypic meaning can be seen as an extension of a nonliteral interpretation (i.e., a metonymic relationship) in which a perceived dominant characteristic of a particular ethnic group is used to refer to the entire group (e.g., Frisson & Pickering, 1999; Gibbs, 1990, 1993, 1994). In fact, Heredia and Blumentritt (2002) showed that social stereotypes can be examined from a psycholinguistic (as well as sociocognitive) perspective and that by doing so several interesting and novel processing effects emerge. We begin by reviewing the relevant sociocognitive literature on stereotype processing and then introduce important concepts from the psycholinguistic literature that bear directly on stereotype processing. Finally, we review a recent study that illustrates how concepts and methods from the field of psycholinguistics can inform and guide the empirical study of stereotypes.

STEREOTYPE PROCESSING

Stereotype Activation and Structure

Broadly speaking, current conceptualizations construe stereotypes as a specific type of cognitive structure that contains information relevant to the categorization of groups of people (Dijksterhuis & Van Knippenberg, 1996; Stephan, 1989). These cognitive structures enable the perceiver to efficiently, simplistically, and often inaccurately make judgments about others. The dominant view holds that information contained within the structure is highly interconnected, and forms large networks of abstract information often referred to as *schemas*. *Social schemas* are networks representing knowledge about members of a given social category and can include such things as perceived physical characteristics, (stereo)typical traits and attributes, and expected behaviors of members of the particular social group. Specific pieces of information (often referred to as *nodes*) within the schemas are thought to be organized semantically and according to frequency and recency of activation. *Activation* occurs when the node is made accessible to working memory and can occur either through consciously controlled processes or through automatic, largely unconscious processes (e.g., Bargh, 1994; Blair & Banaji, 1996). Following initial node activation, a process of spreading activation occurs in which related information about the group is automatically activated until lexical decay occurs (Anderson, 1983; Stephan, 1989).

In recent models of stereotyping, a conceptual distinction is drawn between stereotype activation and stereotype application (Blair & Banaji, 1996; Fiske & Neuberg, 1990; Gilbert & Hixon, 1991). Stereotype activation occurs when the stereotype is brought to mind through various means (e.g., being asked to think about a group of people) or modalities (e.g., viewing a human face or listening to stereotypic remarks). Stereotype application involves making a stereotypic judgment or response—for example, associating the word *competence* with the word *male*. However, for the perceiver to be able to apply the stereotype (i.e., to make the judgment), the stereotype must first be activated. According to this view activation is a necessary but insufficient condition in stereotyping.

Methodological Techniques for the Study of Stereotyping

The primary methodology used in the experimental study of stereotype activation has been semantic priming. In the typical single-word priming experiment, participants are visually presented racially salient words, such as *black* or *white*, and then asked to make a judgment or decision about stereotype-congruent target words, such as *lazy* or *smart*. Reaction times of participants are faster when the prime-target relation is congruent with the negative or positive stereotypes associated with the relevant social category (e.g., Dovidio, Evans, & Tyler, 1986). The majority of studies have used visually presented priming stimuli of different types, including words (primarily trait words, but also nouns related to gender (Banaji & Hardin, 1996; Dijksterhuis & Van Knippenberg, 1996; Dovidio, et al., 1986), scrambled sentences (Bargh, Chen, & Burrows,

1996), names of historical figures (Stapel, Koomen, & Van der Plight, 1997), social category labels (Rothbart, Sriram, & Davis-Stitt, 1996), and human faces (Bargh et al., 1996; Chen & Bargh, 1997).

The particular priming method varies as well, with many studies using the well-known priming technique in which the participant is consciously exposed to the critical prime (*bread*), followed by the presentation of a related (*butter*) or unrelated target (*floor*). However, some studies have used nonconscious (i.e.., subliminal) methods in which the priming stimulus is presented below the participants' level of reliable detection. Devine (1989) used a form of this method by having participants identify the location of the stimuli (stereotype-related words) briefly presented in the participants' parafoveal visual field, quickly followed by a pattern mask. Other studies have relied on masking techniques to prevent conscious recognition of the content of the stereotype-related priming stimuli. For example, masking stimuli have been used to subliminally present photographs of faces of different ethnicities (Bargh et al., 1996; Chen & Bargh, 1997) and trait or nontrait words (Bargh & Pietromonaco, 1982; Locke, MacLeod, & Walker, 1994).

In a related vein, Banaji, Hardin, and Rothman (1993) examined implicit stereotyping using a priming technique in which individuals are exposed to positive or negative trait words that are either semantically relevant or irrelevant to a brief story participants subsequently read (see Higgins, Rholes, & Jones, 1977). The story involved a character named Donald who performed various empirically established, ambiguous behaviors with respect to the trait categories. Participants who were previously exposed to positive traits rated Donald's behavior more positively than participants exposed to negative traits, and vice versa. Exposure to semantically irrelevant positive or negative traits showed no influence on ratings. Using a version of this technique, Banaji et al. demonstrated that implicitly primed, stereotyped information influenced judgments of targets consistent with the stereotype. For example, participants exposed to primes connoting dependence (a stereotypically female trait) subsequently rated a female target more dependent than a male target who performed identical behaviors.

With very few exceptions (see Dijksterhuis & Van Knippenberg, 1996; Heredia & Blumentritt, 2002; for examples of lexical decisions), the dependent measures for most priming-based studies of stereotyping have been reaction times to various kinds of judgments about the target stimuli. The presumption (generally borne out by research) is that reaction times will be faster for stereotype consistent prime-target relations than for stereotype inconsistent, prime-target relations. Examples of the types of tasks used include judgments of pronouns (e.g., is it a male or female pronoun? Banaji & Hardin, 1996), judgments of proper nouns (e.g., is it a male or female name? Blair & Banaji, 1996), and judgments of whether a target stimuli *could ever be true* of the prime category or was *always false* (Dovidio et al., 1986).

Automaticity and Controlled Processes in Stereotype Activation

A great deal of research has examined the extent to which stereotypes are automatically activated and the conditions under which their activation may be consciously controlled (e.g., Banaji & Greenwald, 1995; Banaji & Hardin, 1996; Banaji et al., 1993; Blair & Banaji, 1996; Devine, 1989; Dovidio et al., 1986). Automatic processing of social information has been extensively elaborated by Bargh and colleagues (e.g., Bargh, 1984, 1989, 1994; Bargh, Chaiken, Govender, & Pratto, 1992) who proposed that automatic cognitive processes are those that are largely involuntary, effortless, and unconscious. They run on autopilot, so to speak, and are viewed as relatively static processes that, once initiated, are not constrained by capacity limitations and are not under the conscious control of the perceiver. Specific automatic processes arise from repeated experience with a particular stimulus or stimulus domain and are automatically triggered by exposure to the stimulus (Bargh, 1984).

Controlled processes are aspects of cognition believed to be under conscious, voluntary control and are effortful and limited by the availability of attentional energy (e.g., Bargh, 1989; Shiffrin & Dumais, 1981). Conscious control over activation can occur only if the perceiver is given enough processing time to allow suppression (or inhibition) of activation or if the perceiver has a conscious intention to suppress activation (Bargh, 1989; Blair & Banaji, 1996). An early influential study by Neely (1977) examined specific experimental conditions under which automatic processing of single words can occur. For one condition, participants were presented with words that primed their own semantic category (e.g., BODY–arm); for the second condition, participants were told to expect a target from a semantically unrelated category when given a certain prime word. For example, they were told to expect the name of a type of bird when presented with the BODY prime (e.g., BODY–sparrow). For both conditions, the experimental task was a lexical decision, with prime-target intervals set at 250 ms and 2000 ms. Neely found that for the short prime-target interval (250 ms), the prime facilitated lexical decisions to semantically related target words irrespective of experimenter instructions. At the longer prime-target interval (2000 ms), the conscious expectancy conditions produced facilitation for the expected target and inhibition for unexpected targets regardless of the targets' semantic relation to the prime. Neely (and others) have taken these results to indicate that automatic activation occurs at very brief time intervals (i.e., under very high cognitive constraints); at longer time intervals, conscious attention is allowed to develop and to potentially inhibit the automatic processes (Devine, 1989; Logan, 1980).

Using designs that assess on-line automaticity effects, Blair and Banaji (1996) reported a series of experiments that examined automatic activation of gender stereotypes under baseline conditions of automaticity (i.e., prime-target interval less than 500 ms) and under conditions designed to counteract automatic stereotyping. They used a semantic priming procedure in which the primes were either positively or negatively valenced stereotypically masculine traits (e.g., *bold* and *crude*, respectively), feminine traits (e.g., *gentle* and *fickle*, respectively), or gender neutral non-traits (e.g., *birthday* and *horror*, respectively). Targets consisted of male or female proper nouns. Results indicated automatic activation of the stereotype when the prime-target interval was very brief (350 ms), and no explicit intention to counter the stereotype was created. When given an explicit strategy to counter the stereotypical association, participants were able to significantly reduce (but not eliminate) stereotype priming, even under high cognitive constraint. Further, when given more processing time, in combination with the counterstereotype strategy, stereotype priming was reversed. A second on-line study by Banaji and Blair (1996) revealed that gender stereotypes are automatically activated even when the judgment task is unrelated to gender and even if the participants are unaware of the gender relation of the prime-target pairings.

In summary, the study of the social stereotype—its cognitive structure, processes, and influence on behavior—has been an extremely active area in the extant sociocognitive literature. Drawing on models and methods from cognitive psychology, social psychologists have delineated many of the mechanisms underlying stereotyping, and they have highlighted important areas that need further investigation. Our work, too, is based in the sociocognitive literature. However, we also offer a new and different perspective on stereotypes. It is to this perspective to which we now turn.

FIGURATIVE LANGUAGE AND STEREOTYPES

What is the relationship between figurative language and stereotypes? To illustrate consider the sentence, (2) "Be careful James, those SHARKS will tell you one thing today and tomorrow say something completely different." The term *sharks* in this case is clearly not describing a marine animal. It describes the idea that lawyers are vicious and cunning. This type of figurative language is known as metaphoric reference (Gibbs, 1990, 1994; Onishi & Murphy, 1993; Stewart & Heredia, 2002), and it contrasts with predicate metaphor of the form "A(n) is a B" (e.g., lawyers are sharks). In predicate form, metaphor consists of a topic (e.g., lawyers) and a vehicle (e.g., sharks). When these domains are combined (i.e., "*lawyers are sharks*"), what is common about the two domains comprises the metaphorical meaning of the statement which is referred to as the "ground." Finally, in referential metaphor, the topic and vehicle occur apart from one another. The vehicle is usually made explicit, and the listener must abstract the topic from the previous context. For example, to understand (2), information relevant to the topic (e.g., lawyer) must come before the metaphoric reference; otherwise, it would be extremely difficult to make sense of such an utterance. Notice also that the metaphoric reference can be generalized to all lawyers. In this case, it would be possible to say that all lawyers are vicious and cunning and that one would have to be careful with them, especially when it comes to monetary issues. Such logic could also be applied to other instances in which, for example, all surgeons are viewed as butchers, all women are described as female dogs, and all men are viewed as pigs. In fact, it is not surprising to hear women lament that all men are pigs. We contend that it is possible to view and study social stereotypes as extensions of metaphoric referential descriptions.

In addition, stereotypes can also be viewed and classified as parallel cases of metonymic reference. In metonymy, a salient aspect of an entity is used to refer to the entity as a whole or to some other part of the entity (Frisson & Pickering, 1999, pp. 1366–1367). That is, the name of one thing is used for that of another of which it is an attribute or with which it is associated. For example, in (3) "We need a new glove to play third base" (Gibbs, 1993), the metonymic reference *glove* maps a salient characteristic of one domain. The *glove* in this case is part of the baseball player that in turn represents the entire domain *player*. The connection between the two domains form a relationship between part (*glove*) and whole (*baseball player*). In metonymic comparisons, the two concepts being compared must belong to the same conceptual domain (Gibbs, 1990, 1993, 1994; also see Frisson & Pickering, 1999 for a comprehensive list of different types of metonymy).

How are stereotypes related to metonymic references? Let us reconsider our earlier example of terrorists from (1), "It is important to assure that TERRORISTS do not access airports." The term *terrorist* has become a stereotype attributed to the Arab community. It can be argued that this stereotype is being used as metonymic reference due to the perceived notion that because some Arabs have been involved in terrorist attacks (a salient characteristic of this perceived generalization), it represents the entire domain (all Arabs). Following this reasoning, other ethnic stereotypes are possible such as (4) "Jane stopped and said hello to the BEANER who was reading a novel." In (4), the stereotype may describe a Mexican or a Hispanic individual. The idea here is that this ethnic group becomes associated with the assumed food that they consume. That is, if Mexicans eat beans, they must be described as *beaners*, and this follows the somewhat risible general principle that you are what you eat.

Therefore, stereotypes can be seen as composed of a nonliteral and a literal interpretation. In the case of the stereotype *beaner*, the nonliteral meaning describes the Mexican ethnic group, and the literal meaning describes the direct related association to food. Now, the question of interest is, how are stereotypes processed? Are people able to access the nonliteral sense of the stereotype directly (e.g., Banaji & Greenwald, 1995; Banaji & Hardin, 1996; Banaji et al., 1993; Blair & Banaji, 1996; Devine, 1989)? Or, during stereotype processing, must the literal interpretation of the stereotype be triggered first and only after the nonliteral interpretation can be triggered (cf. Glucksberg & Keysar, 1993; Grice, 1975; Searle, 1979)? Or, can both the literal and nonliteral interpretations be triggered simultaneously? (e.g., Frisson & Pickering, 1999; Swinney, 1979; and also see Simpson, 1994). Before reviewing our work on stereotype processing using this perspective, we briefly review relevant studies in metaphoric and metonymic reference.

EVIDENCE ON FIGURATIVE REFERENCE

Metaphoric Reference

In one of the first studies to investigate this issue, Gibbs (1990) had participants read paragraphs such as (1a) in Table 11.1. The purpose of this manipulation was to determine comprehension differences between metaphoric and literal reinstatements in reading. In the literal reinstatement condition, the final sentence referred to its antecedent with a word that was a synonym of the person or thing being described by the context (e.g., *fighter*). For the metaphoric reinstatement condition, the final sentence referred to its antecedent with a metaphoric term (e.g., *creampuff*) that was semantically felicitous to the context of the passage. The participants' objective was to simply read and comprehend each sentence one at a time. Reading times were recorded at the final sentence of the passage (metaphoric vs. literal). The results from the reading task showed that final sentence containing metaphoric reinstatements took longer to comprehend than the sentence containing literal reinstatements. This result was interesting because, as suggested by the accompanying probe recognition task, participants were indeed able to make the connection between the metaphoric reference *creampuff* and the antecedent *boxer* described by the preceding context.

In a follow up study, Onishi and Murphy (1993) suggested that using the vehicle *creampuff* to reference the topic *boxer* may have required readers to infer semantic information beyond that provided by the story context. To address this possibility, Onishi and Murphy enriched Gibbs' (1990) stimuli so that there would be as little confusion as possible as to whom or what in each story might be serving as the topic of the figurative description. Regardless, in two different reading time experiments, Onishi and Murphy were unable to show that comprehension of nonliteral reference could be as effortless as understanding comparable literal reference. Thus, Gibbs and Onishi and Murphy's results supported the idea that during reading comprehension it is more difficult to understand metaphoric than literal referential descriptions. With respect to whether literal or nonliteral language can be accessed faster, the results from these two experiments suggest that literal processing has precedence during language processing (also see Swinney & Osterhout, 1990; and cf. Gerrig & Healy, 1983; Gildea & Glucksberg, 1983; Keysar, 1989; McGlone, Glucksberg, & Cacciari, 1994).

However, in a recent study, Stewart and Heredia (2002) examined the activation of the antecedent during real-time comprehension of metaphoric reference. Unlike the original studies by Gibbs (1990) and Onishi and Murphy (1993), Stewart and Heredia used the cross-modal lexical priming technique (CMLP; Swinney, 1979), a psycholinguistic task known to be sensitive to semantic and associative relations as well as contextual effects (e.g., Swinney & Osterhout, 1990; Tabossi, 1988, 1996). The CMLP was used to study the activation of the literal and metaphoric referential descriptions throughout the sentence at Positions 1 (at prime offset, depicted by the subscript $_{[**1]}$ in Table 11.1, paragraph 1b), and 2 (1000 ms after prime offset). As participants listened to sentences of the type in paragraph 1b, at the offset of the critical prime *creampuff* (Position 1), for example, a literal-related (e.g., *pastry*) and its controlled-unrelated probe were presented in the middle of a computer screen. This probe re-

TABLE 11.1
Sample Stimuli From Gibbs (1990) and Stewart and Heredia (2002)

Paragraph 1a: Metaphoric Reference From Gibbs (1990, p. 59)

Stu went to see the Saturday night fights. There was one boxer that Stu hated. This guy always lost. Just as the match was supposed to start, Stu went to get some snacks. He stood in line for ten minutes. When he returned, the bout had been cancelled."What happened?" Stu asked a friend. The friend replied,
"The creampuff didn't even show up." (metaphoric reinstatement)
"The fighter didn't even show up." (literal reinstatement)

Paragraph 1b: Metaphoric Reference From Stewart and Heredia (2002, p. 36)

Stu and his buddy went to see the Saturday night fights. There was one fighter they both hated because the guy always lost. Just as the match was about to begin, Stu went to get some snacks. When he returned he saw that the bout had been cancelled. "What happened?" Stu asked. His friend replied,
"Aw, the creampuff$_{[**1]}$ didn't even show$_{[**2]}$ up, I can't believe it!"
(metaphoric probe: boxer) vs. (literal probe: pastry)

Paragraph 1c: Metonymic Reference From Gibbs (1990, p. 60)

Mr. Bloom was manager of a high-school baseball team. He was concerned about the poor condition of the field. He also was worried about one athlete. His third baseman wasn't a very good fielder. This concerned the manager a good deal. The team needed all the help it could get. At one point, Mr. Bloom said to his assistant coach,
"The glove at third base has to be replaced" (metonymic reinstatement)
"The player at third base has to be replaced" (literal reinstatement)

Note. Probes presented at prime offset are noted as **.

flected the literal meaning of *creampuff* associated to bread. The related nonliteral form, contrarily, reflected the meaning of the prime word implied by the context (e.g., *boxer*). The participants' objective was to simply listen to the sentences presented over headphones and pronounce the probe appearing on the computer screen. To summarize, the results revealed significant activation for the nonliteral interpretation and no activation for the literal interpretation of the metaphoric referential prime. That is, it was possible to access the figurative meaning but only when measurement took place immediately after the metaphoric reference term (i.e., the critical prime). These results contrasted with Gibbs' (1990) and Onishi and Murphy's (1993) findings in which readers experienced great difficulty comprehending sentences containing the same nonliteral description. Thus, according to Stewart and Heredia (2002), access to the nonliteral interpretation of a metaphoric reference is possible provided that appropriate and sensitive methods to early stages of language processing are used (cf. Dascal, 1989; Frisson & Pickering, 1999; Heredia, 2002). Next we review two important studies in metonymic reference.

Metonymic Reference

Again, in one of the few metonymy experiments, Gibbs (1990) had participants read a passage such as the one in Table 11.1, paragraph 1c. Reading times were recorded for the final sentence (metonymic vs. literal reinstatement). Notice that in the metonymic referential description, the *glove* is meant to refer to the baseball player being described by prior context. *Player*, contrarily, is the literal and direct meaning of the contextual information preceding the target sentence. Similar to metaphoric referential descriptions, the results showed that participants were faster to comprehend literal than metonymic reinstatements. Although participants had more difficulty in comprehending metonymic reinstatements, evidence by the accompanying recognition task showed that participants were actually able to make the connection between the metonymic reference and the antecedent information related to the player. Although both metonymic and metaphoric referential processing appeared to have behaved in the same manner by showing similar patterns, a subsequent experiment comparing both tropes showed that, indeed, metaphoric referential statements were easier to comprehend than metonymic references. In both cases, the literal reinstatement was easier to comprehend than both tropes. However, in a more recent study using an eye-tracking paradigm (e.g., Tanenhaus & Spivey-Knowlton, 1996), Frison and Pickering (1999) demonstrated that, like other research on ambiguity (e.g., Seidenberg, Tanenhaus, Leiman, & Bienkowski, 1982; Swinney, 1979), both the metonymic and literal referential descriptions can be accessed simultaneously. Clearly, more research is needed in both areas to investigate metaphoric and metonymic reference to rule out the possibility that differences among Gibbs (1990), Stewart and Heredia (2002), and Frison and Pickering (1999) are merely methodological ones. In any case, the studies reviewed in this section provide both a conceptual and methodological framework to study stereotype processing under a psycholinguistic and, more specifically, a figurative language perspective. We now return to our discussion on stereotype processing.

STEREOTYPE PROCESSING

Our exploration of stereotypes differs from that of Stewart and Heredia (2002) and Heredia and Stewart (2002). Again, our general theoretical framework is that social stereotypes can be viewed as an extension of figurative language and, more specifically, to include metaphoric and metonymic relations. In this view, the social stereotype *terrorist* is seen as containing a literal meaning (e.g., *bomb*), which is directly associated with acts of destruction, and a nonliteral meaning (i.e., *Arabs*). The nonliteral meaning, in this case, represents the generalization that when people think about the term *terrorist*, they immediately activate information related to Arabs. In our research, we asked the following questions: How do people process social stereotypes? Are stereotypes processed in such a way that during comprehension only the nonliteral sense is activated? To what extent is prior context necessary to active the nonliteral sense of the stereotype? In the following section we attempt to answer these very important questions.

In perhaps the only study of its kind, we (Heredia & Blumentritt, 2002) employed the CMLP task to examine the automatic on-line activation of stereotypes during spoken language. Participants listened to complete sentences presented aurally, and then they made yes or no lexical decisions to visually presented target words. As previously discussed, this type of task has been widely used in psycholinguistic studies, and its sensitivity to semantic and associative relations, as well as contextual effects, is well documented. In addition, we were interested in using a method that increased the general ecological validity of the study of stereotypes. Specifically, we maintained that exposure to stereotypes normally occurs during the course of spoken conversation (see also van Dijk, 1984, 1987). For example, a common scenario is that a conversational partner makes an offhand racist or sexist remark, or he or she uses a stereotypic term to reference a particular social group or, perhaps, tells a sexist or racist joke that relies on stereotype information for its humor value. The point is that we typically hear stereotypical remarks rather than, say, read them in print form. Although many people subscribe to joke listservs and receive all kinds of jokes describing certain ethnic groups stereotypically, in this case such jokes have to be read. But, Stewart and Heredia (2002, p. 35) pointed out, "speech contains a number of prosodic cues that we as listeners have come to rely on to resolve ambiguity in an expeditious manner." Our goal then was to examine activation of both the stereotype meaning and the dominant meaning during spoken language and as language unfolds (cf. Frisson & Pickering, 1999). The CMLP task is an appropriate methodology to do just this. We used as our dependent measure reaction times to a lexical decision. We wanted to examine real-time processing of stereotypes, outside of postlexical episodic memory influences. A lexical decision task gives us a purer measure of activation, especially when compared to other kinds of judgment tasks that have been used (e.g., Blair & Banaji, 1996; Devine, 1989). For example, in some tasks used in the stereotype literature, participants are given a particular stereotype such as *secretary* and then they are asked to judge whether the stereotype is more relevant to a male or female employee. Selections are made by pressing a computer button labeled *m* for *male* or *f* for *female* as fast and as accurately as possible (e.g., Banaji & Hardin, 1996). To say the least, this technique is hardly an example of an implicit task. Moreover, by using the CMLP we were able to take advantage of the priming effect to assess the extent to which a particular meaning was activated or inhibited. According to this logic, significant priming facilitation signified that the meaning of the particular concept of interest was indeed activated. Third, we systematically manipulated the effects of contextual information on the comprehension of social stereotypes. A well-known finding from the psycholinguistic literature is that lexical activation is faster when the word appears within a contextually appropriate sentence than when it appears in a contextually inappropriate or neutral sentence (Simpson, 1994; Tabossi, 1988; Tabossi, Colombo, & Job, 1987). Here, we report here a series of four experiments that addressed these issues. Table 11.2 shows sample sentences and the experimental manipulations. Target words are presented immediately at the offset (0 ms) of the critical prime (probe $_{[*1]}$) or 300 ms after the offset of the critical prime (probe $_{[*2]}$).

As shown in Table 11.2, for the contextually unbiased conditions (Experiments 1 and 2), the portion of the sentence preceding the critical prime (e.g., *terrorist*) provided no specific information about its nonliteral (e.g., *Arabs*) or its literal meaning (e.g., *bombs*). For experiment 1, we wanted to see if activation of the nonliteral word would occur immediately at prime offset (0 ms). Based on the sociocognitive literature (e.g., Blair & Banaji, 1996; Banaji & Hardin, 1996), we expected that it would. To assure that the nonliteral stereotype meaning was not less familiar than the literal term, thus taking longer time to achieve full activation, in Experiment 2 we presented the critical targets 300 ms after prime offset. We predicted that with greater processing time we would see increased activation of the nonliteral meaning. Finally, for both prime offset conditions, we expected facilitation priming for the literal targets (Swinney & Osterhout, 1990).

In Experiments 3 and 4 (see Table 11.2) we evaluated the effects of contextual information on the processing of social stereotypes. To what extent is the nonliteral word dependent on an appropriate context to trigger its activation? We drew here from the literature on lexical ambiguity to inform our hypotheses and expected that, with the addition of a biasing context, we would see even greater activation of the nonliteral word (e.g., Simpson, 1994). As shown in Table 11.2, in the contextually biased conditions, the term *Middle East* is included in the sentence prior to the critical prime. Our logic was that *Middle East* would bias the sentence toward the stereotype that all people from the Middle East (i.e., Arabs) are terrorists. Moreover, we evaluated time course effects in a contextually biased condition by presenting the targets at 0 ms and 300 ms prime offset. We predicted that with increasing processing time context would become even more powerful in its effect on activation and reaction times would become increasingly faster to the nonliteral words (e.g., Tabossi, 1988; Tabossi et al., 1987).

Across all experiments the literal forms of the critical prime showed facilitatory priming. In fact, the priming effect was very similar across experiments. However, contrary to our predictions, the nonliteral forms generally demonstrated inhibitory priming. That is, we found slower reaction times to the nonliteral meanings of the critical prime relative to unrelated control words. And, as shown in Tables 11.3 and 11.4, reaction time differences clearly indicate a pattern of increasing inhibition of the nonliteral forms. To summarize, in the absence of any contextual information (Experiment 1), processing of nonliteral targets was no different than the processing of unre-

TABLE 11.2
Sample of Sentences Used in the Heredia and Blumentritt (2002) Study

Experiment 1 and 2: Contextually Unbiased Toward the Stereotype

Pete realizes the importance of assuring that TERRORISTS [Probe *1] do not have access [Probe *2] to airports or any other type of security related system.

Experiment 3 and 4: Contextually Biased Toward the Stereotype

Pete has lived in the Middle East and realizes the importance of assuring that TERRORISTS [Probe *1] do not have access [Probe *2] to airport systems or any other related system.

Sample Targets	Related	Unrelated Control
Literal:	BOMB	YARD
Nonliteral:	ARAB	CAIN

Note. From "On-line Processing of Social Stereotypes During Spoken Language Comprehension," by R. R. Heredin and T. L. Blumentritt, 2002, *Experimental Psychology, 49,* p. 211. Copyright 2002 by Hogrefa and Huber. Reprinted with permission.

TABLE 11.3
Priming Effects for Experiment 1 Prime Offset (0 ms)
and Experiment 2 (300 ms)

| Visual Probes | Prime Offset | |
Probes (Targets)	0 ms	300 ms
Literal (bomb)	58*	45*
Nonliteral (Arab)	5	−26*

Note. Lexical decision results are given as (control − experimental) priming reaction times in milliseconds; *p < .05.

TABLE 11.4
Priming Effects for Experiment 3 Prime Offset (0 ms)
and Experiment 4 (300 ms)

| Visual Probes | Prime Offset | |
Probes (Targets)	0 ms	300 ms
Literal (bomb)	55*	50*
Nonliteral (Arab)	−31*	−39*

Note. Lexical decision results are given as (control − experimental) priming reaction times in ms; *p < .05.

lated control targets. However, by increasing the processing time window of the critical stereotype (prime) to 300 ms (Experiment 2), reaction times to the nonliteral targets were significantly reduced, producing inhibition. In addition, when we added a biasing context we saw inhibition immediately (Experiment 3) and even greater inhibition after a 300-ms delay (Experiment 4).

What should we make of this interesting pattern of results? First, we wondered if our participants were simply inadequately familiar with the stereotypes used in the experiments. Blasko and Connine (1993) examined lexical decision reaction times to targets that were either figuratively (*secure*) or literally related (*hard*) to a metaphor ("the family is a rock"). They found that reaction times were slower for figuratively related words, but only when the metaphor was relatively unfamiliar. They also found that when they increased prime offset time from 0 ms to 300 ms they produced decreased inhibition of the figurative form. This contrasted with our results, which indicated increasing inhibition with increased processing time. Note that we also pretested our word pairs (e.g., *terrorist–Arab*) for familiarity. Mean familiarity rating for our stimuli was 4.3 ($SD = .906$), well beyond the 3.9 criterion proposed by Blasko and Connine (1993).

Second, if low familiarity was not a plausible explanation, could it be that the stereotype was simply less dominant than the standard meaning and that during processing it was not only poorly activated, but actually inhibited? The sociocognitive literature on selective attention and person perception (e.g., Dijksterhuis & Van Knippenberg, 1996; Macrae, Bodenhausen, & Milne, 1995; Macrae, Milne, & Bodenhausen, 1994; Neumann & DeSchepper, 1992) suggests this explanation. In general, this literature shows that not only are dominant stimuli automatically activated (i.e., show a pattern of facilitation), but subordinate, less dominant stimuli are actively inhibited. Apparently, as Macrae et al. (1995) noted, the subordinate meaning "is not simply neglected; instead, it is actively dampened through a spreading inhibition process, even to levels below its resting state … one advantage of active inhibition … lies in the suppression of potentially distracting (hence disruptive) mental representations" (p. 399). Perhaps a similar process occurred in our study in which the literal and more dominant meaning was automatically activated, whereas the nonliteral meaning was dampened. With more processing time and a biasing context, this dampening effect was allowed to develop and becomes even more potent in its effect and, consequently, produced even greater inhibition.

Third, we considered the possibility that some sort of controlled processing of the stereotype targets occurred. Controlled processing of stereotype-related information has been reported in the literature (e.g., Blair & Banaji, 1996; Devine, 1989), although it has not been previously demonstrated in on-line tasks under conditions of high cognitive load (i.e., less than 500 ms prime offset) and without a specific strategy to counter the stereotype. Nonetheless, it is conceivable that the stereotype-related primes and associated targets evoked feelings of uneasiness or even discomfort in our participants (who were primarily Mexican American) which then produced an inhibitory response. This is speculative at this point because, to our knowledge, no other study in the sociocognitive literature has examined stereotype processing in an ethnic minority sample. Moreover, it is clear from previous work that (at least in off-line tasks) individuals who are motivated to do so are able to inhibit activation of stereotypes (e.g., Devine, 1989; Kunda, 1999).

What are the theoretical implications of our results? Certainly one is that they point to some sort of inhibitory mechanism involved in stereotyping that remains poorly understood. We propose that further study needs to be conducted to more fully understand the specific mechanisms underlying this inhibitory process. Relatedly, it is reasonable to conclude that automatic

276 ~~   BLUMENTRITT AND HEREDIA

activation of stereotypes may not occur as previously theorized (e.g., Banaji & Greenwald, 1995; Banaji & Hardin, 1996; Banaji et al., 1993; Blair & Banaji, 1996; Devine, 1989; Dovidio et al., 1986), and further work needs to be done to understand under which specific conditions automaticity of stereotype activation occurs. It may be that with certain populations who are particularly sensitive to the effects of stereotyping the accepted boundaries of automaticity (i.e., 500 ms) will need to be revised. What are the real-life implications of stereotype inhibition? Are some people more likely to inhibit stereotypes than others? For example, are there certain person variables, such as prejudice level, that systematically influence stereotype processing? And, perhaps most important, how does inhibition (or activation) at the moment of processing translate into attitudes, impressions, expectations, and behaviors? No doubt these questions have been addressed at the postaccess level of analysis in the sociocognitive literature (e.g., Banaji & Greenwald, 1995; Banaji et al., 1993; Chen & Bargh, 1997; Devine, 1989; Dijksterhuis & Corneille, 2000; Levy, 1996). However, very few (if any) studies have addressed these theoretically and practically important questions utilizing methods that enable investigation of on-line processing of stereotype-related information. It is our contention that psycholinguistic concepts and associated methods provide an interesting way to approach these issues. Before closing our discussion, we address the issue as to whether stereotypes are triggered automatically during the communicative process. In a subsequent study, we attempted to replicate our results of Experiment 2 with the same methods described in Table 11.2, but this time we utilized a naming task instead of the lexical decision task. We used a naming task because naming is thought to provide a deeper and less strategic measure of lexical access (e.g., Hernández, Bates, & Ávila, 1996). Needless to say, we were unable to replicate the results of Experiment 2. These results and the finding that no activation for the nonliteral meaning was evident in Experiment 1 at prime offset, but activation in both Experiment 2 and 3 has lead us to conclude that stereotypes may not be as automatic as once thought. Thus, to comprehend the nonliteral sense of a stereotype, prior biasing context should be provided. Alternatively, about 300 ms are needed to fully process the social stereotype and grasp the implied meaning of it.

FINAL REMARKS

The purpose of our chapter was to provide a novel perspective on how stereotypes can be studied. We believe that stereotypes are closely related to both metaphoric and metonymic referential descriptions. Our overall argument is that theoretical and methodological advances in figurative language and ambiguity resolution could be used as a tool to understand how humans process stereotypes during the communication process. Although we clearly favor research techniques such as the ones described in Heredia and Blumentritt (2002) and Stewart and Heredia (2002), future research would benefit from replicating our results using other reading techniques that rely on priming. It is important to underscore that Heredia and Blumentritt's (2002) results are based largely on Mexican Americans. The next step should be to replicate our results with Anglo Americans. That is, we would like to see our results extended and replicated both cross-regionally (within the United States) and cross-nationally.

We argued the possibility that stereotypes can be seen as extensions of metaphoric and metonymic referential descriptions. Certainly, this view may or may not apply to all stereotypes; that is, some stereotypes may not meet the exact criteria for metaphoric or metonymic referential descriptions. Ultimately, the researcher should decide if the stereotype can be considered a metonymy or a metaphoric reference. Finally, we note that in Heredia and Blumentritt (2002) no distinction was made between possible metaphoric- and metonymic-like stereotypes. And, it is quite probable that our results would not have changed given the similar patterns observed by Gibbs (1990) for both kinds of tropes. However, one direction for future work would be to analyze social stereotypes from a metaphoric and metonymic language perspective. It would be interesting to observe if differential processing effects emerge for different kinds of language-based interpretations of social stereotypes. In summary, we echo the comments of Maas and Arcuri (1996) who observed that "stereotypes are closely—if not inseparably—linked to language. Indeed, it is difficult to imagine language-free stereotyping ... our knowledge of stereotypes will remain incomplete without an analysis of the language that defines a given stereotype" (p. 220). We would simply add to this by reiterating that a very useful and, we believe, potentially fruitful way of studying stereotypes is by viewing them as a special case of figurative language. This will open new research avenues, and new information will emerge.

REFERENCES

American Civil Liberties Union: Freedom Network. (1995, November 9). *ACLU files claim against U.S. government on behalf of Jordanian–American wrongly detained for Oklahoma City bombing.* Retrieved July, 8, 2002, from http://www.aclu.org/news/n1109951.html

Anderson, J. R. (1983). *The architecture of cognition.* Cambridge, MA: Harvard University Press.

Banaji, M. R., & Greenwald, A. G. (1995). Implicit gender stereotyping in judgments of fame. *Journal of Personality and Social Psychology, 68,* 181–189.

Banaji, M. R., & Hardin, C. D. (1996). Automatic stereotyping. *Psychological Science, 7,* 136–141.

Banaji, M. R., Hardin, C., & Rothman, A. J. (1993). Implicit stereotyping in person judgment. *Journal of Personality and Social Psychology, 65,* 272–281.

Bargh, J. A. (1984). Automatic and conscious processing of social information. In R. S. Wyer, Jr., & T. K. Srull (Eds.), *Handbook of social cognition* (Vol. 3, pp. 1–43). Hillsdale, NJ: Lawrence Erlbaum Associates.

Bargh, J. A. (1989). Conditional automaticity: Varieties of automatic influence in social perception and cognition. In J. S. Uleman & J. A. Bargh (Eds.), *Unintended thought* (pp. 3–51). New York: Guilford.

Bargh, J. A. (1994). The four horsemen of automaticity: Awareness, intention, efficiency, and control in social cognition. In R. S. Wyer & T. K. Srull (Eds.), *Handbook of social cognition* (2nd ed., pp. 1–40). Hillsdale, NJ: Lawrence Erlbaum Associates.

Bargh, J. A., Chaiken, S., Govender, R., & Pratto, F. (1992). The generality of the automatic activation effect. *Journal of Personality and Social Psychology, 62,* 893–912.

Bargh, J. A., Chen, M., & Burrows, L. (1996). Automaticity of social behavior: Direct effects of trait construct and stereotype activation on action. *Journal of Personality and Social Psychology, 71,* 230–244.

Bargh, J. A., & Pietromonaco, P. (1982). Automatic information processing and social perception: The influence of trait information presented outside awareness on impression formation. *Journal of Personality and Social Psychology, 55,* 599–605.

Blair, I. V., & Banaji, M . R. (1996). Automatic and controlled processes in stereotype priming. *Journal of Personality and Social Psychology, 70,* 1142–1163.

Blasko, D. G., & Connine, C. M. (1993). Effects of familiarity and aptness on metaphor processing. *Journal of Experimental Psychology: Learning, Memory, and Cognition, 19,* 295–308.

Bodenhausen, G. V. (1988). Stereotypic biases in social decision making and memory: Testing process models of stereotype use. *Journal of Personality and Social Psychology, 55,* 726–737.

Chen, M., & Bargh, J. A. (1997). Nonconscious behavioral confirmation processes: The self-fulfilling consequences of automatic stereotype activation. *Journal of Experimental Social Psychology, 33,* 541–560.

Cohen, C. E. (1981). Person categories and social perception: Testing some boundaries of the processing effects of prior knowledge. *Journal of Personality and Social Psychology, 40,* 441–452.

Darley, J. M., & Gross, P. H. (1983). A hypothesis-confirming bias in labeling effects. *Journal of Personality and Social Psychology, 44,* 20–33.

Dascal, M. (1989). On the roles of context and literal meaning in understanding. *Cognitive Science, 13,* 253–257.

Devine, P. (1989). Stereotypes and prejudice: Their automatic and controlled components. *Journal of Personality and Social Psychology, 56,* 5–18.

Dijksterhuis, A. P., & Corneille, O. (2000). *On the relation between stereotype activation and intellectual underperformance.* Unpublished manuscript, University of Amsterdam, Amsterdam, The Netherlands.

Dijksterhuis, A. P., & Van Knippenberg, A. D. (1996). The knife that cuts both ways: Facilitated and inhibited access to traits as a result of stereotype activation. *Journal of Experimental Social Psychology, 32,* 271–288.

Dovidio, J. F., Evans, N., & Tyler, R. B. (1986). Racial stereotypes: The contents of their cognitive representations. *Journal of Experimental Social Psychology, 22,* 22–37.

Fiske, S., & Neuberg, S. (1990). A continuum of impression formation, from category-based to individuating processes: Influences of information and motivation on attention and interpretation. *Advances in Experimental Social Psychology, 23,* 1–74.

Frisson, S., & Pickering, M. J. (1999). The processing of metonymy: Evidence from eye movements. *Journal of Experimental Psychology: Learning, Memory, and Cognition, 25,* 1366–1383.

Gerrig, R. J., & Healy, A. F. (1983). Dual process in metaphor understanding: Comprehension and appreciation. *Journal of Experimental Psychology: Learning, Memory, and Cognition, 9,* 667–675.

Gibbs, R. W., Jr. (1990). Comprehending figurative referential descriptions. *Journal of Experimental Psychology: Learning, Memory, and Cognition, 16,* 56–66.

Gibbs, R. W., Jr. (1993). Process and products in making sense of tropes. In A. Ortony (Ed.), *Metaphor and thought* (2nd ed., pp. 252–276). New York: Cambridge University Press.

Gibbs, R. W., Jr. (1994). *The poetics of mind.* New York: Cambridge University Press.

Gilbert, D., & Hixon, J. (1991). The trouble of thinking: Activation and application of stereotypic beliefs. *Journal of Personality and Social Psychology, 60,* 509–517.

Gildea, P., & Glucksberg, S. (1983). On understanding metaphor: The role of context. *Journal of Verbal Learning and Verbal Behavior, 22,* 577–590.

Glucksberg, S., & Keysar, B. (1993). How metaphors work. In A. Ortony (Ed.), *Metaphor and thought* (2nd ed., pp. 401–424). New York: Cambridge University Press.

Grice, H. P. (1975). Logic and conversation. In P. Cole & J. Morgan (Eds.), *Syntax and semantics: Vol. 3: Speech acts* (pp. 41–58). New York: Academic Press.

Heredia, R. R. (2002). *Bilingual sentence processing: An examination of context effects and cross-language priming.* Unpublished manuscript, Texas A&M International University, Laredo, TX.

Heredia, R. R., & Blumentritt, T. L. (2002). On-line processing of social stereotypes during spoken language comprehension. *Experimental Psychology, 49,* 1–14.

Heredia, R. R., & Stewart, M. T. (2002). On-line methods in bilingual spoken language research. In R. R. Heredia & J. Altarriba (Eds.), *Bilingual sentence processing* (pp. 7–28). Amsterdam: Elsevier.

Hernández, A. E., Bates, E. A., & Ávila, L. X. (1996). Processing across the language boudary. A cross-modal priming study of Spanish–English bilinguals. *Journal of Experimental Psychology: Learning, Memory, and Cognition, 22,* 846–864.

Higgins, E. T., Rholes, W. S., & Jones, C. R. (1977). Category accessibility and impression formation. *Journal of Experimental Social Psychology, 13,* 141–154.

Keysar, B. (1989). On the functional equivalence of literal and metaphorical interpretations in discourse. *Journal of Memory and Language, 28,* 375–385.

Kunda, Z. (1999). *Social cognition: Making sense of people.* Cambridge, MA: MIT Press.

Kunda, Z., & Sherman-Williams, B. (1992). Stereotypes and the construal of individuating information. *Personality and Social Psychology Bulletin, 19,* 90–99.

Levy, B. (1996). Improving memory in old age through implicit self-stereotyping. *Journal of Personality and Social Psychology, 71*, 1092–1107.

Lippman, W. (1922). *Public opinion.* New York: Harcourt Brace Jovanovich.

Locke, V., MacLeod, C., & Walker, I. (1994). Automatic and controlled activation of stereotypes: Individual differences associated with prejudice. *British Journal of Social Psychology, 33*, 29–46.

Logan, G. D. (1980). Attention and automaticity in Stroop and priming tasks: Theory and data. *Cognitive Psychology, 12*, 523–533.

Maass, A., & Arcuri, L. (1996). Language and stereotyping. In C. N. Macrae, C. Stangor, & M. Hewstone (Eds.), *Stereotypes and stereotyping* (pp. 193–226). New York: Guilford.

Macrae, C. N., Bodenhausen, G. V., & Milne, A. B. (1995). The dissection of selection in person perception: Inhibitory processes in social stereotyping. *Journal of Personality and Social Psychology, 69*, 397–407.

Macrae, C. N., Stangor, C., & Milne, A. B. (1994). Activating social stereotypes: A functional analysis. *Journal of Experimental Social Psychology, 30*, 370–389.

McGlone, M. S., Glucksberg, S., & Cacciari, C. (1994). Semantic productivity and idiom comprehension. *Discourse Processes, 17*, 167–190.

Neely, J. H. (1977). Semantic priming and retrieval from lexical memory: Roles of inhibitionless spreading activation and limited-capacity attention. *Journal of Experimental Psychology: General, 106*, 226–254.

Neumann, E., & DeSchepper, B. G. (1992). An inhibition-based fan effect: Evidence for an active suppression mechanism in selective attention. *Canadian Journal of Psychology, 46*, 1–40.

Onishi, K. A., & Murphy, G. O. (1993). Metaphoric reference: When metaphors are not understood as easily as literal expressions. *Memory & Cognition, 21*, 763–772.

Rothbart, M., Sriram, N., & Davis-Stitt, C. (1996). The retrieval of typical and atypical category members. *Journal of Experimental Social Psychology, 32*, 309–336.

Searle, J. (1979). *Expression and meaning.* Cambridge, England: Cambridge University Press.

Seidenberg, M., Tanenhaus, M., Leiman, J., & Bienkowski, M. (1982). Automatic access of the meanings of ambiguous words in context: Some limitations of knowledge-based processing. *Cognitive Psychology, 14*, 489–537.

Shiffrin, R. M., & Dumais, S. T. (1981). The development of automatism. In J. R. Anderson (Ed.), *Cognitive skills and their acquisition* (pp. 111–140). Hillsdale, NJ: Lawrence Erlbaum Associates.

Simpson, G. B. (1994). Context and the processing of ambiguous words. In M. A. Gernsbacher (Ed.), *Handbook of psycholinguistics* (pp. 359–374). San Diego, CA: Academic Press.

Stapel, D. A., Koomen, W., & Van der Plight, J. (1997). Categories of category accessibility: The impact of trait concept versus exemplar priming on person judgments. *Journal of Experimental Social Psychology, 33*, 47–76.

Stephan, W. G. (1989). A cognitive approach to stereotyping. In D. Bar-Tal, C. F. Graumann, A. W. Kruglanski, & W. Stroebe (Eds.), *Stereotyping and prejudice: Changing conceptions* (pp. 37–57). New York: Springer-Verlag.

Stewart, M. T., & Heredia, R. R. (2002). Comprehending spoken metaphoric reference: A real-time analysis. *Journal of Experimental Psychology, 49,* 34–44.

Swinney, D. A. (1979). Lexical access during sentence comprehension: (Re)consideration of context effects. *Journal of Verbal Learning and Verbal Behavior, 18,* 645–660.

Swinney, D. A., & Osterhout, L. (1990). Inference generation during auditory language comprehension. *Psychology of Learning, 25,* 17–33.

Tabossi, P. (1988). Accessing lexical ambiguity in different types of sentential contexts. *Journal of Memory and Language, 27,* 324–340.

Tabossi, P. (1996). Cross-modal semantic priming. *Language and Cognitive Processes, 11,* 569–576.

Tabossi, P., Colombo, L., & Job, R. (1987). Assessing lexical ambiguity: Effects of context and dominance. *Psychological Research, 49,* 161–167.

Tanenhaus, M. K., & Spivey-Knowlton, M. J. (1996). Eye-tracking. *Language and Cognitive Processes, 11,* 583–588.

van Dijk, T. A. (1984). *Prejudice and discourse: An analysis of ethnic prejudice in cognition and conversation.* Amsterdam: Benjamins.

van Dijk, T. A. (1987). *Communicating racism: Ethnic prejudice in thought and talk.* Newbury Park, CA: Sage.

12

On Mosquitoes and Camels: Some Notes on the Interpretation of Metaphorically Transparent Popular Sayings*

Carmen Curcó
National Autonomous University of Mexico

All languages have proverbs and popular sayings that appear to be metaphorically transparent. Consequently, their interpretation should pose no serious problems for nonnative speakers and second language learners. This work explores an empirical observation: Their metaphorical transparency does not necessarily lead to one single interpretation across subjects. For almost any popular saying there are a number of possible interpretations, all compatible with its linguistic form. Normally, native speakers are unaware of interpretations different from that generally accepted in their community, but these tend to emerge naturally when fluent nonnative speakers participate in joint conversations. For instance, for a Swedish saying that translates roughly as "picking out mosquitoes and swallowing camels," the interpretations of subjects unfamiliar with the expression fell into two distinct groups: For some it meant to attempt something very difficult; for others it meant to pay excessive attention to insignificant details while overlooking serious faults (the standard interpretation in Sweden). The aim

*I am grateful to Ana Villa for her enthusiastic and valuable participation in gathering the data, and to Marilyn Buck for her valuable comments on a previous version of this paper. This research was supported by project IN313001-DGAPA of the National Autonomous University of Mexico.

of this chapter is to explore the extent to which this kind of variation is systematic and, if so, whether it can be traced to specific social, cultural, and linguistic factors. I report the initial results of an exploratory cross-linguistic study, wherein the preferred interpretations that native and nonnative speakers gave to a set of metaphorical proverbs were considered. Subjects came from a diversity of linguistic, social, and cultural backgrounds. Results suggest that complex inferences are at work in the interpretation and learning process of these expressions. Some of them are triggered by lexical meanings and associations specific to the languages with which a particular subject is familiar, while others seem to be derived from cultural practices, social knowledge, and salient values of specific groups.

INTRODUCTION

The study reported here arose from an empirical and accidental observation involving a mild misunderstanding. A group of colleagues were having an informal conversation about work issues. At a certain point, one colleague, who was Swedish in origin but had lived and worked in Mexico for over 30 years, used a translated version of a Swedish proverb and uttered, "I then realized we were sieving for mosquitoes and swallowing camels." The meaning of this statement was unfamiliar to other colleagues, who nonetheless understood her expression and enjoyed it. Or so they thought, as it later emerged that their interpretations fell squarely into two groups: those who had (incorrectly) interpreted it as "we were doing something very difficult and very absurd," and those who had got the intended point "we were getting obsessed about unimportant details and overlooking serious faults." Both interpretations made sense in the context of the conversation. When commenting about this regular difference in interpretation, the Swedish woman remarked that she thought it was because of the influence of the country of origin of participants in the conversation (France, Greece, Mexico, and United States). She advanced the hypothesis that people coming from Protestant countries would tend to recover the Swedish proverbial meaning more easily, because in those countries there is tradition in the religious practice of reading the Bible individually and as a direct source. In Catholic countries, by contrast, people are less prone to read the Bible themselves, and they often have access to its content through priests and public religious activities; thus, the biblical context of interpretation for proverbs with a scriptural origin would be less accessible for them.

    This anecdote gave rise to a more general query about the effect of the accessibility of cultural values, practices, and beliefs on the favored interpretation given to unfamiliar proverbs by foreigners. An exploration into this interpretation process bears directly on a number of issues, and it should have theoretical implications for our understanding of linguistic and conceptual metaphor, proverbs, and the workings of verbal interpretation, in addition to our second language teaching practices. In particular, it could give some indications about the role—if any—of proverbs in testing and assessing linguistic competence in first and foreign languages (Chapman et al., 1997; Cheng, 1996; Nippold, Uhden, & Schwartz, 1997; Ormsby, personal communication, December 2, 2001; Ulatowska, Chapman, Highley, & Prince, 1998), an increasingly important issue that is not addressed here.

The question of how cultural elements impinge on the interpretation of metaphorical proverbs involves many others. How do speakers interpret utterances? Ho do we process figurative language? What is the nature of metaphor? Are concepts metaphorical themselves? What are the essential features of a proverb? What counts as cultural concepts or beliefs? Are they homogeneous across a given population? Is it possible to study cultural representations systematically? None of these questions is unproblematic, and we do not seem to have any definite answers to them yet. In what follows I sketch a few assumptions made throughout this chapter, leaving aside the major controversies surrounding them.

VERBAL COMMUNICATION AND THE INTERPRETATION OF UTTERANCES

Linguistic underspecification seems to be widely recognized nowadays in the semantics and pragmatics literature. Although there are a number of different ways in which it can be understood depending on what is meant by *linguistic meaning*, it remains fairly uncontroversial that every utterance has a number of possible interpretations, all compatible with its linguistic form.[1] There is also wide agreement that, given linguistic underdeterminacy, pragmatic inference is required if a listener is to successfully recover a speaker's meaning. What is less settled is the nature of the principles involved in the pragmatic inferential process (for leading positions, see Grice, 1975/1989; Levinson, 2000; and Sperber & Wilson 1986/[2]1995) and whether pragmatic additions are strictly guided by the underlying structure of the sentence uttered or are relatively free of linguistic constraints (for a discussion, see Carston, 2002; Stanley, 2002; and Stanley & Szabo 2000).

Here I assume that the interpretation of verbal stimuli is guided by the search for an optimal balance between the cognitive gains obtained from processing an utterance and the effort invested by the hearer in doing so. This is what Sperber and Wilson (1986/[2]1995) called the search for an interpretation consistent with the principle of relevance. The automatic search

---

[1]The underspecification thesis can take at least these forms: (a) Linguistic meaning underdetermines speaker meaning (what is communicated), (b) linguistic meaning underdetermines explicitly communicated content, and (c) linguistic meaning underdetermines the proposition expressed (see Carston, 2002, for a discussion).

for relevance is an assumed inbuilt disposition rooted in the human cognitive system.

Among the factors known to affect the processing effort invested in interpreting a linguistic expression are frequency and recency of use, the logical and linguistic complexity of the expression, and the size and accessibility of the intended context of interpretation. This last factor is especially important in the study reported here, as I will show.

I also follow Sperber and Wilson (1986/²1995) in viewing the context of interpretation of an utterance as a psychological construct, a subset of he hearer's beliefs and assumptions about the world that are mentally represented and employed as a set of premises in the derivation of cognitive effects (Sperber & Wilson, 1986, p. 16).

A hearer interpreting an utterance will follow a path of least effort: He or she will start from the smallest set of the most accessible contextual assumptions in which the linguistic expression used can be processed to derive cognitive effects and will stop expanding the context and/or searching for alternative interpretations as soon as enough cognitive effects in exchange for the processing effort invested have been derived. The first interpretation that meets this criterion and is compatible with what the hearer knows about the speaker's preferences and abilities will be selected as the intended one.

Members of the same cultural group share a number of experiences, teachings views, beliefs, and assumptions about the world. Among the set of assumptions mentally represented by any individual, those that are shared by the cultural group he or she belongs to are likely to be more salient and accessible than they are for nonmembers of the culture, although such cultural representations can be entertained by outsiders too. It is the relative accessibility of cultural assumptions mentally represented that has a direct bearing on this study, given that the particular way in which these assumptions interact with the incoming ostensive stimulus (the metaphorical proverb, in this case) will make one interpretation more readily available than other potential candidates that are also compatible with the linguistic form of the proverb.

THE NATURE AND INTERPRETATION OF METAPHOR

Views about the nature of figurative language in general and of metaphor in particular abound, and a number of interesting issues about the relationship between figurative language and thought (see Gibbs, 1994; Katz, Cacciari, Gibbs, & Turner, 1998), and how figurative language is processed have been explored in the psycholinguistics and pragmatics literature by a great many authors. Gibbs (1994, 2001a) offered recent and interesting reviews of contemporary models of figurative language understanding. Here I assume (as does Sperber & Wilson, 1985–1986, 1986/²1995) that understanding metaphor requires no special interpretive abilities or procedures, and that metaphor is merely a particular case of loose talk. When hearers encounter a metaphorical utterance, they search for an interpretation consistent with the principle of relevance in exactly the same manner as when interpreting any other type of utterance. The ostensive use of a metaphoric expression, however, can be viewed as an instruction for the hearer to find relevant common properties between the concepts associated with the topic and the vehicle terms (Gibbs 2001a, p. 326; Sperber & Wilson, 1985–1986, 1986/²1995).

Concepts encoded in the linguistic form of the utterance typically give access to encyclopedic knowledge and stereotypical contexts associated with them. When processed in such contexts, any utterance, whether metaphorical or not, will yield a range of explicatures and implicatures. In the case of a metaphor, hearers find the intended resemblances among concepts use association through metaphor in their search for optimal relevance, inhibiting the recovery of those resemblances whose derivation would detract from relevance. The relevance of a metaphor is thus established by finding a wide array of cognitive effects that can be retained as strong or weak implicatures.[2] In highly standardized metaphors, relevance is achieved through the derivation of a few strongly implicated assumptions. More creative cases involve putting together the encyclopedic entries of encoded concepts to yield a weaker, less determinate range of implicatures for which the hearer takes more responsibility.

We have known for a long time that our similarity judgments are asymmetrical in metaphor. There is good evidence to believe that an important role of the vehicle term in a metaphor is to make more salient a number of features of the topic term (Winner, 1988). But not all features of the vehicle term are equally important in interpreting a metaphor. The subset of characteristics that a metaphor directs our attention to is determined by salience, which in turn is a property linked both to the context of interpretation and to the intention of the communicator. Hence, when people understand metaphors, a great deal of irrelevant information is filtered out (Glucksberg, Newsome, & Goldvarg, 2001).

The study of the interpretation processes underlying our understanding of metaphor poses a crucial question for cognitive science concerning the nature of concepts. Many researchers of figurative language claim that metaphorical language is a direct reflection of the structure of concepts, which

---

[2]Implicatures are said to be strong if they are fully determinate premises or conclusions that must be supplied if an interpretation is to be consistent with the communicative principle of relevance and for whose derivation the speaker seems responsible. Weak implicatures fall on the other extreme of a continuum, being assumptions that the hearer is encouraged but not forced to supply, so that a great part of the responsibility for their derivation falls largely on the hearer's side. The less the responsibility on the part of the speaker, the weaker the implicature.

are themselves thought of as metaphorical (Gibbs 1994, 2001a; Lakoff & Johnson, 1989), and they argue that most of our thinking and cognition is metaphorical too (Lakoff & Núñez, 2002). Other cognitive scientists have strongly argued that concepts cannot be metaphorical (Fodor, 1998; Murphy, 1996). This debate is beyond the scope and purpose of this chapter, but it is certainly one of the fundamental questions underlying the scientific study of metaphor.

THE NATURE AND INTERPRETATION OF PROVERBS

Proverbs are short utterance types—public representations—that people quote with the purpose of addressing some aspect of about human nature, life, behavior, or experience. Because proverbs are public representations widely distributed in human populations, they are cultural representations. It is recognized that human cognitive abilities act as a filter on the representations that are capable or likely to become cultural (Sperber, 1996, p. 70). As often noted (e.g., Gibbs, 2001b), an important number of proverbs are metaphorical. In particular, their interpretation depends on our ability for abstract thought, given that proverbs establish a link between something specific and concrete and a generic, more abstract aspect of human experience.

Perhaps the pervasiveness of proverbs in all human societies is due to our capacity to recognize similarities between what proverbs mean and different life situations. Besides, if Sperber and Wilson (1995) are right that the aim of the human cognitive system is the maximization of relevance,[3] an abundance of proverbs in human societies is to be expected. Proverbs encode concrete manifestations of more abstract themes to which they bear a resemblance relation. They can thus be relevantly used in wide ranges of situations, condensing as they do a huge potential to achieve cognitive effects at a rather low processing cost: Proverbs usually have simple and short linguistic and logical forms. This links their social importance to our most basic cognitive dispositions. Socially, as Gibbs (2001b) put it, proverbs "function as devices to unite speakers, speakers to their communities, and communities to ideas of universal truth in human experience" (p. 167). Their efficiency as public representations and their impact as elements of internal cohesion in a sociocultural group are thus consequences of their extraordinary efficiency as cognitive devices.

Whether proverbs are interpreted through a single generic metaphoric pattern of thought, "generic is specific," as some have argued (e.g., see Gibbs, 2001b; Lakoff & Turner, 1989), or through a general comprehension procedure employed in communication, as would follow from other views (Carston, 2002; Sperber & Wilson, 1986, 1995) is an open issue. In the first

---

[3]Contrast this with the aim of natural language interpretation in ostensive communication, which is merely the *optimization* of relevance.

case, a hearer would map knowledge from specific, familiar, and concrete domains to very general events that are less familiar and abstract as part of a complex conceptual—itself metaphorical—process. In the second case, hearers would recover interpretations guided by their search for optimal relevance in the interpretation of ostensive stimuli and their general knowledge of the world. Here I take the second view. This framework allows for a good understanding of cross-cultural differences in the interpretation of proverbial language. For one thing, it clearly predicts that salient culture specific assumptions can, in principle, intervene in the selection of one of several possible interpretations when subjects are confronted to unfamiliar proverbial language. Notice, besides, that the assumption that proverbs encode information about specific and concrete events that should be interpreted as referring to more general aspects of human life and experience in particular situations is most likely to be part of the knowledge of the world that an individual brings to his or her interpretation process. Hence, the role of this contextual knowledge in interpreting can be acknowledged without committing to the view that there is a single generic metaphoric pattern of thought "generic is specific" responsible for proverb interpretation.

Metaphorical proverb interpretation is, along with metaphor, a context-dependent process, sensitive to the beliefs held by the hearer and the mutually manifest assumptions shared by participants.[4] Interpretation of unfamiliar proverbs presented out of context, or in a very limited one, is a rather unnatural task. However, observing how subjects choose an interpretation in such circumstance offers an advantage: Their choice will rest heavily on the hearers' most firmly established beliefs and salient assumptions, among which cultural representations and values should play an outstanding role. In natural contexts, cultural assumptions may be—and often are—overridden by other assumptions that are more specific to the participants and to the time and place of the utterance.

Note that feature salience is the result of the interpretation process, not a preestablished fact. Notions such as salience should result from instantiations of the optimization of relevance, rather than having to be separately specified. Therefore, they are attached to a particular individual, interpreting a particular utterance token in a particular context of interpretation, at a particular time. However, in comparing preferred interpretations across individuals with different cultural backgrounds and without a biasing context we can safely

---

[4]Sperber & Wilson (1986, 1995) define the manifestness of an assumption to an individual as the degree to which an individual is capable of mentally representing an assumption and holding it as true or probably true at a given moment. The set of assumptions that are manifest to an individual at a given time constitute his cognitive environment. A mutual cognitive environment is one which is shared by a group of individuals and in which it is manifest to those individuals that they share it with each other. Every manifest assumption in a mutual cognitive environment is mutually manifest.

assume that in general culture-specific beliefs are relatively more salient for members of that culture than for outsiders.

Conversely, if Lakoff and Turner (1989) and Gibbs (2001b) are right that unfamiliar proverbs are interpreted by using the "generic is specific" conceptual metaphor, the way in which salient cultural properties play any special role in the process seems less clear. If I understand them correctly, the idea behind the "generic is specific" metaphor is that it provides a general cognitive mechanism for understanding the general in terms of the specific, in which the mapping of the source domain knowledge onto the target domains of experience preserves the cognitive structure of the source domain. This would help us understand why certain cultural representations and values play important roles in the coining of new (or a series of) proverbs linked with specific conceptual domains,[5] but it does not give many reasons to explain why interpretations other than the generally accepted are possible for fluent nonnative speakers and why some of these interpretations appear to be more accessible to certain groups.

Indeed, Gibbs (2001b) acknowledged the importance of cultural assumptions in interpreting proverbs. In discussing some proverbs mentioned in 20th-century African literature, he mentioned, "Each of these proverbs poses riddles whose solution is found in the specific cultural contexts in which they are used. Their rhetorical power comes from people's tacit recognition of the tension between these sayings' concrete messages and their application to abstract themes" (pp. 174–175). In this view, cultural factors determine the interpreter's understanding of the concrete and specific domain, and they would interfere negatively with interpretation whenever this culturally specified knowledge cannot be used in linking it to the generic and abstract.

One important assumption underlying the study reported here is that not only is the concrete and specific culturally shaped, but that abstract themes can be more or less salient to an individual depending on cultural factors too.

In any case, Gibbs' (2001b) view that proverbs are public representations of schemas that characterize an open-ended category of situations and that they function as a variable template that can be filled in different ways is right. Cultural background is one of the many factors likely to affect the actual manner in which the template is filled and a particular interpretation is selected.

CULTURAL FACTORS AFFECTING INTERPRETATION

Cross-cultural psychology has succeeded in many respects as a new academic discipline, but it nonetheless faces some general methodological diffi-

---

[5]For instance, it would help understand why proverbs involving food concepts are so basic to all cultures.

culties. First, cross-cultural psychologists and anthropologists do not completely agree on what precisely should count as a cultural unit of analysis. Clearly, a culture-bearing unit of analysis cannot be defined independently of the level at which the independent variable studied operates, so that appropriate units will vary from study to study. Second, assuming homogeneity of cultures and social groups with respect to the factor studied is usually misleading. Third, the spreading of cultural characteristics through contacts between groups, known in anthropology as *Galton's problem*, is noticeably on the rise as the global era takes over (see Berry, Poortinga, Segall, & Dasen, 1992, for discussion). Hence, in cross-cultural research there is a risk of drawing erroneous inferences based on empirically observed differences across groups, given the difficulties in effectively isolating a cultural homogeneous population and defining a culture-bearing unit. Further complications include the difficulty of ruling out all possible alternative explanations to the differences found.

The study of the variation of selected interpretations to a given proverb reported here is not free of these limitations. Even if one were to find some form of special association between group membership and interpretation selected, tracking such differences to some specific cultural factor is not straightforward. Variation in the selection of an interpretation is likely to arise out of differences in the ease with which a subject can integrate one of the possible interpretations of a proverb with the content of certain individual mental representations, which could or could not be cultural. Concepts and beliefs are representations that can be internalized individually and that are cultural as a result of a great many individuals internalizing them (Sperber, 1996, p. 75). Cultural classifications are set apart by their uniform distributions: Closely similar versions of the same representation are spread throughout a human population. The results report initial explorations. In future studies, cultural assumptions with a potential to affect interpretation will have to be studied independently to ascertain the extent to which they have been replicated and distributed homogeneously across the populations studied. Also, the probes employed in empirical studies should be chosen or designed to match specific target assumptions isolated this way.

DESCRIPTION OF THE STUDIES

In the studies reported here, the preferred interpretations of proverbs given by native speakers of Spanish (familiar with the proverbs) and those selected by a group of foreign students learning Spanish as a second language (less familiar or totally unfamiliar with the same proverbs) were compared. The studies were conceived as initial tools in an exploration of the question whether there are any preferred interpretations and, if so, whether these interpretations are associated with group membership, such as geographical or religious origin, or gender.

Presented out of context, the meaning of a proverb is radically underde-termined, especially if the proverb is unfamiliar to a subject. For proverbs, as well as for any other utterance, it is possible to recognize a number of poten-tial interpretations compatible with their linguistic form, and the choices given by subjects may be influenced by a very wide array of factors, among which cultural background is but one. Future studies will develop more fine-grained tools to explore it.

A set of proverbs was chosen and subjects were presented with two possi-ble paraphrases of each: One that represents the generally accepted use in the community where they are mostly used and another that is compatible with its linguistic form, but that is not standard in the way the first one is.

The first objective was to find out whether Mexican native speakers of Spanish shared a canonical conventional meaning associated with each proverb. Participants were asked to choose one of two possible interpreta-tions: There are no intended interpretations, because probes are not embed-ded in an ostensive act of communication. The study merely looked for more salient and preferred ones. In general, the context in which an utterance is produced disambiguates and helps hearers recognize which of the various possible meanings of an expression is intended. The quest here was precisely about a psychological, individual, culturally determined subset of context that should remain when the discourse and situational contexts are omitted. The second objective was to explore the extent to which certain factors, such as country of origin or religious background, were in some special asso-ciation with the interpretations to the same proverbs selected by foreigners learning Spanish as a second language in Mexico.

STUDY 1: STABILITY OF PROVERB MEANING AMONG NATIVE SPEAKERS

Stability of Meaning Among Mexican Native Speakers of Spanish

The aim of Study 1 was to determine the extent to which there is stability among Mexicans in their interpretation of a proverb. Selection of the gener-ally accepted figurative use paraphrase over the possible figurative use para-phrase was expected as a tendency[6] (see Appendix).

Method

Participants. Twenty-four Mexicans—15 men and 8 women—who were native speakers of Spanish, from middle-class homes, and between the ages of 25 and 30 (mode = 27) volunteered for participation.

---

[6]Generally accepted interpretations were based on the intuitions of a few native speak-ers independently questioned and checked against three handbooks of proverbs and popu-lar sayings.

Materials.   The items consisted of 14 proverbs and a set of two possible interpretations for each (see Appendix for a full list). All proverbs but one are independently recognized as familiar by Mexicans.

Procedure.   The 14 proverbs were included in a questionnaire. Their order of presentation was randomized, as was the order of the possible interpretations. For each proverb, participants were asked whether they knew it and whether they understood the meaning of all the words. They were also instructed to select the interpretation of the proverb they considered closest to its meaning.

Results and Discussion

Frequencies for each answer to all proverbs given by the participants are displayed in Table 12.1. Chi-square tests were conducted for each probe to explore whether the null hypothesis (that Mexicans choose the figurative use paraphrase) can be maintained.

Results show that Mexicans choose the conventional interpretation for 9 of the 14 proverbs, although stability of meaning was shown for a few more of them. For instance, note the consistency of answers to Proverb 4, which do not match the generally accepted paraphrase. None of the subjects chose the expected answer for this probe. There is a straightforward explanation for this outcome. The proverb is not of Mexican origin, but it comes from Spain. In Mexico parrots are culturally associated with nonstop talking, which explains the salience of the possible paraphrase over the generally accepted one in Spain.

Interpretation and Gender.   The same set of data was analyzed to test for a possible relation between gender and choice of answer for the group of Mexicans. The frequencies of response are displayed in Table 12.2. Again, chi-square tests were conducted to see if the null hypothesis that there is no special association between gender and the selected interpretation could be maintained. Results show that, except for Probe 1, there is no significant relation between choice of interpretation and gender of speaker. Thus, although there is some variation in the answers selected by native speakers, this is not linked to their gender.[7]

---

[7]An interesting result emerges from the distribution of answers in Probe 1. The two possible answers differ only in the presence of a syntactic negation in one of them. This issue is, of course, beyond the scope of this chapter.

TABLE 12.1
Frequency of Selection of the Canonical Interpretation
by Mexicans—Study 1

Proverb Number (Ordered as in the Appendix)	Frequency	%	χ^2 Value (Critical Value of $\chi^2 = 3.84$, $p < .05$)
1	15	62.5%	3.3
2	19	79%	1.04
3	11	45.8%	7.04
4	0	0%	24
5	19	79%	1.04
6	18	75%	1.28
7	6	25%	11.57
8	10	41.6%	7
9	17	70.8%	1.75
10	16	66.6%	2.66
11	15	62.5%	3.3
12	12	50%	6
13	18	75%	1.28
14	19	79%	1.04

STUDY 2: STABILITY OF MEANING AMONG NON-NATIVE SPEAKERS

Method

Participants. Thirty-two foreign students of Spanish attending the National Autonomous University of Mexico—16 men, 16 women—participated in the study. They were paid $5. The participants' ages ranged from 18 to 34 (mean = 25.5, mode = 25). On average, they had studied Spanish for 16.75 months (exposure to language ranged from 2 to 6 years). Half of them lived in Mexico for 2 months, and the other half lived in Mexico between 3 and 12 months. Nine of them were studying Spanish as their second language, 10 as their third language, and 7 as their fourth language. For the rest, Spanish was being studied either as fifth, sixth, or seventh language. Their countries of origin included Austria, Brazil, Bosnia, Cameroon, Canada, China, England, France, Holland, Indonesia, Japan, Poland, Slovenia, South Korea, Tanna Vanuatu, and the United States. For the analysis of the data, the subjects in the sample were grouped into four main geographical

TABLE 12.2
Frequency of Selection of the Canonical Interpretation
by Male and Female Mexicans—Study 1

Proverb Number (Ordered as in the Appendix)	Interpretation	Women	Men	χ^2 Value (Critical Value of $\chi^2 = 3.84$, $p < .05$
1	GAP	0	15	
	PFP	8	1	19.99
2	GAP	7	12	
	PFP	1	4	.45
3	GAP	4	7	
	PFP	4	9	.29
4	GAP	0	0	
	PFP	8	15	0
5	GAP	5	12	
	PFP	2	3	.17
6	GAP	7	11	
	PFP	1	5	.99
7	GAP	2	4	
	PFP	6	12	0
8	GAP	3	7	
	PFP	5	8	.13
9	GAP	6	11	
	PFP	2	5	.34
10	GAP	4	12	
	PFP	4	4	1.2
11	GAP	6	8	
	PFP	1	6	1.6
12	GAP	4	8	
	PFP	4	7	.04
13	GAP	7	11	
	PFP	1	5	.99
14	GAP	7	12	
	PFP	0	4	1.68

Note. GAP = generally accepted paraphrase; PFP = possible paraphrase.

areas: Asia (9 subjects), Europe (10) subjects, America[8] (12 subjects, Canadians and Brazilians are included here), and Africa (1 subject). The religious breakdown was as follows: 7 Catholics, 14 Protestants, and 11 non-Chris-

---

[8]Throughout this chapter 'America' includes all countries in the continent and does not refer to the United States.

tians. Half of them had lived in countries other than Mexico, and Mexico was the only foreign country where the other half had stayed for longer than 2 months. According to the language course in which they were enrolled, 15% of them had a basic command of Spanish, 65% were considered intermediate, and 18% were classified as advanced students.

Materials.   The materials used were the same as those in Study 1.

Procedure.   The same 14 proverbs were included in a questionnaire. Their order of presentation was randomized, as was the order of the two possible paraphrases offered as what was believed to be the most appropriate interpretation. For each proverb, participants were asked whether they knew it and whether they understood the meaning of all the words. They were also instructed to select the interpretation of the proverb they considered closest to its meaning. Whenever participants indicated that they did not understand all the words in a proverb, their answer to that probe was not taken into account.[9] The objective was to find out (a) whether foreigners chose the generally accepted paraphrase of a proverb, (b) whether there is an association between being Mexican or foreigner and the interpretation selected, (c) whether there is an association between the geographical location of the country of origin of subjects and their choice of paraphrase, and (d) whether there is an association between the dominant religion of the country of origin of subjects and their choice of paraphrase (in most of the cases, the main religion in the country of origin of a subject coincided with his or her own).

Results and Discussion

As in study 1, chi-square tests were conducted for each probe to explore whether the null hypothesis (that all foreigners will choose the generally accepted paraphrase) should be rejected. Frequencies for each answer given by the group of foreigners to all proverbs are displayed in Table 12.3.

Interpretations of Nonnative speakers.   The null hypothesis—that all foreign subjects select the generally accepted paraphrase, as native speakers do—was rejected for all probes but three (Proverbs 1, 2, and 5), in some cases, $p < .05$, and in others, $p < .01$.

Association Between Being a Native Speaker or a Foreigner and Interpretation Chosen.   We then explored whether there was a special relation between being Mexican or being a foreigner and the type of para-

---

[9]All participants answered a second questionnaire, which presented them with a number of conversational exchanges in written form (contexts) for each proverb. Subjects were asked to choose the context in which a particular proverb would be most adequately used. The results of this study are not reported in this chapter.

TABLE 12.3
Frequency of Selection of the Canonical Interpretation
by Foreigners—Study 2

Proverb Number (Ordered as in the Appendix)	Frequency	%	χ^2 Value (Critical Value of $\chi^2 = 3.84$, $p < .05$ and $\chi^2 = 6.63$, $p < .01$)
1	24	75%	2
2	27	84%	0.78
3	11	34%	13.78
4	14	43%	10.12
5	23	71%	2.53
6	13	40%	11.28
7	10	31.2%	15.12
8	12	37%	12.5
9	11	34%	13.78
10	20	62.5	4.5
11	17	53.1%	7
12	12	37%	12.5
13	13	40%	11.28
14	17	53.1%	7

phrase chosen. For each probe (excluding Proverbs 1, 2, and 5), we compared the answers of both groups and conducted a chi-square test. The results, displayed in Table 12.4, lead us to conclude that there is a significant relation between being a native speaker of Spanish or a foreigner and the interpretations selected for Proverbs 4, 6, 9, 12, and 13. For the rest of the probes, the null hypothesis is maintained.

Effect of Geographical Area of Origin on Interpretation Chosen. To explore whether the type of answers selected were related to the geographical location of the country of origin of a subject, we partitioned our sample into three major geographical areas: America, Europe, and Asia (the only African subject in the sample was excluded from this section of the study).[10] To test the null hypothesis that geographical origin is not related to

---

[10]Murdock (1967, cited in Berry et al., 1992) distinguished six cultural areas on the basis of geography, namely Sub-Saharan Africa, Asia, Australasia, Circum-Mediterranean, North America, and South America. Our categories are a simplification of his system, given the size and composition of our sample. Note, however, that the range of variation within certain cultural areas can be as large as the variation between these areas for a number of dimensions, so we need to explore the crucial dimensions intervening in interpretation in more detail.

TABLE 12.4
Frequency of Selection of the Canonical Interpretation
and the Possible Paraphrase by Foreign Speakers of Spanish
and by Mexican Native Speakers—Study 2

Proverb Number (Ordered as in the Appendix)	Interpretation	Foreign Speakers of Spanish	Mexican Native Speakers of Spanish	χ^2 Value (Critical Value of $\chi^2 = 3.84$, $p < .05$)
1	GAP	Not considered	Not considered	Not calculated
	PFP			
2	GAP	Not considered	Not considered	Not calculated
	PFP			
3	GAP	11	11	
	PFP	17	13	.26
4	GAP	14	0	
	PFP	17	23	16.2
5	GAP	Not considered	Not considered	Not calculated
	PFP			
6	GAP	13	18	
	PFP	16	6	5.8
7	GAP	10	6	
	PFP	20	18	.24
8	GAP	12	10	
	PFP	15	13	.004
9	GAP	11	17	
	PFP	17	7	4.72
10	GAP	2	16	
	PFP	9	8	.15
11	GAP	17	14	
	PFP	12	7	.28
12	GAP	6	12	
	PFP	21	11	4.83
13	GAP	13	18	
	PFP	18	6	5.97
14	GAP	17	19	
	PFP	11	4	2.9

Note. GAP = generally accepted paraphrase; PFP = possible paraphrase.

choice of paraphrase, we conducted chi-square tests for each of the probes (2 possible answers × 3 geographical areas, $df = 2$). The results are displayed in Table 12.5

Effect of Dominant Religion on Interpretation Chosen

To explore whether the type of answers selected were related to the dominant religion of the country of origin of a subject, we partitioned our sample into three major religious categories: Catholic, Protestant, and non-Christian. To test the null hypothesis that the dominant religion is not related to choice of paraphrase, we conducted chi-square tests for each of the probes (2 possible answers × 3 major religious backgrounds, $df = 2$). The results are displayed in Table 12.6.

GENERAL DISCUSSION AND CONCLUSION

For the probes used in this exploration, it was found that there is a very significant amount of stability of interpretation for native speakers. For the four proverbs in which more variation in interpretation was found (Proverbs 3, 7, 8, and 12; see Appendix), it was noticed that one of the alternative responses can be seen as a particular case of the other, a fact that may have led some of the subjects to select the most general one. Further studies should take this into account and test different interpretations derived from more distant conceptual domains, in which the connection to cultural themes is ideally more precise. Variation in responses for native speakers was not significant and not linked to gender factors.

Nonnative speakers showed a pattern of responses that contrasts significantly with native speakers. The null hypothesis that nonnative speakers select the same interpretation as native speakers was rejected in most cases. For 78.6% of the proverbs in Study 2, participants did not select the generally accepted paraphrase, and this was statistically significant in all cases but one, in which only a tendency was found.[11]

A special association between being native or nonnative speaker of Spanish and the type of answer selected for several items was found. For Proverb 4, Mexicans overwhelmingly preferred an interpretation based on the concept of talking, whereas foreigners were divided between this and an interpretation based on the concept of eating. For Proverb 6, native speakers were inclined to choose an interpretation based on the conceptual construction of "nonintrusion in other people's affairs," whereas nonnative

---

[11]Despite the limitations of the conclusions that can be drawn, this finding deserves consideration in second language testing practices, wherein the use of proverbs is sometimes found in proficiency exams. (Ormsby, personal communication, December, 2, 2001)

TABLE 12.5
Frequency of Selection of the Canonical Interpretation and the Possible Paraphrase by Foreign Speakers of Spanish Coming from the American continent, Europe, and Asia—Study 2

Proverb Number (Ordered as in the Appendix)	Interpretation	Foreign Subjects Coming From the American Continent	Foreign Subjects Coming From Europe	Foreign Subjects Coming From Asia	χ^2 Value (Critical Value of $\chi^2 = 5.99$, $p < .05$, $df = 2$
1	GAP	Not	Not	Not	Not
	PFP	considered	considered	considered	calculated
2	GAP	Not	Not	Not	Not
	PFP	considered	considered	considered	calculated
3	GAP	4	8	3	
	PFP	8	2	6	6.14
4	GAP	8	7	3	
	PFP	4	3	6	3.70
5	GAP	8	5	9	
	PFP	4	3	0	4.35
6	GAP	4	4	4	
	PFP	8	3	5	1.14
7	GAP	2	4	5	
	PFP	10	5	4	3.64
8	GAP	7	0	5	
	PFP	5	8	4	7.20
9	GAP	5	3	2	
	PFP	7	3	7	4.12
10	GAP	6	6	8	
	PFP	6	2	1	3.80
11	GAP	9	3	5	
	PFP	3	5	4	3.26
12	GAP	1	1	4	
	PFP	11	5	5	5.07
13	GAP	5	5	1	
	PFP	7	3	8	5.33
14	GAP	6	8	4	
	PFP	6	2	4	2.74

Note. GAP = generally accepted paraphrase; PFP = possible paraphrase.

TABLE 12.6
Frequency of Selection of the Canonical Interpretation and the
Possible Paraphrase by Foreign Speakers of Spanish With Catholic,
Protestant, and Non-Christian Religious Background—Study 2

Proverb Number (Ordered as in the Appendix)	Interpretation	Foreign Subjects With a Catholic Background	Foreign Subjects With a Protestant Background	Foreign Subjects With a Non-Christian Background	χ^2 Value (Critical Value of $\chi^2 = 5.99$, $p < .05$, $df = 2$)
1	GAP	Not	Not	Not	Not
	PFP	considered	considered	considered	calculated
2	GAP	Not	Not	Not	Not
	PFP	considered	considered	considered	calculated
3	GAP	4	6	3	
	PFP	3	8	8	1.06
4	GAP	3	7	4	
	PFP	4	7	6	0.22
5	GAP	5	7	10	
	PFP	2	5	0	5.41
6	GAP	2	6	5	
	PFP	5	6	5	0.95
7	GAP	3	2	5	
	PFP	4	12	5	3.4
8	GAP	1	7	6	
	PFP	6	6	4	3.24
9	GAP	2	4	3	
	PFP	4	8	7	0.031
10	GAP	1	7	6	
	PFP	6	6	4	6.22
11	GAP	4	8	6	
	PFP	2	6	4	0.18
12	GAP	1	1	4	
	PFP	5	11	5	5.07
13	GAP	5	4	3	
	PFP	1	9	8	5.86
14	GAP	7	5	7	
	PFP	0	8	3	7.68

Note. GAP = generally accepted paraphrase; PFP = possible paraphrase.

speakers were split between this and an interpretation based on the conceptual scheme of "life style matching what one can afford." For Proverb 9, nonnative speakers selected interpretations based on the concepts of necessity and surprise, but native speakers preferred the interpretation based on the concept of surprise. Proverb 12 elicited interpretations based both on the concept of ugliness and the concept of humbleness in native speakers; but in nonnative speakers, most choices were linked to humbleness. For Proverb 13, native speakers' interpretations were related to the concepts of kindness and usefulness, whereas nonnative speakers chose interpretations linked to concepts of clarity and understanding. The variations in responses were significant, as shown in the tables, along with other strong—though not statistically significant—tendencies.

Some associations between the type of answer selected and the geographical origin of the subjects were also found. For Proverb 3, Europeans had a significant stronger tendency to select an interpretation based on the concept of price, whereas Americans and Asians preferred an interpretation based on the concept of solution. Proverb 4 elicited answers based on the concept of eating in most Europeans, but Americans and Asians tended to select an interpretation based on the concept of talking. For Proverb 5, speakers of all geographical areas showed a tendency for an interpretation based on the concept of good times, but note that no Asian subject chose an interpretation based on bad times, whereas almost half of the Americans and the Europeans did. In Proverb 7, most Americans preferred an interpretation linked to the notion of boasting, whereas other groups were divided among the interpretation options. The concept of efficiency underlied the choice of interpretation of Europeans in Proverb 8, but Americans and Asians were divided between this interpretation and one based on the concept of bravery. Results also showed that Asians tended to choose an interpretation of Proverb 9 based on the concept of necessity, whereas Americans and Europeans did not have a preferred interpretation. For Proverb 10, Asians preferred an interpretation based on the notions of fitness and ability, whereas Americans and Europeans were divided among the alternative choices. Americans showed a strong tendency to select an interpretation based on the notion of spending for Proverb 11, Europeans preferred one based on the notion of understanding, and Asians were split between the two possibilities. Finally, for Proverb 13, Asians chose an interpretation based on notions of clarity and understanding, whereas Europeans preferred one based on helpfulness, and Americans were divided between the two.

Religious background also was significantly associated to the answers in several cases. For instance, all subjects from mainly Catholic areas selected the no action option in Proverb 1, all Christians selected the interpretation based on the notion of good times in Proverb 5, Protestants preferred an interpretation linked to the concept of boasting over one based on the concept of humbleness in Proverb 7. People from Catholic regions chose an interpretation based on the notion of bravery for Proverb 8, whereas Protestants and non-Christians selected one based on the concept of efficiency. Protestants were significantly inclined to choose the interpretation constructed on the notion of concern for Proverb 10, but Catholics and non-Christians preferred one based on concepts of fitness and ability. For instance, and against the assumptions mentioned in the introduction, all Catholics associated the "picking out for mosquitoes and swallowing of camels" with an obsession for details and with an overlooking of serious faults, an interpretation also favored by non-Christians, whereas Protestants chose an interpretation based on the notions of difficulty and absurdity.

No definite associations between these answers and cultural specificity can be made before more detailed studies consider the cultural representations of the populations studied as such and finer instruments are designed to attest to the salience and impact of these cultural assumptions in the interpretation process, but the results presented suggested some lines along which future research can be designed.

REFERENCES

Berry, J., Poortinga, Y., Segall, M., & Dasen, P. (1992). *Cross-cultural psychology: Research and Applications*. Cambridge, England: Cambridge University Press.

Carston, R. (2002). *Thoughts and utterances: The pragmatics of explicit communication*. Oxford, England: Blackwell.

Chapman, S., Ulatowska, H., Franklin, L., Shobe, A., Thompson, J., & Mc Intire, D. (1997). Proverb interpretation in fluent aphasia and Alzheimer disease: Implications beyond abstract thinking. *Aphasiology, 11*(4–5), 337–350.

Cheng, L. (1996). Beyond bilingualism: A quest for communicative competence. *Topics in Language Disorders, 16*(4), 9–21.

Davis, S. (Ed.). (1991). *Pragmatics: A reader*. Oxford: Oxford University Press.

Fodor, J. (1998). *Concepts: Where cognitive science went wrong*. Oxford, England: Clarendon.

Gibbs, R. W., Jr. (1994). *The poetics of mind*. Cambridge, England: Cambridge University Press.

Gibbs, R. W., Jr. (2001a). Evaluating contemporary models of figurative language understanding. *Metaphor and Symbol, 12*, 295–316.

Gibbs., R. W., Jr. (2001b). Proverbial themes we live by. *Poetics, 29*, 167–188.

Glucksberg, S., Newsome, M., & Goldvarg, Y. (2001). Inhibition of the literal: Filtering metaphor-irrelevant information during metaphor comprehension. *Metaphor and Symbol, 12*, 277–293.

Grice, H. P. (1989). *Studies in the way of words*. Cambridge, MA: Harvard University Press. (Original work published 1975)

Katz, A., Cacciari, C. Gibbs, R. W., Jr., & Turner, M. (1998). *Figurative language and thought*. Oxford, England: Oxford University Press.

Lakoff, G., & Núñez, R. (2002). *Where mathematics come from*. New York: Basic Books.

Lakoff, G., & Turner, M. (1989). *More than cool reason*. Chicago: Chicago University Press.

Levinson, S. (2000). *Presumptive meanings. The theory of generalized conversational implicature*. Cambridge, MA: MIT Press.

Murphy, G. (1996). On metaphorical representation. *Cognition, 60*, 173–204.

Nippold, M., Uhden, L., & Schwarz, I. (1997). Proverb explanation through the lifespan: A developmental study of adolescents and adults. *Journal of Speech, Language and Hearing Research, 40*(2), 245–253.

Sperber, D. (1996). *Explaining culture. A naturalistic approach*. Oxford, England: Blackwell.

Sperber, D., & Wilson, D. (1985/1986). Loose talk. In *Proceedings of the Aristotelian society* (pp. 153–172). Oxford, England: Blackwell (reprinted, Davis, 1991).

Sperber, D., & Wilson, D. (1986). *Relevance: Communication and cognition*. Oxford, England: Blackwell.

Sperber, D., & Wilson, D. (1995). *Relevance: Communication and cognition* (2nd ed.). Oxford, England: Blackwell.

Stanley, J., & Szabo, Z. (2000). On quantifier domain restriction. *Mind and Language, 15*, 219–261.

Stanley, J. (2002). Making it articulated. *Mind and Language, 17*(1–2), 149–168.

Ulatowska, H., Chapman, S., Highley, A., & Prince, J. (1998). Discourse in healthy old–elderly adults: A longitudinal study. *Aphasiology, 12*(7–8), 619–633.

Winner, E. (1988). *The point of words: Children's understanding of metaphor and irony*. Cambridge, MA: Harvard University Press.

Appendix

1. *Ver el temblor y no hincarse* (proverb in Spanish)
   - Seeing the earthquake and not kneeling down (not kneeling down at the sight of an earthquake) (approximate literal translation)
   - To see danger approaching and do nothing to prevent it (generally accepted figurative use paraphrase)
   - To see danger approaching and do something to prevent it (possible figurative use paraphrase)

2. *Dar margaritas a los cerdos* (proverb in Spanish)
   - To give pigs daisies (approximate literal translation)
   - To give something valuable to someone who cannot appreciate it (generally accepted figurative use paraphrase)
   - To encourage someone who has no real hope to succeed (possible figurative use paraphrase)

3. *Depende del sapo la pedrada* (proverb in Spanish)
   - The type of stone you throw depends on the toad you aim it at (approximate literal translation)
   - The charge for a good or service depends on the customer (generally accepted figurative use paraphrase)
   - The type of solution you give to a problem depends on how serious it is (possible figurative use paraphrase)

4. *Perico, corto de manos, largo de pico* (proverb in Spanish)
   - Parrot, short hands, long beak (approximate literal translation)
   - Said of someone who works little and eats much (generally accepted figurative use paraphrase)
   - Said of someone who does little and talks much (possible figurative use paraphrase)

5. *A cada santo le llega su función* (proverb in Spanish)
   - Each saint gets its performance day (approximate literal translation)
   - Everyone gets good times (generally accepted figurative use paraphrase)
   - Everyone gets bad times (possible figurative use paraphrase)

6. *A tu palo, gavilán y a tu matorral, conejo* (proverb in Spanish)
   - To your tree, hawk and to your bush, rabbit (approximate literal translation)
   - People must mind their own business (generally accepted figurative use paraphrase)
   - People's lifestyle must be compatible with what they can afford (possible figurative use paraphrase)

7. *Perro que ladra no muerde* (proverb in Spanish)
   - A dog that barks does not bite (approximate literal translation)
   - People who have fits of temper are usually good natured and noble (generally accepted figurative use paraphrase)
   - People who boast are usually lacking (possible figurative use paraphrase)

8. *A ver de qué cuero salen más correas* (proverb in Spanish)
   - Let's see which leather yields more belts (approximate literal translation)
   - Let's see who is bravest (generally accepted figurative use paraphrase)
   - Let's see who is most efficient (possible figurative use paraphrase)

9. *Hasta el más chimuelo come clavos* (proverb in Spanish)
   - Even the toothless eat nails (approximate literal Spanish)
   - You can get a surprise from the people you less expect it (generally accepted figurative use paraphrase)
   - When in extreme need, people cannot afford to be choosy and demanding (possible figurative use paraphrase)

10. *No hay que meterse en la danza si no se tiene sonaja* (proverb in Spanish)
   - Don't get in the dance if you don't have a rattle (approximate literal translation)
   - Don't get involved in something for which you are unfit (generally accepted figurative use paraphrase)
   - Don't get involved in other people's affairs (possible figurative use paraphrase)

11. *Comen frijoles y repiten pollo* (proverb in Spanish)
   - They eat beans and belch out chicken (approximate literal translation)
   - They have a low income and spend like rich (generally accepted figurative use paraphrase)
   - They're told one thing and they understand another (possible figurative use paraphrase)

12. *A cada capillita le llega su fiestecita* (proverb in Spanish)
   - Every little chapel gets is little celebration (approximate literal translation)
   - Even if a person is ugly, someone will eventually fall in love with her (generally accepted figurative use paraphrase)
   - Even those with a humble background get a moment of glory (possible figurative use paraphrase)

13. *Candil de la calle, oscuridad de su casa* (proverb in Spanish)
   - Street lamp, darkness at home (approximate literal translation)
   - Said of someone who is helpful and kind to others, but not to his own family (generally accepted figurative use paraphrase)
   - Said of someone who is very clear about the problems of other people, but very confused about their own (possible figurative use paraphrase

14. *Estamos colando mosquitos y tragando camellos* (proverb in Spanish, translated from Swedish)
   - We are sieving for mosquitoes and swallowing camels (approximate literal translation)
   - We are overconcerned about details and overlooking serious faults (generally accepted figurative use paraphrase)
   - We are doing something very difficult and absurd (possible figurative use paraphrase)

13

Metaphors in Sign Language and Sign Language Users: A Window Into Relations of Language and Thought

Marc Marschark

*National Technical Institute for the Deaf,
Rochester Institute of Technology, and University of Aberdeen*

As its title suggests, this chapter is about the metaphoric aspects of sign language and the use of such figurative devices by sign language users.[1] Distinguishing and then integrating these domains requires consideration of three primary areas of investigation, each of which is described here to only a limited extent—albeit for different reasons. After a brief history of research into linguistic and psychological study involving metaphor, the chapter focuses on metaphorical qualities that appear to be inherent in signed languages to some greater degree than in spoken languages. Although it could be argued that, in terms of the totality of artistic impression, a spoken language can be as metaphorical as a signed language, the discussion here primarily considers everyday language, a domain in which spoken language often seems to be a dull cousin. Of particular interest here is the issue of metaphor versus iconicity. These two aspects of sign language frequently have been seen incorrectly as a single dimension, likely because iconicity does not occur in spoken languages (its closest parallel is onomatopoeia).

---

[1]Except where noted otherwise, *metaphor* is used metonymically to refer to figurative expressions in general.

The second area of investigation concerns the ways in which various aspects of sign language are used to express ideas in figurative ways. This discussion focuses on common metaphors in sign language. The author's firsthand aspects of this discussion are largely limited to American Sign Language (ASL), although several secondhand examples are included. Beyond these language-specific examples, however, it appears that all sign languages, from Croatian Sign Language (*Hrvatski Znakovni Jezik*) to Italian Sign Language (*La lingua italiana dei segni* or LIS) and from Australian Sign Language (*Auslan*) to Austrian Sign Language (*Österreichischen Gebärdensprache*), have similar means of expressing metaphor, even if their differing linguistic rules make for normal cross-linguistic variation.

The third area considered, and the one most obviously psychological rather than linguistic, concerns processes involved in the comprehension and production of figurative language by individuals who use sign language. Regrettably, this area is perhaps the most wanting of the three examined here. Most notable are the lack of research on (a) the comprehension of metaphor in sign language, (b) the use of figurative language by deaf individuals who use spoken language or by hearing individuals who use sign language, and (c) the development of metaphor in children acquiring sign language as a first language. Although it might be assumed that the lack of such work suggests that there is nothing to investigate (i.e., that a metaphor by any other name smells as sweet), several considerations suggest this is not the case. Rather, a combination of the immaturity of this research area, the relative paucity of psycholinguists (as opposed to linguists and cognitive psychologists) interested in sign language, and some sociopolitical constraints within the Deaf[2] community have delayed what is likely to be a fascinating and informative domain of enquiry, especially as it relates to children. Meanwhile, the study of figurative and artistic use of sign language by adults continues apace in both theater and linguistics.

BIRTHING THE STUDY OF METAPHORS IN SIGN LANGUAGE AND SIGN LANGUAGE USERS

As many of the chapters in this book demonstrate, figurative language has long been recognized as both a reflection of creativity and a window into the language and thought of the user. Paivio (1979) once referred to this metaphorically by saying "For the student of language and thought, metaphor is a solar eclipse" (p. 150). Mac Cormac (1985, p. 2) noted that metaphors can operate as cognitive processes that offer new insights, whereas Wilcox

---

[2]Note that literature in this field uses *deaf* to refer to audiological matters and *Deaf* to refer to cultural matters. The metaphoric character of lower case *d* and uppercase *D* is not lost on many familiar with the Deaf community (see Marschark, 1993).

(2000, p. 35) suggested that we use metaphors to make sense of what goes on around us. If metaphor is such a valuable tool, how is it learned or does it develop spontaneously?

These questions were addressed in an early study by Piaget (1923/1974) which examined the ability of 8- to 11-year-olds to comprehend and explain the meanings of proverbs. Piaget asked children either to describe how each proverb was related to its literal meaning or simply to explain isolated proverbs. His results suggested that younger children create "holistic schemas" or "general images" of the literal contents of a proverb, based on their knowledge of the topic (subject) and vehicle (object) rather than the underlying figurative meaning (p. 151). Although the children in his study "all had the feeling that each proverb had a symbolic sense" (p. 161), Piaget found that it was not until the children started to apply analogical reasoning to the parts of the proverbs and move away from their global, concrete images that they could correctly explain figurative meanings.

Since Piaget's (1923/1974) study, comprehension of figurative language has been seen as an indicator of cognitive flexibility in children, both deaf and hearing. For theoretical reasons, Piaget did not expect hearing children younger than 11 years (i.e., not having achieved *formal operations*) to be able to understand the figurative meanings of proverbs, a correct prediction on his part. Yet, research demonstrating younger deaf children's failures to understand nonliteral language frequently led to the conclusion that they are both concrete and literal in language and thought (Blackwell, Engen, Fischgrund, & Zarcadoolas, 1978; Boatner & Gates, 1969; Conley, 1976; Myklebust, 1964; but also see Marschark & Nall, 1985). As discussed in this chapter, these latter studies typically entailed stimulus materials drawn from the vernacular and presented in print (e.g., "The students studied the poem until they knew it by heart"). The fact that deaf children typically lag behind hearing peers in literacy skills (Traxler, 2000) was ignored or taken as convergent support for the conclusion.

The development of metaphoric understanding in deaf children is considered at length in a later section. At this point, however, it is important to recognize that, at least in part, the negative view of their skills from early work in the area followed naturally from the fact sign languages such as ASL and British Sign Language (BSL) were not recognized as true, natural languages until the early 1960s (Stokoe, 1960; Stokoe, Casterline, & Croneberg, 1965) and did not become an object of study in psychology until the 1970s. By the late mid- to late 1970s, linguists were beginning to examine the structure and rules of signed languages (e.g., see Friedman, 1977, and Siple, 1978), and the first forays into the psycholinguistics of sign language use emerged at about the same time (e.g., Klima & Bellugi, 1979). More recently, the combination of evidence from cognitive psychology, psycholinguistics, cultural anthropology, and neuropsychology has offered new insights into sign language and sign language users, and further studies of sign language have spawned new conceptions about language (e.g., Brennan, 1990; Liddell, 1990; Wilcox, 2000).

As I clarify in the remainder of this chapter, recent studies of signed languages have been augmented by extensive and sophisticated studies of iconicity and metaphor. Meanwhile, creativity expressed in the theatrical and poetic sign productions of deaf native signers has long been taken as a reflection of the flexibility of sign language rather than the language user, a position that appears to be implicit in recent analyses of sign language poetry (e.g., Taub, 2001a; Wilcox, 2000, chap. 7). Thus, despite discussions about the unique figurative potential of sign language, there has been little consideration of potential interactions between sign language and the cognitive or other psychological characteristics of sign language users.

To a considerable degree, this situation appears to have developed because of the absence of discussion about the possibility that individuals who grow up using a signed language might have psycholinguistic or metalinguistic skills different than other hearing or deaf individuals (but see Emmorey, 2002; Marschark, 1993; Marschark, Lang, & Albertini, 2002). The history of research involving deaf individuals has been haunted by a scientific culture that equated speech with language and language with intelligence. Lacking a full understanding of sign language, disagreement and discord both among deaf people (e.g., those using spoken vs. sign language) and between deaf and hearing individuals have created significant barriers to investigations in several potentially interesting domains (Marschark & Spencer, 2003). The related view of deaf people as deficient or inferior also led to an understandable resentment among many deaf people toward those hearing people who sought to study them.

The lack of discourse concerning interactions between language and cognition among deaf adults and children is regrettable for both theoretical and pragmatic reasons. With regard to recent reconsideration of the Sapir-Whorf notions of linguistic relativity, it might be suspected that the modality difference between signed and spoken language might increase the apparent effects of linguistic relativity, just as greater differences between any two spoken languages might produce larger collateral effects than when those languages are more similar. In the case of signed and spoken languages, however, the two co-occur in the same culture (broadly speaking). This similarity of context suggests the possibility that whereas reciprocal effects of language and culture might both contribute to observed differences between two aural–oral cultures, any such effects will be attenuated for a deaf subculture immersed within a hearing culture. Deaf culture thus appears to provide a paradigm case for examining the effects of cultural and linguistic relativity, but such an exercise still has not yet been undertaken. Particularly with regard to metaphor, the kinds of figurative constructions produced, the range of their most common meanings, and their interactions with the educational and cultural backgrounds of deaf individuals would be particularly enlightening.

Consider, for example, Glucksberg's (2001) discussion of ASL as one of several classifier languages that "do not normally have names for superordinate categories" (p. 39). If true, what does this say about the cognitive processes of ASL users? Glucksberg cited the example of the category *furniture* which, he suggested, is signed as CHAIR-TABLE-BED, ETC., that is, as a list of category exemplars rather than with a single, lexicalized category name.[3] In fact, there are some categories, such as *furniture*, that used to lack signed category names, and some others, such as *tools*, that still do. The very existence of such situations suggests that native users of ASL might have somewhat different conceptions of those categories than others and that the organization of their knowledge might well affect problem solving, reading, and memory. Glucksberg noted that the relations of categories are intimately tied to the abstraction of essential properties of objects, and one presumes that a collective lexical or conceptual term for a set of objects might well be more conducive to seeing that set as an abstraction than would a listing of concrete exemplars (cf. Luria, 1976, chap. 5; Piaget, 1923/1974). Although investigations of that possibility are in their early stages, some related findings are now emerging (e.g., Marschark & Everhart, 1999; Marschark, Convertino, McEvoy, & Masteller, 2001), indicating relatively small but consistently significant differences between deaf and hearing individuals in relations among concepts and the spontaneous use of associative connections in a variety of tasks.

Over the last 20 years or so, the use of multiple exemplar category names in ASL appears to have become far less frequent, and now it is relatively rare.[4] In some cases, such as *furniture*, new category name signs have emerged. (For example, FURNITURE entails an inclined F-hand shape (see Fig. 13.1) moved side-to-side in a short arc, whereas PREACH entails the same hand shape moved forward and backward.) Other category names, such as *tools*, are finger spelled, whereas many others have long had common sign names. Still, the potential cognitive impact of such linguistic and morphological differences between signed and spoken languages or among signed and among spoken languages has yet to be determined. To fully un-

---

[3]English glosses of signs typically are written in capital letters.

[4]The apparent rapidity of such changes suggests that sign languages might be evolving faster than spoken languages, but the topic has not been investigated formally.

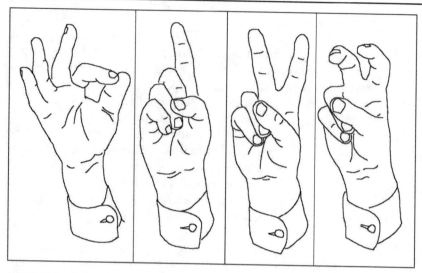

FIG. 13.1   Selected ASL hand shapes (F, 1, V or 2, bent V).

derstand the interactions among cognition, metaphor, and sign language, it is clear that a more complete understanding of metaphors inherent in sign language and metaphors expressed through sign language is needed. An excellent starting place for this discussion is the distinction between iconicity, signs appearing to look like their referents, and metaphor, the symbolic likening of one thing to another.

ICONIC AND METAPHORIC ASPECTS OF SIGN LANGUAGE

For many years, investigators of ASL (and many nonnative users of ASL) downplayed the role of iconicity in the language in an attempt to focus attention on its linguistic status rather than its gestural qualities.[5] But times are changing. Taub (2001b, p. 1) described ASL as involving "an integration of visual imagery with linguistic structure on a scale that no spoken language can equal." She and Wilcox (2000) provided in-depth analyses of the iconic qualities of ASL poetry, and several linguists have extensively investigated the iconic and metaphoric properties of ASL and other sign languages, even if they have not always distinguished among them (e.g., Boyes Braem, 1981; Brennan, 1990; Marschark & West, 1985).

Apparently the first treatment of metaphor and iconicity in sign language was provided by Boyes Braem (1981). In her pioneering and influential ex-

---

[5]*Gesture* in this sense is not intended in the verbal sense described by McNeill (1992), but precisely the opposite: the appearance to many laypersons, including some hearing parents of deaf children, that sign language is not really language at all (cf. Stokoe, 1960).

amination of ASL handshapes, Boyes Braem identified a level of symbolic representation that she referred to as metaphorical. Although many of the uses of devices she identified are now referred to as iconic rather than metaphoric (she described visual metaphors of various handshapes), her work set the stage for later analyses of metaphor and iconicity across a variety of signed languages. Brennan (1990) similarly blurred metaphor and iconicity in her morphological analysis of BSL, whereas Marschark and West (1985) confounded iconic gestures with iconic and metaphoric characteristics of ASL. The latter study also may have underestimated what was seen at the time as an amazing degree of figurative language competence by deaf children (discussed later). Beyond their specific findings, however, these earlier investigations pointed the way toward the need to distinguish linguistic and psychological aspects of metaphor and iconicity in signed languages. To date, only the linguistic distinction has been considered in any detail.

Iconicity of Classifiers

Signs are essentially composed of handshapes, locations, and movements (see the hand shapes of Fig. 13.1, and all three components in Figs. 13.2 and 13.3). Distinguishing the iconic properties of signs and signing from their metaphoric properties requires consideration of the use of these components, within the sign space, to map linguistic form. Inherent in such mapping is the way that signers use classifiers as a kind of *frozen trope* (i.e., figurative devices that have entered into common usage) to describe space and time. Classifiers are particular handshapes that can be used to represent people, animals, vehicles, or objects. The referent of a classifier is first established in the discourse via signs, and the classifier handshape then assumes that role much in the manner of a pronoun, albeit a dynamic one. In ASL, for example, a bent V-hand (see Fig. 13.1) is used represent an animal; or an upside down bent V-hand could indicate a dead animal. (Metaphoric extension of such signs is considered in the next section.)

Emmorey (2001, pp. 148–151) described the three primary categories of mapping between signs and space: (a) *articulators* map physical and conceptual elements, (b) *locations* in signing space map to locations in physical or conceptual, and (c) space *movements* of the articulators map to the motion of elements. Handshapes may be fixed in space, indicating a relative location, a relative time, or a qualitative aspect. Alternatively, movement of the handshape can indicate changes in relative location, time, or quality (e.g., IMPROVE, reflecting "good is up," and DETERIORATE, reflecting "bad is down"). In these cases, the signs entail both iconic and metaphoric characteristics, a *double mapping* (considered later).

Taub (2001b, p. 34) described classifiers as forming "a set of iconic building blocks for the description of physical objects, movements, and loca-

FIG. 13.2   Two ASL signs for PROMOTION.

FIG. 13.3   ASL classifier used to show a bicycle (or other vehicle) riding over a hill.

tions." Beyond iconicity in the shapes of signs is the iconic quality referred to as *virtual depiction* (Mandel, 1977) or *path-for-shape iconicity* (Taub, 2001b). Rather than the hands or other parts of the body offering the iconic ana-logue for some part of an object or event, virtual depiction entails the move-ment of the articulators providing the representational quality, as in the two alternative signs for PROMOTION in ASL shown in Fig. 13.2. When handshapes take on iconic similarity to concrete referents (e.g., the PERSON or VEHICLE classifier), they also can represent the movement of those referents in space—which is what Mandel (1977) referred to as *temporal motion*. Figure 13.3 shows an example involving the VEHICLE classifier.

It should be evident by this point that the perception of iconicity in sign language is not limited to sign language users. Nonsigners often can pick up an occasional sign in an otherwise inscrutable language stream, just as a speaker of English might recognize the odd word in a conversation held in French. For example, a one-hand (see Fig. 13.1) classifier, representing a person descending a staircase might easily be recognized by someone without sign language experience (this is usually referred to as *transparency*).

Klima and Bellugi (1979) asked American hearing individuals with no knowledge of ASL to identify the relations between signs and their English meanings or simply identify the meanings of isolated signs. They found only limited transparency of their 90 stimulus signs, ranging from 9% in a free identification task to 20% in a multiple-choice task. O'Brien (1999) examined iconic and metaphoric characteristics of isolated signs, asking hearing individuals to identify meanings of iconic, metaphorical, and arbitrary ASL signs. She found that although iconic signs were the most obvious of the three, people found metaphorical signs to be more sensible, natural, and transparent than arbitrary signs. Finally, Pizzuto and Volterra (2000) showed 40 signs from LIS, 20 considered transparent and 20 not, to nonsigning individuals from six countries and 12 language communities (both signed and spoken). Overall, at least 50% the non-Italians were able to correctly identify the meanings of 13 of the 20 transparent signs, whereas none of the nontransparent signs reached that criterion (and only two approached it). Deaf individuals from other countries were better able to guess meanings than hearing individuals for all but two signs, but variation across hearing status and country of origin indicated cultural as well as linguistic bases for perception of iconicity (cf. O'Brien, 1999). Taken together, such findings offer some consistency, but there is considerable variability in the ability of nonsigners to see the regularity or bases of signs. Such findings should not be surprising, as they mirror well deaf people's difficulty in mastering the irregular aspects of many spoken and written languages. It would be expected that the most irregular languages, like English, would be particularly difficult for deaf individuals to learn, whereas more phonologically regular languages, like Italian, would be somewhat easier. Unfortunately, differences in deaf education across countries like the United States and Italy make such comparisons difficult, and they have not yet been undertaken.[6]

---

[6]There are, however, suggestive findings showing that dyslexia is more common among hearing children learning irregular languages such as English or French than those learning regular languages such as Italian (Paulesu et al., 2001).

Representation of Time

One of the most potentially interesting metaphoric qualities of sign language is its representation of time. Within all signed languages, temporal information is represented via the use of space in ways that preserve dimensions of relative time. Several different time lines can be found in ASL, and other languages have additional ones or variations of those found in ASL (see, e.g., Engberg-Pedersen's, 1993, description of Danish Sign Language). The most obvious of these time lines is referred to as the *deictic time line*, extending forward and backward from the signer's dominant shoulder to indicate time relative to the time of the utterance (Emmorey, 2001; Engberg-Pedersen, 1993). Whereas signs like NOW and TODAY (and, nonmetaphorically, HERE) as well as time-related signs like WEEK and MONTH are made in the neutral sign space just in front of the signer's body, the deictic time line is used to indicate both past and future. Thus, MONDAY is made relatively close to the signer's body, to the right side of the neutral sign space, whereas NEXT MONDAY is usually signed NEXT-WEEK MONDAY, with the sign WEEK made with a forward moving arc indicating "into the future." Alternatively, the next Monday or two or three Mondays in the future might be made, metaphorically, by signing MONDAY and "bumping" it forward, in the future, one, two, or three times.

A second, fairly obvious time indicator is the *sequence time line*. Extending from left to right across the front of the signer's body, the sequence time line indicates relative placement in a temporal sequence, with the reference point determined by the time of focus of the description, placed (signed) directly in front of the signer. Thus, a recounting of the various steps involved in the preparation of this chapter centered on the "present" task of sitting at the keyboard and composing (as this sentence first is being written) might also include, to the left, going to the library and collecting references, writing notes, and assembling information. To the right might be revising the document and, in a more creative moment, the sign indicating PAPER COMING OFF PRINTER, representing the publication of the chapter in the book.

Somewhat less obvious to naive observers of signing is the *anaphoric time line* (Engberg-Pedersen, 1993). Used to compare or contrast time periods related to the topic of a discourse (Emmorey, 2001), the anaphoric time line extends diagonally through the sign space, from the nondominant side of the signer forward to the dominant side. Unlike the deictic or sequence time lines, the anaphoric time line does not have a neutral here-and-now default. Rather, the events or topics are described relative to each other, as if each was represented by a separate positional pronoun with anaphoric reference relative to others. Describing the evolution of metaphor research, for example, might make better use of an anaphoric time line rather than a sequence time line, capturing the various paradigms and theoretical perspectives that have been seen in the field over the past half century or so, rather than a sequence of specific events relative to a particular time. Starting wherever the focus of the discussion might be (e.g., research on deaf children's sign language metaphors in the 1980s), the signer's body would be placed along the diagonal anaphoric time line relative to other events being described, not in order of mention (i.e., requiring shifting forward and backward in time along the time line).

Beyond these primary time lines are two other uses of a time indicator that occurs in a two-dimensional plane in front of the signer, parallel to the body. The *calendar plane* (Engberg-Pederson, 1993) iconically captures a calendar in some ways, for example, as the sign EVERY-FRIDAY is made by drawing the FRIDAY F-handshape down a column of Fridays on a calendar. CLASS EVERY-MONDAY AND EVERY-WEDNESDAY also would preserve the relative positions in the (horizontal) week. In Danish Sign Language, the calendar plane is used primarily for describing the year, whereas in ASL, it is most often used for descriptions within a week. In addition, the calendar plane serves as a generic indicator of successive topics in a discourse, not necessarily temporally related outside of the discourse, indicating the NEXT in a sequence, moving from higher to lower in the plane (e.g., changing topics in a classroom psychology lecture, which is not particularly tied to time).

In short, the use of space to represent time in ASL and other sign languages offers rich metaphorical opportunities to highlight temporal quality and relative position. Unfortunately, there does not appear to be any research concerning the development of time lines in either deaf children or second language learners of a signed language. The possibility that the depiction of the abstraction of time might result in some cognitive correlates in children (as might the difference between learning to tell time with a digital vs. an analog clock), however, suggests that it might be a fruitful area of study (Stokoe & Marschark, 1999).

METAPHORS IN SIGN LANGUAGE
AND USING SIGN LANGUAGE METAPHORICALLY

The previous section noted that classifier handshapes are frequently used to represent various kinds of objects, often located or moving in a designated environment. As in spoken language, such signs can also be used metaphorically to represent abstract concepts. Indeed, many of the conceptual metaphors found in spoken English are also found in ASL, and presumably a considerable number of those occur in other languages as well. *Conceptual metaphors*, such as "events are movers" (Lakoff & Johnson, 1980; Lakoff & Turner, 1989), involve abstract domains described in terms of concrete domains, with numerous and consistent transfers between them (also see McNeill's, 1992, treatment of metaphoric gestures). Without a sensory basis for understanding and communicating abstract ideas, language users often resort to mapping those ideas on parallel physical entities and relations. The *target* (or topic) domain is that actually being referred to, whereas the *source* (or vehicle) domain is that being used in the description. How it is that children come to understand conceptual metaphors and their psychological utility for language users of all ages are two of the more fascinating areas of psycholinguistic investigation (e.g., Glucksberg, 2001). Unfortunately, they are also beyond the scope of this chapter.

In ASL, many signs for abstract concepts involve visual aspects of objects or actions that are figuratively part of or associated with the abstractions. One of the most commonly cited examples in treatments of metaphor in ASL (as well as in English) is that involving mapping from the abstract domain of communication (the target) to the sending and receiving of objects or ideas (the source), that is, the conceptual metaphor "communicating is sending." In ASL, however, "communicating is sending" involves a double mapping of both metaphoric and iconic components (Taub, 2001a). Thus, in one oft-cited example, an idea represented by a one-hand (see Fig. 13.1) can move from the signer's head to another person but "not get through"—communicated via the sign THINK-BOUNCE, in which the handshape bounces off of a raised flat hand representing the impenetrable mind of another. Alternatively, if the point finally does sink in, THINK-PENETRATE shows the idea (the index finger) slowly penetrating the fingers of the previous blockage. The iconicity of sign language thus is often reflected in the shapes and movements of the hands representing analogous aspects of the referent, whereas the metaphoric quality overlays and binds the abstract (or concrete) relation between the abstract and the concrete referents.

A related example common to ASL, spoken English, and other languages is the conceptual metaphor of "mind as container." In addition to mapping cognitive processes onto containers, either in the head or elsewhere, iconic properties of the ASL metaphor, similar to those in "communicating is sending," provide a double mapping not available in spoken language. Thus, forgetting or overlooking something can be signed by making the EMPTY or VACANT sign across the forehead instead of its usual location on the back of the nondominant hand, indicating MIND-EMPTY. Similarly, a sign for NONE, a zero-hand, usually made with a brief movement away from the body, can be moved to the forehead, indicating the same thing. The feeling of losing a thought is often signed with the 1-hand of a thought gradually sinking through a horizontal flat hand (the conceptual and physical opposite of THINK-PENETRATE) until it disappears completely; recognition of a complete if momentary loss of reason (also known as realizing you have done something really stupid) might be signed by taking the sign for BRAIN (made with two hands), removing it from the head, and, while holding it like an ostrich egg, breaking it onto the floor or whisking it in a bowl.

Wilbur (1987) described the use of the C-hand classifier, normally used to represent size and shape of cylindrical objects, in the "mind as container" metaphor. Made at the forehead, the C shape can open (expand) or close to indicate amount of knowledge. Signers put information into the container, take information out, and a double-handed C comprises the sign BRILLIANT (as in intelligence; there is a different sign for use with light). Liddell (1995) described use of the same hand shape, also used in the sign CULTURE (with the same movement as FAMILY, GROUP, and CLASS), to capture "culture as container," as individuals "carry" their attitudes and behaviors in their perceptions of their own culture.

Related to the "mind as container" and "communicating is sending" metaphors is the "ideas are objects" metaphor. The signs for LEARN and STUDENT (literally, LEARN-PERSON) both involve drawing ideas up from the printed page into the head. INFORM and TEACH both entail taking ideas from the head and sending them outward. As verbs, LEARN, INFORM, and TEACH all can be inflected to denote manner, duration, and so on. But, as a *directional sign*, INFORM also can be iconically inflected in an established sign space to indicate who informed whom, as well as in what manner. Similarly, the directional sign GIVE can be inflected to indicate periodic or continual passing out of papers to members of a class in either a uniform or seemingly random order. As indicated earlier, such combinations of metaphor and iconicity in sign language are referred to as double mapping.

Several investigators (e.g., Emmorey, 2001; Taub, 2001a, 2001b; Wilcox, 2000) have described the double mapping of qualitative information in the use of sign space, which is comparable to the (single) mapping of quality and space in spoken language. For example, the common observation is that "good is up" and more good is more up (see Fig. 13.3). As indicated in Table 13.1, power, status, happiness, quantity, and value are also up in the sign space, either made with upward movements or signed at higher levels in the sign space to indicate relative quality, whereas their want is indicated by downward movement or lower signing (also see Lakoff & Johnson, 1980).[7] The availability and use of double mapping may or may not bestow any cognitive or linguistic benefits to the native or near-native signer, but it certainly provides an added creative characteristic to the artistic use of signing, as in poetry or storytelling, as is described in the next section.

---

[7]The "good is up" relation is not just seen in signed and spoken languages. In Bliss symbols, *good* is represented by an upward arrow, *feeling* by a heart, and *happy* by a heart with an upward arrow beside it (and a caret above the heart).

TABLE 13.1
Examples of ASL Signs

"Positive is up"	*"Negative is down"*
HAPPY	SAD
IMPORTANT	LOUSY
THRILLED	DEPRESSION
INSPIRED	WORTHLESS
BETTER, BEST	BAD
IMPROVE	DETERIORATE
SUCCESSFUL	OPPRESSION
RICH	CHEAP
WIN	LOSE
OUTSTANDING	FAILURE
FAMOUS	IGNORE
APPEAR	DISAPPEAR

Nonmetaphor Trope in ASL

Before moving from the linguistics of figurative language to its psychology, it is worth noting that the other categories of trope typically found in spoken languages are also found in signed languages. As alluded to in the previous section, *hyperbole* (exaggerating magnitude) and *litote* (minimizing magnitude) occur frequently and naturally in most signed languages by modifying sign size or movement, often with accompanying facial expression (Marschark, LePoutre, & Bement, 1998). *Simile* is fairly obvious and iconic in ASL; for example, the sign LIKE is made with a prone Y-hand shape that moves side to side, often between two objects, people, or concepts that have been established in the sign space. *Metonymy* (part representing the whole) is also a common aspect of ASL; a number of signs are represented by an iconic depiction of one of their parts. Signs for many animals, in particular, are metonymic, showing the stripes for TIGER, ears for RABBIT and HORSE, whiskers for CAT and MOUSE, and the trunk for ELEPHANT, among many others. Although such observations are encouraging, apparently the only empirical research to date on nonmetaphoric trope in sign language is the work by Marschark and colleagues (e.g., Everhart & Marschark, 1988; Marschark, West, Nall, & Everhart, 1986), documenting that such constructions are produced by deaf children and by deaf and hearing mothers who sign.

ASL also includes a number of examples of what Goossens (1990) referred to as *metaphtonymy*, or metaphorical use of metonymy. Wilcox (2000, pp. 92–96) described one example of metaphtonymy, THINK-HEARING, which she saw as illustrating "the powerful conflicting cultural influences" experienced by culturally Deaf individuals through their interactions with hearing people and deaf individuals who are not part of the Deaf community. First consider the sign SPEAK, which involves a 1-hand rotating, clockwise, parallel to and just in front of lips. Metonymically, the sign also means HEARING, as in a hearing person (but not in hearing in the auditory sense). The sign THINK has the same movement as HEARING, but it is normally made to the side of the temple inclined to a 45° angle. However, when the HEARING sign movement (horizontal) is made in front of the forehead instead of the lips, the result is THINK-HEARING, a sign that negatively and metaphtonymically refers to a deaf person who thinks and acts like a hearing person. More neutrally, HEARING also is used metaphtonymically in HEARING-SCHOOL, meaning public school. As with other kinds of trope seen within sign language, such documentation hopefully will soon lead to empirical investigation.

COMPREHENSION AND PRODUCTION OF METAPHOR BY DEAF INDIVIDUALS

Over the past 20 years or so, metaphor research has yielded a rich body of literature concerning the psychological processes involved in the comprehension of figurative language. Research involving hearing individuals, both adults and children, has been reviewed elsewhere and will not be reconsidered here (see Gibbs, 1994; Glucksberg, 2001; Katz, Cacciari, Gibbs, & Turner, 1998; Ortony, 1993). Research concerning the comprehension of metaphor by deaf adults and children, however, has been more limited. For adults, there appears to be no published research at all concerning comprehension of figurative language either in sign language or in the vernacular. For figurative language in printed materials, this gap in the literature likely reflects the well-documented finding that deaf individuals have significant challenges in the domain of literacy, with the 50th percentile of deaf 18-year-olds reading at approximately the fourth-grade level (Traxler, 2000). Teachers of deaf students of all ages (including the author) are well familiar with their struggle to understand English metaphors and idioms, at least in part as a result of their relatively impoverished early language experience (see Marschark et al., 2002, chaps. 4, 5, & 8, for discussion).[8] Teachers often work with deaf students on comprehension of metaphors in text, but it is unclear whether the general principles underlying figurative constructions are understood and transfer across domains or types of trope.

---

[8]These generalizations refer to the 95% of deaf children who have hearing parents. Deaf children of deaf parents have rich early language experience and tend to show better academic and reading achievement (see Marschark et al., 2002).

The comprehension and production of metaphor by deaf children has received some empirical attention (discussed later), but research concerning how or when deaf adults comprehend metaphors within sign language is clearly needed. Even if deaf college students and other deaf adults were to show lower levels of performance relative to hearing peers, examination of factors that influence their comprehension could be enlightening. Although there has been a history of assuming that deaf and hearing individuals have identical cognitive processes, we now know that there are some reliable differences with regard to imagery and verbal processes, as well as memory. In particular, despite considerable overlap, deaf and hearing college students have recently been found to show significant variation in the organization of conceptual knowledge, associations among conceptual domains, and the symmetry or asymmetry (relative to hearing peers) in the links between exemplars and their category names (Marschark et al., 2001; McEvoy, Marschark, & Nelson, 1999).

Several investigators have demonstrated that the distance between the domains of a metaphoric *tenor* (that being described, usually the subject) and *vehicle* (that to which a comparison is being made, usually the object) can affect comprehension and memory of metaphors (e.g., Marschark & Hunt, 1985; Tourangeau & Sternberg, 1981; Trick & Katz, 1986). In general, the typical finding is that domains that are farther apart, but not too far, lead to better comprehension, memory, and judgment of a metaphor's quality, supporting interactionist theories of metaphor comprehension (e.g., "Juliet is a rose" versus "Juliet is a bartender" or "Juliet is a fax machine"). Such studies have not been conducted with deaf individuals or, apparently, with individuals presented with metaphors in their second language. In view of the findings indicating less well-bounded and strongly interconnected conceptual domains among deaf individuals, such research might be particularly enlightening, both theoretically and pedagogically.

Metaphor Comprehension by Deaf Children

Deaf children's comprehension of metaphor has historically been examined in deaf studies as a means of evaluating their linguistic and cognitive abilities. Following the early work of Piaget (1923/1974), many investigators examined figurative language abilities in hearing children as an indicator of both linguistic flexibility and a more global cognitive ability to consider the world from alternative perspectives (e.g., Gardner, Winner, Bechofer, & Wolf, 1978). Studies of deaf children occurred naturally from such work, following from earlier studies of nonverbal creativity (see Marschark & Clark, 1987, for a review). In particular, figurative language abilities have been shown to depend on classification skills and, especially, the ability to see relationships across domains as superseding superficial similarities, an area in which deaf children are seen to lag behind hearing peers (Ottem, 1980). Studies by Rittenhouse, Morreau, and Iran-Nejad (1981) and Inman and Lian (1991) showed that metaphor comprehension in deaf children is related to performance in Piagetian conservation tasks, further indicating a link between those skills.

If deaf children think as concretely and literally as early investigators reported (e.g., Blackwell et al., 1978; Boatner & Gates, 1969; Myklebust, 1964), they would not be expected to either comprehend or produce nonliteral language. Alternatively, because of its compactness, figurative language provides an extremely efficient and vivid form of communication that could allow deaf children to communicate ideas that might not be expressible in literal terms. Several investigators have emphasized the importance of this aspect of figurative language for young hearing children who have much to say but meager linguistic resources at their command (e.g., Gardner et al., 1978; Petrie, 1979). Thus, metaphor should be of particular utility to deaf children, across a wider age range, due to their having smaller vocabularies than hearing peers.

Given the deaf children's relative lack of experiential diversity and language skills in the vernacular (Marschark et al., 2002), it would not be surprising to find that they have little skill in understanding the many nonliteral aspects of English (Boatner & Gates, 1969). Conley (1976) was apparently the first to evaluate that assumption, comparing deaf and hearing students on a test of English idiom comprehension. Despite the fact that the vocabulary of test sentences were selected from lower reading levels, she found that the deaf children were significantly poorer in their (English) idiom comprehension than hearing peers, at least at the middle range of reading levels. However, she also found that deaf and hearing children at lower reading levels did not differ significantly in their performance (see also Easterbrooks, 1983).

Iran-Nejad, Ortony, and Rittenhouse (1981) argued that the lack of comprehension indicated in such studies resulted from deaf children's difficulties in understanding written English, rather than in anything specific to nonliteral language (Paul, 2003). They presented deaf 9- to 17-year-olds with short stories in which syntax, vocabulary, and world knowledge were controlled. The students read the stories, which were accompanied by a simple picture depicting the main point, and then selected from a set of four literal sentences, similes, or metaphors the sentence that best completed each story. Iran-Nejad et al. found that even their youngest deaf students could select nonliteral sentences as best completions for the stories, a finding replicated by Rittenhouse et al. (1981) and Fruchter, Wilbur, and Fraser (1984) with deaf children who signed and Rittenhouse and Kenyon (1991) with children who used spoken language.

Payne and Quigley (1987), in contrast, controlled vocabulary and syntax and included thematic pictures in an investigation of comprehension of idiomatic phrases by deaf and hearing students and still found a consistent hearing status difference. Their study involved 10- to 19-year-old deaf students and 8- to 12-year old hearing students. The participants were shown simple pictures (e.g., men holding up a store) and asked them to select the most appropriate verb-particle phrases from among three choices. The phrases included three levels of semantic difficulty: literal (e.g., *walks out*), semi-idiomatic (e.g., *washes up*), and idiomatic (e.g., *gives up*) embedded in five syntactic structures: subject-verb-adverb, subject-verb-adverb-object, subject-verb-object-adverb, subject-verb-preposition-object, and subject-verb-adverb-preposition-object. Payne and Quigley found that the hearing students performed significantly better than the deaf students on all levels of semantic difficulty and for all syntactic constructions. In addition, they found that performance was highly related to reading comprehension ability. More recently, Sawa (1999) had Japanese deaf and hearing high school students paraphrase similes like "The heart is like the sea." Results indicated that almost half of the interpretations provided by the deaf students were either inappropriate or simply restated the simile. Unlike hearing peers, the deaf students were significantly more likely to explain the similes with single-attribute predicates than multiattribute predicates. Sawa and Yoshino (1995) also found that metaphor comprehension and production were strongly correlated among deaf junior high school students.[9]

At this point, it is clear that comprehension of metaphor in the vernacular remains problematic for deaf adults and children. Such difficulty appears to be tied largely to print literacy, although carefully controlled studies still need to be conducted. Further, until studies are conducted concerning the comprehension of signed metaphor by deaf adults and children, both in and out of context, we do not know if there are any differences in figurative comprehension, broadly defined, between deaf and hearing individuals. If deaf individuals show typical patterns of figurative comprehension within sign language, educators should be able to use them to improve comprehension of metaphor in print.

Metaphor Production by Deaf Children

To obtain an indication of deaf children's figurative language abilities outside of spoken and written language, some researchers have focused on the use of figurative expression in their sign language production. Theoretically, what appears to be metaphor expertise on the part of deaf children could be considered (a) a simple reflection of their acquiring the apparently metaphoric and iconic aspects of sign language use (e.g., Emmorey, 2002, p. 82);

---

[9]The Sawa and Yoshino (1995) and Sawa (1999) articles were published in Japanese, and only English abstracts are available. A complete review of their results, therefore, could not be included here.

(b) demonstrative of creative, flexible thinking at least within the context of sign language production (e.g., Everhart & Marschark, 1988); or (c) an indicator of limited (literal) language ability. This last alternative might be considered a straw man, especially because there is so little research on the issue. However, in the context of the discussion of metaphor in sign language and sign language users, it is best thought of as an empirical question that likely has a complex answer (Everhart & Marschark, 1988).

Several studies have shown that when evaluated in sign language, deaf children display linguistic competencies not evident from their use of and evaluation in printed language. This was first demonstrated by Marschark and West (1985), who examined fantasy-based stories signed by deaf children and spoken by hearing children between the ages of 12 and 15 years old. The most important general finding was that there were several types of figurative language used consistently by both deaf and hearing children. In contrast to studies of their comprehension of English idioms, Marschark and West found that the deaf children produced novel and frozen trope just as often as their age-matched hearing peers. The deaf children also reliably surpassed their hearing peers in their frequency of using gesture, pantomime, novel but grammatically acceptable linguistic modifications, and linguistic inventions. Everhart and Marschark (1988) explicitly showed that deaf children's production of trope in sign language significantly exceeded their production in written language, whereas hearing children produced more trope in spoken than written language.

Marschark et al. (1986) examined developmental changes in figurative production by deaf and hearing children between the ages of 7 and 15 years old. Beyond replication of the earlier findings, the most interesting result was the finding of a *literal period* in deaf children's language productions. Previous studies had demonstrated a point at around 8 or 9 years of age when the use of figurative language by hearing children is at a minimum. This hiatus has variously been described as a consequence of perceived academic demands, the emergence of an analytic attitude in concrete operations, and the point at which linguistic and cognitive skills have matured enough that children stop producing apparently figurative category violations that actually stem from conceptual error (i.e., they are intended literally because children do not recognize the metaphoric tension). According to the latter interpretation, it is only after the literal period that true figurative language use begins.

The literal period in deaf children's language observed by Marschark et al. (1986) was its first demonstration within sign language. Perhaps the most interesting aspect of that finding, however, was that the literal period of the deaf sample was observed at around age 12 or 13, 3 to 4 years later than the minimum evident in the hearing sample. This result was consistent with Iran-Nejad et al.'s (1981) suggestion that deaf children's lack of linguistic experience should be reflected in various lags in their language use. More generally, it indicated that the development of linguistic creativity in deaf children follows a similar but slightly delayed course relative to hearing children.

Figurative Production by Deaf Adults

There have been no published studies concerning deaf adults' comprehension of metaphor, and apparently all but one of the investigations of their figurative production have had a linguistic focus. In the one psychologically oriented study, Marschark, Everhart, and Dempsey (1991) explored the figurative language of signing deaf women, speaking hearing women, and bilingual (signing and speaking) hearing women who had ASL as their first language (i.e., learned from their deaf parents). The women all made up and told stories on supplied themes, allegedly to be shown to 4- and 10-year-old children, while being videotaped (the bilingual group told stories in both sign language and spoken language). When all forms of nonliteral language were included (e.g., novel and frozen trope, rhetorical questions, pantomime, and invented signs and words), the deaf mothers produced the most nonliteral language. The two groups of hearing women produced equal amounts of nonliteral content, whereas the bilingual mothers produced more when signing than when speaking. In terms of the frequency of using only novel trope, Marschark et al. found that deaf mothers and the bilingual-speaking mothers produced the most figurative language, followed by the bilingual-signing mothers, and finally the hearing mothers. Although individual categories of novel trope were not considered, the results indicate that the equal or greater frequency of figurative language found among deaf signers was not simply a reflection of some greater flexibility in ASL relative to English. Rather, there is clearly an unexplored interaction among language modality, language user, and metaphor.

Turning to linguistic analyses of metaphor in sign language, Wilcox (2000) provided an in-depth analysis of the structure and metaphoric content of a story entitled, *The Dogs*, by deaf poet Ella Mae Lentz (1995). Published on video, the story uses a fight between a well cared for, purebred Doberman and a stray mutt, chained together and unable to escape each other, as a metaphor for cultural discord within the Deaf community. Wilcox identified several recurring metaphoric and metonymic themes including "the mind is a body," "social relations are spatial relations," "social constraint is physical constraint," and "involuntary social unity is involuntary physical connectedness." Her analysis provides insights into Deaf culture, the beauty and expressiveness of ASL, and metaphor within signed languages. Although it reflects Lentz's obvious creativity and figurative deftness, the analysis was not intended to examine the psychology of the artist. Indeed, this might better be left to a cultural anthropologist.

Taub (2001b) offered a similar analysis of *The Treasure*, also by Lentz (1995), providing a linguistic and metalinguistic analysis of a poem fraught with metaphor and iconicity. In *The Treasure*, Lentz uncovered a beautiful treasure (a metaphor for sign language) buried underground and attempted to share her discovery with others. The way in which she and her discovery are rebuffed, and the treasure eventually reburied, offers both linguistic and cultural insights into ASL and the American Deaf community, similar to those in *The Dogs*. Taub described three categories of structures in the poem, *literal* (nonmetaphorical) signs, *lexicalized* metaphorical signs, and *free* metaphorical signs. Earlier, Marschark and West (1985) referred to the two latter categories as *frozen trope* and *novel trope*, respectively, labels that are more in keeping with the metaphor literature. For Taub's analysis of *The Treasure*, like Wilcox's (2000) analysis of *The Dogs*, it is the linguistic quality of the poem that is of interest, rather than anything about the language user. For the time being, we therefore must await study of the outstanding deaf artists who use sign language as the tools of their craft and less experienced signers who strive to develop such skills.

SUMMARY AND CONCLUSIONS

This chapter has explored the use of metaphor and other trope in sign language and its comprehension and production in sign language users. If metaphor has been seen to be an essential component of spoken language (Lakoff & Johnson, 1980), its centrality in signed languages seems even greater. The iconic property of signed languages, having signs that look or move like what they represent, and their metaphorical qualities, the symbolic likening or highlighting of dimensions across conceptual domains, have been confused in earlier work in the area, but the two aspects of signing are now seen to function together in creating its particularly apt and depictive representations. Iconicity and metaphor are essential components of the visuospatial nature of signing, and the availability of double mapping, the incorporation of both components simultaneously in the same sign, gives sign language a figurative, descriptive quality that makes spoken language pall by comparison.

Iconicity in sign language includes the use of handshapes or motion to demonstrate position, shape, or other qualities of objects. These classifiers can also be used as pronouns that preserve anaphoric relations among other, previously established entities, either variously shaped objects (including animals and people) or abstract entities (e.g., time periods, concepts, and other relations). It likely is the use of iconicity in sign language that sometimes leads hearing people to think that signing is more gestural than linguistic, but the many sign languages of the world are indeed true languages (Stokoe, 1960) that are often accompanied by gestures as well (Marschark, 1994). The degree to which individual signs are transparent to nonsigners varies with the language, the culture, and the particular signs involved. Nonetheless, many of the metaphoric devices found in spoken languages (e.g., "good is up" and "bad is down") are depicted iconically in sign language.

The use of metaphor in sign language has been well documented by those studying various languages, and consistencies across various national sign languages indicate the ubiquity of figurative language regardless of its mode. There have not yet been studies on the development of metaphoric and iconic characteristics in young signers, however, other than a few cross-sectional studies showing similar if delayed patterns of development in deaf children relative to hearing peers (e.g., Marschark et al., 1986). Further studies of metaphor and iconic sign language development could consider the conceptual and linguistic knowledge underlying language use and the possible utility of metaphor and iconicity in teaching hearing as well as deaf children.

A variety of studies, primarily involving school-age children, have demonstrated that because of their literacy-related challenges, and perhaps because of relatively limited world knowledge, deaf children and adolescents demonstrate poorer performance than hearing peers on tests of metaphor comprehension evaluated via print materials. Although such results long were taken as reflecting concrete and literal thinking on the part of deaf people, more recent research—both psychological and linguistic—has shown that deaf individuals and other fluent users of sign language incorporate metaphoric mappings in their sign language and produce figurative constructions just as often as their hearing peers.

Research concerning the comprehension of metaphor in sign language by deaf adults or children is completely lacking. One would hope that results from future work would indicate full comprehension of signed metaphor, comparable to that observed by hearing individuals with spoken metaphor. Nonetheless, recent evidence indicating somewhat different organization and use of conceptual information by deaf as compared to hearing individuals suggests the potential for variation—variation that would be of both theoretical and educational importance. As in the other areas of investigation described in this volume, such work would provide additional windows onto the nature of language and language users.

REFERENCES

Bellugi, U., & Klima, E. (1976). Two faces of sign: Iconic and abstract. In S. Harnad, D. Hoest, & I. Lancaster (Eds.), *Origins and evolution of language and speech* (pp. 514–538). New York: New York Academy of Sciences.

Blackwell, P., Engen, E., Fischgrund, J., & Zarcadoolas, C. (1978). *Sentences and other systems: A language and learning curriculum for hearing-impaired children.* Washington, DC: National Association of the Deaf.

Boatner, M. T., & Gates, J. E. (1969). *A dictionary of idioms for the deaf.* Washington, DC: National Association for the Deaf.

Boyes Braem, P. (1981). *Features of the handshape in American Sign Language.* Doctoral dissertation, Department of Linguistics, University of California, Berkeley.

Brennan, M. (1990). *Word formation in British Sign Language.* Stockholm: University of Stockholm.

Conley, J. E. (1976). The role idiomatic expressions in the reading of deaf children. *American Annals of the Deaf, 121,* 381–385.

Easterbrooks, S. R. (1983). *Literal and metaphoric understanding of four pairs of polar adjectives across four domains by hearing and hearing impaired children at two age levels.* Doctoral dissertation, Department of Special Education, University of Georgia.

Emmorey, K. (2001). Space on hand: The exploitation of signing space to illustrate abstract thought. In M. Gattis (Ed.), *Spatial schemas and abstract thought* (pp. 147–174). Cambridge, MA: MIT Press.

Emmorey, K. (2002). *Language, cognition, and the brain.* Mahwah, NJ: Lawrence Erlbaum Associates.

Engberg-Pedersen, E. (1993). *Space in Danish Sign Language: The semantics and morphsyntax of the use of space in a visual language* (International Studies on Sign Language Research and Communication of the Deaf, No. 19). Hamburg, Germany: Signum-Verlag.

Everhart, V. S., & Marschark, M. (1988). Linguistic flexibility in signed and written language productions of deaf children. *Journal of Experimental Child Psychology, 46,* 174–193.

Friedman, L. (Ed.). (1977). *On the other hand: New perspectives on American Sign Language.* New York: Academic Press.

Fruchter, A., Wilbur, R. B., & Fraser, J. B. (1984). Comprehension of idioms by hearing-impaired students. *The Volta Review, 86,* 7–19.

Gardner, H., Winner, E., Bechofer, R., & Wolf, D. (1978). The development of figurative language. In K. Nelson (Ed.), *Children's language* (Vol. 1). New York: Gardner.

Gibbs, R. (1994). *The poetics of mind.* Cambridge, England: Cambridge University Press.

Glucksberg, S. (2001). *Understanding figurative language.* New York: Oxford University Press.

Goossens, L. (1990). Metaphtonymy: The interaction of metaphor and metonymy in expressions for linguistic action. *Cognitive Linguistics, 1,* 323–340.

Inman, P. R., & Lian, M.-G. J. (1991). Conservation and metaphor performance among children with hearing impairments. *Journal of the American Deafness and Rehabilitation Association, 25,* 28–41.

Iran-Nejad, A., Ortony, A., & Rittenhouse, R. K. (1981). The comprehension of metaphorical uses of English by deaf children. *Journal of Speech and Hearing Research, 24,* 551–556.

Katz, A. N., Cacciari, C., Gibbs, R. W., Jr., & Turner, M. (1998). *Figurative language and thought.* New York. Oxford University Press.

Klima, E., & Bellugi, U. (1979). *The signs of language.* Cambridge, MA: Harvard University Press.

Lakoff, G., & Johnson, M. (1980). *Metaphors we live by.* New York: Cambridge University Press.

Lakoff, G., & Turner, M. (1989). *More than cool reason: A field guide to poetic metaphor.* Chicago: University of Chicago Press.

Lentz, E. M. (1995). *The treasure: Poems by Ella Mae Lentz.* Berkeley, CA: InMotion.

Liddell, S. (1990). Four functions of a locus: Reexamining the structure of space in ASL. In C. Lucas (Ed.), *Sign language research: Theoretical issues* (pp. 176–198). Washington, DC: Gallaudet University Press.

Liddell, S. (1995). Real, token, and surrogate space: Grammatical consequences in ASL. In K. Emmorey & J. Reilly (Eds.), *Language, gesture, and space* (pp. 19–41). Hillsdale, NJ: Lawrence Erlbaum Associates.

Luria, A. R. (1976). *Cognitive development: Its cultural and social foundations.* Cambridge, MA: Harvard University Press.

Mac Cormac, E. R. (1985). *A cognitive theory of metaphor.* Cambridge, MA: MIT Press.

Mandel, M. (1977). Iconic devices in American Sign Language. In L. A. Friedman (Ed.), *On the other hand: New perspectives on American Sign Language* (pp. 57–107). New York: Academic Press.

Marschark, M. (1993). *Psychological development of deaf children.* New York: Oxford University Press.

Marschark, M. (1994). Gesture and sign. *Applied Psycholinguistics, 15,* 209–236.

Marschark, M., & Clark, D. (1987). Linguistic and nonlinguistic creativity of deaf children. *Developmental Review, 7,* 22–38.

Marschark, M., Convertino, C., McEvoy, C., & Masteller, A. (2001, November). *Organization and use of the mental lexicon in deaf and hearing individuals.* Poster session presented at the annual meeting of the Psychonomic Society, Orlando, FL.

Marschark, M. & Everhart, V. S. (1999). Problem solving by deaf and hearing children: Twenty question. *Deafness and Education International, 1,* 63–79.

Marschark, M., Everhart, V. S., & Dempsey, P. (1991). Nonliteral content in language productions of deaf, hearing, and native-signing hearing mothers. *Merrill-Palmer Quarterly, 37,* 305–323.

Marschark, M., & Hunt, R. R. (1985). On memory for metaphor. *Memory & Cognition, 13,* 413–424.

Marschark, M., Lang, H. G., & Albertini, J. A. (2002). *Educating deaf students: From research to practice.* New York: Oxford University Press.

Marschark, M., LePoutre, D., & Bement, L. (1998). Mouth movement and signed communication. In R. Campbell & B. Dodd (Eds.), *Hearing by eye II: The psychology of speechreading and auditory–visual speech* (pp. 243–264). London: Taylor & Francis.

Marschark, M., & Nall, L. (1985). Metaphoric competence in cognitive and language development. In H. Reese (Ed.), *Advances in child development and behavior* (Vol. 19; pp. 49–82). Orlando, FL: Academic Press.

Marschark, M., & Spencer, P. E. (2003). What we know, what we don't know, and what we should know. In M. Marschark & P. E. Spencer (Eds.), *Oxford handbook of deaf studies, language, and education.* New York: Oxford University Press.

Marschark, M., & West, S. A. (1985). Creative language abilities of deaf children. *Journal of Speech and Hearing Research, 28,* 73–78.

Marschark, M., West, S. A., Nall, L., & Everhart, V. (1986). Development of creative language devices in signed and oral production. *Journal of Experimental Child Psychology, 41,* 534–550.

McEvoy, C., Marschark, M., & Nelson, D. L. (1999). Comparing the mental lexicons of deaf and hearing individuals. *Journal of Educational Psychology, 91,* 1–9.

McNeill, D. (1992). *Hand and mind.* Chicago: University of Chicago Press.

Myklebust, H. E. (1964). *The psychology of deafness* (2nd ed.). New York: Grune & Stratton.

O'Brien, J. (1999). Metaphoricity in the signs of American Sign Language. *Metaphor and Symbolic Activity, 14,* 159–178.

Ortony, A. (1993). *Metaphor and thought,* (2nd ed.). New York: Cambridge University Press.

Ottem, E. (1980). An analysis of cognitive studies with deaf subjects. *American Annals of the Deaf, 125,* 564–575.

Paivio, A. (1979). Psychological processes in the comprehension of metaphor. In A. Ortony (Ed.), *Metaphor and thought* (pp. 150–171). New York: Cambridge University Press.

Paul, P. V. (2003). Processes and components of reading. In M. Marschark & P. E. Spencer (Eds.), *Handbook of deaf studies, language, and education* (pp. 97–109). New York: Oxford University Press.

Paulesu, E., Démonet, J.-F., Fazio, F., McCrory, E., Chanoine, V., Brunswick, N., Cappa, S. F., Cossu, G., Habib, M., Frith, C. D., & Frith, U. (2001). Dyslexia: Cultural diversity and biological unity. *Science, 291,* 2165–2167.

Payne, J.-A., & Quigley, S. (1987). Hearing-impaired children's comprehension of verb–particle combinations. *Volta Review, 89,* 133–143.

Petrie, H. (1979). Metaphor and learning. In A. Ortony (Ed.), *Metaphor and thought* (pp. 438–461). New York: Cambridge University Press.

Piaget, J. (1974). *The language and thought of the child.* New York: New American Library. (Original work published 1923)

Pizzuto, E., & Volterra, V. (2000). Iconicity and transparency in sign languages: A cross-linguistic cross-cultural view. In K. Emmorey & H. Lane (Eds.), *The signs of language revisited: An anthology to honor Ursula Bellugi and Edward Klima* (pp. 261–286). Mahwah, NJ: Lawrence Erlbaum Associates.

Rittenhouse, R. K., & Kenyon, P. L. (1991). Conservation and metaphor acquisition in hearing-impaired children. *American Annals of the Deaf, 136,* 313–320.

Rittenhouse, R. K., Morreau, L. E., & Iran-Nejad, A. (1981). Metaphor and conservation in deaf and hard-of-hearing children. *American Annals of the Deaf, 126,* 450–453.

Sawa, T. (1999). Metaphor interpretation by students with hearing impairments. *Japanese Journal of Special Education, 37,* 59–69.

Sawa, T., & Yoshino, T. (1995). Relation between metaphor comprehension and development of a linguistic framework in students with hearing impairments. *Japanese Journal of Special Education, 33,* 21–29.

Siple, P. (Ed.). (1978). *Understanding language through sign language research*. New York: Academic Press.

Stokoe, W. C. (1960). *Sign language structure: An outline of the visual communications systems* (Studies in Linguistics, Occasional Papers 8). Buffalo, NY: University of Buffalo.

Stokoe, W. C., Casterline, D. C., & Croneberg, C. G. (1965). *A dictionary of American Sign Language on linguistic principles*. Washington, DC: Gallaudet College Press.

Stokoe, W. C., & Marschark, M. (1999). Signs, gestures, and signs. In L. Messing & R. Campbell (Eds.), *Gesture, speech, and sign* (pp. 161–182). Oxford, England: Oxford University Press.

Taub, S. F. (2001a). Complex superposition of metaphors in an ASL poem. In V. Dively, M. Metzger, S. Taub, & A. M. Baer (Eds.), *Signed languages: Discoveries from international research* (pp. 197–223). Washington, DC: Gallaudet University Press.

Taub, S. F. (2001b). *Language from the body: Iconicity and metaphor in American Sign Language*. New York: Cambridge University Press.

Tourangeau, R., & Sternberg, R. (1981). Aptness in metaphor. *Cognitive Psychology, 13*, 27–55.

Traxler, C. B. (2000). Measuring up to performance standards in reading and mathematics: Achievement of selected deaf and hard-of-hearing students in the national norming of the 9th Edition Stanford Achievement Test. *Journal of Deaf Studies and Deaf Education, 5*, 337–348.

Trick, L., & Katz, A. N. (1986). The domain interaction approach to metaphor processing: Relating individual differences and metaphor characteristics. *Metaphor and Symbolic Activity, 1*, 185–213.

Turner, M. (1996). *The literary mind*. New York: Oxford University Press.

Wilbur, R. B. (1987). *American Sign Language: Linguistic and applied dimensions*. Boston: College-Hill Press.

Wilcox, P. P. (2000). *Metaphor in American Sign Language*. Washington, DC: Gallaudet University Press.

Author Index

Subject Index